CW00347524

Editorial Note

Professor Wesley C. Mitchell (1874-1948) delivered his famous course of Lectures on Types of Economic Theory at Columbia University during the 1930's. An extremely popular course, it attracted students from all over the world. It was not unusual to find all the seats occupied in the old lecture room of Fayerweather Hall, as students crowded in to hear Professor Mitchell's lucid and penetrating analysis of the contributions of the great economists to the development of economic thought.

Professor Mitchell discussed each leading figure with a characteristic dry humor and warm sympathy that served to bring their ideas to life in a truly remarkable degree. But what he was most deeply concerned with was the dependence of these ideas of the great theorists on the major social and economic issues which "troubled their generations".

This theme, carefully elaborated in the lectures, has not received much emphasis in Professor Mitchell's published work, with the exception of the essays on Bentham and Ricardo reprinted in the Backward Art of Spending Money. (New York, 1936; reprinted in 1949 by Augustus M. Kelley.)

It is fortunate then, that the lectures were stenographically transcribed by John Myers, a student attending the course delivered at Columbia in the fall of 1934 and the spring of 1935. It is perhaps not too much to draw a parallel with the Lectures on Justice, Police, Revenue and Arms of Adam Smith, which were given in the University of Glasgow in 1763 but only made available to readers at large when the notes of an anonymous student were discovered in the 1890's.

During his lifetime Professor Mitchell always disclaimed responsibility for the accuracy of the transcript. In fact in a letter to the present publisher written shortly before his death he denied ever having read the Notes. We feel confident, however, that he was well aware of their great value to graduate students.

The present version has been edited to eliminate obvious errors and occasional obscurities in the transcript. Every effort has been made to preserve the conversational phrasing, even on occasion to the detriment of grammar; (but it should be said that Professor Mitchell always spoke in a classic prose.) In spite of careful study it may be that certain passages remain in doubt and in such cases we would welcome correspondence from former students whose notes of the course may suggest alternative wordings.

We feel that the Notes are of value on several planes. They are probably the best general survey of the development of economic thought; and on that score should be a boon to a whole generation of graduate students. They are an unrivalled stimulus to deeper study of the economic classics. They form a masterpiece of intellectual and social historiography. And finally to former students, they evoke in the mind's eye the unforgettable picture of Professor Mitchell standing before his class, with his clear and penetrating voice, and his ever present smile which seemed to tell of the huge pleasure he drew from discussing his beloved Adam Smith and David Ricardo.

J.M. Gould
A.M. Kelley

TABLE OF CONTENTS

Chapter   Page

I   Introductory Lecture, October 2, 1934.   1
II   Adam Smith's Treatment of the Problem of Economics as
         Contrasted with That of Modern Treatises.   8
III   The Relation of The Wealth of Nations to Economic Science. 11
IV   Adam Smith's Theories Contrasted with Those of the
         Mercantilists   15
V   The Logic of Adam Smith's Theories   23
VI   English Developments in the Eighteenth Century; The
         Phenomenon of Individual Initiative   28
VII   The Development of Government by Public Discussion   34
VIII   Individual Initiative in Local Government; Changes in
         Economic Conditions and Their Effect on Economic Theory   41
IX   The Theory of Mercantilism   48
X   Mercantilism vs. Individual Initiative in the Eighteenth
         Century. Adam Smith's Early Life   53
XI   Adam Smith and The Wealth of Nations   61
XII   The Wealth of Nations: A Philosopher's Reflections on What
         He Saw About Him.   67
XIII   Adam Smith's Influence upon British Politics   74
XIV   The Effect of the French Revolution upon British Politics
         And Economic Conditions   81
XV   Economics Not Independent of Man's Other Interests   88
XVI   Jeremy Bentham: His Influence upon the Development of
         Economic Theory   90
XVII   Bentham's Felicific Calculus   97
XVIII Bentham's Conception of Human Nature 104
XIX   The Felicific Calculus in Practice 108
XX   Malthus and the Principle of Population. 113
XXI   The Essay on the Principle of Population 116
XXII   The Effect of Malthus' Essay; His Later Editions 126
XXIII David Ricardo: His Life and Early Writings; The Bullion
         Controversy 130
XXIV   The Role of the Economists in the Corn Law Struggle.
         Ricardo's Later Essays and Later Life 138
XXV   Ricardo's Later Years – His Principles of Political
         Economy 145
XXVI   Ricardo's Method of Work 154
XXVII The "Postulates" and "Preconceptions" of Economic Theory.
         Ricardo's Preconceptions. 162
XXVIII Ricardo's Conceptions of Human Nature. His Four Levels
         of Analysis 169
XXIX   Reasons for the Popularity of Ricardo's Analysis 177

TABLE OF CONTENTS

Chapter   Page

    XXX   The Philosophical Radicals: Their Activities and Political
           Position 184
    XXXI   Political Events and How They Aided in Bringing About the
           Reforms which the Philosophical Radicals Advocated 191
    XXXII The Passage of the Great Reform Bill of 1832 199
   XXXIII Similarities and Contrasts Between the Processes of Social
           Reform and Reform in Methods of Production in England . . 207
   XXXIV   Politics, Social Reform, and Political Economy in the Period
           from 1832 to 1848. 215
    XXXV   Further Remarks on the Period Preceding John Stuart Mill;
           His Early Life 223
   XXXVI   The Life of John Stuart Mill. 230
  XXXVII   John Stuart Mill's Principles of Political Economy. 240
 XXXVIII   Some Shortcomings of the Classical Economists 248
   XXXIX   John Stuart Mill's Method of Analysis 254

* * * * *

I

I feel moved this year to begin this course on current types of economic theory by making some general remarks upon the present state of the world at large and its bearing upon the would-be science of economics. One of the results of any survey of the development of economic doctrine is to show that in very large measure the important departures in economic theory have been intellectual responses to changing current problems. That is, the economic theorists who have counted most in the development of thought have been men who have been very deeply concerned with problems that troubled their generations. Their theories have been attempts to deal scientifically with these problems, to point out promising means of practical action.

Now that is a conclusion that I think will without doubt be patent to everyone before the end of this course. But I delight in giving the conclusion away at the very start because I think to have the matter stated in this unequivocal form at the outset will help you to read with greater interest and success the various books which will be suggested.

I even go further and give two or three illustrations to make the point more concrete. The first type of economic theory that we shall take up for discussion is that presented by Adam Smith in The Wealth of Nations which was published in 1776. Now Adam Smith lived at a time when a great system of national economic planning was gradually disintegrating and when the practice of individual initiative on the part of adventurous business men was becoming a mass phenomenon. This rise of individual initiative was hampered to some extent, though less than the reading of the statutes might lead you to expect, by the multitude of directions which the government sought to impose in practicing its policy of national planning - was hampered to some extent by the multiplicity and minuteness with which the government sought to direct what private individuals should do.

Now Adam Smith was primarily a philosopher. He lived at a time when economics was just beginning to disassociate itself rather clearly from the general body of philosophical interests. And as a philosopher he became convinced that the general principle of trying to control the activities of private individuals was inimical to the growth of the wealth of nations. He set forth with masterly lucidity the proposition that the wealth of the nation would grow most rapidly if the government practiced a minimum of interference with the operations of private people, if it left every man substantially free to choose for himself whatever occupation seemed to him most conducive to his private interest. That centered economic theory upon the problem of the production of wealth and how best the production of wealth might be fostered. The answer was: by letting things substantially alone. You see, Adam Smith was dealing with a practical issue, the overmastering economic issue of his time; and he came to very definite conclusions regarding the policy which it would be wise for an individual to follow.

The second man whose economic doctrines we shall consider is Malthus, who at the very end of the eighteenth century and the early years of the nineteenth century was a leading authority on the problem of population. Malthus lived at a time when the industrial revolution was beginning to produce its marked effect upon the growth of population. We heard a great deal, of course, about the frightful hardships which the rise of the factory system imposed upon the lower classes and no doubt most of what we heard was a valid account of actual events which took place. But the population figures assure us that despite the horrors which many of the Blue Books revealed, the numbers of the people were increasing with unaccustomed rapidity during the period when the new machine technique and the factories were becoming an important part of the daily life of Englishmen. More than that, the figures show us that the reason for the increase in the population was not owing to stimulation of the birth rate; it was primarily because of the decline of the death rate, because most of the people seemed on the whole to have lived under conditions which reduced mortality, particularly reduced the number of deaths of infants and small children. So the population expanded because the birth rate remained constant and the number that died declined.

Well, now this increase of the population gave rise to very grievous problems. It led immediately, combined with other events taking place, to a great increase in pauperism, in the taxes which were imposed upon the property owners in the British parishes to support the poor. And Malthus, another philosophic mind, reflecting upon this situation, came to his momentous conclusions about what he called the principle of population, and argued these conclusions through to his definite ideas regarding proper policy for the treatment of the poor, the enforcement of responsibility upon individuals for looking after themselves, the granting of relief only in cases of persons unable to support themselves by their own efforts. A second example of a great economist who got his problem from the current events of the day and who treated his problem in such a fashion as to suggest lines of public policy.

The third critically important writer, whom we shall take up on a more extended scale than Malthus, is David Ricardo, who changed the perspective of economic theory by announcing that the principal problem of political economy is the problem of distribution. Adam Smith, as I said, centered his attention upon the production of wealth. What Ricardo regarded as the matter that required chief attention was, in his own language, the manner in which the annual produce of the nation is distributed among the three classes: the capitalist, the laborer, and the landlord.

This shift in the perspective of political economy which occurred through David Ricardo is the reflection of a shift in the British problem. In David Ricardo's time the momentous economic issue in Parliament was the issue presented by the so-called Corn Laws, laws which imposed duties upon the importation of the staple food products into Great Britain; and these laws were believed by all hands to mean an increase in the price of food, an increase in the price of food was believed with equal simplicity to involve high money wages; high money wages meant larger costs of production; and larger costs of production meant to the manufacturing and commercial interests a disadvantage in competing with foreign goods at home and in competing with other countries for foreign markets. So the whole rising commercial interests of the country were deeply concerned lest the economic policy practiced by the government should hamper the growth of their operations. And, on the other hand, the landlord interest, which was predominant in Parliament, thought that the Corn

Laws by diminishing foreign competition in agricultural products helped keep up their rent. The issue was clearly drawn. It was one concerning the distribution of income between the capitalist, the employing interest, on the other side. Well, that was the problem with which David Ricardo dealt with in such masterly fashion; and it was through the influence of Ricardo's writings that the problem of distribution came to occupy that central place in economic speculation which it has held ever since.

John Stuart Mill represents not only a further stage in the development of economic theory but likewise a further stage in the development of economic life in Great Britain. He was writing a book which appeared in 1848. He was writing at a time when Great Britain was rapidly consolidating its position as the workshop of the world, as the greatest of manufacturing nations. And he was much concerned with the outcome for the future. It seemed to him that there was grave likelihood that the unsatisfactory economic organization of his own day would crystallize and become more or less permanent. That would have been, from his viewpoint, a great tragedy. So he got to thinking far more seriously than his predecessors about the differences between what we call in these days the laws of production, that Adam Smith had done so much to bring out clearly, and the laws of distribution, which Ricardo had formulated so sharply. It occurred to him that there was a fundamental difference between the principles which controlled the production of wealth by mankind on the one hand, and the principles that controlled the distribution of wealth among mankind on the other hand.

To Mill the laws of production had very much the character of physical laws; they were fixed, they were immutable. Nothing that any man could do would alter the fact that after land has been cultivated to a certain point further application of capital and labor will yield a relatively diminishing return. Nor would anything that man can do alter the fact that the scope of production is limited by the capital which can be used by the producers. On the other hand, however, he came to the conclusion that the like is not true about the laws of distribution of wealth. They depend upon human institutions. In a genuine sense they are man-made; and because they are man-made they are susceptible of alteration by human arrangement. So he saw a hope in the future through the possibility of designing with due care the kind of institutions which would bring about a distribution of income far more conducive to the general welfare than that which prevailed in his own day and age. And he had in mind the particular type of organization which he thought held the greatest promise for the future, the scheme of producers' cooperation with which we shall become familiar later on.

After John Stuart Mill's time economics seemed for a considerable while to lose a large measure of its contemporary interest. It retired more or less into academic halls. It was cultivated primarily by professors. It became more and more a specialty with its own body of erudition with which any one who wanted to discuss economic problems had to make himself familiar before he ventured to express an opinion in public. And as economics took on this character it seemed in good part at least to change from being a vigorous criticism of current economic practices, as it had been notably in the cases of Adam Smith, of Malthus, of Ricardo, of John Stuart Mill, and to be in danger of becoming a defense, in some sense at least, of the existing situation.

This economics of the last half of the nineteenth century and the first part of the twentieth century with its increasing logical perfection is a just intellectual reaction to the general conditions that prevailed in Great Britain, the country that has done most for the development of economics, and in con-

siderable measure in the other countries of western Europe and North America.
For it was a period during which the expansion of that type of economic activity
which had got started with the Industrial Revolution beginning in Adam Smith's
time seemed to be producing results which on the whole were rather satisfactory.
The increase in population that had begun to be notable in England even by the
turn of the eighteenth century occurred also in continental Europe. And of
course in North America the rate of increase was far faster than in any European
country, not only because there was a relatively high birth rate and lowered
death rate, but also because of the enormous stream of immigrants from the
European shores westward across the Atlantic.

There was evidence of increased well-being; it could be shown that
decade by decade the standard of living was rising in these countries of western
Europe and North America. The working classes were escaping in increasing measure from frightful conditions under which they had lived for centuries.
Their wages were not rising rapidly but the cost of living continued on the whole
to diminish. As the new methods of production and transportation developed their
efficiency, that was a second indication of increasing well-being. And then,
of course, there was a fairly steady decline in the average hours of work which
could be demonstrated with a fair degree of success and some approach to precision by the use of statistics. It appeared that man was taking the enormous
advantages which science and invention in the commercial application of new
methods yielded him as a producer, was taking this advantage out partly in
increasing his numbers, partly in raising his standard of living, and partly in
shortening his hours of toil.

It was very easy in those days to be highly optimistic about the
future. It was perfectly natural that men whose business it was to analyze the
workings of economic institutions should come to the conclusion that they on the
whole rendered very satisfactory service to the mass of mankind. And if they
held these conclusions they were but influenced in trying to demonstrate the
benevolence of the scheme of organization that then prevailed. Among the opti-
mists it was quite natural that the Americans should be more or less in the lead
of the procession for there was no country in which the improvements in the economic condition of the mass of the people seemed more rapid or more striking than
in the United States. So I think that even this rather learned kind of economic
theory which developed in the days after John Stuart Mill may be said, like its
more vigorous and interesting simpler predecessors, to represent an intellectual
reaction to the conditions of the day.

And if that is true about the dominant orthodox type of economics which
flourished in the latter part of the nineteenth and the early twentieth, it is
just as true about the unorthodox critical types which were not lacking. Whatever one may say about the net effect upon the mass of the population at large,
there were numerous classes that had only a very small share in the improvements
which humanity was making. And these people always had their spokesmen, since the
time of Adam Smith. Still more emphatically in the days of Ricardo when the results of the Industrial Revolution were being made clear, there were writers who
took a viewpoint, based particularly on the interests of the working classes, and
attacked the social injustice that was being worked upon the mass of the manual
laborers. A former Columbia student in a brilliant dissertation has called
these writers the "Ricardian Socialists".* Their analysis of the way in which

*Lowenthal, Esther, The Ricardian Socialists, New York, 1911. "Studies in
History, Economics and Public Law, Faculty of Political Science of Columbia
University," Vol. XLVI, No. 1, whole No. 114.

economic processes worked did a great deal to influence that German genius Karl
Marx who presently took up the same line of work.

Marx's Das Kapital is to be taken as one of the most influential books
of the nineteenth and twentieth centuries, not only so far as social movements
are concerned,but also on account of the important contribution to economic analysis in the technical sense. His economic contemporaries of the orthodox persuasion found it difficult to realize the scientific significance of Marx's position. They preferred to regard him primarily as a radical agitator making
class appeals,a man whose fundamental principles were erroneous and who therefore could not hope to arrive at valid intellectual results.

Now all this by way of giving some body to the statement which I have
made at the outset of the hour to the effect that economics from the time when
it began to be organized with some pretensions of being a science has been in
very large measure a reflection of current social developments; that in the hands
of its most notable developers it has been a series of dealings with current
problems of outstanding importance. And it has been worked out into conclusions
of a rather substantial sort regarding public and social matters. It has dealt
definitely with what ought to be done.

In saying all this of course I am not detracting from the intellectual
merits of the economists themselves. It is comparatively easy as one follows
the development of a science to get the impression that the successive stages in
its building up are due to the appearance from time to time of geniuses who had
more insight than their predecessors. That may be in considerable measure a
valid account of developments in the sciences which have to do with subject
matters that are themselves more or less stable, though I fancy that one who
knows the history of mathematics, of physics, and of chemistry could demonstrate
that in good part these sciences, particularly on their experimental side, could
not possibly have developed as they have except for what happened in the world
of industry and trade.

But leaving that matter aside, it is perfectly clear that when you
come to a science that deals with a subject matter itself continually developing
you can scarcely expect that its growth will be due simply to the forthright
process of logical excogitation. The working out of new problems goes on.
Intellectual genius has its part to play in economics, and the men whose names
I mentioned are simply citizens of the times who presumably because of their
superior intellectual gifts, combined with the circumstances that brought them
into touch with questions of the day, were able to produce what seemed to their
contemporaries and to their successors the most cogent analysis of these questions.

What has been true of the development of economics in the past is
likely I think (and here of course I have to speak with far less assurance) to
prove true of the development of economics in the future. That is, it seems
to me that as we look forward we have good ground for supposing that the further
growth of our science will be shaped in very large measure by the appearance of
new social problems and the reaction of trained minds toward these problems. If
that is the case, then I think I can say now with more assurance that the times
in which we live are likely to produce a very considerable stimulus to the growth
of economics, a stimulus far more effective than was produced, let us say, in
the period between John Stuart Mill and the Great War. For during these latter
years we have found that economic organization has been subject to very considerable changes, that these changes have presented to all the populations

where economics is most assiduously cultivated a host of problems, problems some of which have at least a distinctly novel guise.

The relative importance of different issues has been shifted and a great many ingenious minds, not only minds trained in economics but many minds trained in other branches of science have been and are today endeavoring to work out the problems of the moment in somewhat the same fashion as Adam Smith,Malthus Ricardo, John Stuart Mill, Karl Marx and his contemporaries, endeavoring to work out the problems that were presented by the times when they were at the peak of their powers. For during the War we saw in the United States, as also in the other belligerent countries, the great experiment of economic mobilization which involved for the time being a degree of economic planning more far-reaching and more drastic than the economic planning which was breaking down in Adam Smith's day and which he protested against so effectively. And since the War, beginning back during the war days, we have seen the great Russian nation attempting vigorously to substitute a communistic form of organization for a capitalistic form, using the analysis of Karl Marx supposedly as its guide in these endeavors. Then we have seen in other European countries the rise of a fascist organization in which, to be sure, there is no attempt to suppress private property and the pursuit of profits. Here we have an endeavor to organize economic activity primarily on a nation-wide basis, but in which all the forces of the country, all its economic energies from the side of property owners as well as from the side of the laboring classes are supposed to be comprised in one great corporate state and to have the conditions under which they shall do their work prescribed for them in a far more thoroughgoing fashion than has been true of the nations of the western world since the decline of mercantilism. And in this country, of course, to go to the case that interests us most closely, we have, after a period of high prosperity, seen a depression so severe that it is scarcely to be matched in our whole business history; and in the last ten months we have seen a series of attempts on the part of our national administration to organize new plans not only for lifting us out of the depression but also plans to modify our past economic organization in rather substantial fashion.

Now these changes in economic organization are presenting to us problems that the generation that followed John Stuart Mill did not see at all or that had been solved in a rather satisfactory fashion. It is not by any means as clear to us nowadays as it was clear to our predecessors before the War that the plan of economic organization celebrated by Adam Smith and perhaps worked out in the broadest fashion in this country, results in giving the highest possible, highest attainable level of welfare. We are beginning at the very least to ask ourselves questions and if we do not ask ourselves questions there are plenty of our friends and associates to thrust these questions upon our attention. We want to know whether the capitalistic form of organization makes it possible to provide employment for all willing workers at a living wage. That is, we are deeply concerned with the phenomenon that during the heyday of our prosperity was commonly called that of technological unemployment. We want to know whether it really is true that this form of economic organization prevents mankind from utilizing to the full the great advantages which science has applied to industry. There is abundant skilled testimony in favor of the opinion that provided we can have a market for all the goods that we can make, with our present knowledge, our present labor force, and present industrial equipment, it would be possible for us to increase the national income by a very substantial amount above the best records that we have ever attained.

Well, are these engineers right? We are a bit concerned as we watch the Russian experiment, as in these last few months we have watched the efforts of our own government, we have been concerned with the question whether a planned economy really is effective. Have we drawn too hasty a conclusion from the downfall of mercantilism? Was Adam Smith really right when he argued that if everyone were left to choose the occupation which is most advantageous in his own eyes the wealth of the community as a whole will improve at the most rapid rate? If Adam Smith was right in that opinion with respect to the conditions in his time, have conditions perhaps not changed in such a fashion as to justify very substantial modifications in the conclusions to which economists for three or four generations assented with very little difficulty? We want to know whether business cycles with their concomitants of recurring depressions in which a very considerable fraction of the working classes are unemployed for long periods and in which a very considerable proportion of our investors lose part of their savings cannot be obviated by more skilful economic organization.

We ask whether or not the country really has suffered from the plenitude of industrial equipment, whether the real problem is that capital is saved so rapidly and invested so heedlessly in new undertakings as to depreciate the values of our older producing establishments at a rate so rapid as to bring economic ruin upon many business men and investors. And we want to know particularly whether the troubles that come upon us are due to inherent defects of the economic organization that we have had, whether these troubles are primarily the aftermath of the Great War, or whether, as some think, they are due to unwise governmental interference with the operations of free men.

All these questions that we are debating center in problems of economics and they are making the subject of economics (and particularly economic theory which is supposed to give the general view of large issues such as I have been talking about) a matter of far deeper social concern to men of the present than it was to our fathers and our grandfathers.

The subject which has been primarily a dweller in academic halls is being dragged out into the market-place. Issues that have been debated in learned journals are being discussed violently in legislative halls and in places where business men consort, at conventions of labor unions. And those of you who are now young and looking forward to the future have, it seems to me in view of these facts, a peculiarly heavy responsibility to face, a responsibility of endeavoring to equip yourselves thoroughly for constructive work in a task which the world needs to have solved far more desperately than it needed such aid or was conscious of needing such aid in recent generations.

The chief task of this course is not to acquaint you with the history of economic theory in the last one hundred and fifty years. It is primarily to acquaint you with the way in which economics has developed as part of humanity's struggle to deal with the problems that evolving social life has brought upon us, to deal with these problems by trying to think them out, by seeing how successive generations have faced their problems, what they thought to be the central points of difficulty, the matters of grave social concern, and how they have dealt with these problems to which they have attached such importance – that will be the thing we shall attempt. Your part in the course should be primarily a searching, critical reading of some of the great masterpieces of economic analysis.

II.
ADAM SMITH'S TREATMENT OF THE PROBLEM OF
ECONOMICS AS CONTRASTED WITH THAT OF MODERN TREATISES

As I said Tuesday, the first type of economic theory that we take up for discussion in this course is the original form of English classical political economy as represented by Adam Smith's The Wealth of Nations. That book was published in 1776. It has been republished many times since. The best edition for study is that which appeared in 1904 edited by Professor Edwin Cannan, and published in this country by Dutton's. Professor Cannan was long in the chair of political economy at the University of London, and he is one of the most scholarly and conscientious editors of our time. His edition is an admirable piece of work. You can, however, find plenty of one volume editions which are decidedly less expensive. The Wealth of Nations is of course a large and formidable book. It is a book of which you can without much loss skip certain portions; but it is a book which you should not read in brief extracts but which you should read as a whole, omitting only chapters that possess at the present time antiquarian detail.

In discussing this type of economic theory and the types that we shall take up later on, my purpose is not to expound the details of economic doctrine. These details are matters that you can learn far better by reading the book than by listening to second-hand oral exposition. Those of you who want to profit by the course, I can say with perfect assurance at the outset, will find your profit primarily in your readings. You have an opportunity and an incitement to become personally acquainted with the greatest masterpieces of economics. A good many students find that reading by themselves is difficult and sometimes not a highly fruitful undertaking. One device to make your reading more interesting, to sharpen your minds as readers, is to join a discussion group. Numerous students in the past have told me that they have gained perhaps more from participating in discussions of the classics of economics with fellow-students than they have gained in their formal courses. For if you join a group of that sort and make a regular practice of exchanging views about the books that you are reading, you will find that the questions which your fellow-students raise will call to your attention matters that you may pass over rather lightly, and that in trying to explain and perhaps defend your interpretations you will have occasion to think rather more actively about the material that you have read than you are likely to think if you do your reading all to yourself. So I commend very heartily the practice of forming discussion groups which are much more successful seemingly if they are kept fairly small.

The questions that I am going to take up about The Wealth of Nations are questions as to the choice of problems, how Adam Smith focused the type of economic theory which he gave us around the question of the production of wealth, how he came to regard production as the central problem of economics, how his work influenced his contemporaries, how it reacted upon economic practices and how it influenced his successors.

Of course nowadays we think of economics as centering primarily not about the problem of production but about the problem of value and distribution. If you look over a considerable number of recent text-books on economics or elaborate treatises upon the subject, you will find, I think, that there is no one framework followed but that the framework most in favor is one which starts with the problem of value. that sets forth the view that values are always determined by the forces of supply and demand, and proceeds then to discuss the conditions under which the demand for commodities varies, and afterwards to take up the various factors that limit supply under differing conditions. When this exposition of the theory of value has been completed, the next topic undertaken is commonly the theory of distribution; and the theory of distribution is ordinarily treated as a series of problems in value, that is labor's share in distribution, wages, is discussed as the factor which determines the value of human services of different sorts when sold by the man who renders them to an employer. And once again the discussion turns to the various factors which influence the demand for labor of different sorts and the supply of it. Rent is similarly treated as a problem determining the value of the uses of land. Interest is treated as the problem determining the value of the uses of capital. And profit is treated as the problem determining the value of services rendered by a business organization.

Now in the course of a discussion organized in that way the subject of production comes in for treatment at several points. When a writer is discussing the conditions which limit supply in periods of moderate or great length, he commonly selects the cost at which goods are produced as the factor requiring most elaborate attention. And in studying cost of production he ordinarily sheds a good deal of light upon the general problem of production. And once again, when a man comes to his book dealing with distribution, with labor, and with interest, and profits, he has occasion to make remarks which throw some light upon the sphere of production. But there is many a modern treatise on economics in which there is no separate discussion of production. That topic which was the very center of Adam Smith's interest gets incidental treatment, rather than systematic treatment. What the writer has to say is broken up into bits, partly in his discussion of value at large and partly in his discussion of the various shares in distribution.

Adam Smith did not neglect entirely - indeed, rather far from it -this problem of value and distribution which has become the center of interest to economic theorists. But he treated value and distribution incidentally in the development of his general discussion of the factors which determine the amount of wealth produced in a country. He begins by pointing out that the production of wealth is enormously enhanced by what he calls the division of labor. When division of labor is practiced on a large scale, it is necessary for people who follow particular trades to exchange their products with that of others. The pinmaker who performs one of eight or ten operations in the making of a pin - we find that celebrated case mentioned in his book - of course produces nothing except one part of a pin; and he must get his food, clothing, shelter, entertainment, and whatever else he consumes, by exchanging the service that he renders for goods which have been produced by other people.

So division of labor necessitates exchange, and exchange, to be efficient, must take place in organized markets, and in these markets goods are traded for one another at varying prices. These prices at which goods exchange, Adam Smith tells us, can be analyzed into their component parts, which are rent, and wages, and profits. So you see, a discussion as oriented upon production as the central feature arrives at an analysis of the factors which determine prices and that analysis of prices leads on to a consideration of the shares in distribution, the three shares which were recognized in Adam Smith's time, for he does not give us a separate treatment of interest as separate from profits.

Adam Smith thus reverses the modern emphasis. With him production is the matter of chief concern; value and distribution are treated as incidents in the analysis of the conditions affecting production, whereas nowadays - and this is the great change in orientation which David Ricardo introduced in his Principles of Political Economy published in 1817 - the center of interest is value and distribution. What he said about production is ordinarily introduced in the course of an analysis of the factors which determine the prices at which commodities are exchanged for one another; and in the course of the subsequent analysis of the factors which regulate wages, rent, interest, and profit.

That then was Adam Smith's central problem. Now he treated this problem in a way which is relevant to his day; and it seems to us in a fashion rather peculiar. I think it fair to say that his treatment of the problem of production was a treatment from the viewpoint of the stateman. He talked about production as a problem of statecraft. He gives in the course of The Wealth of Nations two or three definitions of political economy. One of them is particularly interesting from the present point of view. It occurs at the first sentence of his fourth book "Of Systems of Political Economy":

> Political economy, considered as a branch of the science of a statesman or legislator, proposes two distinct objects: first, to provide a plentiful revenue or subsistence for the people, or more properly to enable them to provide such a revenue or subsistence for themselves; and secondly, to supply the state or commonwealth with a revenue sufficient for the public services. It proposes to enrich both the people and the sovereign.

That is, from the modern viewpoint, a very quaint conception of what political economy proposes to do. Nowadays we think of it as being or as aspiring to be a science; and we think of sciences as aiming to give us understanding of how phenomena are related to one another. Economic science is conceived to be that branch of human knowledge which gives us an understanding of how economic processes work. And we often are at considerable pains to argue that the economist as such should have nothing to say about what ought to be done. Economics we often claim does not propose to enrich anybody. All it does is to give to a student such a knowledge of economic processes as will enable him to draw certain conclusions, if he is interested in practical affairs, about how a country may prosper. The art of applying this knowledge to practical affairs is from this point of view best left to men who have mastered principles of political economy, but men who are not themselves investigators. The investigator by temperament may be likely to be a very poor hand at directing operations. On the other hand, the practical man is very commonly a poor scientist. Well, nothing of that sort is characteristic of Adam Smith or of the men of his generation. To him political economy was legitimately considered as a branch of the science of the statesman or legislator; and as such it proposed to enrich both the people of the country and the sovereign.

This problem of political economy considered as a branch of the science of the statesman is one that came to Adam Smith directly from his experience in his time. English policy in economic matters in the closing quarter of the eighteenth century was still substantially directed by national planning, the scheme of national planning that is called in our text-books on economic history Mercantilism. Those of you who have studied the devolopment of European countries in general and England in particular during modern times must have read expositions of the Mercantilist system. This is not the place in which to go into the details of that elaborate scheme of statecraft for enriching nations. You learn much of the detail indeed from Adam Smith himself because a very considerable proportion of the whole book is taken up by an exposition of the errors of Mercantilism, in the course of which you will find many of the details followed by Mercantilist statesmen set forth somewhat fully.

The system of Mercantilism had been going on in England for more than two centuries when Adam Smith wrote. It had gotten into fairly systematic form by the latter years of Queen Elizabeth. It was strengthened under James I and Charles I. Cromwell took it over and added to it emphasis upon the Navigation Laws, laws which were intended to win a larger part of the carrying trade from the Dutch in order that Britain might become more powerful upon the seas. The Civil War, of course, relaxed administration in England, and it was not reestablished after the Restoration in as systematic a form as it had been practiced in the days of Queen Elizabeth and Cromwell. But still these old regulations stood upon the statute books. And a man who discussed public policy would take it for granted that it was as much the duty of the statesman of the day to look after and supervise the economic interests of the country as a whole, to regulate them in detail, as much the duty to do that as it was to look after foreign affairs in the modern sense or to see that the game of politics was played in a proper fashion. Economic legislation was one of the chief tasks which the administration had continually to consider.

III

THE RELATION OF THE WEALTH OF NATIONS TO ECONOMIC SCIENCE

As I said at the beginning of the course, I have no intention of discussing in detail the economic analysis presented in any of the classics that we read. You can follow that analysis far better in the text yourself. My function is primarily to point out certain of the general features of the books that we take up and to discuss in particular their relation to the time out of which they came, of which they were a part.

I have already had occasion to remark that the order of The Wealth of Nations differs widely from that which is adopted in later treatises. I now want to discuss the relation of The Wealth of Nations to economic science at large. We speak commonly of political economy as a science and we often speak of Adam Smith as the father of political economy. We have some misgivings of imputing the paternity of economics to Adam Smith because there are other claimants for that honor. There are people who would say that the real father of political economy is Quesnay; there are others who would say that of a slightly earlier Franco-Irishman, Richard Cantillon, who published an Essay Upon the Nature of Commerce in General in 1755, an essay that shows remarkable powers of organization. And there are still others who would say that if you are really looking for a father of modern political economy you should go back a little further still to Pierre Boisguillebert, a French writer of numerous tracts,* whose unsystematic exposition does contain not a few of the observations and reflections that made Quesnay's work and Adam Smith's work seem so pregnant to contemporaries.

But waiving that question of who started political economy, it is interesting to observe the pattern in which this particular science grew up. We nowadays I think regard most of our highly developed sciences as growing mainly by a cumulative process of accretion; one man makes a discovery which suggests problems to other people; many set to work to see whether the first discovery is really valid. They work on the problems which the first discovery suggests, and presently additions are made to the one that started this innovation in research. And such innovations are being continuously made. We rely with a high degree of confidence upon the more or less steady process of the increase of scientific knowledge through the efforts of a very large number of trained investigators.

Now when some one of these investigators makes a particularly momentous

---

*Detail de la France sous le regne present, 1695, to which was added dissertations on Grains and Richesses and published in 1707 as Factum de la France.

discovery and we think of that discovery as possibly marking off a new epoch
in research, those who know most about the history of science are usually in a
position to point out that this discovery which was likely to seem to the lay-
man as a stroke of genius, as a matter of such exceptional significance, after
all is really representative of the tamer researches, the solid advances of
the preceding years. And once the momentous discovery is made, it takes its
place in the vast growing body of knowledge, plays its part in initiating new
research. So that, to repeat, it is easy to think of science as growing rather
steadily through the piling up of detailed discovery upon detailed discovery;
and the larger the body grows, the relatively less is the addition which any one
man can make by his own work to what is known in his own field.

It would appear, at least at first blush, as though economics had not
developed in that fashion. It does not matter whether you take the rise of political economy from the time of Adam Smith or the time of Quesnay, from the time
of Cantillon or from the time of Boisguillebert, it still remains true that if
you take any one of these men, you are impressed by a very considerable compass
of the work at the outset. It does not look like a humble beginning. It does
not seem to rest upon a large number of small discoveries that have been made by
successive generations of workers. But in good part an impression of a difference between the way in which political economy grew up and the way in which the
more advanced sciences grew is a delusion. I say in good part a delusion, for
obviously all these great innovators had at their disposal the results of a vast
amount of human observations. Every one who lives in the world is familiar
through his own daily activity with the fundamental economic processes. Each
one of them is engaged in valuing objects and trying to determine their relative
importance for various uses which we have for goods. Every one of us is familiar,
at least in some degree, with markets. We have to pay prices. Each one of us
gets his income from some source, and he knows something at least about how that
income is obtained, the sources from which it comes, the factors that determine
its size.

And then of course any one who thinks at all seriously about economic
matters, who observes with his own eyes not only his own economic behavior but
that of the people among whom he lives can see the processes of production and
exchange going on, he can learn not a little about the way in which the values
that are produced are distributed among the various people who contribute to the
process of production. In a certain sense he does not need to the same extent
as a physicist does special equipment for observation. To this day there are
economists who tell us that laboratories are not required for our purposes, that
the thing that is necessary is not to see how materials behave under artificial
conditions such as can be observed in experiments; the really significant thing
is to look within ourselves, by our own economic valuations, by our own experiences of the irksomeness of prolonged labor, and then to look abroad and see
how actual men deal with one another. And if the economist needs any special
methods of observation, the proper materials for him are not the kind of materials that might conceivably come out of laboratory; rather they are those wide
records of human behavior that are contained in statistics, for statistics can
extend the range of observation far beyond the reach of any man's eyes no matter
how far the man is able to travel, no matter how ready his access to people in
different social classes.

Further than that, these people who began to systematize economic inquiries had at their disposal a very considerable literature. The Mercantilists
whom Adam Smith criticizes so effectively produced a vast pamphlet literature.
They were not systematic writers, but Adam Smith could find much in English and
French, and those who wanted to in Italian and in Spanish and German treatises
that had been appearing for a century or two dealing with particular branches

of trade, going into detail regarding what the writers thought were proper governmental policies to encourage manufactures or to keep down rates of interest, or to stimulate the industry of the lower classes, to prevent the consumption of goods from rising to what they regarded as an extravagant scale. He could find an abundant literature on the colonies, on technical questions of money, on technical questions of organization, and so on without number. And for that matter he could go further back and see economic questions debated in philosophic fashion by the fathers of the Church. And of course if he thought it worth while he could consider what the Greek philosophers, Aristotle in particular, had to say about such matters as money and trade.

It was not this knowledge of economic facts that was new in The Wealth of Nations, or in Quesnay's Tableau Economique, or in Cantillon's Essay, or in Boisguillebert. What was new was the organization of a vast amount of knowledge which was more or less common property and which could be extended in detail just so far as an investigator wanted to observe or just in so far as he wanted to spend his time reading earlier pamphlets and tracts. The new thing was the organization of knowledge. What Adam Smith did was to show his contemporaries what were the leading problems of economic policy and what they knew about economic policy could be systematically grouped around a few leading ideas. And by this organization of knowledge he gave an enormously increased effectiveness to matters that were familiar to the mass of his fellow-countrymen. He showed his followers how, starting out from the organization he created, to extend the range of their knowledge, to make it wider, wiser, and more precise; and by the success of his own analysis he stimulated them to argue these questions which he had taken up.

Other sciences are not without examples of a similar sort. I do not know the history of biology in any detail, but I get the impression that what Adam Smith did for economics was in many ways like what Charles Darwin did for biology. If you read The Origin of Species you will find that Darwin cites an enormous amount of detailed evidence consisting largely of precise observations that had been made mostly by highly trained investigators, regarding the growth of plants and animal forms, regarding the similarity between parents and offspring or the differences that appear between them. Now that information was of course not common knowledge in the community as a whole to the extent that Adam Smith's information about the economic problems was because of course it is only the specialist who is likely to give very close attention to problems of a biological sort, whereas all are forced by circumstances to give at least a little reluctant attention to economic questions. But still Darwin did have at his disposal a great deal of material in the same sense that Adam Smith had large amounts of material at his disposal. And what Darwin did was to organize those old materials by suggesting a new framework which lent a new significance, a framework which seemed to offer an answer and which suggested a hope of further investigations that needed to be made, investigations which had a very large part in making biology what it has become.

We do not, however, regard anybody's knowledge as full-fledged science until it gets beyond the stage of setting familiar materials in a new framework, of introducing points of view and of drawing only rather broad and general conclusions. The sciences which we find most useful, which we represent as the fine product of intelligence are sciences that are able to give their conclusions a high degree of precision, that is, sciences that have advanced to the stage of quantitative statement, that can measure the relative importance of the factors which they regard as of most important consequence, that can measure the effects which different causes produce. That was the stage that Darwin did not reach and you will find of course that some of the more radical experimental biologists

of later time regard Darwin's achievement rather slightingly. I have heard
men say that after all Darwin's work stands closer to theology than it does
to science; that he suggested ideas which he tried to support by evidence but
that he has no real proof to offer, that proof can be had only by precise experiment. So a science remains insecure and of comparatively little worth
until you reach the stage where you can determine with a high degree of exactness what are the relations among the processes that concern you.

Adam Smith certainly did not profess to reach this stage of exactness.
His discussion runs almost altogether on what has been in later years called the
qualitative plane. He makes comparatively little measurements, and that despite
the fact that before the close of the seventeenth century a pretty strong beginning had been made at what was then called political arithmetic. That beginning is to be found among members of the group that constituted the great
Royal Society of which Sir Isaac Newton was the crowning glory. They were men
who believed that just as Newton's extraordinary scientific work had derived
its significance from the precision of his mathematical formulations, so in
carrying science into the study of social affairs we must build upon the determination of quantity, that we must eschew discussion of matters which can
be talked about only in vague and general terms. They held that only knowledge
of what happens in any department of society that can be counted, or weighed, or
measured is of consequence to the future.

The most memorable figure among these early exponents of political
arithmetic was Sir William Petty. Those of you who are interested in this department of economics will find a deal of interest in turning back to Sir
William Petty's rather hazardous numerical speculations about the number of the
population, the amount of the national wealth, and matters of a similar order.
Petty was by no means the only one interested in political arithmetic. Vital
statistics was getting its start in the time of Sir Isaac Newton largely through
statistics based upon bills of mortality, that is, death certificates. And other
later writers had begun to carry on this tradition. But unfortunately for them
they ran against the great difficulty of finding proper measurements upon which
to base their discussion when they got outside of a very narrow realm. And the
controversies that were carried on, even within Adam Smith's own lifetime, among
the leading political arithmeticians indicate how uncertain and insecure were
the efforts to build up quantitative knowledge.

Among Adam Smith's slightly younger contemporaries was a celebrated
pamphleteer, Dr. Richard Price, who dealt rather liberally with figures as well
as with political arithmetic. Dr. Richard Price, about the time Adam Smith was
writing The Wealth of Nations, undertook to prove that the population of England
had fallen off thirty per cent since the Restoration. And he arrived at that
astonishing numerical result by comparing the receipts from the hearth-money
tax in the days of the first Charles and the receipts from the inhabited house
data in later years. Well, needless to say, the data were not really comparable
and that it is certain that Price was wrong. At the same time William Eden,
using different materials, obtained largely from parish registers, was trying to
show that the population of England had been growing and growing somewhat steadily during this very period when Dr. Price claimed it was declining.

Well, in view of the fact that there could be differences among two
of the leading authorities of the day on a problem so simple as it seems to us
nowadays, and certainly so fundamental, as to whether population was falling
rapidly or whether it was increasing rather rapidly, in view of the fact that
such differences of opinion could exist, it is not surprising that Adam Smith remarked in one passage of The Wealth of Nations:"I have little faith in political arithmetic." To him it seemed that for the time being that lead which had

been worked on so confidently by able contemporaries of the great Sir Isaac
was a lead that had turned out to yield comparatively slight results. The
results it yielded seemed to him very precarious. So it was natural that he
turned back in his organization of knowledge to a simpler scheme, trying to
make out what the factors in the problem were, even though he could not have
determined with any degree of precision their relative importance, trying to
demonstrate how these factors tended to go in the processes of social life,
even though he could not measure the effects which should be attributed to the
several factors intelligently. It did seem to him that he could prove on the
basis of general argumentation, not supported by quantitative evidence, a
conclusion of the utmost practical importance and of great intellectual interest,
mainly the conclusion that the wealth of a nation would be promoted with vastly
greater effectiveness by the "simple and obvious system of natural liberty"
than it would be perfected by national planning of the Mercantilistic sort.
And so he gives us an organization of knowledge relatively elementary in the
sense that it made very little pretensions at precision, but very significant
in the sense that even without exact formulation it seemed to establish with a
high degree of certainty conclusions of vast import.

IV

ADAM SMITH'S THEORIES CONTRASTED WITH THOSE OF

THE MERCANTILISTS

At the first meeting of the class I presented the view that the
several types of economic theory which we shall become acquainted with in this
course differ from each other primarily in respect to the problems that are
put into the forefront by the successive authors. Their difference lies primarily in the perspective in which they see the several leading problems of
economics. And secondly, they differ from each other in respect to the common
conception of human nature which successive writers upon general economic theory
have entertained. We start with Adam Smith not because he represents the beginning of economic theory —needless to say that is not the fact— but because
his formulation was the earliest which has exercised a very potent influence
upon the work that is being done in later times. In very large measure Adam
Smith summed up and presented in superior form the contributions of his predecessors, and the people who have made constructive contributions to economic
theory have in general not felt themselves under the need of going back earlier
than The Wealth of Nations in their own researches, though again, needless to
say, the historians of economic theory have done a great deal of work with his
Physiocratic and Mercantilist predecessors.

In accordance with the view of what differentiates the types of economic theory from each other, our first question about Adam Smith is: what problems
did he put into the forefront of the discussion, what was the perspective in
which he saw the questions which economics treats, what was the general outline
of the subject in his eyes? That question is very simply answered: it is
answered, as I said at the first meeting, in the very title of his book The
Wealth of Nations. The problem which Adam Smith conceives to be the master problem for an economist is the problem how can the growth in the wealth of nations
be most facilitated? A little more specifically, what line of policy is most
conducive to the increase of the wealth of nations? And the answer to that
question concerning the policy most conducive to the increase of wealth is again
simply summed up in the term which has become famous, the two words laissez
faire, in the belief that the wealth of nations will increase most rapidly if

every person is allowed the fullest opportunity to decide for his own individual self what is the best way to use his labor and whatever capital he possesses. In other words, the best policy for governments (and, of course, when you talk about economic policies you are, in Adam Smith's day at least, certain to be concerned with the problem of the policies of government) is to interfere as little as possible with the occupations and investments of its citizens.

And the next question we want to ask about Adam Smith's type of theory is what conception of human nature did he entertain? You find that the conception of human nature that he entertained had a very great deal to do in determining the answer that he gave to his question about the best policy for increasing national wealth. His conception of human nature has been briefly summed up by Walter Bagehot* in the statement that he thought that there was a Scotchman inside every man, a person who was intent primarily upon pushing his own fortunes and who possessed a high degree of shrewdness in deciding what he could best do.

Now Adam Smith's problem of how the wealth of nations can most effectively be promoted was a problem that he got directly from his predecessors, the Mercantilists, that rather ill-defined group of somewhat unsystematic writers who treated a series of questions of public policy in an economic order. To the Mercantilist the one important thing to anyone interested in what we now call economics was the question: what is the right policy of the government to pursue in order to increase the national wealth, or the national power? They were primarily concerned with the national wealth because they considered national power as resting on an economic foundation. And the answer that they gave to the question as to what was best policy was almost always an answer in terms that could recommend themselves to most politicians of the age. It was that the government ought actively to undertake to guide the activities of its citizens into those lines which were conducive to national well-being. They recommended a series of ingenious regulations concerning the terms on which goods might be imported from abroad or exported. They went far in the development of a very elaborate and detailed tariff policy. They believed that the government should definitely encourage certain lines of manufacture by direct grants of bounties or monopoly privileges in some cases, and should do everything in its power to build up a great mercantile marine.

The Mercantilists also thought the government should acquire colonies and run the affairs of those colonies in the interests of the home country; that the colonies be required to buy commodities in the home country; and, on the other hand, the colonies be forced to export their raw products to the home country instead of trading with any nation with whom they could make the best bargains. They believed the labor force of the country, that is, most of the work-

*"Adam Smith and Our Modern Economy" in Economic Studies by Walter Bagehot, (1895) p.125. The paragraph referred to reads as follows: "Adam Smith approximates to our modern political economist, because his conception of human nature is so limited. It has been justly said that he thought 'there was a Scotchman inside every man'. His Theory of Moral Sentiment, indeed, somewhat differs in tone, but all through The Wealth of Nations, the desire of man to promote his pecuniary interest is treated as far more universally intense, and his willingness to labour for that interest as far more eager and far more commonly diffused, than experience shows them to be. Modern economists, instructed by a larger experience well know that the force of which their science treats is neither so potent nor so isolated as Adam Smith thought. They consistently advance as an assumption what he more or less assumes as a fact."

ing people, should in a broad degree be the wards of the government; that the government should determine the conditions for entrance to every trade; that it should adopt sufficient apprenticeship rules in order to see that in each trade there be adequate workmen and no more than adequate. That the government should lay down the terms of admission to any occupation. That the government should regulate or supervise, at least in the large, the wages that were obtained. And so for almost the whole realm of economic life; that the government should have a detailed economic policy which required active intervention in the affairs of the community in a thousand and one ways, all with the great purpose of achieving exactly the aim Adam Smith wanted to achieve; the most rapid possible increase in the country's wealth.

So Adam Smith, while having the same problem as the focus of his attention as the Mercantilists, arrived at a very different solution from the one which they recommended. He arrived at a very different solution despite the fact that he had, in part at least, the same working conception of human nature that the Mercantilists had. The real difference between Adam Smith and the Mercantilists arose from the fact that Adam Smith held that when every man was following his own advantage the net resultant was bound to be that which was most conducive to national welfare for the simple reason that the wealth of the country was, in his eyes, the sum total of the wealth of its inhabitants; therefore, anything which promoted most effectively the wealth of the individuals who belonged in the community was the policy which must of necessity contribute most to the growth of the national wealth. The Mercantilists held that if every man tried to do those things which were for his own advantage very grievous national ills would arise unless some statesman who was looking out for the fortunes of the individuals in the interests of the welfare of the whole commonwealth, should formulate a general plan and by ordered regulations get it effected.

Now I want to make what I have been saying rather clearer by reading you some extracts, first from The Wealth of Nations and second from the best representative of Mercantilist lore. I start with a passage in The Wealth of Nations which shows you the basis for Walter Bagehot's remark that Adam Smith thought there was a Scotchman inside every man:

> . . . The uniform, constant, and uninterrupted effort of every man to better his condition, the principle from which public and national, as well as private opulence is originally derived, is frequently powerful enough to maintain the natural progress of things toward improvement, in spite both of the extravagance of government, and of the greatest errors of administration.*

Adam Smith is there, you see, taking it for granted that every man behaves like the Scotchman of the cartoon and the movie; he is characterized by well-nigh constant and uninterrupted effort to better his condition. And he also takes it here without argument that this is the principle from which public and national as well as private fortune is derived.

Now I will read you a passage a little longer which comes somewhat later in the book:

> Every individual is continually exerting himself to find out the most advantageous employment for whatever capital he can command. It is his own advantage, indeed, and not that of the society, which he has in view. But the study of his own advantage naturally, or rather

*The Wealth of Nations; Bk II, Ch. 3 Cannan ed., vol. I. p. 325; Everyman ed. vol. I p. 306; Modern Library ed. p. 326.

necessarily leads him to prefer that employment which is most advantageous to the society.*

And then a page or two later he explains somewhat the reason why he thinks that
the individual's "study of his own advantage naturally, or rather necessarily
leads him to prefer that employment which is most advantageous to the society."
The reason that he gives runs as follows:

> But the annual revenue of every society is always precisely
> equal to the exchangeable value of the whole annual produce of its in-
> dustry, or rather is precisely the same thing with that exchangeable
> value. (p.413)

In more modern terms: the national income is the sum of the income of the people
who belong to the nation.

> As every individual, therefore, endeavours as much as he can
> both to employ his capital in the support of domestic industry, and
> so to direct that industry that its produce may be of the greatest
> value; every individual necessarily labours to render the annual
> revenue of the society as great as he can. He generally, indeed, neither
> intends to promote the public interest, nor knows how much he is pro-
> moting it. By preferring the support of domestic to that of foreign
> industry, he intends only his own security; and by directing that
> industry in such a manner as its produce may be of the greatest value,
> he intends only his own gain, and he is in this, as in many other cases,
> led by an invisible hand to promote an end which was no part of his in-
> tention. Nor is it always the worse for the society that it was no
> part of it. By pursuing his own interest he frequently promotes that
> of the society more effectually than when he really intends to promote
> it. I have never known much good done by those who affected to trade
> for the public good. It is an affectation, indeed, not very common
> among merchants, and very few words need be employed in dissuading them
> from it.

Then, going on with the argument, -and he is here talking about the inexpedience
of national interference with foreign trade by means of tariffs - he said:

> What is the species of domestic industry which his capital can
> employ, and of which the produce is likely to be the greatest value;
> every individual, it is evident, can, in his local situation, judge
> much better than any statesman or lawgiver can do for him.

The emphasis there, you see, is on the fact that every man knows his own circumstances vastly better, in Adam Smith's language, in his local situation he
is a better judge as best to employ his capital than anybody in the distant
capital of the country can judge. It is evident with Adam Smith that it takes
no evidence to substantiate the argument.

> The statesman, who should attempt to direct private people in what
> manner they ought to employ their capitals, would not only load
> himself with a most unnecessary attention, but assume an authority
> which could safely be trusted, not only to no single person, but

*The Wealth of Nations; Bk. IV, Ch. 2; Cannan ed., vol. I p.419; Everyman
ed., vol. I, p. 398; Modern Library ed. p. 421.

to no council or senate whatever, and which would no-where be so
dangerous as in the hands of a man who had folly and presumption
enough to fancy himself fit to exercise it.* ·

You see how bold and sweeping that argument is from Adam Smith's eyes; everybody quite ovbiously is pursuing his own interest; everybody, it is evident,
in his own local situation is a better judge of where his economic interest
lies than any statesman could be. Therefore, the individual will get on best
if he is left alone by the government. But the income of the nation as a whole
is nothing but the sum of the income of the individulas who compose the nation.
Therefore, the policy which is most advantageous to individuals must be the
policy which is most advantageous to the nation. There is the great fundamental argument for laissez faire.

ˏ   Adam Smith goes through his discussion, but points out that there
are certain exceptions to this general rule, but the exceptions are not numerous and they are all defended on the grounds of considerations which must take
primacy as contrasted with considerations of the nation's wealth; above all,
great questions of national security. He is rather inclined to defend economic regulations the end of which is to make the nation secure. It is worth
sacrificing some of the larger wealth that you might otherwise obtain for this
fundamentally important aim. But except for matters of that sort the government
should pursue the policy of laissez faire, that is, the policy of giving every
individual citizen an opportunity to pursue his own economic interests unham-
pered save that no one must pursue his own individual interest in ways that deny
his fellow-citizens similar opportunities.

        I want to read another passage, hardly less celebrated than the one
I just read. It occurs almost at the end of the Fourth Book in which he is
examining elaborately the economic system recommended by the Physiocrats, a
system which we shall see a little later on had something in common with his
own and from the study of which he profited a great deal. He winds up his remarks with these ringing words:

        It is thus that every system which endeavours, either, by ex-
        traordinary encouragements, to draw towards a particular species of
        industry greater share of the capital of the society than what
        would naturally go to it; or, by extraordinary restraints, to force
        from a particular species of industry some share of the capital
        which would otherwise be employed in it; is in reality subversive
        of the great purpose which it means to promote. It retards, instead
        of accelerating, the progress of the society towards real wealth and
        greatness; and diminishes, instead of increasing , the real value of
        the annual produce of its land and labour.

        All systems either of preference or of restraint, therefore,
        being thus completely taken away, the obvious and simple system of
        natural liberty establishes itself of its own accord. Every man,
        as long as he does not violate the laws of justice, is left per-
        fectly free to pursue his own interest his own way, and to bring
        both his industry and capital into competition with those of any
        other man, or order of men. The sovereign is completely discharged
        from a duty, in the attempting to perform which he must always be
        exposed to innumerable delusions, and for the proper performance

*Ibid; Bk. IV. Ch. 2., Cannan ed. vol. I, p. 421; Everyman ed., vol.I,,pp. 400-
401; Modern Library ed., p. 423.

of which no human wisdom or knowledge could ever be sufficient;
the duty of superintending the industry of private people, and
of directing it towards the employments most suitable to the
interest of the society. According to the system of natural
liberty, the sovereign has only three duties to attend to; three
duties of great importance, indeed, but plain and intelligible
to common understandings; first, the duty of protecting the
society from the violence and invasion of other independent
societies; secondly, the duty of protecting, as far as possible,
every member of the society from the injustice or oppression
of every other member of it, or the duty of establishing an
exact administration of justice; and, thirdly, the duty of
erecting and maintaining certain public works and certain public institutions which it can never be for the interest of any
individual, or small number of individuals, to erect and maintain; because the profit could never repay the expense to any
individual or small number of individuals, though it may frequently do much more than repay it to a great society.*

It was in the eighteenth century that you find the great prophet of
the coming day in economics talking about natural liberty in following your
material interests, in just that same large and evident way concerning which
his admirers in the United States and presently in France began to talk about
political principles, and the two ideas really had a great deal in common. He
says the government has just three duties: one is public defense, second the
administration of justice, and third the maintenance of public works such as
roads and bridges, perhaps the post-office, probably not the schools. Had
Adam Smith lived a generation or two later he might have considered public
schools as fit item falling under his third head here, public works and institutions.

By way of contrast to this philosophy of Adam Smith, let me read you
some passages from his contemporary, another Scotchman, Sir James Steuart. Sir
James Steuart had been a Jacobite in his younger days and as such had been
banished. That had led him to spend a good part of his life upon the Continent.
He was as typically a Scotchman as Adam Smith, very much interested in economic affairs, a very close and detailed observer of economic policies in all the
countries with which he had been acquainted in his enforced travels, and a
very systematic writer. In his middle age he was allowed to return home and he
set himself to work writing a great treatise on economic policy which he called
An Inquiry into the Principles of Political Economy: Being an Essay on the
Science of Domestic Policy in Free Nations. This was published in 1767. You
see, that was just nine years before The Wealth of Nations came out, and I
think it is fair to say that Sir James Steuart's Inquiry is, broadly speaking,
about the most systematic summary of Mercantilist wisdom which was compiled.

If the Scotchman inside every man is the central figure in Adam Smith's
economic philosophy, the statesman occupies a similarly central position in Sir
James Steuart's philosophy. It is his task not only to develop schemes of statecraft but also to see that these schemes are obeyed, put into actual practice.
The first passages that I will read you concern the question of the means by
which the statesman is to get his schemes of national economic policy acted
upon. And you will see that in this explanation Sir James is presenting a conception of human nature very similar to the one which Adam Smith presented,

---

*Ibid.; Bk. IV, Ch. 9; Cannan ed., vol II, pp. 181-185: Everyman ed., vol. II,
pp. 180-181; Modern Library ed., pp. 650-651

though there is a different point, a critical point of difference.

> The principle of self-interest will serve as a general key to this inquiry; and it may, in one sense, be considered as the ruling principle of my subject, and may therefore be traced throughout the whole. This is the main spring, and only motive which a statesman should make use of, to engage a free people to concur in the plans which he lays down for their government.

Indeed, he starts with self-interest like Adam Smith but at once proceeds, without arguing, to hold that this is a principle of which the statesman should make use.

> From this principle men are engaged to act in a thousand different ways, and every action draws after it certain necessary consequences. The question therefore constantly under consideration comes to be, what will mankind find it their interest to do, under such and such circumstances? . . . .

> The best way to govern a society, and to engage every one to conduct himself according to a plan, is for the statesman to form a system of administration, the most consistent possible with the interest of every individual, and never to flatter himself that his people will be brought to act in general, and in matters which purely regard the public, from any other principle than private interest.

> Public spirit, in my way of treating this subject, is as superfluous in the governed, as it ought to be all-powerful in the statesman . . .

You see there is close kinship with Adam Smith there, that assumption that public spirit is superfluous in the governed.

> at least, if it is not altogether superfluous, it is fully as much so, as miracles are in a religion once fully established. Both are admirable at setting out, but would shake everything loose were they to continue to be common and familiar. Were miracles wrought every day, the laws of nature would no longer be laws; and were every one to act for the public and neglect himself, the statesman would be bewildered, and the supposition is rediculous.

> I expect, therefore, that every man is to act for his own interest in what regards the public; and, politically speaking, every one ought to do so. It is the combination of every private interest which forms the public good, and of this the public, that is, the statesman, only can judge . . . . . .

There you see the critical difference comes out. "It is the combination of every private interest which forms the public good", just as to Adam Smith the wealth of the nation is the sum of the wealth of the individuals that compose it. The difference between the two men is that one takes for granted that the pursuit of private interest will, in his own language, promote that of society, while the other has the shrewd conviction that the public good must be looked after by people who make this their one great task, that is, by statesmen, for without a definite plane the pursuit of private interest would lead to public injury.

Were the principle of public spirit carried farther; were
a people to become quite disinterested, there would be no
possibility of governing them. Every one might consider the
interest of his country in a different light, and many might
join in the ruin of it, by endeavoring to promote its advantages...

Now as I suppose my statesman to do his duty in the most
minute particulars, so I allow every one of his subjects to
follow the dictates of his private interest. All I require is
an exact obedience to the laws. This also is the interest of
everyone; for he who transgresses ought most undoubtedly to be
punished; and this is all the public spirit which any perfect
government has occasion for.*

Here is another passage. It is not possible to get from Sir James
Steuart anything that puts his central philosophy in concise form as The Wealth
of Nations for the reason that Sir James was not gifted with Adam Smith's grasp
of ideas and that he did not have Adam Smith's genius of exposition. I suppose
few writers have ever lived who were more skilful in setting their views in
broad and persuasive fashion than Adam Smith. So, to repeat, I cannot get anything that is quite as nice an exposition of the central viewpoint here. You
have to take passages which bear upon details and see what they imply. Here he
is discussing what happens when a country begins to go backward. a trading
nation.

. . .so soon as matters begin to go backward in a trading
nation, and that by the increase of their riches, luxury, and extravagance take place of economy and frugality among the industrious;
when the inhabitants themselves foolishly enter into competition
with strangers for their own commodities:

You see, these are silly things people are inclined to do if left unguided; increase of riches will betray them into extravagance, and they foolishly enter
into competition with strangers for their own commodities.

. . and when a statesman looks cooly on,

which is exactly what Adam Smith says the statesman should do while people are
attending to their own affairs

. . with his arms across, or takes it into his head, that it is
not his business to interpose, the prices of the dextrous workman will rise above the amount of the management, loss, and
reasonable profits, of the new beginners; and when this comes
to be the case, trade will decay where it flourished most, and
take root in a new soil . . . .**

That is, you will have wages rising to an unprofitable level, you won't any
longer have a thriving industry, and the country will be impoverished.

One other passage. Here he is talking not about the decay of once
flourishing things but about how to develop infant industries; he talks about
infant trades.

*An Inquiry into the Principles of Political Economy, London, 1767; vol. I
pp. 162-165
**Ibid.; vol. I, p. 236

> The statesman who resolves to improve this infant trade into
> foreign commerce must examine the wants of other nations, and con-
> sider the productions of his own country. He must then determine,
> what kinds of manufactures are best adapted for supplying the first,
> and for consuming the latter. He must introduce the use of such
> manufactures among his subjects; and endeavour to extend his popu-
> lation, and his agriculture, by encouragements given to these new
> branches of consumption. He must provide his people with the best
> masters; he must supply them with every useful machine; and above all,
> he must relieve them of their work,

That does not mean shorter hours. It means he must make a market for their products.

> when home demand is not sufficient for the consumption of it.*

The statesman, thus, must do it all.

Now Sir James Steuart was undoubtedly expounding the view which was
not only traditional in England, which was not only embodied in the country's
existing scheme of legislation, but also the view that was accepted as plain
common sense. Adam Smith, on the other hand, in holding that the statesman
should sit still with his arms across and look calmly on while people were
following their own interest, challenged in the most direct fashion the laws
of England relating not merely to all imports and exports of commodities to
foreign nations but also substantially to all the laws relating to the management of the country's colonies, the enormous mass of legislation relating to
the conduct of the various trades, the time-honored scheme which was supposed
to regulate the wages of people throughout the country; laws for preventing
prices from being carried to exorbitant heights, laws which were supposed to
protect borrowers from the necessity of paying usurious rates of interest. He
was challenging a whole scheme of life which had grown up in England and which
rested on exactly the sort of thing that Sir James Steuart was systematizing.
It was a message that struck intelligent people in his generation like a fresh
wind from the mountains. It makes a very different impression upon us nowadays,
primarily because Adam Smith succeeded, or rather his successors succeeded in
getting Adam Smith's philosophy accepted in very large measure by modern countries, most of all by England itself. It became for a considerable time the
dominant economic gospel of his country, a doctrine which became dominant but,
on the other hand, a target of criticism. Our minds, of course, have been formed in that era when people are beginning to react against the philosophy which
was to the minds of most people so novel in the days when The Wealth of Nations
was published.

V.
THE LOGIC OF ADAM SMITH'S THEORIES

At the last meeting I pointed out the sharp contrast between the
opposing views of Adam Smith and his Scotch contemporary, Sir James Steuart,
upon the question how best to facilitate the increase of national wealth. We
find Sir James Steuart standing for the traditional policy that a statesman
should develop a grand scheme of economic mobilization and frame the necessary
laws and regulations to compel the citizens of the country to do those things
which he as a statesman saw were conducive to national economic prosperity.

*Ibid., vol. I, pp. 302-303.

And Adam Smith we found working for a thoroughgoing policy of _laissez faire_, what he himself called "the obvious and simple system of natural liberty". Today I want to discuss the question how Adam Smith came by his strong faith in the superiority of the simple and obvious system of natural liberty as a means of promoting national prosperity over the traditional system of guidance by a statesman.

Now the question which of these two lines of policy is in fact more conducive to national welfare is a question which in the realm of fancy might be decided by factual observation. If you could find two countries one of which adopted the _laissez faire_ policy and the other of which had a thoroughly worked out system of Mercantilism, countries which in other respects were similarly situated, and if you could then get reliable statistical measurements of the annual produce of the two nations over a half century or a longer period you might be able to say with considerable confidence that you had demonstrated the superiority of one system or the other.

Well, needless to say, that was not a method of proof open to Adam Smith. There was in his day no country in the world which was actually following the policy of _laissez faire_. And if there had been one such country, it would have certainly differed in a variety of respects from the rest of the nations of the world which were pursuing Mercantilist policies. And anyone who doubted the conclusions that were based on observation of the _laissez faire_ country and the Mercantilist countries might have ascribed the difference between their relative prosperity to some one of the other ways in which they differed from each other. You might have said this country has a better climate, or more energetic people, or the people are Protestant instead of Catholic, or there is a different form of government. Heaven knows how many different explanations might be found.

That way of working simply was not at all feasible; and Adam Smith did not arrive at his faith in the superiority of _laissez faire_ by any such direct process, at least of observation. He demonstrated his conclusions by argument; what he gives us is a syllogism. And the real question to be faced by any one interested in finding out whether his opinion is sound or not would concern the legitimacy of the assumptions on which that syllogism rested. For like all syllogisms it was built by combining certain premises and on the basis of the premises drawing what appeared an inevitable conclusion.

So let us look at these premises and see where Adam Smith got them. The first proposition on which his syllogism rests is that there is a Scotchman inside every man, to quote his own phraseology again: "The uniform, constant, and uninterrupted effort of every man to better his condition" is assumed. He says every individual is continually exerting himself to find out the most advantageous employment for whatever capital he can command. That is an assumption concerning the character of human nature. Adam Smith is taking it for granted and he uses very strong language that every individual is characterized by a uniform, constant, and uninterrupted effort to better his condition.

Now is that assumption a valid one? How did Adam Smith convince himself that this is true of people at large? Do you accept the assumption yourself as applying to the community in which you live? If you question it, on what grounds? And do you question it simply by pointing out that there are exceptions to the rule, that there are such people as tramps, for instance, that in more fortunate surroundings there are spendthrifts? Include every individual, does it? Or do you question the word "continually" and say that a good part of our time we are, after all, quite intent on finding the most advantageous employment for our capital or trying to better our condition, but that we also engage in

other pursuits out of which we get more satisfaction. Or would you be inclined to say this is a rather fundamentally wrong picture of human nature;
that men, as a matter of fact, lack that hard rationality which Adam Smith
ascribes to them, that they are by no means so energetic, so alert to their
own advantages as he assumes? Suppose you do differ from Adam Smith, how could
you maintain your position against him? Quite clearly this is an assumption,
isn't it, -an assumption which you can challenge, which I suppose most modern
people would be inclined to challenge, at least in the very rigid form in which
Adam Smith put it forward, but an assumption which we find it exceedingly difficult to replace by some different statement which we can approve.

Adam Smith had to get that from his own rather casual observation of
the community of which he was a part, supplemented by the prevailing ideas of
the students of human behavior of his time, just in the same way we get whatever ideas we hold of human nature: observations, first, of our disposition
which we are rather prone to think common; second, by observation of the people
about us; and third, whatever contact we have with definite inquiries into the
field of human motive, how people act.

The second proposition in Adam Smith's syllogism is that every individual is the best judge of how to spend his own time and labor, notably a
better judge than a statesman can be. Once more to quote his own language:

What is the species of domestic industry which his capital
can employ, and of which the produce is likely to be the greatest
value, every individual, it is evident, can, in his local situation,
judge much better than any statesman or lawgiver can do for him.

- -better judge of the most advantageous course of economic activity to follow.
Well, here you see Adam Smith treats his view as a matter that admits of no discussion. It is clear that a statesman, though he may be a vastly abler individual than Tom Jones, still would not know Tom Jones's circumstances in his
knowledge of the local circumstances which puts him in a better position to
judge what he had better undertake than somebody living in London might judge.

Let me ask again, is that proposition evident to you? And if it is
not evident, why do you doubt it, what is your ground? Is it evident to you
that something quite different from what Adam Smith said on this head is the
truth? And if so, how can you defend your position if somebody questions it
as we are now questioning what Adam Smith said? Presumably if whatever view
you entertain is questioned, you will find very considerable difficulty in
adducing evidence which will convince the skeptic of your opinion. What can
you resort to, after all, in the way of convincing evidence of the broad issue
as to whether a statesman is a better judge as to what to do than a given individual? And what if you again perhaps after all find that your difference
from Adam Smith came down to the quantitative matter that some individuals can
judge better than the statesman can do but some individuals cannot? And what if
you come to think the question would be: what proportion of the individuals
would be better judges and what proportion of the individulas in the community
require guidance of the sort that can be provided by a statesman?

That is one of the matters of course on which we do not have any definite information to this day. We do not have observations that we can rely
upon to decide such issues, presumably even if we should spend an hour in discussing the question. We would find that we are debating with each other and
debating on a basis where it would be exceedingly difficult for us to find
any definite criterion to which we could submit our diverging views, and the
verdict of which we would accept unhesitatingly. There are plenty of questions

on which mens opinions differed in Adam Smith's day and about which people did carry on rather lively controversies and which nowadays we can answer in a very effective fashion. For example, two of Adam Smith's rather distinguished contemporaries interested in economic matters were interested in whether the population of England had increased or decreased since the revolution of '69. Dr. Richard Price thought there had been a decrease and he brought forward what seemed to him adequate statistical evidence. Various people, among them William Eden, held there had been a decided increase in the population, and they again had statistical evidence upon which to base their view. Nowadays if anyone wants to know whether the population of Great Britain had decreased or increased since 1850, there would be a very simple way of settling the question, for there is definite systematic information gathered to which any interested person would turn at once if the question were raised, and evidence of such a convincing sort that any man at all competent to engage in such discussion would be quite willing to accept as decisive, whatever his own personal preliminary views on the subject may have been.

Well, that is true about simple matters like the movement of population. We are in a position nowadays to discuss such matters with more security than most learned people in the last quarter of the eighteenth century. But there are plenty of issues, live and fundamental matters like the one concerning the superiority of individual judgment over statesmanlike guidance which we still cannot meet in the same certain, definite and decisive fashion.

Adam Smith's third proposition is that the annual revenue of every society is always precisely equal to the exchangeable value of the whole annual produce of its industry, or rather, is precisely the same thing as that exchangeable value. Now the context of this quotation shows that when he was speaking about the annual revenue of every society being precisely equal to the exchangeable value of the whole industrial output of the country, he was thinking of the industry of the individual citizens composing the country; that is, the national income is the sum total of all incomes. And he takes that as a matter of actual identity.

Well, that is another assumption. The real question of course is whether the government as such is not one of the great producing agencies. I say the government as such, and nowadays of course we are inclined to think that governments are producing agencies. As a matter of fact, this is one of the earliest of Adam Smith's propositions to be challenged. Still another Scotchman, Lord Lauderdale, slightly younger than Adam Smith, in reflecting upon The Wealth of Nations thought that Adam Smith had made a fundamental error in identifying national wealth as the sum total of individual wealth. He pointed out that there are important parts of the wealth of the country that are not owned by individuals.

When you stop to think about it, Lauderdale is obviously right. Nowadays you find people who are interested in such matters as ascertaining the national income of the country estimating on no very secure statistical basis the income that is produced by various branches of government, from the local school districts up through the municipal, county, and state governments, to the Federal government. And you will find that the people interested in studying the real incomes of wage-earners point out that quite apart from what wage-earners buy, they get a very substantial income in the shape of what are, so far as their individual occupations are concerned, free goods. Education of children is provided for them by the states; they have in most cities various forms of recreation; there are the roads and parkways that they enjoy; - a great diversity of things, quite apart from what is definitely given to the poorer members of society in the way of charity from public agencies.

Every one of Adam Smith's assumptions, then, if you take them up in detail and begin to examine them critically may seem to you to be open to question. If you do question them you may convince yourself - I think you will find it very hard indeed to show just how far your view is correct and just how far Adam Smith's view is wrong. The notable thing is that Adam Smith was able as a singularly realistic observer of life in a broad sense, as a singularly keen philosophic mind, to assume that human nature is of a very alert, rational type, intent upon pushing private interests; that he can assume without hesitation that everybody is the best judge, or is a better judge of how to promote his own fortunes than any statesman could be. And when he can assume that the wealth of the nation is simply the sum total of the income of the individuals that compose it - if you grant Adam Smith these assumptions, then his conclusion follows inevitably, for there is nothing wrong with the syllogism, that is, the logical part of it is sound. Whatever questions you have are questions that relate to the legitimacy of the assumptions which are used in the syllogism.

Now let me go back to the fact that with even less argument one of Adam Smith's abler contemporaries came to precisely opposite opinions, and that this other man, Sir James Steuart, was speaking for the common sense of his time, the current beliefs of the intelligent public. Certainly the beliefs of the ruling classes were the beliefs that Sir James Steuart was expressing. And Adam Smith's claims for the simple and obvious system of natural liberty were the claims of a radical, so far as philosophic speculation was concerned, challenging in a most vigorous fashion views that were then current. Adam Smith's views, if accepted, would imply all sorts of sweeping practical changes in the government of the country. As a matter of fact, they involved a good deal more than economic changes. If Adam Smith's view of human nature is right, then you have a good case for a system of democratic government such as England at that time was far from possessing. If you really could attribute to every individual this keen desire to promote his own welfare, then quite clearly every individual ought to have a chance in deciding what the public policies of the country should be, -and that means, at the very least, manhood suffrage.

What I now want to discuss is how Adam Smith came to entertain this daring faith, a faith that he seemed to hold implicitly, although the assumptions which it involves may seem to us very questionable. In order to make that clear I have got to remind you, and in some detail, of how the economic life of Great Britain was developing. I said that Sir James Steuart was speaking for British traditions, one might say European traditions. And yet it is, I think, perfectly true that Adam Smith's faith in the superiority of individual initiative and enterprise was only a philosopher's rationalization of a practice which was becoming very common in the England of his day, a practice which people found themselves engaged in, though it often ran counter to the laws, and from which they derived individual benefit, often times with compunctions in the belief that what was good for themselves was injurious to the body politic, but which men were continually doing on a broad scale. And then comes a philosopher who says what the people are doing is not wrong but exactly what ought to happen. By rationalization of what most energetic members of the population were doing in practice, Adam Smith did a great deal to stimulate the increase of individual initiative, its rapid spread. It was because Adam Smith's book was in a genuine sense an endorsement of a practice becoming most familiar it turned out to be one of the most influential books published. It was followed in a far shorter time than Adam Smith dreamed possible by a drastic change in the tenor of England's economic policies, ushering in a new day within two generations or thereabouts after The Wealth of Nations had been published.

The new theory was an intellectual reflex of a new practice of individual initiative in economic affairs, -new at least in its scope and in its disregard of repressive conventions; a new practice that was growing up in England during Adam Smith's time. The faith that Adam Smith had in individual initiative as opposed to reliance on the sagacity of the statesman was the result of his reflections on what he saw about him. A review of developments in the eighteenth century will illustrate this, and serve as an example of the way in which our thought on economic matters changed.

The eighteenth century in England was a period of peace as things went. There were within the hundred some fifty-six years in which the country was not engaged in any considerable foreign war; a relatively peaceful period, in which men's minds turned in larger measure than in preceding generations to thoughts of their economic interest. It was not only a period in which there was relatively little foreign war, but a period in which the domestic turmoils of the seventeenth century had been settled, so that the country internally, as well as for more than half the time externally, was not distracted by those matters which war, domestic and foreign, always brings to the forefront. What use the English people made of this relatively quiet and peaceful time to develop their economic interests is the matter which I shall take up when we meet again.

VI

ENGLISH DEVELOPMENTS IN THE EIGHTEENTH CENTURY
THE PHENOMENON OF INDIVIDUAL INITIATIVE

The development of economic theory is part of the development of men's minds, men's intelligence. That is the result of a social process; and if we want to see this in its real significance for us, we must endeavor to understand the circumstances out of which the development came. Men began to think very seriously about economic problems and to conceive the idea that their thoughts concerning these problems could be arranged on the model of the already established sciences; that they could be systematized and made into a more or less coherent discipline.

With the aim of giving some degree of concreteness to that general statement, I shall endeavor today and possibly at the next meeting or two to show the circumstances which I conceive to be of particular importance in leading to the rise of classical political economy in England. I already started that undertaking at the last meeting by beginning to recite a few of the very important facts of British history which appear to be relevant to our purpose - facts, most of which are already known to you, but facts which I think were very likely never assembled and reflected upon as bearing upon the way in which men were endeavoring to treat their economic problems.

The first of these very important facts is the one that I mentioned at the last meeting: that the eighteenth century in England was, as things went in European history at that time, a period of peace - a period in which there were no very serious civil disturbances in the country, and in which, so far as international relations were concerned, England was at peace for rather more than half the time.

Under these circumstances, arts of life developed at a more rapid pace than had been the case in the preceding centuries. Of course, all students of economics are particularly familiar with the changes which were taking place in the economic organization and industrial methods of the time. In the sixteenth, still more in the seventeenth century, British commerce had been growing on a large scale, and the like was true of the domestic trade. This expanded market contributed to and was itself enhanced by certain changes which were taking place in the methods of commercial organization. The eighteenth century was a period in which the older, rather small scale methods of organizing an industry for production and distribution of wares were giving place to something corresponding more closely to the modern capitalistic models. That movement which is frequently referred to as the Commercial Revolution, and concerning which we shall have more to say at a slightly later stage, is one of the matters commented upon in all modern books upon English commercial history covering this period.

Still more familiar as a subject of discussion in economic histories are what are usually called the Agricultural Revolution and the Industrial Revolution. The Agricultural Revolution meant, on one side, some important improvements in the arts of growing crops and breeding animals, - improvements such as more thorough cultivation of the soil, the introduction of certain new crops which were of particular advantage, I believe, in producing nitrogen, and more systematic crop rotations, as well as very material improvement in the breeds of sheep and cattle and hogs, and for that matter of horses. On the other side, this Agricultural Revolution was closely connected with a new form of organization, and just as the Commercial Revolution was largely a matter of reorganization on a large scale, so the Agricultural Revolution was changing the relationship of people interested in farming. The most notable feature of the whole process was its connection with the inclosing of the old commons or open field, -the diminution of the proportion of the land which was cultivated on the manorial system and the diminution of the land which was held on small estates; the increase of large estates run more or less for profit.

With regard to the Industrial Revolution the great inventions are among the topics that all of us have had called to our attention on many occasions. And we know that by the close of the eighteenth century the attempts to apply these new inventions, these new machines, in industrial processes were leading to new forms of organization in industry. The basis was being laid for the rise of the factory, for its rapid development as a great factor in the country's production.

Now all that is of first rate importance to us and so familiar that I need no more than call your attention to these economic developments as a very important part of the general picture. I want also to remind you that the eighteenth century was also a period of initiative as a mass phenomenon in almost all the arts of life. The eighteenth century was the golden age of English pottery, the age of her great furniture makers. It was the time when Handel was writing his great oratorios. Portraiture perhaps reached its height with Gainsborough, Reynolds, and others. It was a time, too, of the appearance of new types in literature. The novel is, I think fairly said to be an eighteenth century invention -the novel in its modern form took shape in England, at least. Robinson Crusoe was published in 1719, Pamela in 1740, Clarissa Harlowe in 1747, and Tom Jones in 1749. It was also at this time that a new type of biography made its appearance at the hands of James Boswell whose life of Dr. Johnson is not only a classic because of its merits but because it was the first time that any man had conceived of setting forth a life of someone else in such intimate and effective a fashion. It was also a time of popular history; there appeared Hume's History of England, Roberts's History of Scotland, and Gibbon's Decline and Fall of the Roman Empire. These books were for the world models of exposition concerning the past of the race, which made quite a different appeal, suggested quite a different outlook on life from the kinds of histories that had been provided theretofore.

life from the kinds of histories that had been provided theretofore.

Perhaps even more important for our purpose was the fact that the eighteenth century was the time when journalism was gradually assuming its modern form. The first daily paper in England that lasted more than a week was first published in 1703. That was presently followed by a series of periodicals which exercised a very great influence upon politics as well as upon literature, such as The Tatler, The Spectator, The Guardian, and their followers. The Gentlemen's Magazine was set up in 1731, and was the forerunner of the whole host of monthly periodicals which have followed it. Also the newspapers were gradually becoming a very important organ of political discussion. The famous Letters of Junius appeared in a newspaper beginning in 1767, and before the century was out, newspapers of the modern type were making their appearance. That is to say, newspapers which made their appeal and their money by uniting two functions, that of news on the one hand and advertising on the other. The attempt to combine these two things in a single sheet was, it appears, a London development which came in the decade between 1770-1780. In that decade, indeed, two of the famous newspapers were set up: The Morning Post in 1772, and the London Times in 1788; and they were followed in 1794 by the Morning Advertiser.

It was also a period when there was very lively interest in realms of thought rather closely related to economics. The eighteenth century is one of the most brilliant periods in British philosophy; and the British philosophers of that time were men who were discussing many questions which had much more than a meta-physical merit. Locke died in 1704 - his activity belongs in the preceding century; but, of course, there were Hume, Bishop Berkeley, and William Paley; these are men who belong to the eighteenth century; and if you know their works at all, you realize how genuinely these men, like their predecessor Locke, united a very keen interest in the discussions of the day with an interest in such problems as the canon of causation.

It was also a period when political theory was being discussed in a more definite and systematic fashion than had been common before in England - discussion not so much of current problems of the day but just as a matter of how modern communities can manage best to conduct their own government. Burke of course, is the great outstanding figure of the latter half of the eighteenth century in this respect.

It was also a period when the law was undergoing notable transformations. It was in the eighteenth century that Mansfield was Lord Chief Justice of England, and he organized the commercial law of Great Britain, adopting a practice which apparently seemed like a rather important innovation in English legal practice. When he had cases of the commercial order coming before him, he called upon men in the various lines of business to come in to explain for the benefit of the Court their various ways of handling matters which were strange to English law, - matters relating to negotiable paper contracts of one sort or another which had not been familiar in earlier British practice, and thus endeavoring to give us decisions largely upon the basis of prevailing practice as explained by these people, with an eye, of course, to his own views concerning what was the most desirable form for this practice to assume in order to increase the efficiency of business and public interest in the long run. The eighteenth century was also the time of Sir William Blackstone whose Commentaries until perhaps to our own generation have constituted the most important text-book of the law, not only for Englishmen, but also for men of those countries which have inherited the British legal system.

Philanthropy was another field in which you see notable developments. Rather early in the century James Oglethorpe organized a grand scheme for colonizing Georgia with people who consisted largely of condemned criminals, and arranged the colony in such a fashion that their life under the new conditions would reform the character of the colonists.

Somewhat later you have the beginnings of prison reform on a grand scale through the labors of John Howard. Jonas Hanway started the movement for taking more effective care of children and guarding them against exploitation. And the close of the century saw the beginning of the great campaign for the abolition of slavery in the British colonies, Sharp, Clarkson, and Wilberforce starting the movement in the 1780's - a movement which achieved success around the 1820's.

It was also through philanthropic effort that a movement got started which has developed gradually into compulsory education for children of all classes. In the early part of the eighteenth century a very small proportion of children in Great Britain were able to read and write. The beginning of this education seems to have been due primarily to the enterprise of the Sunday School Society; its aim being primarily to enable students to read their Bibles, but of course one who could read the Bible was also able to read a newspaper.

And the like is true in general. The even tenor and somewhat worldly life of the Church of England was invaded by the work of John Wesley and George Whitefield, the two preachers who did so much to arouse their admirers to spiritual interest; one of whom, John Wesley, was a most extraordinarily able organizer, a man who succeeded in creating an organization which gathered momentum for several generations after his death.

And what is true of the arts, of literature, philanthropy, and religion is true, perhaps in less striking fashion, in science. Newton died in 1724, and he had, of course, no successor of his standing in England. It is fair to say that the primacy in mathematics crossed the Channel; the great mathematicians of the age were the men connected with the French Academy. But in many branches of work many Englishmen were working in a most effective fashion. Bradley discovered the aberration of light and Sir William Herschel undertook the revision of the calendar. The eighteenth century was the time of Joseph Black, of Joseph Priestley who discovered oxygen, and of Henry Cavendish, that curious aristocratic scientist whose name has become immortalized. It was also the time of James Hutton in the field of geology, and of John Hunter in surgery.

Some of the scientific ideas began to be used in the treatment of human ills. To see what changes had come about, I might mention the curious fact that one of the leading physicians of his day, Richard Mead, who published a Latin treatise on disease that was translated into English in 1748, discussed among others the diseases caused by the sun and the moon; and while those were views that could be held by some of the eminent members of the profession in the middle of the century, the end of the century saw the announcement of the efficacy of vaccination, the study of pathology, and the use of dissection. John Pringle made a study of scurvy and other diseases in the army. These were studies that laid the foundations of modern medicine.

In the field of adventure, the eighteenth century was full of unusual activity. In 1768 Cook roved the Pacific to New Zealand and Australia; in 1791-95, Vancouver commanded an expedition to the northwest coast of America; Matthew Flinders surveyed the Australian coast, and James Bruce explored Africa.

These explorations and the extension of British commerce were accompanied by a very rapid growth of the Empire. Gibraltar was taken by the British, and in the course of the century the conquest of Canada was completed; Ceylon and Malta were added to the British dominions; and British rule in India was rapidly and dramatically extended by Clive and Hastings. In the course of the century, one group of colonies showed their enterprise by setting up an independent government.

While England was successfully fighting Spain and France, she was also winning naval supremacy from the Dutch. British commerce came to surpass that of the Dutch, and London gradually displaced Amsterdam, both as the commercial and as the financial center of Europe.

Now the moral of all of this for our purpose is that in the course of the eighteenth century you find evidence of the fact that individual initiative was becoming a mass phenomenon. Every one of the rather notable events I mentioned is, of course, associated with the name of some remarkable person or several remarkable persons. But the fact is, of course, that these remarkable peopel who get mentioned in the later histories stand for a very much larger number of people, who perhaps met with less fortunate circumstances, or had less vigor, or slighter enterprise, or were less lucky, it may be; but who nevertheless were doing the same sort of things. We know, for instance, definitely that while the great outstanding agricultural reformers were Jethro Tull, Lord Townshend, and Coke of Holkham, there were thousands of other farmers who were trying experiments in cultivation, -who were working with new methods of rotation and were endeavoring to improve the breed of their farm stock. So, too, while the list of the great inventions is a short one, you find in the British records that the number of patents for mechanical discoveries in one year was 1457. It was a time when a great many people were turning their thoughts to the devising of new mechanical contrivances.

And certainly it was a period when the common man had an excellent chance to rise. If you look over the list of the remarkable characters of the eighteenth century, you find that a very large number of them outside the field of politics particularly were men of rather humble origin. All the inventors were such, and the literary and artistic men as well. In fact, scientific men in good part came from rather humble origins. It is mainly in politics that you find that the opportunities for achieving the highest ranges of distinction appear to have been largely allotted to people of aristocratic birth, and even in the realm of politics the rule is far from absolute. Warren Hastings, for instance, learned his letters in a charity school, and Edmund Burke was the son of an Irish attorney.

Not only were the English in the eighteenth century characterized by a rather extraordinary development in initiative in many difficult lines of endeavor, but also by their extraordinary voluntary cooperation. They were not nearly so much characterized by self-seeking in the sense of men who are playing a low-handed game, but by the fact that they could invent when they had a common purpose to pursue, in which they could play a big game and play it most effectively. You find great examples of this capacity for organization without the aid of a statesman to help them, without the kind of aid that Sir James Steuart believed necessary. You find splendid examples of this ability to organize in many different fields. For example, Oglethorpe's colony in America. It was a remarkable piece of work to bring a great many different sorts of people to cooperate in achieving an end, the importance of which could not have made a very extraordinary appeal to a large proportion of them. But even more extraordinary was the organization of the Methodist Church which John Wesley set going.

And so, too, even in politics you find that the celebrated struggle of John Wilkes in his contest with parliament and the Court was started by a series of voluntary organizations which sprang into being spontaneously from the outside and kept their members together in the face of authoritative opposition of the most disconcerting sort.

And then there was the East India Company which faced its complicated task of governing India on one hand and carrying on a profitable trade with the country on the other hand. The English East India Company was supervised in comparatively minor measure by the government, and through its agents always seemed able to effect schemes for meeting any of the emergencies that presented themselves, upon the spot – schemes, the character of which would vary according to the needs of the case.

And, of course, we see examples of this organizing ability appear en masse in the new business enterprises which were arising, not only in London but in the provincial centers. Perhaps the most extraordinary example of British capacity of this sort, however, was shown by the relative success of the British, the French, the Spanish, and the Dutch attempts to colonize America. Now Great Britain was for effective purposes, of course, the late comer in the American field. First the Spaniards and later the French had come to control a very large part of the new continent, had established what looked like firmly set and powerful organizations; and presently the Dutch, though they did not have very large colonies, did secure possession of the best harbor on the coast and the best route into the interior. The British came later than these people, but events show that in the long continued series of contests the British in America were decidedly stronger than their earlier rivals; and that was not, it would appear, because the British colonists were backed more effectively by their government than were the Spanish or the French. It was primarily because the British colonists themselves took a deeper root in the country. They came not to hunt gold like the Spaniards, nor furs like the French, nor to make dividends for a joint stock company like the Dutch. They increased their number very rapidly, and by their capacity to meet the conditions that were presented by a strange environment, cooperating with each other, they were in the end made the stronger than those in whose countries the direction was kept more largely in the hands of people who correspond to the statesmen whom Sir James Steuart and most English contemporaries, theorizing about the subject would have told you were indispensable to the country's increase.

In short, individual initiative was becoming a mass phenomenon. It was united with an extraordinary power for a more or less spontaneous cooperation. The advantages and the sheer superiority of a system which gave scope to individual initiative, and had led people to associate themselves together freely, must have been matters which were impressing the minds of thousands of men in Great Britain, before the time when Adam Smith began to formulate a new economic philosophy, expounding the simple and obvious system of natural liberty. Adam Smith's theoretical exposition of the new basis of economic organization was a set of philosophical reflections upon the advantages of practices which he had seen carried on by his contemporaries, practices the advantages of which his contemporaries who were engaged in business, at least had learned by trying them out, and advantages which they saw threatened from time to time by the conflict between what they discovered it was advantageous to do and certain laws and regulations that had come down from the past and that embodied exactly the kind of old-fashioned wisdom which Sir James Steuart stood for.

But before coming to Adam Smith's own share in the life of his time, I want to call your attention to another feature of the British situation as a whole which I believe of significance in regard to the rise of the social sciences, and that is the gradual development of government in England - of government by public discussion. There were many political experiments of the English people in the eighteenth century; and the instability of English institutions contrasted strongly with the stability of French institutions, for instance.

George I was a person who knew very little about English politics, and he could not therefore intervene effectively in the government of the country. The first George, and even the second George, were people whose knowledge of the English language was deficient, and they knew so little about English conditions and were so much more interested in Hanover that English political life was allowed to take a course determined primarily by the interests of the leading British politicians. The king became a figurehead in large measure, and cabinet government became the rule.

Now, of course, the Parliament had long become the determining power in England. With this series of changes it had clearly become the king-maker. The House of Commons had established its primacy over the House of Lords, and now that the character of the first two Georges kept them relatively out of active participation in the task of ruling England, the administrative work was taken over by a committee of the House of Commons, for that is what the Cabinet meant. Of course, this exalted the power and the prestige of the House of Commons to a far higher point than it had assumed before. It meant that the British were developing a system in which they were basing their most fundamental laws and were making the most fundamental changes on the basis of votes that were cast by people who were elected.

And with that came party government, - party government which in the eighteenth century was nominally along the Whig and Tory line. The Whigs had been responsible for the introduction of the Hanoverian line. The Tory party developed later and found its numerical strength among the country squires and the lower clergy. Now these two parties controlled the government alternatively, according as one or the other could command more votes in the House of Commons. And so the whole political life of the country became centered in a body which discussed the issues before it, - in a body which had members who represented, at least nominally, all the different parts of the country, a body of people who had to appeal to the suffrage of their fellow-citizens.

Now, of course, the British system as it existed in the eighteenth century was a system which because of the peculiarities of the suffrage admitted only a small part of the people directly to participation in choosing members of Parliament, but for all that it was a system which gave the populace a certain organized interest in public affairs, and also left to the populace a very much greater influence on political decisions regarding policy than you would think if you looked only at the character of the suffrage.

VII

THE DEVELOPMENT OF GOVERNMENT BY PUBLIC DISCUSSION

England in the seventeenth and eighteenth centuries was developing a government by public discussion, -a fact which seems to me to have contributed largely to the rise of a widespread interest in the social sciences in general and in economics in particualr.

Concerning that movement, I want to remind you of the facts with most of which you must be familiar. As I said, this government by public discussion had come to center in Parliament, - more particularly in the House of Commons. Parliament had gone to the length of reestablishing the crown on the basis of a contract with the nation. And by virtue of the fact that the holders of the office of king for generations were precluded by their slight knowledge of English and still slighter knowledge of England from taking an active participation in affairs, the administrative power as well as the legislative, had come to center in Parliament. That administrative power was exercised by the Cabinet which grew up in the reign of George I and which was itself a committee of Parliament. It was a committee whose continuance in power depended upon its ability to command a majority vote in the House of Commons which by long established tradition held the power of the purse.

Now that meant nominally, of course, that the representatives of the English people sent to the House of Commons were the people who decided upon the administrative as well as the legislative policy of the nation. They met to debate the various matters which were before the nation - the various problems of policy presented from session to session; to decide by their collective wisdom upon the best course to adopt. Now that is, you need scarcely be told, a very idealistic picture of the situation. In the first place, the decisions in the House of Commons were by no means made on the basis of a rational discussion of the issues, any more than they are made in any assembly of human beings, - particularly in this case because in the eighteenth century votes in the House of Commons were controlled in very large measure by practices which we would now describe as corruption. There was actual bribery in money for the less distinguished members whose votes were wanted. There were other and more attractive inducements to persons of higher rank, such as appointments under the crown which, of course, were controlled by members of the Cabinet, and which were used as bribes. And for their sons and relatives there were sinecures in the government; well paid government posts in which the duties amounted practically to nothing. There were positions in the colonies; there were positions in the Church, for church patronage was used as freely as lay patronage. There were also lucrative positions in Ireland; there were places in the government of England itself in which a fortune could rapidly be acquired; particularly the paymastership which in times of military operations was a position that returned to its incumbent a really princely income. And than there were, of course, the coveted positions of social distinction in the Court. For peers there were higher ranks in the peerage itself. There was the garter and all sorts of methods of rewarding faithful devotees who were faithful to the ministry in power; and the free use of these various means of securing support was developed in the course of the eighteenth century, particularly the early part of it, on a grand scale. The righteous King William himself at times bought votes. The first of the prime ministers, Sir Robert Walpole, reduced bribery to a science. Practically all of his successors for two generations carried on the same practice. Even the elder William Pitt, despite his extraordinary personality, found his position in the House menaced and allied himself with the Duke of Newcastle who was a master in the arts of corruption. And when King George III made his historic attempt to try to replace into the hands of the monarch the right to choose his ministers, he carried on that vigorous campaign of his by a most systematic scheme of giving rewards to men to vote for his favorites and seeing that people who opposed his measures had no hand in the spoils.

Of course, that system of corruption did much to prevent the government from being run on the basis of a rational discussion of questions of the day. But nevertheless, as we shall see, this is simply a modification to be noted as important, to be sure, but not to be taken as so serious as really to

-36-

invalidate the statement that the British nation as a whole had developed its
political institutions to a point where a legislature supposed to be chosen
to represent the different parts of the country -- England, Wales, and Scotland,
and part of the time Ireland, -- was deciding the issues that came along by
discussing them, supposedly on their merits.

It was not only in Parliament, however, that this discussion was carried
on. Public affairs were debated in country houses, at quarter sessions, and at
vestry meetings where members of the ruling class were assembling socially or
to carry on the work of local government. It was discussed in London drawing
rooms, in London clubs, in coffee houses. And not only was it discussed in
public houses and taverns all over the country, but a flood of pamphlets appeared
on every interesting question of the day, testifying to the wide dispersion of
interest in questions before the country -- testifying to the belief that a great
number of the population would be sufficiently interested to read debates which
were carried on by persons belonging to different parties. And the newspapers had,
as I have said, got under way in the early part of the century and assumed their
modern form toward its close. These newspapers, with the large attention which
they gave to the treatment of current political issues are a further testimony
of the rapidly increasing interest which the population was taking in questions
of the sort which now-a-days are becoming the subject of discussion by people
interested in the social sciences.

This increase in the public interest and in the power of public opinion is
perhaps most extensively exemplified by the struggle for public debates in
Parliament. The time had been when parliamentary proceedings were regarded as
confidential; when it was improper even for a member of Parliament to disclose
to any outsider what went on behind the doors. Still less was it proper for any
outsider to take a record of the proceedings and make them public. Thus we find
laid down in a handbook of parliamentary procedure written by J. Hooker in Queen
Elizabeth's times that a member of Parliament ought to keep secret and not discuss
the things done in the Parliament with any person not a member. This rule of
secrecy had been slowly relaxed. Members began to print their important speeches
for the benefit of their constituents; and in 1641 the House agreed to publish
its votes and orders though not its debates. Also the various members, -- for
example, Andrew Marvell who represented Hull from 1660-1678 -- made a practice of
sending regular reports of the proceedings to their constituents, a service which
seems to have been very much followed by many people in the provinces. And this
activity carried on by certain members of the House was presently developed by a
class of more or less professional reporters. They were called news-letter
writers -- men who frequented the lobbeys, made summary reports of the proceedings
and then sent copies of these reports to subscribers, charging two or three guineas
per annum for the service, subscribers being largely country gentlemen and merchants who for business reasons wished to follow what was going on in Parliament.

This practice of newspaper reporting was tacitly acquiesced in for one
generation, but after one had given offense, the House in 1694 ordered that
henceforth no outsider should presume to meddle with the debates or proceedings
of this House. Still, the practice was too profitable to be stopped, and though
the House enforced this order from time to time and occasionally punished some
offender, the practice increased. And this increase naturally became more and
more common in the eighteenth century with the rise of newspapers and periodicals.
The magazines in particular published fairly full reports of the debates, but to
protect themselves they made a practice of giving only the first and last letters
of the speakers' names. And when in 1733 the House declared it was a high
offense to publish debates, the _Gentleman's Magazine_

merely began reporting proceedings in the "Parliament of the Empire of Lilliput"
and other journals followed suit. And by that patent subterfuge they escaped
official notice.

.. A new phase of the struggle began with the rise of modern newspapers
in the 1700's. They took sides with the people against George III on the question whether the House of Commons or the king should control the choice of
ministers. That, of course gave grievous offense to the king, and since his
ministry at the time had secured a majority of votes in the House of Commons,
the House was induced to take up the matter, particularly when in 1771 several
of the London newspapers dropped all disguise and began publishing the speeches,
and most particularly those which gave offense to public feeling because they
represented the royal side in this great constitutional issue. The House of
Commons arrested the fighting journalists. The city officials, representing
the populace of London that was almost unanimously supporting the newspapers, endeavored to protect the journalists who had been arrested, whereupon the House
of Commons ordered the city officials themselves to be sent to the Tower of London. Then the London mob demonstrated in the most vigorous fashion in favor of
the imprisoned officials, and public agitation was so serious that the House of
Commons saw that it was beaten. The reporting of debates remained nominally
illegal, but offenders after this time were not punished.

That story is interesting as showing the increasing interest that
the country was taking in the proceedings of its chosen delegates. Interest that
by a little before the time The Wealth of Nations was published won the great
victory of allowing a full undisguised account to be published daily in the
papers. And, of course, we may assume that the public which had won this jealous-
ly guarded right from the House of Commons -- even when the majority was on the
King's side -- was a public which was quite able to make the control over the
House of Commons felt.

Of course, we take it for granted that control over a legislative
body on the part of the public rests primarily upon rights of election, and the
members of the House of Commons, of course, were elected. But that was not the
chief means of control which the English populace had in the eighteenth century,
because of the fact that the suffrage on the basis of which members of Parliament
were elected was so curious. When Parliament got under way in the Middle Ages,
there is reason to believe that some effort was made to apportion the representation allowed to different parts of the country on the basis of the population. Just how far that was the case is, I believe, not quite clear; but whatever had been the original intent, it is quite certain that by the time of Adam
Smith the apportionment of seats in the House was most uneven as compared with
the people who were represented in the different constituencies. This apportionment on a geographical basis had not been revised for a century or more.
And in that time the population of England had shifted very greatly, so that some
of the constituencies now represented places where the remaining inhabitants
were very few; and on the other hand, throughout the country there had grown
up great centers of population which were not represented at all.

The whole scheme of representation was very complicated. There were
ninety-two knights of the shires who sat as representing English and Welsh
counties, and four hundred and twenty-one burgesses who sat as representing
English and Welsh towns and universities, and finally forty-five members for
Scotland. The ninety-two were chosen under a franchise which required a property
qualification for voting of a forty shilling freehold. It was primarily the
better-to-do people in the towns and the landowning class that had a right to
cast votes for county members. Despite this restriction of the suffrage, the
counties were regarded as offering, on the whole, the best opportunity for

public opinion to make itself felt, and many of the suffrage reformers of the eighteenth century would have felt quite satisfied if they could have establish- ed the burgesses on as representative a basis as the counties. In these towns the system was extremely varied. Suffice it to say that it was estimated that toward the close of the century there were fifty-one constituencies that had less than fifty voters, and one hundred and thirty that had less than three hundred voters apiece. On the other hand, there were a few places where by old tradition any person present on election day was allowed to cast a vote.

It was a very complicated situation, one which made it quite possible for a large proportion of the members returned to the House of Commons to be chosen, not by the people who lived in their constituencies, but by a patron. A patron was a person who in some manner had come to control the election in a parlia- mentary constituency. Where the number of voters was fifty or less, it was comparatively easy for some local magnate, usually a landlord, through the ex- ercise of influence, or by discreet use of bribery in some, to get control of the elections. And in several cases the constituencies were controlled by money. Even the boroughs controlled by influence could be secured by someone who came down with a bagful of guineas and knew the proper person to see.

This situation toward the end of the century was declared to result in the fact that one hundred and sixty-two peers and commoners, together with the Treasury - the patronage branch of the ministry - through their opportunities for distributing local patronage in the towns, were able to control elections. It was said that these one hundred and sixty-two peers and commoners, with the Treasury, could name absolutely one hundred and seventy-two members, and could control one hundred and thirty-two more under most circumstances. Three hundred and six represented a majority of the House of Commons.

Out of this situation there arose a lively traffic in boroughs and cities in the House of Commons. The "pocket boroughs" were recognized as private pro- perty at law, that is, boroughs that were controlled through ownership of pro- perty in some way or other. These "pocket boroughs" were bought and sold, be- queathed in wills, and recognized as assets in the estates of bankrupts. But the borough managers, as a rule, bought and sold not their boroughs, but seats in Parliament. Sometimes they would sell a man a seat for a single session, sometimes for the lifetime of a Parliament; and in the eighteenth century Par- liament, unless for some reason prorogued earlier, ran for seven years. This traffic was carried on by the borough brokers in London who were well-known to the initiated; and there were times when the London brokers, not finding pur- chasers for the property that had been entrusted to them, sent traveling sales- men out among the country houses trying to find some person with money to invest, or who wanted to get a seat for a promising son; or perhaps some business man had done well and would like to gain the social esteem which would come with a seat in the House and would be willing to pay a higher price. In fact, seats were advertised for sale in the newspapers before the close of the eighteenth century rather freely. And people who knew the situation could tell pretty well what a seat was worth. Prices kept rising in the eighteenth century. Edward Porritt says* that the earliest quotation came in 1747 when the price seemed to be about fourteen hundred pounds for a seat. In the early days of

*The Unreformed House of Commons, Cambridge, 1903; I, 357. "But the earliest eighteenth century quotation which I have found for a nomination for a borough, made in a businesslike way, is of the year 1747. James Tilson, of Hampton Court was in that year offered a nomination at Cricklade, for fourteen hundred pounds: and it was a condition in a regularly drawn up contract of sale that the four- teen hundred pounds were not to be paid over 'until Mr. Tilson had sat fourteen days in the House of Commons without a petition being presented against him,

George III, a seat was worth two thousand pounds, In 1799, Lord Castlereagh said* that a seat was worth four thousand pounds, From 1807 to 1832 the price kept rising so that people might be expected to lay out five thousand or six thousand pounds for the life-time of a Parliament, or eighteen hundred pounds a year if they bought seats by the year, which was generally regarded as a rather safer practice inasmuch as in the earlier part of the nineteenth century several of the Parliaments failed to sit out their full terms.

Now borough management was a business and was carried on for profit. The profits were made, not in the local constituencies, but were made in Westminster. A man who controlled a considerable number of seats was a man whose wishes the ministry had to consider, and the result was that the successful borough managers acquired fortunes as well as nobility. For example, Dodington (1691-1762) who owned half a dozen votes, namely from the Cornwall district, ended his life as Baron Melcombe. Sir James Lowther who controlled nine votes, commonly known as "Lowther's ninepins" became Earl of Lonsdale. So, also Henry Dundas became Lord Melville. In fact, nearly half of the members of the house were people who owed their seats to patrons, and two-thirds of the peerages which had been created from the accession of William and Mary in 1688 to just before the accession of Victoria, were granted to borough managers for political support. The government even had to have a patronage secretary. Men complained that party lines did not count in a Parliament where so many votes were for sale.

That business in boroughs, of course, again appears to mean that after all the English scheme of governing by public discussion was perhaps a somewhat empty pretense. Unquestionably the corruption practiced in Parliament was closely connected with this borough mongering. It is a qualification of the statement that the English people were debating the proposals before them. And yet, after all, it is only a qualification, for in some ways this scheme of borough mongering made it easier for public opinion of the sort which was not provided for by traditional British institutions to make itself felt. Certainly the sale of seats made it far easier and simpler than it presumably would have been otherwise for the business interests of the country to get representation in Parliament. According to the old English ideas, the proper man to seat in Parliament was, of course, a landlord. The landed interest held an unquestioned control; and according to the theory, the man of landed property was the type of person who should represent the nation and decide upon its policies. Well, comparatively early the landed interests had found it advisable to admit a certain number of lawyers into Parliament. Their special skill had, of course, its inestimable value in a law-making body. In the course of the seventeenth century, successful business men had begun to work their way in through the purchase of seats-- goldsmiths, and the bankers who developed out of the goldsmiths. Brewers bought seats. Then after 1688 the nabobs from India began to get representation. (Nabob was the name given to persons who had gone to India and acquired a fortune there). A little later the caribs acquired fortunes in the West Indies, as the nabobs had in British India. Later still, manufacturers began to get in. The Foleys were the first family to succeed in getting a member elected. They were iron masters who bought land. Then in 1790 Sir Robert Peel, a great cotton manu-

or been confirmed in his seat in the case of a hostile petition.' It was a further condition that Mr. Tilson 'must come to the borough, or some proper person with the money,' and that the out-of-pocket expenses of the election, not exceeding fifty pounds, must be advanced by the candidate." Cf. Hist. MSS. Comm. 13th Rep., App., pt. III, 118.

*Porritt. op. cit., I, 358. Cf. Castlereagh Correspondence, II, 150

-40-

facturer who also bought land, elected himself, or had himself elected. He
was the first of the manufacturers of the modern type to get into Parliament,
and his son, the great Sir Robert Peel, was the first representative of the
manufacturing class to get into Cabinet rank.

So Parliament was by the sale of seats itself enabled to represent
the shifting economic power of the country, presumably rather more effectively
than it would have if all elections had been carried on according to the traditional scheme. Of these men who bought their way, some were very excellent
members. We shall have occasion to see, for instance, that it was in this way
that Ricardo entered Parliament; and he was not by any means the only man who
bought his way in because he had a very keen interest in public affairs as well
as desire for the social distinction that membership carried with it.

It is also important to observe that because this Parliament was
largely controlled by political bosses, so far as any other than the landed
interest were concerned, it was largely made up of people who could afford to
purchase seats, and it was in very large measure sensitive to opinion - not
merely the opinion of the comparatively small number of the populace who had
votes but to public opinion at large. We have unquestionable evidence of that.
The beat is that every now and then, in response to public pressure, Parliament
would change its decision upon matters even of highest importance. For example,
Sir Robert Walpole gave up an excise act in 1733 because of extraordinary agitation which it stirred up out of doors. An attempt to reform the coinage was
blocked by another demonstration of public wrath. A bill for the naturalization of the Jews was withdrawn in 1754 because again the public took it amiss.
The great contest which Wilkes won against the King in Parliament was due to
the fact that he had the support of the mob. It was, as I have already had
occasion to say today, the demonstration of the London mob in favor of the
journalists that intimidated the House and King in 1771 and established the right
of the public to know what was going on in the legislature. Once more, the end
of the Revolutionary War - the war with the American colonies - seems to have
been brought about because the public rebelled against the continuation of a
struggle regarded as useless, in spite of the fact that the king and his ministry
were determined to go on. Once more, in 1788, an act intended to improve the
elections by providing for registration of county freeholders had to be repealed.

These are simply outstanding evidence of the fact that the Parliament
itself, despite the lack of anything like a popular suffrage, despite the presence of so much corruption in the election of members and in the relations between the members of Parliament and the ministry, Parliament was still responsive
to public pressure. And if you want further evidence you have to notice how
amenable to public opinion every Parliament grew toward the end of its seven
year term - how careful ministers were to get able pamphleteers to present their
cases before the public, employing such men as Swift, Addison, Defoe, and Samuel
Johnson to write defenses of measures which they thought might invoke public
censure. You will find further evidence in the fact that governments were quite
ready to buy newspapers and particularly after the newspapers had attained very
considerable influence with a wide public toward the end of the century.

Well, why was it that this Parliament was so much afraid of public
opinion? It seems to have been primarily the general turbulency of Englishmen
in the eighteenth century. I had occasion to notice last time that in the
seventeenth century matters had gone to extremes; government had been upset and
set up again in a new form two or three times. In the eighteenth century matters
never went to such extremes, but there were occasions when it seemed that they
might. The English people were very much given to rioting. For example, in 1736

the Edinburgh crowd lynched a captain of the city guard, a man who was charged with having fired on the mob some time before in the performance of official duty. In 1753 there was a series of anti-Jewish riots produced by the act for naturalizing the Jews, and leading to the repeal of that act. In 1762 Lord Bute, the prime minister, had his coat torn and he was burned in effigy in a good many towns. In 1770 Lord North, the prime minister, and Charles James Fox, his supporter in the quarrel between the City of London and the king, were rolled in the mud at the gates of the Parliament House by the mob. In 1784 the Gordon riots broke out in London. They were anti-Catholic demonstrations in which a good many buildings were burned and a considerable number of people were killed. In 1791 there were the "church and king" riots in Birmingham. In 1780 the populace was inflamed against the Catholics, so now they were against the Unitarians. Among other atrocities, they wrecked Priestley's laboratory — the laboratory of the man who discovered oxygen. In 1795 the king himself was pelted in his carriage on his way to Parliament. In 1800 there were scarcity riots in many of the towns.

These are only a few of the conspicuous riots in a century filled with many other minor disturbances. It seems to have been the fear of these activities on the part of the populace at large which was an effective factor in making government by public discussion a reality instead of a more or less empty name.

The aristocratic theory in regard to yielding to public pressure is very interesting. What people liked to believe on the subject was very neatly put by the Bishop of Rochester in 1795 who said he did not know what the most of the people had to do with the laws but to obey them. He found it expedient under pressure to explain his views more or less away.

The Lord Chancellor in 1755, in introducing the bill to repeal the naturalization act for the Jews, although he had previously supported the act, justified his stand in these words: "However much the people may be misled, yet in a free country I do not think an unpopular measure ought to be obstinately persisted in. We should treat the people as a humane and skilful physician would treat his patient. If they nauseate, we should think of some other remedy or withhold the prescription until time, which changes circumstances, has removed the nausea."

Now all this means that in the eighteenth century the English nation was moving away form the superior sagacity of the statesman, whether king or minister, and toward reliance on the wisdom of the people -- away form the social philosophy of Sir James Steuart and toward the philosophy of Adam Smith.

VII

INDIVIDUAL INITIATIVE IN LOCAL GOVERNMENT: CHANGES IN ECONOMIC
CONDITIONS AND THEIR EFFECT ON ECONOMIC THEORY

I dwelt at the last meeting on the gradual process by which the english people were developing a government of discussion, a process which implies, of course, that the people were taking a larger initiative as individuals in the general process of determining the policy which the country should follow, and they were doing that as the result of along series of struggles which were very costly to the folks who participated in them. It meant that the country was drifting away from faith in the superior wisdom of the people who under the older political regime happened to be in position to govern them as statesmen, and toward a position where they were trusting far more in their own insight, believing far more that the ordinary citizen had a right to make his own interest felt, had the capacity to judge what was good for himself and his enterprise,-- gradual advance toward the theoretical position which is found in the economic theory of Adam Smith.

Now what had been happening in the development of the central government of England had been happening also in a more confused fashion with reference to local government. Our conventional history of England, of course, centers around the Crown, and Parliament, and it is only in comparatively recent times that any attention has been paid to the development of local institutions. What we know about them in these later times is very largely due to the investigation of Sidney and Beatrice Webb whose five volumes* on local government constitute not only a vast repertory of information, but is also a pioneer work. There is no time, of course, to go into any detail here in treating these problems, but I think what England was doing in the way of recasting her local institutions is for our purpose not less significant than what she was doing in changing parliamentary institutions; and for that reason I do think it necessary to call your attention to the general trend of development.

The local government of England was carried on by the counties, of which there were fifty-two, and by the parishes into which the counties were divided. In the eighteenth century nobody knew how many there were in the country, though it was generally believed in 1688 they numbered nine thousand. They were first counted in the census of 1821 when they were found to number almost ten thousand seven hundred. Local government was carried on also on the manors which were not merely agricultural units but also administrative government units for certain purposes; and it was carried on in the towns, most of which in medieval times had governments the nature of which was determined by special charters granted them by the Crown, renewed and amended from time to tim And finally, as we shall see, there were growing up in the course of the eighteen th century a new set of authorities created by special act of Parliament, instead of authorities which the Webbs call "statutory authorities."

Now these various units of the local government were supposed to be local representatives of the central government. The general theory of the schem in the Middle Ages had been that the king should appoint his officers in all the counties and that these officers should be responsible for maintaining the king's peace, for maintaining the king's highways, for sustaining the established church, for caring for the poor, and the like; also, of course, for collecting the king's revenue. And in order to see that the local authorities did their duty, the king had a set of itinerant courts which moved around through the provinces and reviewed the work of the local officials. That, I say, had been the medieval scheme.

In the time of Elizabeth and James I, the crown had endeavored to perfect the organization by issuing books of orders directing the work of the justices of the peace who were the chief local authorities inside the counties-- the men to whom the parish authorities reported. Those books of orders issued from year to year were supposed to outline in more or less detail the duties of the justices. The itinerant courts inquired in the performance of their duties by the local officials. For the towns a scheme of regulation under charters which were granted by the crown was maintained. But during the Civil War,

*English Local Government from the Revolution to the Municipal Corporation Act, London, 1906-08, 2 vols. in 3.
English Local Government, the Story of the King's Highway, London, 1913.
English Local Government: Statutory Authorities for Special Purposes, London, 1922.

of course, the control of the central government over the local officials had broken down. The Crown passed into abeyance for the time, and neither the Commonwealth nor the Restoration succeeded in restoring the old scheme, so that there was a large opportunity for the local authorities to go their own way, an opportunity of which they proceeded to take advantage. Of course, the local government had to be carried on, and when the grip of the Crown over the local officials relaxed, the officers in the various parts of the kingdom had to use their own judgment in very large measure. It was a great tribute to their efficiency as a whole that the general character of local government under these circumstances did not suffer a very serious backsliding.

What happened under these circumstances was, to begin with the lowest unit, that the manorial courts, the administrative organization for handling affairs in the village communities, were dwindling away. Their decline was primarily a result of the fact that the medieval scheme of agriculture was gradually giving way to more modern methods of carrying on cultivation, particularly where manors were inclosed and then redistributed in larger allotments and let out to farmers who cultivated it largely by the use of hired labor; and especially where the interest of the owner became primarily concerned with getting revenue out of the land by renting it. In these places there was no longer necessity for the medieval scheme of seeing that the villains performed the work allotted them or paid fines for their negligence. There was much less reason for maintaining these manorial courts even as courts of petty justice. Work of that sort passed naturally into the hands of the justices of the peace because the lords of the manors had far less pecuniary interest than formerly in keeping the courts up. This meant that the county officials, and especially the justices of the peace, gained in power and prestige. There was continued rise in the standard of honor and local esteem of the justices. They had a somewhat narrow class standard of their duties and applications; they served without salary, but the position was one of sufficient social eminence to make almost any country gentleman glad to receive a commission and willing to perform the duties which that involved, -- the duties of acting as local magistrate and punishing offenders.

Throughout the researches into the local government of nearly every county of England, from the period of the Revolution to the passage of the Municipal Corporations Acts in the nineteenth century, Mr. & Mrs. Webb say they failed to discover a single example of anything approaching the rule of the boss. It was an aristocratic scheme of governing by the local magnates in a class spirit, but after all, seemingly with considerable attention to the job and with a rather high standard of interest.

Parish governments in the rural districts of the country continued to run on with very little change in their old routine. The parish authorities were the vestry. The typical vestry was made up of the incumbent, the local clergyman, three or four farmers, maybe a small freeholder, or perhaps the innkeeper or the miller. These people filled vacancies in their own number; they appointed from their number the authorities, overseers of the highways, etc. They reported upon their collections of local rates and their expenditures to the neighboring justices of the peace who passed their accounts. That system in the rural districts went on with comparatively little change because the character of the life the people were living in the rural districts was not greatly disturbed.

But in other places, particularly in the towns that were springing up, the changes in the problems that were presented for solution were great and required very great corresponding changes in administrative machinery. Now those towns which had received royal charters had a set of local officials which were

determined in each case by the special terms of their charter, and these charters were by no means highly standardized; so that the situation, if we may
apply an American term, of the English municipalities was very diverse. In some
cases it was of a character which enabled a small group of insiders to exercise a comparatively close control. And the Webbs found in not a few cases
that municipalities operating under old charters developed boss rule of the
American type in a somewhat extreme degree; that they presented the various kinds
of corruption in politics with which we are too painfully familiar. In other
cases there were large centers of population gradually growing up in places which,
therefore, had no royal charters, so that the government had to be carried on in
some other fashion. It was carried on in some cases by the parish officials,
the vestry, which in some rather notable instances constituted people who took
a very definite and public-spirited lead and managed to give their towns an excellent and progressive government - one full of initiative, with sufficient
power of inventiveness to meet the new problems as they came up. In other cases,
quite naturally, the opposite was true and the vestries proved themselves quite
incapable of meeting the new problems, and in some cases they developed boss rule
of quite as malignant a sort as was found in any of the towns that had old
charters. So that in the municipalities in the course of the eighteenth century
there was a most extraordinary range of form of organization and of efficiency.

This situation led to one of the eighteenth century developments which
I think is of particular interest from our viewpoint. Where the local governments
were ineffective or notoriously corrupt, so that the public interest was being
sacrificed in a fashion that even the most patient populace could scarcely stand,
the remedy that was most often taken was not to attempt to reorganize the existing authorities, but rather to organize one new set of authorities after another
to deal with special problems. In some places the question of burning interest
in a locality would be the paving of the streets, at least in the center of the
town; and, of course, pavements became indispensable as towns grew. When the
local population distrusted its local government so much that it did not believe
that it would honestly get the streets paved, the people would join together
and petition Parliament to set up a new set of authorities by a special act, -
a new set of authorities whose business it was to see that certain streets were
paved. In other cases it was not perhaps pavement but the need of embanking
a river that flowed through the town, or the need of getting a fresh water supply.
A great variety of local needs were provided for in this way: special appeal to
Parliament to create by a law passed referring to that particular town and giving
authority to perform the particular service which was required.

It is very characteristic of the attitude of Parliament all through the
eighteenth and the early part of the nineteenth century toward local problems
that it almost never intervened to regulate local government except on petition,
so far as it undertook to exercise any authority for county affairs. It usually
acted at the suggestion of justices of the peace on petition from them. So far
as it intervened in municipal affairs, it almost always intervened in response
to a definite request. Now, of course, this means that the local government of
England was in the course of the eighteenth century carried on much more definitely by local initiative than it was by parliamentary control. The changes came
about through a gradual cessation of the old policy of central government control
- a cessation that began with the Civil War and the abolition of the Crown, but
continued afterward with Parliament simply acquiescing in a scheme by which the
local units of the country ran themselves, and attempting to effect alterations
almost only when the local authorities said that something must be done and told
Parliament what that something was. To such local requests Parliament was
usually responsive.

Now I think this means just as definitely as what was happening in Parliament that the English people were growing into the habit of depending upon their individual judgment, of looking to their own initiative to solve their problems. There was very little explicit philosophy of all this movement; very little attempt to rationalize what was going on. And naturally the social philosopher who could explain and justify to Englishmen what they were doing on their own initiative would be likely to be held as a great discoverer, as Adam Smith was.

So far I have been discussing primarily the machinery that the country had in its central government and its local governments for treating the problems of the day. Now I want to say something specific about the character of the problems which had to be faced by Parliament or by the local governments. And here, of course, I shall not endeavor to treat social problems at large, but primarily economic problems of the day. I do this largely because English political economy from the time of Adam Smith up to the present has had its course of development shaped in very large measure by the current issues of the day. We are likely to think of a science as coming down as a birthright and growing by logical development. We might very well have our minds fixed on a subject like mathematics. If some discoverer starts a new idea, that certain idea has certain implications which might be accepted by following writers, and each will get his chief inspiration from the account of the writer before him. It is a process of intellectual development.

Now that is not a really true picture of mathematics, and it is probably even less true of a science like physics or chemistry. In economics I think it is quite a mistake to believe that this birthright intellectual development has occurred. The passing on of ideas from one to another and the development of these ideas by successive generations as an intellectual stunt has been in economics a secondary rather than a primary factor. The thing which has most of all stimulated the minds of successive generations of economists has been to endeavor to contribute to the understanding of the problems with which their generation as a whole was concerned. It is quite probable, especially since economics has become an academic subject, that we have had our academic writers whose attitude seemed to be primarily that of improving the theories which their predecessors have put forward, endeavoring to free those theories from inconsistencies and carry them to a somewhat higher stage of development. This viewpoint you find given most emphasis in the histories of economic doctrines; that Ricardo improved on Adam Smith, and was followed by John Stuart Mill, who in turn produced the violent intellectual action in Jevons; and that Marshall is an attempt to reconcile the two lines of analysis represented by Ricardo, on one side, and Jevons on the other; and so on.

That I think is a rather false picture. The most important factor has been that the generation of Ricardo faced problems of a different sort from that of Adam Smith; and it was because he reflected a different set of circumstances that Ricardo changed the perspective of economic theory. Thus, it is because successive generations have faced different problems than Ricardo did that they have worked out new ideas, new sides of the subject and given opinions which differ from those of the classical group. That is one of the themes that is going to run all through my lectures, and I am just beginning the discussion of it when I present to you the general picture of the kind of economic problems which faced Adam Smith's generation - the kind of problems which he had been thinking about all his life before he began writing The Wealth of Nations.

These economic problems were caused primarily by changes in the economic life of the people, changes that were coming about through a cumulative process. They were changes in the way people worked, the way in which they organized for their work, the way in which they got the things they needed to consume, as well as changes in the way they produced what they had to sell, that made a great difference. These changes were going on at a decidedly rapid rate in the eighteenth century. In order to see what the changes were, we have to go back a bit and see what the situation was before the series of changes began.

Of course you have all studied English economic history, and you have in mind a general picture of the economic life of the people in the Middle Ages. At that time the English population was predominantly agricultural. The great mass of the folk were villains or serfs who were living in manorial communities, holding certain lands from the lord of the manor, raising crops although paying rent which consisted oftentimes in some slight measure of money but consisted far more in working the land which the lord kept as his own demesne, and also rendering a variety of other services for the rental. Over these village communities the landlord exercised administrative rights; he held the courts; he was the immediate local authority as well as the person to whom the land immediately belonged, so far at least as the peasant was concerned, although in theory the land belonged to the king. In the towns, which were small and not very numerous, there was a population made up largely of handicraftsmen, whom it would seem in the earlier part of the Middle Ages cultivated more or less land outside the walls of the towns but who, as the Middle Ages progressed, came more and more to divorce themselves from agriculture and spend their time in the performance of simple manufacturing processes. The guildsman sold what he made in much larger measure than at the present time, making goods only as he got orders for them. And, of course, there were a few people definitely engaged in commercial transactions in the larger towns - the merchants. As time went on, the number of these merchants became greater and they became more and more separated from the manufacturing class of craftsmen. The craftsmen worked, as a rule, in rather small shops, the typical master employing perhaps a journeyman or two, perhaps three or four apprentices, according to the scale of his operations, training them in the exercise of the mystery which he followed, in return for their labor.

In all this scheme there was comparatively little trade, save in a few articles that were indispensable, like iron for ploughshares, and also in the articles of luxury which the small number of large landowning families could afford to consume. And what trade there was, was carried on largely by barter. Now starting with a picture of this sort, we have a gradual process of transformation toward a more modern scheme of economic organization; a process in which I am inclined to think the most important factor was the increasing use of money. This we see exemplified in many different ways in the relations between the Crown and the people, and among the people themselves. So far as the Crown is concerned, we find the king, as he discovers the advantages of having a money revenue, tries more and more to pass over from the old scheme of taking only commodities for his own use and that of his Court and accepting services to maintain the defense of the realm, to a scheme by which he gets money from the people and then uses the money to buy commodities and services. For example, in the days before the Norman Conquest the dues had been levied largely in kind. Comparatively early the royal officers found it was more advantageous to replace the value in kind by money and commutation - to use the technical term - of dues in kind into dues in money started comparatively early. Another and far more momentous step was taken when the king reestablished the military system on a monetary basis. Instead of relying on the feudal levy, the Crown found that it was advantageous to levy upon the lords and allow them to levy upon their retainers in turn certain monetary dues, so that the institution of "scutage" came into use, each knight paying a fee to be exempted from the performance of the military duty he owed. This revenue was used by the Crown to sustain a mercenary army, an army paid with money, and which the king found in practice more efficient. These men whom he paid he could discharge at will, and on the whole this plan resulted in a more satisfactory arrangement.

And so, too, the king in the early days had gotten a very large part of his revenue directly from the proceeds of his manors, the land which was held by the Crown; but he found that it was most advantageous to give up the old system by which the villains to whom the land was let in comparatively small allotments raised crops for him on the royal demesne, and go over to the system of having the villains pay money rent. Under the old system the king and his court were compelled to live a good part of the year an itinerant life in order to consume the food and forage which the royal manors produced. Obviously it was enormously inconvenient and caused serious difficulties, for when the king had important business in a particular place it was necessary to consider whether he could obtain food and forage there before going. It was far better to get a revenue which he could expend wherever he needed for reasons of state or wanted for personal reasons to be, - expend for things that he and his immediate company required.

Now that process of commutation of labor into money payments spread from the royal manors to the other manors, and it was the most important single step in the transformation of the organization of medieval England to the organization of England as we have it now, for it meant that the masses of the people themselves came to get the one great thing they needed: their land for a money payment; and it meant also that in order to get that money they were selling their produce. It meant that the masses of the people very gradually and very slowly, over a period of some hundreds of years, acquired the habit of living by making a money income and expending it. It meant that the masses of the people were gradually led into a life where they had to learn a sort of calculation, to practice the economic virtues of planning, of thrift, management, and foresight; in other words, the scheme of life where they were exposed to a discipline that was making them more and more like Adam Smith's ideal citizen, the shrewd, enterprising Scotchman.

Needless to say, this process of transformation, particularly this process of the gradual education of the mass of the people, was an extremely slow one, a process that succeeded far better with some individuals than with others, and the individuals who proved to have the knack of living this calculating kind of life were the people who gradually came to the fore in England. They were the people who rose out of the peasantry to become farmers; the sort of people who, when the old manors were gradually inclosed, got the right to use, in return for a money payment, the larger allotments into which the estates were now divided. And the people who could not make a go of this general scheme of living were the people who sank in status to become the hewers of wood and the drawers of water, - the proletariat. And even they, as time went on, had to live on money wages, though in the farming districts they supplemented their wages in large part with food and the right to occupy quarters which the farmer provided. Even these people were in some measure compelled to learn the art of living on money incomes.

In the towns, similarly, the people who proved to have the greatest aptitude for the new method of life which the money economy afforded became the great merchants. At a later time they became the manufacturers, - the sort of people out of whom our present business classes arose. Now, of course, this aptitude, like all other aptitudes, runs in families. In every generation there is a considerable turnover in people who have this particular set of gifts which give them success in a society that is organized in increasing degree on a money-making basis. But all the time the scheme was one which offered pretty good opportunities for a man who was not well-born to come to the fore, provided he happened to be a person of affairs as well as of business shrewdness. The old quasi-caste system was very gradually and not altogether but in large part broken down and superceded by a system in which it was private initiative and individual capacity that counted.

Now the point I am coming to is this: that by the time of Queen Elizabeth the characteristic medieval orders of society had disintegrated in very considerable measure and were being succeeded by the attempt to work out the very comprehensive set of new economic policies for the country as a whole. These economic policies quite naturally sought to take just as full advantage as possible of the money economy. This scheme of arranging economic relationships which seemed to possess such great advantages from the point of view of practically all the classes caused the idea to prevail in the minds of statesmen that just as men get rich by making money, so a country gets rich by making money, and just as a merchant's affairs would prosper if they were assiduously supervised in all details, so a country's affairs would prosper if assiduously supervised by the country's managers, namely the statesmen. There developed gradually a most thoroughgoing attempt to see what the country's resources were and to guide them in such a fashion as to produce the greatest advantage for the community as a whole, the community being conceived in rather a businesslike fashion.

IX

THE THEORY OF MERCANTILISM

I have represented the general philosophy of Sir James Steuart as a systematic presentation of the traditional policy of Great Britain, a policy which based the country's economic organization upon statesmanlike plans, the policy which held that it was as much the duty of the government to effect the sort of economic mobilization of the people in times of peace for the benefit of the national welfare as it was the duty of the government to effect the mobilization of its military resources in times of war. On the other hand, I held that Adam Smith's new philosophy, representing the simple and natural order of liberty as the best way of promoting the wealth of nations was a rationalization of practices which were becoming very common in England in his day.

By way of making that clearer I started to remind you at the last meeting of certain broad features of the economic history of England, features that all of you who have studied English economic history are acquainted with but which perhaps you have not connected very closely with the development of economic theory. I had begun to sketch in the most schematic fashion the economic organization of England in the Middle Ages. That economic organization gradually broke down and as it broke down it was superseded by a new scheme of economic organization which took a very definite form as early as the reign of Queen Elizabeth. That is where I pick up the story today.

The new scheme of organization differed from the old one primarily in that it was so much more highly centralized. If you were an English-

man in any walk of life in the Middle Ages, your occupation, the general
character of your activities, the general character of the living that you
could make, was determined for you primarily by the customs of the manor on
which you were born, if you were one of the nine out of ten people who lived
in the country; primarily by guild regulations and municipal ordinances if
you were one of the tenth of the population who lived in an incorporated town.
Now the new scheme which, as I say, had become fairly definite in its outlines
by Queen Elizabeth's time, was just as much a regulation of the life of the
people, but it was a regulation conceived and supposedly supervised by the
central government. If you had lived in the time of Queen Elizabeth or James I,
your career would have been marked out for you, but a little less definitely.
And this time it would have been marked out for you by the general statutes
of the land, and by the hierarchy running from the local justices of the peace
or municipal officers up to the Privy Council of the sovereign.

I want to outline certain leading features of this general scheme
of economic organization on a national scale. One of its foundation stones was
a definite scheme of labor policy, a scheme which was intended to see to it
that every boy who was born into England should get proper training for an
occupation that would contribute toward the public welfare, and follow it.
One of the great points of this labor policy was to make sure of an adequate
supply of labor, and it was necessary in the eyes of the people responsible
for this scheme of policy that the central government itself should take care
to see that there was an adequate food supply. That is a question which does
not worry modern governments in peaceful times. In those days it was the business
of government itself, the central government, to see to it that the population
be adequately fed. And to provide for that the Statute of Artificers, passed
in 1563, provided that all able-bodied men might be called upon to serve as
agricultural laborers unless they could prove exemption on some specified
ground, specified grounds being membership in crafts or in classes of society
which were supposedly engaged in more important, more skilled work than farming.
Indeed, at times of harvest even the artificers who belonged to the guilds could
be called upon to get in the crops.

In order to make sure that the supply was not only adequate but
that it did not fluctuate too much, the law required that agricultural labor
should be hired by the year. If you took a job on a given estate, you were
under contract to stay until your full term had expired. And there were penalties imposed for leaving service before the expiration of your contract. Nor
was your employer at liberty to discharge you; he might punish you in other
ways, but was not supposed to set you free. And if you did leave his service
at the end of the year, you had to get from your past employer a testimonial
which any new employer to whom you applied was supposed to call for and examine
before taking you into his service.

To provide for an adequate supply of skilled craftsmen in trades
that required longer training, the performance of apprenticeship was required.
The general rule was that every boy who did not belong to the gentry should
be apprenticed to a trade and serve for seven years. But the boy did not have
free choise of the trade that he followed. Any boy might be apprenticed to
husbandry no matter how humble his parentage, but if he wanted to get into
one of the guilds of a better standing like the goldsmiths or the clothiers,
or the mercers, he had to show that his father was a sixty shilling freeholder;
or rather the father who wanted to apprentice his son to one of these trades
had to show that he was a sixty shilling freeholder, that is, that he had a
title to some piece of real property the rental value of which was sixty shillings a year. That seems small on the basis of modern monetary value, but it

meant a very modest competence in Elizabethan days.

Also the central authorities thought it necessary to provide what wages should be paid in differebt occupations. They put that matter in the hands of the local authorities and these local authorities were supposed to act under the supervision of traveling judges. The traveling judges, in turn, reported to the Privy Council; so that theoretically the wages were fixed locally, fixed by people responsible to a set of traveling officers who in turn reported to the chief officers of the Crown.

According to the statute, each year in each locality and in each incorporate town the justices of the peace were to assemble before the Tenth of June, and call ing to them such discreat and grave persons as they wished, they were to meet and confer together respecting the plenty or scarcity of the times and other circum- stances necessary to be considered, they could limit the wages of any kind of manufacturing labor, skilled or unskilled, by the year, week, or day, with or without food. And then after having fixed this scale of wages for different occupations in their locality, they might, if they saw fit within six weeks, pro- vide the scales of hours.

Now you observe that these judges were to take advice respecting the plenty or scarcity of the time and other circumstances necessary to be considered. That is, supposedly they would fix wages more or less in accordance with changes in the cost of living. If prices went up it was theoretically their duty to assure the working classes money wages high enough to give them their accustomed standard. And, on the other hand, if the cost of living went down, then money wages might be reduced. It was, in theory at least, not all an attempt at oppression but supposedly an attempt to guarantee that wages should not be raised in such a way as to jeopardize the national welfare and that, on the other hand, they should not be reduced so as to plunge the working people and their families into distress

A very elaborate scheme of poor relief was also provided. In the old days in England the dispensing of charity had been mainly in the hands of the Church, but the monasteries in England had been dissolved under Henry VIII and it became necessary to provide some scheme for taking care of the poverty-stricken after whom the monasteries had looked theretofore – at least it was regarded as their obligation. Well, the new scheme provided that this important function should be performed by the local officers, the justices of the peace, the overseers of the poor in each parish. To provide the necessary funds, the justices of the peace and the mayors in the towns were authorized to levy what were called the parish poor rates, that is, taxes upon property in the parish. They were authorized to appoint overseers whose duty it was to manage the expenditure of these funds. In expending them the scheme was that the overseers were to provide necessary stocks of raw material on which the able-bodied poor could be kept busy so that they migh in good part defray the cost of their keep. They were to buy materials like wool and flax and the necessary working equipment, and the people under their charge were to spend their time working up these raw materials, the sale of which it was supposed would lighten the poor rates.

People who were unable to work were supposed to be cared for without the necessity of exerting themselves; but the authorities were very much more concerne with those who were able to work and did not want to do so. Valiant beggars, in the phrase of the time, able-bodied men who did not want to work were to be whipped at the cart's tail and sent to houses of correction. Their life was to be made miserable for them in accordance with their merits. This

general scheme of poor law legislation as codified in Elizabeth's Statute of
1601 remained the fundamental poor law of Great Britain until the Act of 1834
was passed, the law which was inspired in large measure by the investigations
of Malthus.

So much for labor. You see that is a very comprehensive scheme to
make sure that the country has properly trained labor forces adequately paid,
but not paid too much, that people who would not work should be duly punished,
that those that were unable to get jobs at the prevailing rates of pay should
be still kept at work on materials provided by the public authorities — a
very elaborate scheme.

The law took as careful consideration of the various fundamental industries
of the country. First agriculture, the great source of food supply. In those
days England lived primarily upon the crops that she raised herself. And it was
also to be seen to that not only was there a sufficient labor supply for agriculture but also that the grain raised was sold at a price which would be remuner-
ative to the farmers on the one side and not unduly high for the consuming masses
on the other hand. The law, therefore, put the trade in grain into the hands of
a set of licensed dealers who were called bodgers. These bodgers, like all
licensed dealers, were licensed in order that they might be responsible to public
authority; and if they did not abide by the regulations they would of course lose
their license and be subject in various cases to additional penalties.

The determination of the price of grain was not left to the bodgers, but
in each market was determined by an official who was called the clerk of the
market. It was his business, in view of the current conditions of demand and
supply which the bodgers as the dealers were supposed to know about, to set the
price to legal weights and measures, so that consumers would get what they were
supposed to; to inspect the quality of the grain offered for food; and to punish
all offenses against the laws. The export of grain from England was promoted,
except in years of scarcity. When harvests were short, the government would
suspend altogether the outflow of grain, — at least that is what it attempted to
do. It also provided that no exports should go to the Queen's enemies, -- one
of the attempts to weaken Spain which by that time was ceasing to be a self-
supporting country agriculturally.

The government also had an elaborate industrial policy. They tried to
stimulate various branches of production which they thought would add to the
economic welfare of the people: the mining of metals that were required; improvements in the art of metallurgy; the making of comparatively novel products
like brimstone and saltpeter; the introduction of new processes or products
such as improved types of cloth; making of better glass; more effective cutlery,
paper, etc. The general method employed, so far as the introduction of new
arts was concerned, was first, when that resort was feasible, to encourage the
immigration of skilled artisans from other countires. That was in those days
often easy enough because of the religious troubles of the time. England had
become a Protestant country and in countries where there were religious wars
skilled artisans of the Protestant persuasion looked naturally to England as
as asylum. In circumstances where that attraction did not suffice, the government often moved companies of foreign workers at its expense and provided
settlements for them. It tried to make them comfortable in England and to use
them as teachers of the native population, so that these important arts might
become indigenous.

Another method employed was to grant patents of monopoly to enterprisers who had invented or acquired the rights to inventions of industrial value, patents which through the monopoly privilege were supposed to make the exercise of the new trade profitable for sufficient length of time to get it firmly established.

Also the government was very much concerned with the foreign commerce of the country. It was very necessary in their eyes that that should be regulated in very great detail in order that they might secure a favorable balance of trade, a balance of trade which would keep the country's workers profitably employed and bring into the country a flow of the precious metals. Precious metals were not, as is often said, in the eyes of the Mercantilist statesmen the only form of wealth, but in their eyes it was obvious that if you have gold and silver you can buy with it most of the things that you require. In order to regulate foreign trade, the general scheme was to put commerce with different parts of the world into the hands of regulated companies, that is, companies to carry on foreign trade which were set up under public regulation very much as the domestic trade in grain was put into the hands of licensed bodgers who acted under the supervision of clerks of the market. Thus, for example, the trade with Germany was supposed to be in the hands of the merchant adventurers, or the Hamburg Company, with Russia in the hands of the Muscovy merchants, with Turkey in the hands of the Levant Company -- great privileged mercantile concerns. The North American fur trade was in the hands of the Hudson Bay Company, the one survivor of these great English mercantile concerns of the sixteenth and seventeenth centuries. There was also the great East India Company which became the largest of them all; and several having to do with the African trade. Commerce just across the Channel with Holland and France was not supposed to require the same sort of regulation.

If you were a merchant in those days and you wished to deal with one of the more distant parts of the earth, you had to do it by getting admission to one of these great regulated companies, pay the standard dues, and supposedly abiding by the restriction which the law placed and sharing in the payments which were required to the government.

The colonial system was used as a general part of this commercial policy. Colonies were planted very largely for commercial motives. It was expected of them that they should provide markets for English manufactures, on the one hand; sources of raw material supplies for English workers, on the other hand; and, third, all their carrying trade was to be carried on in English bottoms. That was one of a considerable number of measures intended to increase the country's mercantile marine, a matter of far greater importance to national defense in those days than now because of course in those days the difference between a stout merchant vessel and a man-of-war was not very marked. In time of war all good mercantile vessels were taken by the navy and put to naval uses with comparatively little difficulty. So having a great merchant marine meant having potentially a powerful navy.

In order to build up this navy not only was the carrying trade with the colonies kept in English hands, but also very special efforts were made to develop fishing. Fishing was also attractive to the Mercantilist statesman on the ground that it supplied a cheap and wholesome part of the diet and also provided goods for which there was a good foreign demand. In order to stimulate fishing, people were required by law not to eat meat on certain days of the week; If they did not eat meat, then the fish were likely to have a market; and our not very closely honored convention nowadays of eating fish on Friday runs back to a time when that was by law the diet of all good citizens.

Then there were the Navigation Acts proper which required in general that British merchants should carry on their foreign trade in British bottoms and in particular that they should avoid employing ships and seamen of rival nations.

Now all these schemes for the economic welfare of the country, and I have mentioned only the most significant of the many which were in effect, constituted what came to be known as Mercantilism; a scheme of economic regulation by national statesman with the aim of making the country strong economically and therefore strong in a military sense. It was really a sort of scheme of economic mobilization in the time of peace which finds perhaps its best modern counterpart in the efforts which were made during the Great War in all the belligerent countries to mobilize all the economic resources in supporting the military program.

What national power required, as these statesmen saw it, was first of all a large population; second, that population should be abundantly provided for in a material sense; and well controlled by the central government, so that it could be turned to whatever uses public policy required. The scheme required also a large marine wherewith anything that was required could be obtained promptly in adequate supplies. And the means by which this policy of power was pursued, as you see, were encouragement of agriculture, training of the workers, regulation of wages, regulation of prices of food and some other things, very careful regulation of foreign trade, of shipping and of the colonial ventures of the country as part of the general scheme; the introduction of new industries - anything which in the eyes of the people who felt responsible, as Sir James Steuart represents his statesmen to be, would affect the economic strength of the nation as a whole.

X

MERCANTILISM VS. INDIVIDUAL INITIATIVE IN THE EIGHTEENTH
CENTURY. ADAM SMITH'S EARLY LIFE.

At the last meeting I sketched very briefly the whole scheme of industrial regulation that was adopted in England in the reigns of Queen Elizabeth and King James I, and which endeavored to provide for the industrial training of the population through the scheme of apprenticeship. It determined what classes of occupations sons of fathers following certain branches of industry might enter; it provided for the supposedly fair but not undue remuneration of the wage-earning classes through the fixing of wages by the justices of the peace; it tried to get all the able-bodied people at work by punishing idleness, and on the other hand tried to keep the deserving poor from distress. The scheme tried to encourage those branches of mining and manufacturing which were deemed by the statesmen most advantageous to the country at large, through granting bounties, imposing duties upon imports, giving inventors or others who were to develop certain trades monopoly privileges. The scheme imposed still more minute regulations upon commerce, endeavoring to see that the country's exports should reach the largest possible excess above their imports, so that a steady stream of the precious metals might flow into the country; and it regulated the business of the colonies in such a fashion as to contribute toward the economic prosperity of the motherland; and also adopted elaborate shipping regulations with the same aim in view. This whole elaborate scheme constituted the English form of mercantilism.

Mercantilism has often and properly been called the policy of power.
We get our most vivid realization of it, I suppose, from what happened through
the war, for in the last century or two the modern world has known nothing
corresponding to this ambitious plan for managing the economic life of nations
upon a sustained scheme, save for the hasty experiment which almost all the
leading nations of the world were forced to adopt under the stress of the recent
great conflict. When it did appear an indispensable national necessity that all
the economic strength of the countries which were fighting each other should
be mobilized and utilized to the utmost, then the preference for individual
initiative was for the time being surrendered, and we put again into the hands
of our statesmen, in this country as well as in Germany, and France, and England
and Austria, and Russia, the task of telling us what we should do, of regulating
in considerable detail and in the most drastic fashion occupations of the
people, the prices at which they should exchange goods, striving to make everybody work or fight, striving to prevent the use of luxuries. In short, we
reintroduced in haste a great many of the most characteristic features of mercantilism, this time not with the primary object of getting a large stream of
the precious metals flowing into the nation, but primarily with the object of
letting the nation attain its utmost fighting power.

Now in thinking about mercantilism, economists quite naturally laid
more stress upon that particular object of getting a large supply of the preciou
metals than upon the general object of enhancing the nation's power. The desire of getting a favorable balance of trade to be paid in gold and silver was
not an end in itself, but a means toward this more general end. It was a sort
of political interpretation of the advantages of securing a money economy. The
successive generations of statesmen had seen how much more the nation prospered
when the king got his revenues in money instead of in commodities; when his
military force was constituted of trained professional soldiers who were paid
salaries obtained in lieu of the performance of the old military duties. When
they had seen how much more effective even agricultural operations were when the
were conducted on a money basis instead of by an exchange of services for the
right to use lands, when they had noticed the manifold advantages of active
trade, they quite naturally thought, in somewhat naive fashion, that the nation
as a whole might get powerful as it got rich, just as a merchant acquires power
along with his wealth. And so, into their schemes of national aggrandizement
which had for untold generations been the general aim of statesmen, they incorporated this new economic measure of trying to get a plentiful supply of the
monetary metals; and in that aim they were led to pursue such a great diversity
of special aims; - all these elaborate regulations and standardizations of the
lives of the population.

I think perhaps we can obtain the clearest idea of the difference
between this general viewpoint and the viewpoint which was eloquently assumed
by Adam Smith, and which is still the viewpoint that most of us hold most of
the time when thinking about economic matters, by noticing the attitude of the
mercantilist writers toward the problem of labor. That is a comparatively easy
thing today because a few years ago Professor E.S. Furniss of Yale made a very
extensive study of seventeenth and eighteenth century pamphlets on trade in
the Yale library, and produced a book which he called rather curiously The
Position of the Laborer in a System of Nationalism*. It is really a series of
citations from mercantilist writers in the seventeenth and eighteenth centuries
in England concerning the proper policy that should be adopted with reference to

* Furniss, Edgar Stevenson, The Position of the Laborer in a System of Nationalism: A Study in the Labor Theories of the Later English Mercantilists, Boston,
1920.

labor. The first point in this policy which Furniss notes is the insistence upon the importance of the laborer to the country. That is a matter which is asserted in as strong terms as any modern orator might adopt in addressing a trade union convention. But the laborer is important not for his own sake but for quite other reasons. The common viewpoint is very neatly and succinctly phrased in an essay of John Bellers:*

> Regularly laboring people are the kingdom's greatest
> treasure and strength, for without laborers there can be no
> lords; and if the poor laborers did not raise much more food
> and manufacture than what did subsist themselves, every
> gentleman must be a laborer and every idle man must starve.

So the laborers are really the foundation stone upon which the national economy rests; but they are important only because gentlemen cannot exist without them. It was also a part of the doctrine that laborers should be kept steadily employed. Another writer said that "labor is to be regarded as a capital material, a raw and undigested commodity, placed in the hands of supreme authority whose disposition it is to improve, manage, and fashion it to more or less advantage." Laborers are not free people who are to live their own lives but they are raw materials, and it is the statesman's duty to see that they are utilized as well as may be. It is, of course, the statesman's responsibility to provide employment for all and, on the other hand, it is the people's duty to labor. "This duty should be taught early."

An anonymous pamphlet on The Management of the Poor (1767) runs:**

> Whenever either the legislature or private persons employ
> their care about the children of the poor, the principal part
> of their plan should be to inure them to the lowest and most early
> labor.

Another writer, William Temple, says:***

> When these children are four years old, they shall be sent
> to the country workhouse and there taught to read two hours a
> day and be kept fully employed the rest of their time in any
> of the manufactures of the house which best suits their age,
> strength and capacity. If it be objected that at these early
> years they cannot be made useful, I reply that at four years
> of age there are sturdy employments in which children can earn
> their living; but besides, there is considerable use in their
> being, somehow or other, constantly employed at least twelve
> hours in a day, whether they earn their living or not; for by
> these means, we hope that the rising generation will be so
> habituated to constant employment that it would at length
> prove agreeable and entertaining to them.....

And besides this rather drastic scheme of training which should be given to the most of the children, it was necessary that after that they be kept

---

* An Essay toward the Improvement of Physick, with an Essay for Imploying the Able Poor; London, 1714; p. 37.
** p. 16
*** An Essay on Trade and Commerce. London, 1770; pp. 266 ff.

poor in order that they be kept busy, as Arthur Young, the author of the celebrated <u>Travels in France</u> wrote in his eastern tour in 1771:*

> Every one but an idiot knows that the lower classes must be
> kept poor or they will never be industrious; I do not mean, that
> the poor of England are to be kept like the poor of France, but,
> the state of the country considered, they must (like all mankind)
> be in poverty or they will not work.

And this view, "that is known to every one but an idiot," really explains a good many opinions which were widely prevalent, even among enlightened men in the eighteenth century; such, for instance, as proposals to reduce wages, based on the opinion that whenever wages were high it meant an increase in idleness and loss of national strength. It was considered necessary to keep the lower orders from feeling above the humdrum routine tasks which the mass of men must be kept to. Endeavors were made to stop popular amusements which not only wasted time but were in danger of taking on a professional character, and the use of luxuries such as tea and sugar by the laborers was viewed with alarm. It was thought that when their consumption increased appreciably it was a sign that the working classes were adopting useless luxuries; a sign that the country would be a good deal better off if their wages be reduced to the level where they have no temptation to use articles which had to be imported at a cost to the country as a whole.

This general scheme of mercantilism, though it continued to find active and able defenders throughout the eighteenth century right down to the time of Adam Smith, as these pamphlets and as Sir James Steuart's great exposition of mercantilism as a whole makes sufficiently clear, this system though it continued to be regarded as theoretically outlining the proper economic policy for the country to pursue, had in fact been gradually disintegrating in a great many of its features. It was disintegrating, I think, quite clearly because certain changes in the daily life of the people were making it profitable to a great many individuals to do things forbidden by mercantilist legislation. Increasing hundreds of thousands of Englishmen were finding that laws adopted for the meritorious aim of increasing the country's strength really prevented them as individuals from finding a most profitable use of their capital and their time. And an Englishman in those times was much like a modern American in that he was always ready to respect laws which complied with his own convenience and to disregard those running counter to his own interests.

And so, while these laws remained on the statute books, and while they had theoretical defenders, we find in all classes of society there came to be an increasing disregard of the fundamental principles of mercantilist policy by a rapidly increasing number of the population. For example, under the mercantilist system a large part of England's foreign trade was reserved for exploitation by certain private companies. That was one of the approved schemes for seeing that the trade carried on was trade of a sort which would tend to increase exports and keep down imports so as to give the country a large favorable balance of trade. But where a monopoly privilege was given to certain companies by the government for exploiting trade, that company quite naturally tried to get monopoly prices, to pay as little as it possibly could to the people from whom it was buying wares in foreign countries and to sell wares when they were brought into England at as high a price as could be obtained. And quite naturally, these profits were almost an irresistible lure to

* Farmer's Tour Through the East of England, London, 1771; IV, p. 361

enterprising British merchants. Ans so you find what in those days was called
"interloping" developing on an ever growing scale. Men who had no connection
with the chartered companies, the privileged monopolists of certain branches
of trade, would by hook or crook try to send their vessels out to these regions
in order that they might get their share of the supposedly fabulous profits.
And that was a practice which they illegally pursued, and it increased as time
went on.

        Everybody who has studied American history knows of similar examples
of the disregard of the requirements of the mercantilist system on this side of
the water and how far from law-abiding our colonial ancestors were with reference to the requirement that they should not trade directly with the sugar
islands of the West Indies belonging to France or Spain; how they should, instead of that, carry on the great bulk of trade directly with the home country;
and not trade, except in a few cases which were excepted on good mercantilist
principles, with people of other nations. Well, the American colonists, finding
an advantage in sending their produce to these islands, where the population was
largely slaves, and importing molasses from which they could make rum, which
they in turn could exchange in Africa for slaves, found it to their interest to
engage in the profitable traffic, and the British government found it extremely
difficult to interfere with the proceeding.

        So too, in England the system of mercantilism involved the imposing
of very heavy duties upon the importation of certain wares for which, never theless, there existed a very great market in England; and that resulted in a system of smuggling which was developed to a stage which I suppose even the infractions of the law against the importing of liquor at the present time gives
only a faint idea of. It was carried on even by government officials and
clergymen.

        This summer I happened to meet an Englishman whose family lived on
the southern coast of England, and who had been clergymen for a long while.
He told me that the church in which his family was most interested was regularly used as a warehouse in which smuggled brandies and French wines were
stored, and that frequently enough the church services themselves were interrupted by the arrival of some messenger belonging to the smuggling gang who told
them a company of soldiers was moving their way, and the whole congregation
was dispersed to move the smuggled goods to a safe place. That kind of thing
was going on through all classes of society.

        There were thousands upon thousands of Englishmen who were pur-
suing profitable trades without having gone through a regular apprenticeship.
There were thousands of people disregarding completely the guild regulations
which prohibited a man who had not been duly initiated in a certain mystery from
exercising the trade in question. From top to bottom, then, the English population, while maintaining in theory its reverence for this general scheme of
having the statesman determine what was best for the country as a whole, were
ready as individuals to do what they found profitable. It was, I think, fundamental, this pursuit of private profit, whether it ran counter to law or not;
and was responsible for a change in practice, a change that came a considerable
time before the change in theory. Adam Smith, when he came forward as the
philosophic champion of a doctrine that justified a system under which everybody would be free to follow his own interests, found the minds of men prepared
for that recipe because it was itself the justification of what they found themselves doing, -- doing rather reluctantly, in some cases against their conscience.
But the promulgation of that kind of thought led men to believe that the laws
were wrong and ought to be changed, and what they had been doing was not only

right and profitable for themselves, but advantageous to the country as a whole.

One of the characteristics of the time, however, was that Parliament in the eighteenth century paid comparatively little attention to economic problems. Nowadays, I suppose, a person who reads congressional debates will get the impression that in most years the chief problems that concern the legislators of this country are problems of an economic order, or at least the problems that come up for treatment are treated largely in their economic aspects. If, on the other hand, you look over such records as we have of the debates in eighteenth century England, you get the impression on the whole that economic problems were not of first-rate importance in the eyes of the legislators. Now and then they could be induced to give their attention to some matter, particularly if that matter could be made in some way a burning issue between the two parties. But they were very much more concerned with the old problems of the balance of power in Europe, the question of foreign policy, and also with constitutional questions. The great issues of eighteenth century British Policy arose from the issues connected with foreign wars, and of course all these had to do with maintaining England's prestige in the balance of power and trying to improve that position.

The great questions were those that centered upon the wars and also around the relations between the king and Parliament. For a long while the great question was whether the efforts of George III to assert the old prerogatives of the Crown should succeed; whether the king should be allowed to choose his ministers, or whether they should continue to be, in fact though perhaps not in name, a committee chosen by the House. And then there came up that long continued and most interesting problem connected with the name of John Wilkes, as to whether a parliamentary constituency should be allowed to choose its own representative; whether Parliament or Parliament and king together could refuse to seat a man who had been elected by a certain constituency. And then there came to the fore for some years as the leading question of the day the struggle with the North American colonies, -- a question that had its economic side, a question which nowadays historians are very likely to treat in economic terms, but a question which was not discussed in eighteenth century England primarily in terms of economic issues but in terms of the Colonists' rights or rather in terms of the colonists' duties.

There were of course, economic questions considered, such for instance as the perennial fear that the national debt was growing to such proportions as to promise the ruin of the country; and questions of taxation methods, of trying to improve the way of collecting duties upon imports. But, broadly speaking, it is almost the fact that the eighteenth century at least until the time of the second William Pitt, that is, some time after the appearance of The Wealth of Nations, eighteenth century England had, so far as the parliamentary record is concerned, hardly any great constructive measure of an economic sort to offer.

To sum up the situation as a whole; We have a community that was, in comparison with past times, living in large part a life of peace; a community that was turning its attention more and more to bettering its economic condition; a community in which people were more and more largely developing initiative and voluntary cooperation in pursuit of their enterprises; in which the government itself, though running on in the old forms, was gradually becoming a government by public discussion; and in which the central government was taking less and less hand in local affairs, leaving them more and more in the management of local people; and in which the old traditional scheme for regulating the economic life of the people was being infringed upon in countless ways by countless individuals; and in which - and this is the last word I have to say before taking up Adam Smith's adventures - in which the government was scarcely intervening to check the changes that were going forward; in which the government was acquiescing tacitly in the breakdown of a plan in which probably almost all members of Parliament continued to believe theoretically.

The British have a great system of what are called "dead letters," - laws which stand on the statute books, which nobody takes the trouble to repeal, but which also nobody takes the trouble to enforce. Now, as the eighteenth century wore on, more and more of the economic legislation came to have that status of "dead letters." Now and then, people whose interests were interfered with by infractions of the law would protest to Parliament and ask that Parliament see to it that its own laws be respected. There were plenty of people of that sort; for instance, the people who were interested in the privileged trading companies found the persons of interlopers in their part of the trading world a most unwelcome development. They would demand that the privileges they were paying for should be confined to themselves and these lawbreakers be kept out. Every now and then a craft guild that found its market was being taken away by some enterprising business man who found a new way of producing things and who employed certain people to make things who had not had proper apprenticeship and admission to the guild, would appeal to Parliament and ask that the laws regarding apprenticeship and guild membership be enforced. The manufacturers of England who thought that their interests in the colonies would be compromised by the illicit trade that the colonists were carrying on with the West India Islands belonging to other powers, or manufacturers in England who feared that the colonists were going to set up iron works of their own and would become independent of British cutlery, etc. would appeal to Parliament and ask that it enforce the laws it had itself passed. And merchants who dealt in goods properly imported into England found that smuggling was likely to cause them serious losses. They did not go into the smuggling trade; and they were going to appeal to Parliament to see that the laws requiring that all goods which came in should come in through the customs house and be subjected there to the proper levies, should be enforced.

Parliament, made up of men who had the usual amount of logical consistencies in their make-up, could always see the point that the laws should be enforced and often enough it lent a willing ear and tried to take some measure to see to it that the statutes were enforced. But more and more often as the century wore on, when a petition in favor of enforcing the old laws was presented, people appeared on the other side and began arguing as plausibly as they could through their representatives that the new ways of doing things after all were not injurious to the country. That happened perhaps most often with reference to the efforts of the craft guilds to get their ancient privileges respected. Business men who found other ways of producing things that were better and cheaper than the craft guild's methods would appear in opposition to a petition of that sort and often-times make a case which a set of gentlemen acting as a parliamentary committee, though they knew little about all this, could hardly disregard, and then Parliament disregarded the petitions and let matters alone. In a most confused sort of way the situation kept drifting on in the direction of freer and freer practice of individual initiative, in the direction of less and less practical enforcement of the scheme of statesmanlike control over the country's economic life as a whole.

Now that was the situation in which Adam Smith had grown up, and what I have next to do is to review briefly his individual experiences before the time when he set himself to discuss these large issues of trade on a philosophic basis. Among the numerous lives of Adam Smith, the best is one by John Rae.* If you look in any considerable library, you will find other lives, older and more recent, but I think none of the more recent ones undertake to be as comprehensive as this very carefully documented study.

Adam Smith was born in a small Scotch town called Kirkcaldy in 1723. About his father we know very little except the fact that he was a lawyer, - what was called in Scotland a "writer to the signet," - he had been the Judge Advocate for Scotland and Comptroller of the Customs in the Kirkcaldy district. These things indicate that he must have been a man of influential connections because anyone who did not have them would not in those days have been likely to get such appointments. His mother was the daughter of a well-to-do landowner. His father died a few months before Adam Smith was born, and he was the only child in the family. He was brought up at home then by a widow, and throughout his life he had the closest of personal relations with her. Most of the time he lived with his mother until her death, and she lived to the age of ninety, at which time he was sixty-one. He never married.

He was sent to the Kirkcaldy school which had a very good reputation, and at the age of fourteen he was ready to enter Glasgow College. Now when Adam Smith entered Glasgow College, it was a place of remarkable intellectual activity. Smith was particularly influenced by Francis Hutcheson, a great teacher, who was the first to give up the practice of lecturing in Latin in favor of English. He was a philosopher who discovered in nature the Benevolent Deity of the eighteenth century, a Deity whose will was to be found, not merely by consulting the Sacred Scriptures, but also to be found by inquiring into the good of mankind. If you could find out what measures made for the good of mankind, for what Hutcheson called "the greatest good of the greatest number", a very famous phrase which he is said to be the first to use, you could find out what God's will was. Such was his philosophic brand of theology and in those days a teacher of moral philosophy was almost as much of a theologian as of a philosopher. His brand of philosophic theology led him quite naturally to inquire into a whole series of social problems, among which economic problems had their place. Hutcheson lectured on certain economic themes in his general course on natural jurisprudence, and took, on the whole, a very liberal stand although on technical points he was a Mercantilist.

This influence of Hutcheson on Adam Smith is represented by all his biographers as being decidedly an important feature in forming his views, beginning at a time when he was pretty young. And another personal factor to which a good deal of influence is ascribed is Adam Smith's early and long acquaintance with David Hume. David Hume was some twelve years his elder; he was beyond a question a man of extraordinary intellectual power. He came to be regarded as the first philosopher of his age, not merely in Scotland and England but on the continent of Europe. He was a man of most delightful personality, a man of very wide interests, a writer upon history and economics and art as well as upon philosophy; a man to whom Adam Smith became very closely attached and with whom he spent a great deal of his time.

At the end of his four years in Glasgow College in 1740, Adam Smith won a Snell exhibition. There were five of these exhibitions granted only by Glasgow College. They were fellowships which carried a stipend of L 40 a year and enabled the holders to spend five years in Balliol College, Oxford. So after his four years at Glasgow, Adam Smith moved down to Oxford and studied there five years. He came to Oxford just at the time when its intellectual lethargy pre-

*Life of Adam Smith, London, 1895

sented the sharpest of contrasts to the intellectual activity of the Scottish universities. In The Wealth of Nations there is a passage in which Adam Smith says that nobody was then taught, or could so much as find "the proper means of being taught, the sciences which it is the business of those incorporated bodies to teach." And that harsh verdict which Adam Smith passed upon Oxford is one that is equally expressed by Edward Gibbon and Jeremy Bentham, who followed him at Oxford after no long interval.

Adam Smith, however, did not waste his time; he was a born student. He spent long days in the library at Balliol College reading classics, reading French and Italian belles lettres, and he was even caught reading his friend David Hume's Treatise of Human Nature, an indiscretion for which he was reprimanded and the book confiscated.

XI

ADAM SMITH AND THE WEALTH OF NATIONS

At the close of our last hour I began a brief account of Adam Smith's personal share in the life of his time. Indeed, it seems that he made very few friends at Oxford. In all this time he lived a very quiet studious life, devoting a great deal of his attention to belles lettres. He was there not only when the work of instructing was very unintelligently treated, but also at a time when there seemed to be no outstanding characters among the students. His biographers have spent a good deal of time looking over the lives of Oxford students and only one man in the University, in Balliol, his college, at that time, who later became distinguished was another Scotch lad, Douglas, who later in life became Bishop of Salisbury.

The Snell exhibitions were supposed to lead to a clerical career, that is, at the end of a man's tenure he was supposed to take Holy Orders and return to labor in the Scotch Church. But Adam Smith had gradually developed scruples against taking Holy Orders; these conscientious scruples stood in the way of a career in the Church, and for that matter in a University career in England, for very few people not in the Church could expect to get University fellowships. So he returned to Kirkcaldy and settled down again to live with his mother.

He hoped to get a tutorship, that is, an opportunity to teach the children of some of the magnates of Scotland, but his diffidence and his poor dress stood in his way and no such opportunity was opened to him. After two years, however, he secured a chance to deliver a course of lectures on English literature in Edinburgh, and that proved one of the turning points in his life. At Edinburgh in the course of lectures on English literature he had a distinguished audience. His lectures were highly appreciated and won considerable reputation. From reports made at the time, we know something about the views he entertained upon this interesting subject. He held that Shakespeare had written good scenes but had not written any good plays; the best tragedy in any language was Racine's Phaedrus: Dryden was a better poet than Shakespeare; Milton's shorter poems were of no account; indeed his opinions upon the merits of English literature were those of the eighteenth century. They differed very widely from our own. When William Wordsworth wrote the preface to his Lyrical Ballads, he remarked that Adam Smith was the worst critic, David Hume not excepted, that Scotland, a soil of which that sort of weed seems natural, had produced. He gave these lectures on English literature three winters in success-

ion, and during the last of these winters he gave a course of lectures on economics
in which he advocated the doctrines of commercial liberty.

The success of these lectures led to his appointment to a chair at
Glasgow in 1751, when he was twenty-seven years old. The professor of logic
had died and Adam Smith was promptly appointed to the vacant post. Next year
he was transferred from the chair of logic to the more desirable chair of moral
philosophy. As professor of moral philosophy he received an income from the
endowment which probably averaged ℒ 70 a year, and in addition he received fees
from the students who attended his course. These fees it is believed never
exceeded ℒ 100, so that his income, both from the endowment and from the fees
was probably in the neighborhood of ℒ 170. The college provided him a home,
and Smith took in an occasional boarder. His mother and his aunt lived with
him. This income seems low to us now-a-days, the sum of money running say in
the neighborhood of six or seven hundred dollars a year, together with a house
and whatever profit he made from the boarder, but we must remember that at that
time the general range of incomes in Scotland was very low. The best paid position in the Scotch Church was only ℒ 138 per annum.

Glasgow College when Smith went there as a tutor had about 300 students of whom 80 or 90 took Smith's general course on moral philosophy. In addition to that general course he had what was called a "private class," a class
of more advanced students, some 20 in number. On the average he used to lecture
from half past seven to half past eight to his large class, to hold a quiz at
eleven, and then to meet his private class at twelve twice a week. In addition,
he had a good deal of personal intercourse with his students and exercised considerable influence upon them. He was one of the most successful tutors in
Glasgow.

The moral philosophy course which he gave year after year consisted
of four parts, the first dealing with natural theology, the second part with
ethics, the third part with justice, and the fourth part with expediency. In
the first part devoted to natural theology the lecturer adduced the principles
of the being and the attributes of God and developed the principles of the human
mind upon which religion is founded. In the second part of the course devoted
to ethics he developed the principles which were presently to be in his <u>Theory
of Moral Sentiments</u>, about which I shall say more in a moment. In the third part,
belonging to justice, he traced the gradual progress of jurisprudence and the
effects of measures which contribute to the subsistence and the accumulation
of property. Finally his discussion of expediency was a discussion of political
regulations which are based not on justice as such but on expediency, -- regulations which were calculated to increase the riches, power, and prosperity
of a state. This brought up for discussion questions of commercial and financial
policy, ecclesiastical and military establishments, and so on. It was this
fourth part of his course of lectures on moral philosophy which gradually developed into <u>The Wealth of Nations</u>. We know a good deal about this course because a very full set of notes taken by some member of this class in 1763 has been
preserved. In 1896 it was edited and published by Professor Edward Cannan under
the title of Lectures on Justice, Police, Revenue and Arms Delivered in the
University of Glasgow by Adam Smith.

From the beginning, in his discussion of such economic problems as
could be brought into the course on moral philosophy, Adam Smith expounded the
principles of free trade, and it was ascribed to his influence that this doctrine
became current among the business classes in Glasgow. Sir James Steuart, whose
Treatise on Political Economy I mentioned in the early part of the course, returned from exile in 1763 and lived for a time at Glasgow. While there, he

tried to persuade the Glasgow merchants to support the theory of protection which, of course, appealed to him; but he said that he became tired of repeating arguments to the Glasgow "theorists" as he called them, whom Smith had converted to the free trade heresy.

Glasgow was at that time a rapidly rising commercial center of some 23,000 inhabitants. It had for an indefinite time been a residential town, but there was a group of unusually enterprising business people there. There interest was largely in the tobacco trade with the West Indies. Glasgow became a point of supply for the tobacco-growing colonies, a point to which tobacco was shipped from the colonies, and from which the tobacco after more or less manufacturing was distributed to the various centers of consumption. In connection with that tobacco trade, the town developed a number of manufacturing enterprises. It imported iron from Russia and Sweden and made it into hoes and spades for the colonists in Maryland; it tanned hides and made saddlery and shoes for use upon the plantations. It was also developing linen works, copper and tin works, and pottery, carpets, silk, and leather glove manufactures on a modest scale.. In 1750 the first bank was opened in Glasgow, and two years later another was found necessary. In 1759 the merchants of the place began improving the navigation of the channel of the River Clyde so that vessels could come up to Glasgow itself. They installed a drydock in 1762, and in 1768 they began work on a canal to connect the Clyde with the Forth. A town then, you see, full of observant merchants and manufacturers; a town, the business of which was increasing rapidly.

Adam Smith entered into rather intimate associations with his enterprising fellow-townsmen. In particular he joined a weekly discussion club of which the express designs were to inquire into the nature and principles of trade in all its branches. Thus, though not engaged in business himself, he had an uncommonly good opportunity to watch the processes of trade as they were carried on by one of the most enterprising groups of business people to be found anywhere in the United Kingdom. I suppose there is no doubt whatever that his weekly discussions for a long period of years with these business people had a great deal to do with the development of his interest in economic problems, and probably the formulation of the views which he came to entertain in regard to them.

Another factor in his development was the ripening of his acquaintance with David Hume, an acquaintance which you remember began when he was a lad in college and brought him the embarrassment of having David Hume's Treatise of Human Nature taken away from him. Hume was not only the first philosopher of Europe at this time, he was also the most enlightened writer upon economic themes, at least the most enlightened English writer upon economic questions before Adam Smith's own day. The two men seem to have been most congenial, although Hume was some ten years older than the economist. Every now and then Smith would run over from Glasgow to Edinburgh where Hume was living, though the journey then was some thirteen hours, and he spent most of his vacations in Hume's house. Thus he came to know not only Hume himself but also to maintain an intimacy with Hume's Edinburgh circle, a circle which, I may add, was composed of people whose chief interest was decidedly different from that of the Glasgow group, so far as economic questions were discussed, and Adam Smith joined this select society in Edinburgh. The chief interest in Edinburgh was in agricultural problems and about them Adam Smith had an opportunity to think almost as much in Edinburgh as he thought about mercantile and manufacturing problems in his own home.

In 1759 Adam Smith published his Theory of Moral Sentiments. As I said, this book was a outgrowth of the second part of his course on moral philosophy, the part that dealt with ethics. It was an eloquently written essay of two

volumes which argued that moral approbation and disapprobation are, in the last
analysis, expressions of sympathy with the feelings of an imaginary and impartial spectator. Even what our own conscience tells us about the rightness
or wrongness of our actions is a reflection of the views which some impartial
or sympathetic spectator has concerning what we have done. And that sympathy with
the views of an onlooker is the basis on which all our moral feelings rest in the
last resort. This treatise upon ethics was most neatly adjusted to the taste
of the age. It was filled with illustrations; the argument was developed in
leisurely and rather copious fashion. It was written with considerable effort;
easy to read, entertaining; was almost as much of a literary as it was a philosophical performance, and it promptly won an enviable reputation for the author.
Within Adam Smith's lifetime it passed through six editions, and made him widely
known in England and in France as well as in Scotland. It also led to a considerable increase in the number of students who attended his classes in Glasgow.
The old Scotch and Irish contingent was added to by men who drifted in from England, the Scandinavian countries, and even from Russia.

What was more important was that the publication of The Theory of Moral
Sentiments led to the next important change in Adam Smith's method of life. The
book came into the hands of Charles Townshend who was then Chancellor of the
Exchequer; and, as David Hume wrote to Adam Smith, Townshend passed "for the
cleverest fellow in England." He was a brilliant parliamentary light, now perhaps remembered because he was the person who took responsibility for imposing the duty upon tea in the North American colonies, the duty which led to
the Boston Tea Party and contributed to the more serious consequences which
followed. Townshend some years before had married the Countess of Dalkeith who
was a great heiress and the widow of the oldest son of the Duke of Buccleugh.
Before marrying Townshend she had two sons, and when the old Duke died, her infant
son came in for the title, becoming the Duke of Buccleugh. To ensure that the
young noble got a proper education, Charles Townshend, his stepfather, set his
heart upon getting the author of The Theory of Moral Sentiments to take a grand
tour with the young duke and give him the proper sort of introduction to life. So
Townshend approached Adam Smith upon the subject, and in 1763 when the boy was
old enough, Smith resigned his professorship and accepted the tutorship. That
meant a very material improvement in his circumstances. He was paid a salary of
L 300 a year and promised a pension of the same amount for his whole life, and of
course his expenses while traveling were to be paid. More than that, it gave
him an opportunity to visit the European countries he had not yet seen.

So rather regretfully he resigned his professorship and in February, 1764
set out with the duke for France. Their first task was to learn to speak the
French language. They went south to Toulouse and devoted themselves in no very
hasty fashion to acquiring familiarity with the language. While he was in the
south of France, Adam Smith wrote to David Hume, "I have begun to write a book
in order to pass away the time. You may believe I have very little to do." And
the book thus begun in 1764 gradually grew into The Wealth of Nations; and it in
turn was founded upon that section of the old moral philosophy course which had
dealt with the principles of expediency.

After leisurely travels through France and Switzerland, during which
Smith had an opportunity to observe economic conditions there, different from
those with which he was familiar in Scotland and in England, the party reached
Paris about Christmas in 1765. Their arrival in Paris occurred at the end of
David Hume's two years of triumph in that city. Hume had been looked upon as a
sort of demigod in the Paris salons. He had become acquainted with all the leaders in the literary and fashionable circles, so that he was in a position to introduce his friend Adam Smith and Smith's noble pupil to the people worth know-

ing. That he did at once, so that Adam Smith promply formed the acquaintance
of the group of men in Europe who were most concerned with the problems about
which he was now actively thinking, that is, the group of Physiocrats.

About the Physiocrats, of course, you must all know a good deal, and it
is no part of my present task to say anything concerning their views. What is
important to recall, however, is that Dr. Quesnay, a physician attached to the
court, had been brought to think rather more systematically about the problems
of economic policy as they presented themselves to the monarch of a country, than
any of his predecessors; that he had come to the opinion that by all odds the
most important, not to say the exclusive source of wealth was to be found in
agriculture, and that the king who wished to raise his people to the highest possible level of affluence should do all that he could to promote agriculture, among
the steps necessary to be taken being to allow almost complete liverty of private initiative. Around him Quesnay had gradually gathered a band of distinguished disciples, and more or less on the outskirts of this band and very sympathetically related to them was Turgot, the celebrated official who while Adam
Smith was in Paris was himself writing a treatise, which was presently published,
on the formation of riches.

When Adam Smith reached Paris, the Physiocrats were in the first flush
of their first brief practical success. They had captured a journal, the Journal
de L'Agriculture du Commerce et des Finances, of which one of their number, Dupont,
that Physiocrat who later in life emigrated to the United States and set up the
great powder business at Wilmington, was made editor in June, 1765. They had persuaded the government to issue an edict in 1764 which promoted the exportation of
grain, and they were looking forward to exercising a very considerable degree of
practical influence upon economic policy, hopes which were destined to an early
and bitter disappointment. For nearly a year Smith stayed in Paris, seeing a
great deal of this group as well as being on more or less intimate terms with the
various sets of philosophers who were having such a good time in discussing unorthodox things of various sorts.

He returned to England rather hurriedly, due to the misfortune that
the younger brother of the Duke of Buccleugh was killed and the party had to go
back to London in November, 1766. When they got back Adam Smith's duties as a
tutor came to an end, and he was left at liberty to pursue his own interests with
the pension of ₤300 a year. He spent a considerable time in London, working
largely at the British Museum where he had opportunity to get certain materials
concerning colonial questions about which his information had theretofore been
unsatisfactory. Then in 1767 he went back to his old home at Kirkcaldy, and there
he lived the greater part of his time the next ten years with his mother, working
on his book. He did interrupt these years in Kirkcaldy, however, with some rather
long stays in London but, substantially speaking, he buried himself in the country
and devotd himself to his writing. We do not know very much about his progress,
though there are occasional letters of his which throw some light on how he liked
his quiet life. For instance, he wrote to Hume soon after settling down that he
was immersed in study which was his only business, that his sole amusement was
taking long solitary walks by the seaside, and that he had never been happier in
his life. He seems to have completed his first draft by about 1770, but he went
on altering and amplifying parts of it for six years more. He suffered some
very ill health. He wrote to a friend in 1772 of interruptions that were caused
partly by bad health. Besides, he was always a slow worker. In a letter to a
publisher that was found not long ago and printed in the Economic Journal, September, 1923, he remarked; "I am a slow, very slow workman, who do and undo everything I write at least half a dozen times before I can be tolerably pleased with
it."

In 1773 he took the manuscript to London and spent three years there.

His stay was a good deal more extensive than he had expected. While there he saw
quite little of Edmund Burke and Benjamin Franklin; he was admitted to the
Literary Club presided over by Samuel Johnson, a club which included among other
members Edmund Burke, Sir Joshua Reynolds, and Edward Gibbon. Finally, in March,
1776 The Wealth of Nations was published as a two volume quarto, selling for
L1:16s. The book had taken ten years to write, if you count only the years from
1766 when Adam Smith had given up his tutoring of the young duke and devoted his
time almost exclusively to it. It took a good deal more time if you go back to the
time he began writing in Toulouse, and it had been really developing in his mind
probably from the beginning of his professorship in Glasgow, perhaps even from that
one course of lectures upon economic topics which he had delivered in his twenty-
ninth year at Edinburgh -- a book, you see, that developed in a very deliberate
fashion.

The Wealth of Nations had a very rapid success. The whole of the first
edition was exhausted within six months. Before Adam Smith died, four other editions had been printed and sold. It was translated three times into French before the end of the eighteenth century and twice into German. It was translated
also into Italian, Danish, and Spanish, and it was pirated in Ireland. It met
as warm and perfect a welcome from the intellectual world in England as any book
of a serious nature that appeared within a hundred years of its time. Our concern,
of course, is largely, in fact mainly, with this book, but before taking up that
theme, let me add a few words about Adam Smith's later years.

He stayed in London for a little time after the book was published, enjoying his triumph, and in 1778, early in that year, he was appointed to a
commissionership of the customs in Edinburgh, a rather lucrative post in the govern
ment employ. This post was a very desirable one from Adam Smith's viewpoint and
seems to have been a direct reward to the author for the benefits which Lord North,
then Chancellor of the Exchequer, had obtained from reading The Wealth of Nations
in preparing his budgets for the years 1777 and 1778. Lord North, by no means
agreeing with Adam Smith's general views, had found certain technical suggestions
on the matter of taxation which he took directly out of the book and incorporated
in the budget. So that when Adam Smith's friends suggested the desirability of
making him Commissioner of the Customs in Edinburgh, he lent a willing ear. His
salary in this post was L 600 a year. Smith retained his pension of L 300 from
the Duke of Buccleugh; he also had half the selling price of the later editions of
The Wealth of Nations, besides his royalties on the editions of The Theory of
Moral Sentiments which the market kept absorbing. Indeed, he enjoyed in the later
years of his life a revenue which for the time and place was almost princely, so
that he was able to live a most agreeable life. He dispensed very liberal charity
and he associated with the leading men of his day. While Glasgow was notable for
its enterprising merchants, Edinburgh was notable for its intellectuals. It was
the home of such men as Hutton, the man whose work did most to introduce the modern
type of geology, and Black, one of the most distinguished surgeons of the day.

It was altogether a very calm and happy old age that he passed, his work
not being exceedingly irksome. Just before his death he called in the most intimate of his remaining friends -- for David Hume had died in 1776 shortly after
The Wealth of Nations had appeared -- and asked them in his presence to burn sixteen volumes of manuscript. This they did without asking what those books contained, and with that act started a mystery which has exercised the minds of
economists ever since. The general supposition is that as Adam Smith had developed
the second part of his course on moral philosophy into his Theory of Moral Sentiments and the fourth part into The Wealth of Nations, so in his later years he spent
his leisure in developing the third part into a treatise upon jurisprudence, and
that the sixteen volumes, not developed to such a point that he was willing to have

them published, may have contained that work. But inasmuch as Black and Hutton did not look into their friend's books, it can only be speculated as to what the world lost in the burning. He died finally on the 17th of July, 1790.

The point of this sketch of Adam Smith's life for us is, I think, to observe that The Wealth of Nations was the carefully elaborated product of a college professor, a professor of moral philosophy, a man whose training had been in classics and literature, and in philosophy; a man who had never taken any active share in business up to the time he published his work, and who even to the close of his days was never a business man, though he did become a public official. But though its author did live this quite reflective life, he was a man who associated closely with several quite different circles of people, -- people whose leading interests were remarkably diverse. He had his long friendship with that curiously stimulating philosopher, David Hume, and his associations with his professional colleagues in Glasgow. For that matter I might mention that among those with whom he came in contact was James Watt who was the mathematical instrument maker to the college while Adam Smith was the professor of moral philosophy; and while Adam Smith was lecturing on jurisprudence and economics, Watt was making those experiments which led to his important improvements on Newcomen's steam engine.

In closing I will say, he had had the active interchange of views with the merchants and manufacturers of the place, and conversations with the people interested in agricultural problems around Edinburgh. And then he had been given the opportunity to travel in France and Switzerland, and to observe economic life under a political system markedly different from that at home, economic conditions in a geographical environment which was different from that of Scotland or England. Also, his French travels had brought him into close intellectual contact with the intellectually most vigorous set of people who were trying to develop economics on a systematic basis. With all these many contacts Adam Smith had finally gone home to his mother's house in the quiet Scotch village and spent some ten or eleven meditative years in elaborating in a finished manner all the numerous ideas which he had gathered. The result was then a book which had a curious degree of finish for a book that marks as large an effort in human thought as does The Wealth of Nations. You expect people who are breaking new ground to show in their books a certain amount of crudity. It is eminently true of the next influential work in economics which we shall have to consider -- David Ricardo's Principles of Political Economy; that is a hasty, raw, imperfect sort of performance. Adam Smith's The Wealth of Nations is from a literary point of view an admirable performance, urbane, well rounded out in all its parts, exactly the kind of work that you might expect, so far as its manner is concerned, to come from the hand of a college professor.

XII

THE WEALTH OF NATIONS: A PHILOSOPHER'S REFLECTIONS ON WHAT
HE SAW ABOUT HIM

Today I wish to say something about The Wealth of Nations, though I do not plan to discuss the economic doctrines which this celebrated book contains. Those doctrines you are acquainting yourselves with by reading the book as a whole. My aim is to emphasize certain characteristics of the book and presently to show in some detail what practical influence it exercised. The Wealth of Nations is certainly one of the most influential books which has ever been published, -- influential both in shaping public policies not only in England but also in other countries, and influential likewise in promoting the development of thought. Yet it is a very curious book in its makeup. As I said early in the course, when we read it, we usually, as students of economics, read it to see what Adam Smith thought concerning certain technical doctrines, particularly the theory of value and the theories of wages, profits, and rent. It was not, however, because of interest in these topics that the book was read so widely by so many important people in its own time. They consulted it rather to see what Adam Smith had to say about the problems which concerned them: about such matters as the currency and banking, colonial administration, the Settlement Laws -- that curious set of regulations which prevented a poor man from moving from one part of the country to the other, -- about the Navigation Acts, about the Canons of Taxation.

Now the book has a good deal to say about economic theory and a great deal to say about public policy. It is a curious compound such as you will find matched in this respect by very few modern treatises. It is a book, indeed, without a systematic plan. In the generation that followed Adam Smith you expected to find that a treatise upon economic theory would be arranged in an orderly manner, beginning probably with a discussion of the production of wealth, followed by a discussion of exchange, then a discussion of distribution, and perhaps closing with a discussion of the consumption of wealth. Now-a-days, when you open an economic treatise you expect to find it organized on the lines of the discussion of value, perhaps opening with a discussion of what constitutes value, duly developing the reasons why we want goods on the one hand, and the factors which regulate the supply of goods on the other hand. And then it will proceed to discuss the distribution of wealth as a series of problems in value: wages is the price paid for labor, and the price for labor can be discussed in terms of the general theory of value as supply and demand. So interest is the price paid for the loan of funds and can be discussed in terms of the supply and demand of capital. Rent is the price paid for the use of land and can be discussed in terms of the supply of and demand for land. And profit is the price which people get for undertaking the work of business management, and can be discussed as a problem of the demand for and supply of business ability.

In The Wealth of Nations you find a plan, and one that unfolds, as Adam Smith writes in a natural, plausible fashion. That is just because Adam Smith had considerable literary ability. Logically, the plan is very curious when you look at it as a whole, and indeed the lack of arrangement, as they called it, was one of the chief criticisms which Adam Smith's young disciples in the generation that followed him made of The Wealth of Nations. It was a criticism naturally that was very prominent in the minds of his French disciples, for we credit the French with having a keener sense of logical proportion than we usually have. It was J. B, Say who in his Cours d'Economic Politique Pratique published in 1803 introduced the order that commended itself to economists for another generation or two, the order which begins with production and goes on through exchange and consumption.

Let us see what Adam Smith's own order was. Book I he calls "Of the causes of improvement in the productive powers of labour, and of the order according to which its produce is naturally distributed among the different ranks of the people." That is, he begins with production and distribution; and this is the longest section of The Wealth of Nations. Book II he calls "Of the nature, accumulation, and employment of stock," -- stock being the term which he used in substantially the way capital is now used in economic treatises. Here is his discussion of capital which would be expected now-a-days to go into a discussion of production and distribution; here is the discussion of capital taken up after he has taken up the productive powers of labor and the order in which the product is distributed. Then he writes a still shorter book, Book III, called "Of the different progress of opulence in different nations," a book on the factors which stimulate or retard the increase in national wealth. Then he turns to an essay in criticism, Book IV, "Of systems of political economy," a book in which he discusses at very great length and with destructive effect the prevalent Mercantilist notions of economic policy, and in which he also discusses more briefly and more sympathetically the ideas peculiar to the Physiocrats with whom he had come in intimate contact, as we saw, during his year in Paris. The work closes with Book V, "Of the revenue of the sovereign or commonwealth," a discussion of taxation.

The explanation of this curious order seems to be a very simple one; that Adam Smith never really emancipated himself very much from the general scheme which he had followed in his course of lectures on moral philosophy at Glasgow University. Apparently he was one of those professors who not only gave the same course year after year, but also one of those who, when he came to write a book, wrote an expanded version of his lectures. The course was divided, you remember, into four parts, of which the fourth part dealt with public policies based upon expediency, taking up police, revenue, and arms. And in The Wealth of Nations Adam Smith dropped his reference to police, seeming to feel that that was, after all, not a matter of first-rate consequence for his purpose, but he expanded the lectures dealing with means of securing cheapness very much. And they grew into his discussions of the division of labor, of the accumulation of stock, of the progress of opulence; and negatively they appeared in another form in his extended criticism of Mercantilist doctrines. He also, of course, expanded his old remarks on revenue. They grew into the closing book of The Wealth of Nations, "Of the revenue of the sovereign or commonwealth."

The most important change from the scheme of the lectures was the introduction of an exposition upon the way in which the produce of a country is distributed among the several ranks of the people, that is, the introduction of the discussion of distribution. And that introduction shows, if you will notice its manner, how hard Adam Smith seemed to be put to it to bring the topic in at all. He begins with his glowing, famous disquisition upon the division of labor and the great advantages which men derive from that in increasing the effectiveness of production. He goes on to point out that the division of labor rests upon exchange. An efficient exchange calls for the use of money and, of course, the use of money brings in the idea of prices, and the idea of prices enables him to discuss the component parts of price. Now that discussion of the component parts of price contains what Adam Smith had to say about the theory of distribution, for the component parts of price are wages, rents, and profits.

The introduction of this theory of distribution which presently became in the eyes of technical economists the most important part of the book as a whole seems clearly to have been due to Adam Smith's converse with the Physiocrats. If you will look at that reprint of a student's notebook of his lectures as given in 1763 which I mentioned on Tuesday, you will find no trace of this discussion of the component parts of price, that is, no trace of the theory of distribution. But when Adam Smith got to Paris, met Dr. Quesnay, and conversed with Turgot, who was at that very time writing his admirable little book on the formation of riches, he found that this physiocratic group was making much of a topic which had played seemingly a very slight role in his own construction of economic problems. Quesnay had hit upon the general conception that the real wealth of a country consists not at all as the Mercantilists had said, - perhaps without really meaning it, but repeating it, - in the amount of gold and silver, but that its real wealth consists fundamentally in the supply of useful commodities which are turned out by its laborers year after year. He hit, in other words, upon the idea which is represented by Alfred Marshall's conception of the "national dividend". And in discussing this "national dividend" he was led to take up the question how it is distributed among the people who cooperate to produce it, - among the laborers, and the landowners, and the employing classes. Now Adam Smith came back from Paris apparently much interested in this idea, and in reflecting upon the matter at large during the ten or eleven years when he was writing The Wealth of Nations in Kirkcaldy, he worked up his reflections upon the Physiocratic doctrine into his own discussion of the component parts of price. So, to repeat, we apparently owe this particularly important section of The Wealth of Nations - that is, particularly important from the point of view of the influence of that book upon the further development of economic theory - to the influence which the Physiocratic group exercised upon Adam Smith.

By odds the most important part of the book, however, so far as influencing practical affairs is concerned, and in the larger sense so far as influencing our thought about social problems is concerned, is the general view which Adam Smith expounded on so many pages and with such force concerning the fundamental principles of economic policy, - the general view which we now usually characterize by the French phrase laissez faire. That was a view which was no less characteristic of the Physiocrats, and even of certain opposing schools of economists, than was the doctrine of the national dividend or the doctrine of the single tax upon land. But Adam Smith did not derive his faith in laissez faire from his contact with the French economists. As I had occasion to remark incidentally, Francis Hutcheson, his teacher at Glasgow College, had much to say concerning the advantages of free enterprise, although on technical economic questions he maintained orthodox Mercantilist views. Adam Smith, apparently from the beginning of his teaching, had been an ardent exponent of the view that after all every man can judge what is to his own advantage far better for himself than any statesman can judge for him, and that inasmuch as the wealth of a country is the sum total of the wealth of the citizens who compose it - a view, by the way, which soon came in for criticism at the hands of later disciples of Adam Smith, but a view which Adam Smith entertained - it must follow that the wealth of nations will increase most rapidly if every man is allowed to follow whatever occupation seems best in his own eyes, and be allowed to invest his capital in whatever enterprise he thinks will prove most profitable.

That opinion, as I said, Adam Smith had heard propounded by Francis Hutcheson. It probably got its energy in his own thinking very largely from his thirteen years of intimate association with that enterprising group of Glasgow merchants and manufacturers with whom he associated in the political economy club in Glasgow. It was a conviction which may have been confirmed by his intercourse with the Physiocrats, but a conviction that had its roots deep in English experience.

Now I have quite failed in the purpose of most of the lectures that I have given so far if I have not made you realize how a philosophic mind reflecting upon varied developments in English life during the eighteenth century would naturally and rapidly come to the conclusion that the country's welfare was really being promoted by the mass phenomenon, mass practice, of individual initiative, and that one of the chief obstacles to be encountered, actually obstructing progress in national welfare, was the mass of old laws and regulations which endeavored to exercise an artificial control over the occupations and investments of the people, - laws which would have constituted a very much more serious obstruction than they actually did had people been foolish enough to observe them.

Adam Smith, drawing this lesson from English experience, was, as I have intimated from time to time, really giving his fellow-countrymen a sort of rationalization of practices which they had developed, probably without much thinking about them, - practices which were doubtless carried on by many a man whose theories of public policy continued to run in the old channels of his mind. It is by no means an exceptional experience in human nature that we readjust our practical activities under pressure by necessity or the stimulus of opportunity very much more readily than we adjust our general conceptions. That is quite true of all of us, as can be shown by a homely illustration in connection with our religious life. If you talk to a man about the matter of Sunday observance, you will find in a large number of cases that what he will tell you citizens should do upon the Sabbath is not at all an accurate picture of his usual Sunday occupations. He keeps certain old doctrines which he learned in his youth, and when he discusses the matter formally he presents those old-fashioned views, but does not observe them very well in his own life as a matter of personal behavior. There were tens of thousands, probably hundreds of thousands of Englishmen in Adam Smith's time who were following the lead of their private interests in economic matters, and following them without devoting much thought to general economic principles - following them while probably if anybody led them into a discussion of economic principles they would find themselves formulating views which would condemn their own conduct.

That frame of public mind, that social situation, goes very far to account for the enormous success that The Wealth of Nations achieved so promptly - goes far to account for the fact that so many editions were called for, and the further fact, of which I shall say more presently, that The Wealth of Nations was soon after its appearance to exercise a very definite influence upon English legislation and administration. But before passing on to this topic of the immediate practical influence exercised by the book, I want to make one other remark about The Wealth of Nations, as a whole.

We like to speak of economics as a science, and we like to speak of Adam Smith as the father of political economy. In our more careful moments we have perhaps some reservations about both remarks. We know that Adam Smith was preceded by Quesnay; that Quesnay was preceded by Cantillon; that Cantillon was preceded by a whole group of at least half-enlightened Mercantilist writers upon public policy. And yet when we have made all these deductions, it does remain a fact that The Wealth of Nations was in a very genuine sense the start, the foundation of modern economics. Even in this qualified sense of the beginning of a new science, it is very different in character from the beginnings to which we trace back most of the natural sciences. If you will contrast this epoch-making book in economics with the epoch-making changes that were made in Adam Smith's own lifetime, or soon thereafter, in the science of chemistry, you will get an idea of what I mean. Chemistry was an older science that economics, but one of the men who were living and had done scientific investigation even before Adam Smith was Lavoisier, the great French chemist who established the science upon a new basis by overthrowing the phlogistic theory, the old idea about combustion, and by using more methodical ways of performing chemical experiments and more accurate procedure in weighing and computing. What this chemical investigator did was to try a set of rather simple experiments, to add a new view of one fundamental chemical process, and to announce his result in a memoir of no great size. From the outset it took a comparatively great step forward, leading to the improvement of our knowledge of one detail in chemistry. And the further growth of chemistry was characterized by a succession of steps of that character, few of which had anything like the general significance of Lavoisier's great experiments. Chemistry grew up by a detailed process of accretion of associated knowledge concerning one set of reactions after another.

On the other hand, the history of political economy is marked primarily by a series of changes in viewpoint. It is not so much that Adam Smith, or Ricardo, or John Stuart Mill, or Jevons, or Alfred Marshall has related some one new fact of very broad significance, such as the facts Lavoisier ascertained concerning combustion, as it is the fact that these successive writers have had a more or less novel way of looking at the more or less common stock of knowledge. In Adam Smith you will find an exposition of very many facts. He has much in-

terest   in a realistic treatment of the questions which he handles, and his
book is,for instance, one of the best sources of information we have concerning
the organization of the Bank of Amsterdam. His account of several of the historical events of particular interest to economic historians is a valuable piece of
work. But after all, in these historical researches he is primarily giving us a
very skilful summary of knowledge which was available to many people. It is not
the new facts which he adduces, when he adduces any facts which are really new,
that are of importance. It is rather that in dealing with a body of actual
knowledge more or less common to people of his generation he dealt with it from
a novel viewpoint adapted to new purpose. That is, The Wealth of Nations is in
fact more like a philosophical treatise than it is like a scientific memoir. And
that has been true, I should say, of the successive very influential books on
economics which have appeared since Adam Smith's time. The science has not gr
up at all by a process of experimentation. It has been influenced but not
decisively influenced by our growth of knowledge. It has been influenced most by
our way of interpreting certain information of which all of us are more or less
masters, - information of a sort which we can very readily accumulate from all
sorts of sources aside from books on economic theory - a way of thinking about
things rather than an organized body of steadily growing ascertained knowledge.

Now and then in the history of science you come across a book that has
this same characteristic. I think this is true of Darwin's Origin of Species;
and it is very characteristic of modern biological research that most of the
active investigators now regard that great classic as a piece of extremely skilful dialectics rather than as adding greatly to our real knowledge of how the
species of animals which now inhabit the world have gradually developed. The
kind of scientific work which is more characteristic of the growth of science as
a whole is represented far better by Gregor Mendel's experiments in growing different types of peas and other experiments that he made and on the basis of which
he formulated what are called the Mendelian Laws. That is very much more typical
of the general characteristics of scientific development than is a book like
Darwin's Origin of Species.

That fact that the greatly influential books on economic theory had
been primarily the presentation of new viewpoints and only secondarily the result
of increasing knowledge of facts, accounts for the fact that a book like The
Wealth of Nations, so large, so finished, so imposing in all respects, could be
written about the subject at so early a date. Men cannot discover new facts
very rapidly. No one man ever discovers a great many. You cannot systematize
a science on the basis of anyone's discoveries. But a philosopher, a man who has
new insight into relations, a man who is relating a great accumulated body of
common knowledge which he is not trying to render particularly more precise, but
about which he is reflecting, - a man of that kind can bring forth a new system
rather rapidly. That is what Adam Smith did. His book is the result of excogitation rather than investigation. It sees new relations of facts, rather
than teach us more about economic life. It is a series of reflections, conclusions drawn by reasoning, rather than an addition to our actual knowledge of economic properties. And as a book of that sort it comes before us, being commonly
referred to, and as it seems to me with some right, as the first of the great
modern books on economic theory, prompting us to call its author the father of his
science. But a father whose child is no infant. If you will want to draw fanci-
ful analogies, you will have to think of the birth of Minerva from the brain of
Jove, springing full-armed into the world. It began at once to exercise a
powerful influence upon the course of affairs.

Now to repeat: All this is said with full realization of the fact that
Adam Smith was not the first person by any means to think about economic problems.

with the recognition of the fact that many of his ideas, probably in detail almost all of them can be traced back into earlier writings, often for a long, long way; but none the less you do not find all this work organized as Adam Smith organized it. He did organize it. And because the object was one of organizing materials in existence he could do the job so quickly and with such finish; and that constitutes his great achievement, an achievement that was great because organizing knowledge on economic matters, seeing it in new perspective, was the one great service that a man of his time could effectively render.

There had started in the England of a hundred years before Adam Smith's time a movement to treat economics in a way far more analogous to the methods characteristic of the physical sciences. That group of men organized the Royal Society, the group of whom Sir Isaac Newton was the most illustrious, included among others Sir William Petty, a man of medical education, of wide philosophical interests, who applied his highly ingenious inquiring mind in many ways, - for he was a character resembling Benjamin Franklin - among which was a discussion of many economic problems. And following the natural bent, reinforced by his close association with the mathematicians and physicists who formed the core of the Royal Society, he tried to treat economic questions distinctly on a quantitative basis. That is, he set out as he put it, to "bottom" his discourses upon number and measure, to use statistical methods, but he produced a high score of speculative discussions on economic problems which were not "bottomed" on number and measure. The fullest result of Petty's labors was the publication of his Political Arithmetic, a book which tried to treat not only economic but also political questions on a statistical basis.

Now this attempt to apply rather rigorous quantitative methods to the discussion of economic problems had not lacked other followers, and if you will look in any of the books which deal with the history of statistics you will find that there followed Petty a long succession of people who worked in the statistical fashion upon economic problems, making most rapid progress with vital statistics. But that attempt to treat economic problems in precise fashion had, after all, not progressed greatly. It is very characteristic of what had happened that in Adam Smith's own lifetime one of his acquaintances, the celebrated Dr. Richard Price, was demonstrating statistically that the population of England had declined since the Revolution of 1688, and Arthur Young was demonstrating statistically that the population of England was increasing rapidly.

These two demonstrations flatly contradicting each other were possible because neither investigator had adequate data. Dr. Richard Price rested his conclusion primarily upon certain tax returns. There were hearth taxes, and then window taxes, and he thought he could figure out the number of houses and so the number of families, and so the number of people. Arthur Young used certain parish records which, while better, were after all merely samples, and not very representative samples at that.

Adam Smith, under such circumstances, naturally came to the opinion, which he expresses in a brief aside in some passage in The Wealth of Nations, saying: "I have little faith in political arithmetic". That is, the time when it was possible to treat questions of the sort that Adam Smith discusses with such great skill and so effectively by methods approximating precision, did not come, and could not come, until the materials for such work existed on a far larger scale and of a far better quality than that in which they were found when The Wealth of Nations was written. The way that Adam Smith had of discussing economic questions from a philosophic viewpoint on the basis of his innate convictions concerning human nature was the one method which could at that time be practiced with a large measure of success, unless a person wanted to confine himself to a comparatively few minor issues.

And if now-a-days we are inclined sometimes to look askance at the drawing of such sweeping conclusions as Adam Smith reached on the basis of his cogitations from general principles, we should remind ourselves of the practical impossibility of treating those problems at that time by any other method than the one he followed.

XIII

ADAM SMITH'S INFLUENCE UPON BRITISH POLITICS

I have been trying for the last two or three weeks to show that The Wealth of Nations grew out of the general social developments of the time and country in which it was published. Now I want to show how this product of the general social process of intellectual and practical developments was in turn affected by Adam Smith's formulations. If the general view that I am presenting is a sound one, then of course it follows that anything which does appear as a prominent factor in the common life of a group of people such as the English population then constituted is never simply an end product. It is always simply one feature of a cumulative development, and if it has any force, effectiveness, it is going to influence what comes after it. That I think is very definitely true of The Wealth of Nations. Perhaps we are not going to far when we say, and I am inclined to take the position, that Adam Smith's economic philosophy was after all a scholar's reflective formulation of ideas that were already acted upon rather than systematically thought about among a considerable proportion of his contemporaries. But the very fact that your ideas are formulated for you, the very fact that the things you are doing are rationally justified is likely to have a considerable influence on your future conduct.

Now one side of the influence exercised by The Wealth of Nations very promptly after its publication is known with curious definiteness. We have on record that certain technical, not very important, actions of the government were suggested within a few years by ideas propounded in that book. And then very soon afterwards, within less than a decade after Adam Smith's death, we find that far more important measures were debated, and debated by responsible statesmen who used Adam Smith's reasons, quoting Adam Smith himself, as an explanation of the changes they proposed. And more intensive study (for which we have not here time) would unquestionably make it certain that not only in these large conspicuous measures - the new laws that were passed - but that in a thousand lesser matters concerned rather with administration than with new legislation, the reasoning of The Wealth of Nations kept men fixed on a line of conduct they had rather waveringly been following before, and emboldened them to go farther and farther in the direction which common sense seemed to justify, though the actions ran directly counter to precedent.

To begin with the very tangible influence which The Wealth of Nations exercised at once on government policy: In the next year after it was published, that is, in 1777, Lord North, who was then Prime Minister and Chancellor of the Exchequer, was drawing up his budget, and as usually happens in planning the budget, he was looking for new sources of revenue. He was particularly eager as Chancellors of the Exchequer are, to find forms of taxation which would result in a considerable yield to the Exchequer, and taxes which would nevertheless not be particularly burdensome to the people taxed, or at least would raise no serious outcry. He obtained valuable assistance from The Wealth of Nations. He imposed two new taxes of which he got the idea from The Wealth of Nations; one a tax on man-servants which Adam Smith recommended with particular fervor, and the other a tax on property sold by auction. In the next year Lord North got still more im-

portant help from Adam Smith's suggestions, for he introduced an. inhabited house
duty, an important tax, whereas the tax on man-servants and property sold at
auction were matters of no very large consequence. He introduced the inhabited
house duty and also a tax on malt which corresponds more or less to our internal
revenue duties on beer. Adam Smith's biographer, John Rae, thinks it was primarily in recognition of this assistance which he derived from <u>The Wealth of
Nations</u> in drawing the budgets for 1777 and 1778 that Lord North appointed Adam
Smith commissioner of the customs in Scotland.

We also know that Adam Smith was consulted by Henry Dundas and by the
Earl of Carlisle in 1779 about a general question of economic policy that was
then very troublesome. Henry Dundas, you may remember I had occasion to mention,
was one of the political jobbers of the time. He was then the man of patronage
in Scotland for the ministry of Lord North, and then he was a sort of political
manager in Scotland for William Pitt. As a Scotchman, he was well acquainted
with Adam Smith and with his claims to attention. Now in 1779 the question about
the commercial relations between Ireland and England came to the fore. In those
days there were rather heavy protective duties imposed in England on the importation of manufactured goods from Ireland. The general British policy in trading
with Ireland had been not very unlike the general British policy in trading with
their transatlantic colonies, a policy of trying to get Ireland as a valuable
source for raw materials which should be brought into England and manufactured
there, and the products of which could be distributed to Ireland and other customers. The British manufacturers, like manufacturers in other countries which
enjoy the blessings of a protective tariff, were very much afraid lest the Irish
should set up independent manufacturing plants of their own and should take away
their business. And so they were very much alarmed when a proposal was made to
reduce materially the English import duties, for efforts had long been made to
keep Ireland as a source of raw materials and a market for English manufactures.

This whole problem was put before Adam Smith by Henry Dundas and the
Earl of Carlisle, and Adam Smith wrote to Lord Carlisle a notable memorandum
which you will find, if you are interested, in Rae's <u>Life of Adam Smith</u>.* He
concluded in this vigorous fashion:

> Should the industry of Ireland, in consequence of freedom
> and good government, ever equal that of England, so much the better
> would it be not only for the whole British Empire, but for the
> particular province of England.

As we shall see, the time presently came when William Pitt tried, though not with
much success, to realize these ideas of Adam Smith about the advantage to England
from vigorous development of manufactures in Ireland.

We also have an interesting and rather mysterious communication that
Adam Smith was consulted by William Pitt in 1792 upon some economic problem, the
nature of which is not disclosed. This communication comes from a letter written
by a prominent barrister of the time, George Wilson, to Jeremy Bentham, July 14,
1787. The letter reads as follows:

> (Bentham had in the early part of 1787 sent from Russia the
> manuscript of his <u>Defense of Usury</u> written in antagonism to
> Smith's doctrine on the subject, to his friend George Wilson,
> barrister, and Wilson a month or two later - 14th of July
> writes of "Dr.Smith," who can, I think, be no other than the
> economist:)

* p. 351-2

Dr. Smith has been very ill here of an inflamation in the
neck of the bladder, which was increased by very bad piles. He has
been cut for the piles, and the other complaint is since much mended.
The physicians say he may do some time longer. He is much with the
ministry, and the clerks of the public offices have orders to furnish
him with all papers, and to employ additional hands, if necessary, to
copy for him. I am vexed that Pitt should have done so right a thing
as to consult Smith, but if any of his schemes are effectuated I shall.
be comforted.*

We also know that Adam Smith came presently to be quoted as an authority
in Parliament. That may seem to us now-a-days rather a slight matter, but in
the eighteenth century it created some surprise that any responsible statesman in
Parliament should think that his views gained any additional weight or authority
by being substantiated by quotations from some theoretical writer. The first man
who cited The Wealth of Nations in a parliamentary debate was Charles James Fox.
That happened in 1783. He afterwards admitted, with somewhat unusual candor,that
he had never read the book, and also that he had a very poor opinion of economics
at large. Nevertheless, he was quite willing to use what he supposed to be Adam
Smith's influence on his side. It was not long, however, before Adam Smith came
to be quoted in Parliament in rather intelligent fashion.In 1787 that happened in
a couple of debates, one on the commercial treaty with France, and one on the proposal to farm out the post-horse duties. He was also quoted in 1788, and in 1792
when William Pitt was introducing the budget and dilating on the advantage of progressive accumulation of capital, he pronounced a formal eulogy upon the writer
of The Wealth of Nations. As I say, he was dilating on the advantages of the progressive accumulation of capital, and in the course of his subject he said:

> Simple and obvious as this principle is, and felt and observed
> as it must have been in a greater or less degree, even from the earliest
> periods, I doubt whether it has ever been fully developed and sufficiently
> explained, but in the writings of an author of our own times, now un-
> fortunately no more, (I mean the author of the celebrated Treatise on
> The Wealth of Nations whose extensive knowledge of detail, and depth
> of philosophical research, will, I believe, furnish the best solution
> to every question connected with the history of commerce or with the
> systems of political economy.

Adam Smith was referred to in the later years of the eighteenth century
with increasing frequency. Buckle** has taken the trouble to go through the debates and note other instances of this sort. If you will look in his first volume
page 167ff.,you will find that he has collected no less than sixty references to
this particular book in the years that elapsed between its publication and 1800.
Indeed, the fourteen years that immediately followed the publication of The
Wealth of Nations seemed to promise sweeping reforms in economic and political
organization, reforms that were precisely in line with Adam Smith's recommenda-
tions.

For this rapid acceptance of the general principles of the book, changes
in politics were in part responsible, in minor part presumably, but they did have
a considerable immediate effect.Lord North's disastrous ministry which carried on
the war against the North American colonies collapsed in 1782, collapsed largely
in consequence of increasing public anger over the feeble and ineffective military operations and resentment at the growing cost of carrying on what seemed to
be a hopeless struggle, supplemented by increasing anger at the rather high-handed

---

* Wilberforce Correspondence, i., 40; quoted by Rae, op.cit., p. 406
**Buckle, Henry Thomas, History of Civilization in England.

fashion by which the king was getting votes in favor of the ministry he was support-ing. When public irritation had finally reached the point where even the king saw that it was dangerous to continue in the policy he allowed Lord North to go, and his ministry was succeeded by that of the Marquess of Rockingham.

The first task of this ministry was to institute the negotiations which led to peace with the North American colonies and the recognition of the United States. Their second task was to institute a series of reforms, reforms, the chief aim of which was to strike at the worst sources of political corruption which George III and his ministers had used so effectively to keep the North ministry in power. The government presently brought in and passed a bill which excluded government contractors from Parliament, that is, a bill which made it impossible in the future to reward obsequious members of the House of Commons or the House of Lords by giving them profitable contracts. Another bill disfranchised customs and revenue officers. That seems to us perhaps a striking measure, but at the time it was declared that there were less than seventy constituencies in England where the customs and revenue officers did not hold the deciding voice in determining the return of candidates to Parliament. That meant that the government in power, by instructing its appointees in the customs and revenue service could make sure that the members returned in those constituencies would be men who would support their policies.

Edmund Burke, who under this ministry was Paymaster General, brought in also a bill for economical reform in which he abolished numerous sinecures, that is, offices that carried pay but carried the performance of no serious duties—offices which had also been used to reward political henchmen; — and which limited the pension list to L 90,000 per annum, and so limited the money a ministry could use to reward with pensions those who gave political support; and it prohibited the use of the secret service fund for political purposes. It was charged, and probably with justice, that the ministry had actually used the secret service funds, not for proper purposes of national protection, but actually for paying hard government cash to people whose votes they needed. Burke also, though himself Paymaster General, carried another measure which prohibited the incumbent of that office from lending out the government balance for his own benefit. This had been a common practice. Henry Fox, the father of Charles James Fox, had accumulated a fortune due to the fact that he had held this position for a rather long period of time when the government was carrying on war upon a grand scale. During periods of active military operations, of course, the Paymaster General had to have at his disposal all the time a rather large working fund, and as matters then stood and as politics was practiced, Fox and for that matter his successors had lent out this balance. They kept it in banks instead of keeping it in the government office and the interest which the banks paid went into the Paymaster General's own private pocket. Edmund Burke brought in a bill terminating that abuse.

Also, William Pitt brought up the fundamental question of reforming Parliament on a broader scale, trying to change the suffrage laws in such a fashion as to give different constituencies greater equality so far as number of representatives was concerned, to allow places which had grown rapidly in population a proportionate number of members, and to abolish the more notorious "rotten boroughs." This bill which Pitt brought in was indeed lost, but it was lost by a majority of twenty votes only, and that was the best that Parliamentary reformers succeeded in getting until 1830, shortly before the Great Reform Bill of 1832 became a law.

The reforming career of the Rockingham ministry, however, was presently terminated very early. They came into power in March, 1782 and in July Rockingham died. He was succeeded by the Earl of Shelburne, one of Adam Smith's earliest disciples among statesmen, a convinced free-trader, a man better known to history under the title he presently bore, the Marquess of Lansdowne. But Shelburne could

not get along with Fox, and in April, 1783 his ministry fell and was succeeded by
a new ministry in which the prime minister was nominally the Duke of Portland,
but in which the real power was supplied by a coalition between Charles James Fox
and Lord North. Now this coalition was bitterly detested by the king and it was
exceedingly unpopular out of doors, primarily because during the American War
Charles James Fox had been the most vigorous parliamentary opponent of Lord North.
He had criticized that statesman's policy and his character in about as vigorous
terms as could be used without going far beyond all bounds of parliamentary re-
straint; so that when these two men struck hands and united in giving support to
the ministry nominally headed by the Duke of Portland, it seemed as though they
were both of them burying what had been credited as their principles and were
willing to sacrifice all their genuine beliefs if only they could keep the reins
in their own hands.

Public feeling about the inequity of the new political combination was increased when the Portland ministry brought in a bill for reorganizing the government of British India. The question regarding the justice and wisdom of the
policy pursued by the British East India Company in governing that great depen-
dency across the sea with its millions of inhabitants had been one of the burning
questions of English politics for a decade or two. Fox's and North's bill provided
that certain leading officials in India should be appointed, not by the British
East India Company, but should be appointed by the British Government. That was
taken to be a Whig job. It was thought that what Fox and North were after was to
substitute for the old sources of corruption which the Rockingham ministry had begun to sweep away with public approbation a new source of corruption, - that they
would reward their faithful henchmen with places in India in which fortunes might
rapidly be accumulated, perhaps not at the expense of the British taxpayers, but
certainly at the expense of the Indian populace. And people who were incensed
with the ministry, probably glad to find a rational and highly moral ground on whic
to criticize it, made much of this piece of corruption which they held to be in
process. This grievance against the Lord North ministry united the Crown and the
English people in opposition, but North and Fox had apparently secured a majority
in Parliament. Both of them practiced parliamentary arts with exceeding skill,
North being one of the masters of corrupt personal politics, and Fox being one
of the greatest parliamentary tacticians who has ever lived. And it seemed for a
while as though the ministry would succeed in carrying this bill, maintaining its
position in the face both of popular clamor and the king's anger.

Well, now, the king, who was himself a very shrewd politician, took a bold
step. He asked William Pitt, the son of the great Earl of Chatham, and who was
then but twenty-four years old, to become prime minister, and Pitt with extraordinary courage accepted the task, knowing full well that nothing which the king
could do to support him would enable him to obtain a parliamentary majority. But
his plan was to accept the government and carry on in the face of certain defeat
of all important government proposals for a short while, and use his position as
the responsible head of the government, as the person who could control the
measures introduced in large measure, to make the public realize exactly how
obstructive, how selfish, was the policy of the coalition which was defeating them.
Being himself no less an artist in parliamentary tactics than Charles James Fox,
he succeeded for several months not, to be sure, in getting any important legislation enacted, but in exciting the popular fury against the North-Fox combination
to higher degree. And then in March, 1784 he thought the time had come. He got
the king to prorogue Parliament and call for a new general election. That is,
they appealed from the men who were defeating them on the benches of Parliament
to the nation at large.

The general election of 1784 that followed was one of the most memorable parliamentary struggles of the century. It resulted in a sweeping victory for the king and Pitt, so that after the election was over Pitt returned to power with a large majority back of him, in a position to carry out the policies which he had at heart. And that meant, so far as we particularly are concerned, that another one of Adam Smith's disciples was occupying the most influential position in the British government, -- a man of far greater talent, far greater power, than Shelburne, the Marquess of Lansdowne, -- a man who remained in power for eighteen years, his ministry having lasted longer than any other in the British record save the preceding ministry in the early part of the eighteenth century headed by Sir Robert Walpole.

Pitt took advantage of his new political strength to begin to introduce reforms of the sort that Adam Smith had advocated on a large scale. One of his earliest steps as Chancellor of the Exchequer was to begin offering loans to public subscription. Before that the loans of the government had usually been negotiated privately. That had been another means by which the ministry in power had been enabled to distribute very valuable favors to its supporters. That is, people would be allowed to buy government stock at prices substantially below current quotations, and sell that stock for their own profit. When the practice was adopted of calling for competitive bids every time the government went into the market to raise money, the source of corruption was stopped and, what in Pitt's eyes was doubtless as important, the government got much better terms.

Also, Pitt attacked the great problem of smuggling which, as I have said, had become an evil on a grand scale. He attacked it by precisely the methods which Adam Smith advocated, that is, by reducing the temptation to smuggle; he cut the duties -- the import duties -- on the most important classes of goods which were the subject of the smuggling trade, and cut them heavily. For instance, the duty on tea which had amounted to about 119% ad valorem, that is, which more than doubled the price which the English consumer had to pay, was cut to 12½%. The result was that smuggling became an unprofitable business so far as tea was concerned, and the great reduction of the rate of duty was followed by a considerable increase in the government's receipts from the duty. All the tea that had formerly been smuggled now passed through the customs, and the increase in the amount that went through the customs was sufficiently great to offset the reduction of the duty by about nine fold.

Pitt also went into an elaborate system of tax reforms, the object of which was largely to simplify administrative procedure and readjust the taxes in a fairer way, according to the ability of people to pay. He also adopted -- and this is one of the most curious, and in the end it became the most celebrated of his reforms -- a sinking fund scheme. One of the leading economists of the day, Dr. Richard Price, the man whom you may remember I mentioned as having proved that the population of England had declined from 1688 to the 1780's, had written a very ingenious book in which he seemed to prove that if the government would only devote a certain part of its revenue every year to payments into a sinking fund and then credit that sinking fund with interest and let the interest accumulate, they would through the magic of compound interest after a time raise the sinking fund to such huge proportions that they could pay off the debt with ease. It was a mathematical fallacy, but Dr. Price who was a clever mathematician was fully taken in with it and so were William Pitt and also the financial experts of that generation. The adoption of this delusive scheme of paying off the government debt through the creation of a sinking fund was one of Pitt's most popular measures, and it was not until at least a generation had passed that anybody succeeded in providing convincing demonstration that the whole delusive scheme had increased the cost of carrying the national debt. It really meant that the government in a great many cases had been contracting new loans and paying higher rates of interest for money being paid into the sinking fund at low rates of interest.

Pitt also attacked the question of free trade between England and Ireland, bringing in a bill along the lines which Adam Smith recommended. But here he did not succeed. The first Parliament of Ireland -- in those days there was a separate Parliament; the Union had not yet been effected -- the first Irish Parliament to which the measure was proposed accepted Pitt's scheme. Then it was presented to the English Parliament, and there it was amended in so many ways through the pressure of the protected British manufacturing interests that it had to be resubmitted to the Irish Parliament, and when resubmitted it promised so little improvement in the relations that the Irish Parliament rejected it.

Pitt had much better success in working toward free trade with France. Through William Eden, later Lord Auckland, he negotiated a commercial treaty with France which did not, indeed, establish free trade between the two countries, but which went far in the direction of diminishing the reciprocal duties which were imposed upon the importation of goods into the two countries. And that bill Pitt got accepted in Parliament by a large majority.

He also brought in a measure for parliamentary reform. This scheme provided that the British government should buy thirty-six "rotten boroughs", the most notorious constituencies where a few people were able through control of property rights of one sort or another practically to appoint members of the House of Commons. The bill provided that the government should purchase these thirty-six of the rottenest boroughs and that the seventy-two seats thus gained should be distributed among the larger counties and part of them given to the City of London and the City of Westminster, both of which were shockingly unrepresented on a population basis. This bill was beaten in Parliament, beaten largely by Pitt's own nominal supporters. And he seems to have acquiesced in the defeat of that measure rather easily. It appears he was much less excited about the evils of the unfair suffrage when he was himself prime minister and able to take the opportunities which the old system afforded to maintain his party in power; he was much more excited when he was in opposition than when he was prime minister.

Finally, Pitt encouraged his supporters to bring in a bill for the abolition of the African slave trade, the first important step in the direction of dealing with the problem of slavery in the British Empire. That measure was supported by Edmund Burke and by Charles James Fox. That is, it was a measure on which party lines were not drawn, and it was accepted by the House without much trouble.

So you see how the whirligig of politics brought into power from time to time men who were decidedly sympathetic toward the general view of public policy that Adam Smith had advocated. Reforms were achieved, and achieved within less than a quarter of a century after The Wealth of Nations was published.

But this era of reform, first under a Whig and then under a liberal Tory administration, was cut short in 1789 by the outbreak of the French Revolution, and we have to notice how that great step toward the liberation of another people reacted upon the British reform movement.

When the news came of the first great steps in the French Revolution, pretty much the whole British nation celebrated the event as a great step toward the liberation of mankind. The leaders of opinion among the English people had close personal relations with many of the more prominent intelligent men in France, and the men with whom they were in closest touch were men, a large proportion of whom had suffered from oppression under the absolute monarchy. They were men who had themselves been exponents of liberal ideas, very often of liberal ideas in the

English way, and it seemed to the leaders of British opinion that at last the
French nation was accepting men of the kind they knew personally and trusted, and
whose ideas were like their own, and that the monarchy was going to be reformed .
after the English fashion; that the shocking financial abuses would be checked; that
a larger measure of representation would be allowed to public opinion; that France
might recast her political institutions along the lines of British policy. And
apparently much the same view of the situation was taken at first by most Englishmen,
so that the first reaction to the opening guns of the Revolution in England was .
almost universally sympathetic. But very soon a change came — a change which
rapidly altered completely the English emotional attitude and which had a profound
influence upon the domestic as well as upon the foreign policy of the British
Government, but that story I must tell at the next meeting.

XIV

THE EFFECT OF THE FRENCH REVOLUTION UPON BRITISH POLITICS AND ECONOMIC
CONDITIONS

At the close of our last meeting on Tuesday I was speaking about the reaction of the French Revolution upon the progress of the social sciences in England.
I said the outbreak of the Revolution was hailed with widespread sympathy on the
English side of the Channel . The leaders of English public opinion had for years
been cultivating rather close personal relations with the leaders of thought in
France. Men like Voltaire had spent considerable time in England and were greatly
admired there. On the other hand, men like David Hume, Edward Gibbon, the author
of The Decline and Fall of the Roman Empire, Charles James Fox, the great Whig
orator, and, as we have seen, Adam Smith had spent considerable time in France, and
had been received there most graciously. And French thought, particularly on social
and philosophic matters had been very much influenced by English thought. Newton's
Principia had led to an enormous development of mathematics. He was the god of
the French mathematicians, quite as much as of the English. Locke's scheme of
philosophy had likewise exercised an enormous influence. And at the time Hume, in
his turn, came to be a factor of real moment in the intellectual development of
France. Broadly speaking, the whole group of the Encyclopedists showed the influence of English thinking and English attitudes, and in large measure they avowed
themselves warm admirers of British political institutions. And then a thousand
lesser people had traveled in France; had formed personal acquaintances with various French families, and had in turn received them at their homes in England. The
relations were of a rather intimate sort, — more intimate than we are likely to
think.

For the French Government, on the other hand, the English people had no
high respect. It seemed to them tyrannical in the last degree. The excesses of
court life, the disorder of the French finances, the attitude of the court towards
religious and intellectual problems, seemed to the average Englishman really very
shocking. And most of the people with whom the eminent Englishman at least had
entered into relations were people who had suffered or were in danger of suffering
persecution from the royal government.

So then, the French people rose and promised to reform their antiquated
scheme of government by setting up parliamentary institutions that had real vital-
ity, presumably, in Englishmen's eyes, modelling their new constitution upon the
British constitution. Most Englishmen looked upon the movement with warm sympathy.
Almost immediately upon the fall of the Bastille, there broke out in England a warm
discussion of political principles in which the writers showed a very sympathetic
attitude toward the pending developments in France. Of the publications which revealed this freedom of mind in a most conspicuous fashion, two at least remain

famous to this day: Thomas Paine's celebrated pamphlet on The Rights of Man
which was published in 1791, and the second part in 1792; and William Godwin's
Political Justice, also published in 1792. William Godwin, you may know, was the
author of Caleb Williams, one of the most famous of the eighteenth century novels,
and perhaps you remember him better as one of Shelley's fathers-in-law. His
Political Justice, however, is not a book of visionary principles, but of a man
who had a large and most attractive vision, a man who saw mankind gradually perfecting his institutions and by perfecting his institutions perfecting his own
nature, having before himself an illimitable vista of steady progress.

A very sudden change came over British opinion upon the outbreak of what
we call the Reign of Terror, for presently the sort of people with whom individual
Englishmen had made friends lost their position of leadership in the great social
upheaval and began marching one after another to the guillotine. And particularly
when the king attempted to escape from the control of his people and was brought
back and himself condemned, a spasm of horror ran over the former English friends
of the Revolution. The feeling was intense to a degree that probably we can hardly
have understood had not something similar occurred in our own lifetime. I think
most of us felt a certain measure of horror about the bloodier features of the
great social revolution in Russia, but when we felt about that we felt as people
who had no close connections with anybody concerned — that must be true at least
about the great majority of us. Had that thing happened within a country separated
from us only by a narrow channel, had it happened in a country with whose literature
we were in some measure familiar, had the persecutions been visited upon persons
we knew intimately, how much greater would not our revulsion of feeling have been?
Most of us at first beheld the Revolution in Russia with gratification as a step of
another people taken in the direction of liberty, and still our sympathy in very
many cases turned into a feeling of horror when the course of the Revolution was
stained with blood. That sort of feeling certainly developed in England; it became extremely intense, and presently led to consequences which have a direct bearing upon our particular theme.

The first consequence was that all the theoretical champions of the French
Revolution either changed their minds or were discredited; and in the second place
pretty much speculation on social philosophy, including political economy, was for
a time discredited. Matthew Stewart, one of Adam Smith's younger friends deemed
it inexpedient to give a course of lectures that had been announced for him at the
University of Edinburgh on the ground that if he discussed a subject of that sort
at all he could hardly avoid touching upon subjects which it was unwise to develop
in public.

In politics the change had even more serious effects. It split the Whig
Party — split it into two hostile camps. The bulk of the old Whigs followed Edmund Burke and the Duke of Portland into the Tory camp, some 110 members of the
House of Commons who had been classified as Whigs. These became supporters of the
government which was opposing the Revolution with all its forces. There was left
about a third of the party, estimated at perhaps fifty votes, to follow Charles
James Fox and Sheridan, the playwright, and Grey, the man who in due time became
the Lord Grey of the Great Reform Bill, — to follow these three leaders in the
Commons as still standing for what they conceived to be genuine liberal principles.
And in the House of Lords the number of people who still maintained that despite
its excesses the movement of the French people in the direction of self-government
was likely to prove in the long run a blessing to themselves and mankind was even
smaller. There were a few such peers, notable Lord Holland, Lord Lauderdale, the
Scotch economist, and Lord King, that curiously independent mind in the body of a
member of one of the great English aristocratic families.

Not only were the Whigs split but also, as I have intimated incidentally,

the Tory Party under William Pitt's leadership was diverted from the policy of
rapid social and economic reform which they had been following since Pitt's
accession to power in 1784, and turned from that policy to one of uncompromising
conservatism. That change of mind is perhaps best represented in what Pitt himself said regarding the reform of Parliament. You recall that before he had become Prime Minister he had introduced a bill providing for an inquiry into the
abuses of the suffrage, and that after he had become Prime Minister he had introduced a measure to buy a certain number of "rotten boroughs" (36) and redis-
tribute their seats among the more populous unrepresented areas, – a bill which,
to be sure, was defeated, and defeated largely by the efforts of his own followers. He was, however, supposed, at least in theory, and on the basis of his record, to be a champion of parliamentary reform. In 1800 he had occasion to refer
again to this topic in a speech, a subject which came up in connection with quite
a different topic, the Union between England and Ireland. In the course of his
remarks he said:

> . . . if any thing could in my mind counterbalance the advantages
> that must result from it, (the union), it would be the necessity
> of disturbing the representation of England: but that necessity
> fortunately does not exist. In stating this, Sir, I have not for-
> gotten what I have myself formerly said and sincerely felt upon
> this subject; but I know that all opinions must necessarily be sub-
> servient to times and circumstances; and that man who talks of his
> consistency merely because he holds the same opinion for ten or
> fifteen years, when the circumstances under which that opinion was
> originally formed are totally changed, is a slave to the most idle
> vanity. Seeing all that I have seen since the period to which I
> allude; considering how little chance there is of that species of
> reform to which alone I looked, and which is as different from the
> modern schemes of reform, as the latter are from the constitution;
> seeing that where the greatest changes have taken place, the most
> dreadful consequences have ensued, and which have not been con-
> fined to that country where the change took place, but have spread
> their malignant influence almost in every quarter of the globe,
> and shaken the fabric of every government; seeing that in this
> general shock the constitution of Great Britain has alone remained
> pure and untouched in its vital principles. . . – when I see that
> it has resisted all the efforts of Jacobinism, sheltering itself
> under the pretence of a love of liberty; when I see that it has
> supported itself against the open attacks of its enemies, and
> against more dangerous reforms of its professed friends; that it
> has defeated the unwearied machinations of France, and the no
> less perservering efforts of Jacobins in England, and that during
> the whole of the contest it has uniformly maintained the confidence
> of the people of England; – I say, Sir, when I consider all these
> circumstances, I should be ashamed of myself, if any former opinions
> of mine could now induce me to think that the form of representation
> which, in such times as the present, has been found amply sufficient
> for the purpose of protecting the interests and securing the happi-
> ness of the people, should be idly and wantonly disturbed from any
> love of experiment, or any predilection for theory. Upon this sub-
> ject, Sir, I think it right to state the inmost thoughts of my mind;
> I think it right to declare my most decided opinion, that even if
> the times were proper for experiments, any, even the slightest
> change in such a constitution must be considered as an evil.

– the most thoroughgoing condemnation of the plan which he himself had formerly advocated, - a change of mind which he himself attributed to the influence exercised upon his opinion by observing the results of the French Revolution.

Of course, the English Government did not maintain a passive attitude with reference to events in France, but presently plunged into war with the Republic. The long series of French wars began in 1793 and they lasted, with a brief peace in 1802-03, until the Battle of Waterloo was fought in the middle of 1815. During this long military struggle, England kept control of the seas primarily because of the great victories of Nelson at the Battle of the Nile and Trafalgar. She provided subsidies for her Continental allies in the successive coalitions that upset first the French Republic and later Napoleon. She sent a succession of expeditionary armies to the Continent, armies that suffered a long series of reverses until after Napoleon's disastrous Russian campaign, and in consequence of this great and long-continued military effort she assumed an enormously heavy economic burden. The taxes which were imposed mounted to extraordinary figures. There was a rapid increase in the public debt, an increase so rapid that many Englishmen thought the outcome would necessarily be some form of repudiation. The specie payments upon the paper currency then in use - the notes of the Bank of England - were suspended, and the country suffered from the evils of an irredeemable paper standard, and the value of the irredeemable notes in gold, of course, declined. There was a great inflation of prices. The price level was not only high, but most unstable, and English economic life had to contend with great monetary uncertainty.

Also, British commerce was seriously interfered with, a matter which to the island empire was of the greatest consequence. It became part of Napoleon's policy to prohibit, so far as he well could, intercourse between Great Britain and those portions of the Continent which he controlled. Also, while the British kept the seas they could not prevent French privateers from doing much damage to their merchant marine. And this brought a series of losses upon the British nation as a whole which in proportion to the resources of the time were rather serious. This great economic burden, - the burden of carrying on war itself - rendered more serious by the monetary instability, by the oppressive taxes, by the heavy load of the increasing debt, by the interference of the French with commerce, this heavy economic load the country was able to bear in large measure because of the continued progress in the arts of production.

By the time when the French wars began, what we usually call the Industrial Revolution was beginning to gain considerable headway in Great Britain, particularly in the textile industries, and presently and to a lesser extent in certain other industries. Revolutionary improvements were effected in the arts of production. It was in large measure because Englishmen at the time of the war were learning how to produce all kinds of goods that they needed with much greater efficiency than theretofore, that they could go through the struggle without more serious strain than they in fact had to endure.

Also, agriculture was making great strides through that period - a matter of particular consequence since even before the war England had become in average years a grain importing country. That is, the nation was already dependent , in years when the British harvests were not exceptionally abundant, upon foreign sources of supply for the bulk of its food, and, of course, with the means of transport then available these food supplies came commonly from rather nearby parts of Europe. Well, when England was at war with France, she could draw comparatively little wheat from that country, and when Napoleon controlled not only France but also a large part of Europe and most of the seaports on the Baltic, his attempt to cut off the Continental supplies of grain to England was in considerable measure effective. Now to meet the threatened deficiency in food supply, English agriculturists pushed forward vigorously with the extension of improvements in agricultural technique which had been introduced in the latter part of the eighteenth century, and encouraged by the high prices which prevailed for grain. In view of the restriction of imports it was quite natural that the domestic price of grain should rise faster than the general level of prices, and the English landlords began turning a larger proportion of their estates into arable land. A good many fields which in the days before the war no one would have thought profitable to use for purposes other than grazing or as meadow land were fertilized in various ways and put down to wheat. A good many swamp districts were drained. A vast step indeed was taken toward improving the British farm lands so as to yield a considerable increase in domestic supplies of grain.

In view of what happened during the Great War, it is interesting to observe that during England's much longer and perhaps equally severe struggle with the French, the government adopted no such policy of economic mobilization as was resorted to in 1914 to 1918, not only by England but by most of the other belligerents. You might have thought, in view of the strong tradition of Mercantilist policy, particularly for the many statesmen who had not been converted to a set of rather new-fangled theories, that it was their duty to safeguard the economic welfare of the country as a whole. You might have thought that the first notion of such men, when entering upon a war would be that this was above all others an occasion when the government should lay down an economic policy for the country as a whole. They undertook almost nothing of the sort. There was some legislation passed which touched upon economic problems, quite naturally, but there was no systematic concerted scheme to direct the economic energies of the people primarily to rendering the country strong for military purposes.

Practically the British government relied, so far as its economic policy was concerned, upon _laissez faire_. It let matters take their course. And in view of what was under way in a number of important manufacturing industries, and in view of the changes that were taking place in British agriculture, it may well seem in retrospect that their policy was wise. It is, however, none the less, I think, a notable fact that the great occasion for reintroducing as a leading principle of British statesmanship, a policy of Mercantilism on a scale justified by war needs was allowed to pass without a serious effort of the kind.

All this concerns the country's war policy. But the domestic policy underwent a change. Not only was the Tory government strengthened by the accession of the greater part of the Whigs converted from a policy of reform to one of maintaining the _status quo_, but they were also quite naturally led into a policy of active social repression. And naturally a few of the later developments of the French Revolution led a great many Englishmen to fear that as the mob had gotten the upper hand in France, so it might get the upper hand in England; - to fear that the seductive principles of republicanism would cross the Channel, that the lives and property of Englishmen would be no more secure than were the lives of their former French friends.. And that fear became intensified when it became known that certain societies had been set up by friends of the French Revolution to discuss its principles and presumably to inquire whether some such policies as the French were embarking upon, with more and more boldness, might not advantageously be adopted on their side of the Channel. The particular bogy of the time was the Corresponding Society. That was an organization in which the bulk of the membership belonged to the artisan classes, the intelligent English artisans who were beginning to take an active interest in all sorts of social questions and whose minds were greatly stimulated indeed by the knowledge that men of their station in life were coming to exercise considerable influence upon public affairs in France.

Now the Corresponding Society was a somewhat mysterious organization. It had little groups of members scattered about in different parts of the country, and an effort was made to perfect some kind of mechanism by which these local groups might keep in touch with each other. Everything concerned with the organization was of the character to make people who had gotten into that panicky frame of mind, which war is likely to breed in any case, to think that here was some very dangerous threatening secret organization which was preparing for a great social overturn in England. It is very enlightening, concerning the general condition of British society at that time, that there was an organization with very similar ideas, but a society which on account of its membership excited scarcely any alarm. This organization was called the Friends of the People, and its membership was made up of men like Lord Grey and the Earl of Lauderdale and people who belonged in their ranks of life. Now, of course, no English gentleman was going to be much afraid of any opinions that were expressed by a Scotch or an English peer or the sons of aristocratic families. They might deduce republican opinions, but when expressed by aristocrats such as they were, the matter would be different than when they were expressed by an artisan; but after all. the general theory of England was that Englishmen were free, and for purposes of freedom the free Englishman was, of course, the man of station and property. There was a very fine and long-established tradition of open discussion, of candor, of intellectual independence. among people of that rank in life, and even amidst the terrors excited by the French Revolution it was possible for men of the sort who would be admitted to the Friends of the People, with its rather high subscription rates, to maintain their position without anticipating serious trouble.

So there were days when it seems not improbable that even Lord Grey and Lord Lauderdale might be subjected to prosecution. There was no question, however, in the minds of the government concerning the danger of the Corresponding Society, -- that organization made up primarily of artisans. And to avoid that danger, William Pitt's government brought in the Treason and Sedition Bills of 1795, commonly known later as the Pitt and Grenville Acts: laws in which the right of free speech, the right of free press, and the right of public meeting were for the time being practically abolished.

What is even more interesting from the point of view of the economist, is that in 1799 and 1800 the government went further and passed what were commonly known as the Anti-Combination Laws. Now these were measures which prohibited any sort of combination among either journeymen or employers for regulating the conditions of employment. Nominally, the Anti-Combination Acts were quite impartial as between the employer and the employee. The men who hired labor were just as much forbidden to combine in order to regulate the terms of employment which they would give as workingmen were prohibited from combining in order to get better wages or conditions. But the enforcement of these acts was anything but impartial. There is said to be no single case on record of the Anti-Combination Acts having been put in force to check combination among employers, and there are many cases on record of workingmen being punished under these acts.

There is no direct connection between the economic question of the desirability of having both employers and men free to organize as they see fit, in order to arrange the terms on which labor is paid and sold; no direct connection between this economic question and the political issues which were then uppermost in England -- but the indirect connection is clear and very important. The political temper of the time aided the British employers in getting laws passed to help them in their dealings with their hands. For the time being, the employing interests of England struck up a sort of alliance with the agricultural interests which were also employers, although on a less magnificent scale, and which agricultural interests dominated Parliament,-- an alliance which was cemented by the passage of the Anti-Combination Acts. That measure meant that men of property were stand-

ing together in defense of what they regarded as the most fundamental interest of
the country - the interest in security of property - the interest in maintaining
the power of the more intelligent classes. Thus you see that the ministry which
had in its early days been distinguished, beyond any of its predecessors, for a
liberal reformist policy was made in a few years, primarily because of the changes
which the events in France made in English government policy and opinion – into
a repressive administration. And when Pitt finally died and passed from power, it
was quite natural that the conservative, not to say repressive, policy should be
maintained, at least as long as the war lasted. Indeed, it was maintained for a
considerable time afterward. There occurred than what Lord Dicey has picturesquely
called "the period of legislative stagnation" in England.

We think of English history as characterized by a gradual but steady evolution of institutions, an evolution whose trend for centuries has been in the
direction of gradually increasing the democratic element in British life. However,
for something like a generation at least that policy was interrupted, - not altogether suspended, for even during this period of legislative stagnation there were
certain measures adopted in Parliament which look to us now-a-days as steps toward
the making of the England which came into being in the latter part of the nineteenth century. For example, despite vigorous protests from people who thought
more about what happened to King David when he tried to take the census than they
thought about the needs of administration, the government in 1801 took the important step of beginning to make the decennial counts of the inhabitants of the country, a policy which was expanded more or less steadily until the British census has
come to be scarcely less elaborate than that of our own United States.

In the next year, 1802, the first of the long series of Factory Acts was
passed. Under the nominal leadership of Sir Robert Peel, the father of the more
famous man whom we know as the author of the great Bank of England Act of 1844,
the man who passed the most critical of all the British free-trade measures, –
under the leadership of Sir Robert Peel and largely through the inspiration of
Robert Owen, the government was induced to enact a bill seeking to protect young
children from certain abuses that were characteristic of the early factory system
– a bill limited in its scope and poorly executed, but nevertheless the beginning
of a long line of legislation which is one of the outstanding features of British
accomplishment in the course of the nineteenth century.

The slave trade was definitely abolished in 1807. The first reform in the
savage British criminal code was adopted in 1808; and in that same year Parliament
authorized the establishment of the Royal Lancasterian Society, one of the first
evidences of parliamentary interest in the elementary education of the children of
the masses.

But after all that is a small amount of reform for a period in which the
Industrial Revolution and agricultural changes were altering the living conditions
of the English population at an extraordinarily rapid rate. The result of this
general policy of inaction was that the adaption of British legal institutions
and administrative practices to the changes which were coming about in living
conditions were checked for a time, and since the changes went on irrespective of
what the laws upon the statute books were, there resulted an ever increasingly
acute need of change. Had it not been for the war, the odds are that something
like William Pitt's early policy would have been characteristic of most of the
British administration throughout this whole time, interrupted now and then, presumably by minor reactions. But since the world events did check that attempt to
bring the formal government institutions of the country into harmony with the
changing social needs, a situation came about in which it was increasingly clear
to the more intelligent Englishmen that measures of a sweeping sort would have
to be adopted.

Now this means that while for a time the pursuit of the social sciences was discredited because it seemed to be infected by French ideas, the course of events presently produced a situation in which the thoughts of Englishmen were concentrated in larger and larger measure than at any time theretofore upon precisely the type of problems which are considered by economists.

XV

ECONOMICS NOT INDEPENDENT OF MAN'S OTHER INTERESTS

In histories of political economy, economics has often been treated as if it were independent both of the practical interest of mankind and as if it were independent of man's other intellectual interests. That is, the story is told as if it is the story about the theories entertained by successive thinkers concerning the production, exchange, and distribution of wealth; as if these theories were notions that were excogitated on a logical basis by men of unusual penetration and by men who were specialists in economics to such an extent that their minds were untroubled by notions that they had derived or had learned concerning any other set of human interests.

Now this picture of economics as growing up in isolation is, it goes without saying, a false picture. Its validity would be contended for by no man. And if at times certain writers have discussed the development of economics in isolation from practical affairs on the one side and from man's other intellectual interests on the other side, it is solely because they thought that there was an advantage in this intense specialization. From some points of view it is possible that there is an advantage if their interest lies solely in the technical features of the development of economic theory. If you think that those are matters of such transcendent interest that you had best devote your whole attention to them, shutting out from view, at least temporarily, whatever you know about social history on the one side and intellectual history on the other side, then you will find a picture in which you have nothing to disturb your contemplation of this central interest very much to your taste.

But needless to say, that is not the way in which one can really understand the development of man's ideas about his own economic behavior. And I am happy to say that at least one of these errors, the error of divorcing the development of economics from the social history of the time and country in which developments took place, is becoming less frequent. So, though I lay a good deal of stress upon the fact, for instance, that The Wealth of Nations grew out of social conditions existing in eighteenth century England, was also intimately related to the further development of social conditions at the end of the eighteenth century and in the course of the nineteenth century, I do that not so much to supply a picture which is entirely omitted from modern books as in an effort to give a valid background which will make The Wealth of Nations more comprehensible as you read it, while giving it a larger significance in your thinking.

But I am sorry to say that the second error of treating economics as if it were a wholly independent science is one that still commonly persists. That this is an error seems to me scarcely less obvious than that it is an altogether inadequate presentation of the facts to treat economics as independent of social conditions and social history. For economics, after all, is only one of several sciences that try to throw light upon human behavior. It treats one aspect of man's life, the aspect of man's life which is concerned with his efforts to get a living, his efforts to turn the material resources of nature to his own service in production, and then, on a more liberal scale still, primarily his dealings with other men in organization for the production of wealth and in exchanging the product among the members of the community as a whole.

Well, quite obviously this side of life is important, important not only in the sense that we are all of us fundamentally dependent upon the processes by which we get means for supplying our own biological needs but also in the sense that the way in which we get our living reacts upon our own minds, makes us creatures of a more or less definite sort. You have only to observe a little patiently the characteristics of people who belong to different occupations and you see plenty of evidence how the kind of work upon which a man has spent so many hours in making his living over so long a period of time reacts upon his attitudes toward a great many other things than his work itself, -- how his economic activities affect his scales of social value, affect the things that he takes for granted as matters of course, the things which he is inclined to think of as immutable principles of a higher than economic origin, And yet, important as it is, this study of men in the activities of getting a living does not profess to be in any sense a competent account of human behavior as a whole.

Beside economics we have in these latter days more or less independent sciences dealing with the political behavior of men, dealing with their general social behavior. Then if you want to go a little further afield you find the subject of anthropology which of course up to this time has dealt in a very general way with the somatic and social views accepted by simpler types of society. And then of course in another sense you have the long complicated record of the past that is offered you by history; and then in still another sense you have studies of special institutions like educational institutions; and you have much labor expended in developing particular techniques of research, particularly in recent years statistical methods of study.

Economists, like all people who are trying to add to knowledge, are forced to specialize, and that means that they do not profess to be masters in fields outside their own. And indeed most economists would be very reluctant to hear anyone hold them responsible for a really thorough knowledge of all phases of their own field. To that they do not pretend. Yet they would admit that in attempting to give a valid account of man's economic behavior they have to take into account the fact that he is also, as Aristotle said, a political animal; that he is also a member of society, and that his economic behavior as such is influenced in no small measure by the political framework within which he belongs, under which he lives and is influenced in no less degree by the general social conditions of his time. So that the economist who attempts to make economics a really valid account of the way in which people actually behave in any given society must at least pay some attention to the current political and social conditions. And if he is wise he will think about these social and political as well as economic conditions which he is discussing as influenced by developments through the past.

All of which means, of course, that in thinking about economics and its development we really do have occasion, as is becoming clearer and clearer the more we learn about economics, to pay attention to other aspects of human behavior. And most particularly and intimately does economics depend upon those branches of human knowledge from which we derive our general ideas about human nature. For it is quite obvious that you cannot build up any constructive account of how you would expect human beings to behave without implying some fairly definite conception of human nature. That is eminently the case with all types of economic theory which are in any sense speculative.

I think it is logically possible perhaps to build up an economics which rests upon an analysis of actual observation and does not go beyond the effort to generalize about these observations, which does not go further than to say that in actual fact men are prone to do thus and so under given circumstances. But, needless to say, that is not the way in which economic theory has been built up. Our economics has not been primarily a vast body of systematic, ordered observations upon human behavior. It has been much more a set of speculative statements which outrun the observational basis. It consists much more of statements concerning how a given writer expects men to behave under given conditions and, as I say, expectations as to how human behavior will run are guided in their larger issues by the beliefs which the speculator entertains concerning human traits.

It is by no means common for an economic theorist to realize this fact clearly enough so that he endeavors to set out in specific terms what assumptions concerning human nature he entertains in his own mind. Almost always these basic assumptions on which the whole argument turns in the last resort are left unmentioned, and he is very likely to be unconscious himself that he is making any assumptions of a psychological sort. It you tell him that he is making such assumptions he may perhaps be inclined, at least at first, to regard that statement as an accusation and to deny it, perhaps with some show of feeling. But none the less the fact is perfectly plain that every time we formulate some expectation as to how people are going to behave under certain conditions, that formulation rests of necessity upon some notions we entertain regarding human nature at large. In practice these notions with which we work vary much from case to case; and many of the differences of opinion regarding public policy which divide us run back to different tacit assumptions which we entertain regarding the relative promise of different traits in the mind of mankind.

I make these remarks at this point partly because I think they have a very direct bearing upon any thorough consideration of any type of economic theory; also in part because they explain the reason for giving the next two or three lectures. I am going to turn aside as it may seem to you from economists proper to a man who, though he did write at least one rather important economic tract, nevertheless cuts a very small figure in histories of political economy, a man whose name indeed is calmly omitted entirely. This man is Jeremy Bentham.....

XVX

JEREMY BENTHAM: HIS INFLUENCE
UPON THE DEVELOPMENT OF ECONOMIC THEORY

At the close of our last meeting I said that today I should discuss certain ideas of Jeremy Bentham's. Now Jeremy Bentham was a man who, while he wrote upon economics, while he was indeed the author of one of the minor economic classics, the Defence of Usury, was nevertheless not a man who took any large personal share in formulating the theories of political economy. Moreover, he was a man about whom, as a rule, very little and generally nothing is said in histories of economic doctrine. Yet, unless I am gravely mistaken, he was one of the men who has exercised the most potent influence upon the development of economic theory. That influence is due to the fact that he formulated far more explicitly and clearly than anybody else the conception of human nature which prevailed among his contemporaries. And his contemporaries were two generations — perhaps one might almost say three generations — of men active in working on economic problems, for

Bentham lived to be a very old man. His first book was published in the same year as The Wealth of Nations, and one of his latest books was edited by John Stuart Mill.

Throughout all that time, and particularly through the generation of Ricardo and the years in which John Stuart Mill was growing up, he was in very close touch with the group of economists. The problems to which he gave his greatest strength were problems in which they were interested, though not problems of an economic sort for the most part. And he was the person who gave the clearest expression to the conception of human nature which they all entertained.

Now ordinarily we do not think of a person's conception of human nature as belonging to his economic theory, and perhaps we should not. But is it not apparent that any person's system of economics must be based upon his conception of human nature, tacit or expressed, so long as his system of economic theory consists of reasoning about what people will do? It may be that you will build up an account of economic behavior by methods of objective observation, using your statistical materials, without professing to know much about what goes on inside people's heads. It is also conceivable to treat economics as we treated problems in animal psychology in the good old days; to read your mind into the mind of the animal, supposing its feelings and ideas much like yours, but that he has not the power of expressing himself. And you think about why the animal does things. Well that is the way we have usually worked at economic theory; and, of course, in working economic theory we have the advantage, presumably, that our minds are much more like the minds of the people whose behavior is discussed. But the modern way of working animal psychology is to experiment with animals; to watch what they do, and then base conclusions upon your observations. It is possible to develop economic theory that way. Most of our economic theory consists of reasoning about what people will do under certain circumstances; and whenever you do that you are, whether you know it or not, - and most of the theorists have been too deeply conscious of the fact, - whether you know it or not, you are shaping your whole system of economic theory by your tacit conception of human nature.

Taking an example: Why did Malthus fear so darkly the result of man's instinct for procreation, whereas William Godwin did not fear it at all? The reason is simply that Malthus had a conception of human nature in which the sexual passion was a dominating instinct. He was sure that with the most of mankind they were going to yield to this impulse to marry and to get children without paying any adequate attention to the consequences which early marriage and a large family might produce, first for themselves and second for everybody else. Godwin, on the other hand, in his conception of human nature put the general idea of the possibility of perfectibility into the foreground. He thought of men in his own time as creatures little lower than angels and rapidly increasing in their self-control. He believed that if there were dangers to be feared as the result of a rapid increase in population, men would avoid them by regulating their conduct in a sensible and moral fashion.

I have said that Bentham formulated the ideas of his generation concerning human nature more clearly than anybody else. He helped them to understand what they were talking about. And for that reason he exercised a very great influence upon the development of economic theory. There is another, I think even more important reason for seeing what his opinions about economic theory were. That reason is that the conceptions which he himself entertained of how men guide their conduct are conceptions of the sort that we very readily form in our own minds, particularly if we do not happen to be addicted to candid and constant observation of ourselves, to an honest type of introspection; and particularly if we ourselves make no psychological studies or do no psychological reading. The idea he had about human nature is an idea that is extensively prevalent now-a-days, particularly among business men and engineers, people who have to deal with human nature as such, not in a formal way but by direct appeal. Advertising men are likely to be more free from this particular set of delusions about human nature than people who are not trying to influence what people do. The politician is less likely to fall into this particular type of error than is the engineer. The politician has to learn much more nearly what we are like and how people's minds can really be influenced.

The general conception which Bentham had is one that is widely prevalent today. It is one that we find is extremely convenient to use in our reasoning, and one which we are likely to fall back into if we are not conscious of the dangers to which we are exposing ourselves. As a matter of fact, I think we shall conclude before the course is over that the bulk of orthodox economic theory as we have it at the present time rests upon a conception of human nature which is not very different from that which Jeremy Bentham drew up in such a formal shape. Indeed as late as 1914 Professor Frank A. Fetter of Princeton, in publishing the second edition of his text-book of economics, a book that he called The Principles of Economics, said in the preface that one of his aims was to free economic theory from the delusions to which it had been subject ever since the days of Jeremy Bentham. I think no one can read that book without feeling that the bulk of Professor Fetter's own writing shows the need of such emancipation from Benthamite error very distinctly.

Who was Bentham, and what were these ideas? He was born in London in 1748, his father being a prosperous solicitor, a man of large practice and of considerable means. He hoped to make his son a barrister. The boy was exceptionally precocious. He was sent to Oxford at twelve years of age, and at Oxford he had about as good a time as Adam Smith had had not very long before, and of Oxford entertained an opinion at least as low as Adam Smith. After his residence at the University, he was sent to Lincoln's Inn, one of the great law schools in London, and carried on legal studies there for a considerable time. When he was ready to enter practice, his father as a solicitor was able to get a case or two for him, but the boy very promptly made it clear, even to his paternal eyes, that he was altogether unfitted for the rough and tumble of active practice. And so he was allowed by his father to lead the life he liked, a sort of cloistered life in London, dedicated to the pursuit of his favorite studies which were matters touching upon social ethics in the large sense, particularly the social ethical problems which are so prominent in the various legal fields.

In the course of this cloistered life Bentham began to compose with great regularity, a practice which he kept up throughout the rest of his eighty-four years; so that he became a singularly prolific writer. The first of his books to be published was called A Fragment on Government. That came out in 1776, the same year as The Wealth of Nations was published. It was a spicy attack on Blackstone's Commentaries which, though published not very long before, had already become one of the sacred books of the lawyers, and was working its way toward that prominent place as a legal text-book which it held long in England and also in the United States. Bentham, however, was quite sure that Blackstone's Commentaries, while possessing certain literary merit, and while perhaps correct as a statement of legal principles, was nevertheless essentially vicious in its philosophy. As he put it, the capital blemish of that work is this grand and fundamental one, antipathy to reformations (now-a-days we would say reform); for Blackstone was a man who worshipped the British Constitution with an idolatry that no American lawyer can exceed when he contemplates our own fundamental instrument of government. Perhaps you will realize this if I read the concluding passage of the Commentaries:

"Of a constitution so wisely contrived, so strongly raised, and so highly finished, it is hard to speak with that praise which is justly and severaly.its due: the thorough and attentive contemplation of it will furnish its best panegyric. It hath been the endeavor of these commentaries, however the execution may have succeeded, to examine its solid foundations, to mark out its extensive plan, to explain the use and distribution of its parts, and, from the harmonious concurrence of those several parts, to demonstrate the elegant proportion of the whole. We have taken occasion to admire at every turn the noble monuments of ancient simplicity and the more curious refinements of modern art. Nor have its faults been concealed from view; for faults it has; lest we should be tempted to think it of more than human structure; defects chiefly arising from the decays of time or the rage of unskillful improvements in later ages. To sustain, to repair, to beautify, this noble pile, is a charge intrusted principally to the nobility and such gentlemen of the kingdom as are delegated by their country to parliament. The protection of THE LIBERTY OF BRITAIN is a duty which they owe to themselves, who enjoy it; to their ancestors, who transmitted it down; and to their posterity, who will claim at their hands this , the best birth-right and noblest inheritance of mankind."

Well, of course, the man who took that view of the merits of the British Constitution could not be eager for what Jeremy Bentham called "reformation". And Jeremy Bentham's *Fragments* were an attempt to indicate broadly how the Britishhh Constitution ought to be reformed. His principle was to try all the questions which arose on considering constitutional law by one grand criterion: the "greatest happiness" principle. His phrasing is this fundamental maxim: "the greatest happiness of the greatest number, that is the measure of right and wrong." Now you may recall that in discussing Adam Smith I noted that his teacher Francis Hutcheson is generally reputed to have been the first English writer to adopt explicitly this principle of greatest happiness as the basis for his social speculations. It comes out in a far more definite form in Bentham's writings, and there it gets its widest, its most extreme application. He adopts it as the fundamental basis by which one should be occupied in considering even constitutional problems.

The book made something of a sensation. It had been published anonymously, and people began to speculate as to who had ventured upon this spicy attack on the great Judge Blackstone. There were some people who pleased Bentham very much by attributing the book to Lord Mansfield, and to other scarcely less eminent legal lights. But Bentham later on wrote with some bitterness that when it was discovered that the book had been written by a nobody the sensation died away.

Bentham kept working at his problems, and in the course of time he prepared that one of his books which is still kept in print, one of the classics in the field of social ethics, a book which he called An Introduction to the Principles of Morals and Legislation, a book that, I dare say, a large proportion of you have been asked to read in courses given in the Departments of Sociology or Philosophy. To the end of his days, this book remained the most systematic formulation of Bentham's general principles, though these principles were developed in some measure in other writings and were applied over an extraordinary range of problems. It is the book which it is still best to read if one wants to get in small compass the gist of Bentham's conception of human nature, and I commend it earnestly to the attention of all members of the class.

This book was printed privately in 1780 and circulated among Bentham's personal friends. It gave him considerable standing, and emboldened him in 1789 to try again the hazard of a publication. You see, he had been disappointed by

-94-

the way in which his _Fragment_ had dropped out of sight as soon as people found it had not been written by a great lawyer, and for that reason, presumably, he did not at first publish the _Principles_, but in 1789 he did so. He could not have chosen a more unlucky time; the French Revolution broke out; the reading public was concerned with those tracts written by Edmund Burke, Thomas Paine, and William Godwin, and Sir James Mackintosh, — books discussing the absorbing events that were taking place over on the Continent. While the public mind was preoccupied with that spectacle, they did not feel concerned over a general treatise upon ethical principles.

Bentham was again grievously disappointed and he turned in a most character istic passion to one of his other interests; that was prison reform. Bentham had a good deal of the mechanical inventor in him. His brother Samuel was, in fact, one of the rather important inventors of the early nineteenth century. He was connected with the British Admiralty; went to Russia for a considerable time at the invitation of the Empress, and organized the arsenals and supply works for the Russian Admiralty, and then returned to Great Britain where he had a very large share in designing the first set of woodworking machines, that is, machines that were arranged in series so that one machine would take up a piece of work where it was left by the preceding machine and then carry it on, so that an elaborate process could be carried on always by machinery.

Jeremy Bentham had a good deal of Samuel's mechanical ingenuity, and the most notable of his inventions was the Panopticon prison house. That was a model penitentiary designed in such fashion that the officers of the penitentiary could at all times have a perfect view of what every inmate of the penitentiary was doing; and Bentham proposed to use this perfected scheme of observation as a basis for elevating the moral characters of the lprisoners. While he was no per-fectionist, his conception of human nature was to lead to the conclusion that the human kind can be made over rather rapidly by establishing right associations. He proposed that the director of the Panopticon should supply the inmates with these "incitements" — we would now-a-days say "those stimuli" — which would make for desirable mental actions. And by keeping everything else that would interfere with the process of making those new associations out of sight and out of the mind of his prisoners, he would be able rather rapidly to convert them into decent characters. Bentham, in a playful way, described the Panopticon as a mill for grinding idle men industrious and rogues honest.

He came to have such faith in the scheme that he proposed to take over the prisoners of England and put them into Panopticon buildings, and rid the country of its criminal class. He became so much obsessed with this scheme that, finding it difficult to get proper financial backing, he used a large proportion of the ample fortune his father left him in getting a site for a Panopticon building and putting up an experimental structure; but he thought all along that he had pledges from influential people in the government that when the proper time came the govern-ment would take over his Panopticon building and reimburse him for his own outlays, — promises which he never had secured in sufficiently formal shape, and promises which, after the most intense and painful struggle, were performed in only partial degree. So that the latter part of the eighteenth century was for Bentham a bad time.

The year 1802 was the turning point in his career. By that time he was fifty-four years old. He was the author of books that had been published but had not been read or sold. He was the inventor of a patent prison scheme in which he could not really interest the influential men. He was in embarrassed financial circumstances. He felt himself more or less without friends, — a disappointed man. But in that year a reputation was made for him on the continent of Europe.

In 1788 Bentham had met a certain Swiss refugee, Pierre Etienne Louis Dumont; and Dumont had become the earliest and one of the most ardent of his disciples. Dumont was a good deal of a book-maker, the master of a pleasing fluent style; and he set himself to produce a treatise in French for Continental use which would reveal to people unacquainted with the English language the revolutionary and important ideas of his master. That book of Dumont's Traite de Legislation Civile et Penale, was published in 1802. It made a Continental reputation for Bentham, and that reputation presently came home and made Bentham an influential figure in England.

It helped rapidly to gain him disciples, for presently he was the center, the revered center, of a group later to be known as the Philosophical Radicals, a group that included among its members a considerable proportion of the ablest men of his time. It included James Mill, the father of John Stuart Mill. It included Ricardo. It included Francis Place, the great radical who had so large a share in bringing about the economic reforms of the 1820's and 1830's. It included Sir Samuel Romilly, the first of the great criminal reformers in Parliament. And many other people who, while less important to us, counted heavily in their own times.

Later on it will be part of our task to see what this group of Philosophical Radicals accomplished. In the meantime I simply note that the group began to form around Bentham in the early part of the nineteenth century. It was made up of men interested in all the branches of what we now call the social sciences, and men who were as active in practical reform as they were active in developing their intellectual opinions. The Philosophical Radicals, as we shall see, succeeded to a most extraordinary degree in getting most of the measures which Jeremy Bentham labored for accepted and incorporated into the British Constitution. If you want to get a lively idea of what a great practical influence Jeremy Bentham exercised upon legal development in England you had better read Professor A.V. Dicey's Lectures on the Relation between Law and Public Opinion in England during the Nineteenth Century, a book in which he says that people now fail to realize adequately how much Bentham's influence accomplished, mainly for the reason that nearly all of his ideas by let us say the 1870's and '80's had become part of the legal structure of his country.

Our concern now is with the ideas of human nature which he expounded, with ideas which underlay the Fragment on Government published in 1776, expounded in systematic fashion in An Introduction to the Principles of Morals and Legislation, published in 1789, and applied by him and his disciples to the discussion of all sorts of constitutional and criminal problems in the law, to problems dealing with criminals, problems of education, to problems of marriage, to problems of the church, particularly in its relation to the state, to all the problems of political science and to the problems of economics.

The distinguishing characteristic of Bentham's conception of human nature, what makes it so exceptionally important to the social sciences and so exceptionally interesting to us, is that it is a conception on which Bentham proposed to base the science, that is, the social sciences, - what we have now come to call the social sciences; they were not so called in his day. For these branches of knowledge, he had an ambition far larger, far more amazing , than Adam Smith, for example, had ventured to entertain. After all, political economy with Adam Smith was more a branch of philosophy than a science. Bentham thought that he saw a way of raising our discussion of all social problems to a scientific level, and by scientific level he meant something that would correspond at not too great remove from what the great Newton had accomplished for the physical sciences. That is, he proposed to show what are the forces which control human behavior, and then he proposed to show how these forces could be measured, and through measurement, how a science of calculation could be built up. His dream was to develop a science of human behavior carried on by means of calculation, much in the way in which Newton had developed the science of astronomy by dealing with the force of gravitation and by showing how the force of gravitation can be calculated. Bentham says explicitly in some of his notes that he had dreamed of becoming the Newton of the moral world.

Now what are the forces which control human behavior, the forces which it is feasible to measure? That is stated with the most delightful explicitness in the most famous passage of the Introduction to the Principles of Morals and Legislation:

> Nature has placed mankind under the governance of two sovereign masters, pain and pleasure. It is for them alone to point out what we ought to do, as well as to determine what we shall do. On the one hand the standard of right and wrong, on the other the chain of causes and effects, are fastened to their throne.

There are then two forces which control human behavior; pleasure and pain. How can these forces be measured? Bentham says that they can be measured by taking account of the several dimensions, for pleasure and pain are multi-dimensional forces. When you are thinking about a single individual you have to take account of four dimensions. A Pleasure has (1) intensity, it has (2) duration. It has some measure of (3) certainty if it lies in the future. And it has some measure of (4) propinquity, that is, it is nearer to us or farther away. Then if you are interested in the tendency of acts, whether performed in order to get pleasure or avoid pain, you must add two other dimensions: (5) fecundity of pleasure, that is, the quality which certain pleasures have of reacting upon us so that these pleasures when enjoyed in the future grow weaker or stronger. And it has (6) purity, that is, in many cases pleasures are mixed with some element of pain, and pain with some element of pleasure. A man may get a certain pleasure from drinking wine, but with that pleasure is mixed the resultant pain in his headaches. Finally, when you are not thinking about one individual but of a community, you must take account of (7) the extent of pleasures, that is, the number of people they affect. You see at once that the calculation of pleasure and pain must be a rather complicated process, because you have to take account of all these dimensions and each one must be taken account of in units appropriate to itself.

What then is the unit that we employ in measuring the intensity of pleasures? Bentham considers the problem and concludes that the unit for intensity must be the slightest sensation. On introspection we can determine what acts are pleasurable and painful, and then pleasures which are more intense should be reckoned as containing so many of these barely perceptible units. Duration can be measured naturally in units of time; in seconds, or minutes, or hours. Just as a pleasure is the greater the more units of intensity it has, so the pleasure is the greater the longer it endures. Certainty is to be measured by nearness. Pleasures we are enjoying at the present time are certain and can be represented by unity; pleasures which we expect in the future are uncertain in various degrees, and we can represent their relative certainty by fractions, diminishing as the certainty becomes more. Propinquity can be represented by unity when a pleasure is just at hand and by a diminishing series of fractions as the pleasures in contemplation are farther and farther away. The farther away a pleasure is, the less its force in determining our conduct at a present moment. Fecundity is that quality that some pleasures have of growing if we learn really how to take advantage of them, and can be represented by additions to the future pleasures representing the increased magnitude they will have for us. And so with purity; there you must subtract from a pleasure any pains which are mixed with it, calculating those pains in the same way you calculate pleasures, allowing for their intensity, certainty, and propinquity. And in dealing with pains you must reckon the amounts of pleasure they contain and subtract these pleasures in order to tell how much they influence your conduct.

Finally -- and here we come to one of Bentham's, I think, really grand ideas; grand for that time -- when we deal with extent we must take every single human being as one; count all men alike. The pleasures that are to be obtained by the humblest of his majesty's subjects is just as important in the calculus as the pleasures of majesty itself. All human beings should be counted alike; though if Bentham would have been more careful he would have drawn the conclusion that the better the machine the more important he is in terms of the felicific calculus. That refinement he had indeed overlooked.

You see then that Bentham supposes that men are governed by two forces of opposite sorts, forces which have several dimensions; each dimension, however, of a character which is susceptible of measurement; and he supposes moreover that men all do calculate more or less, some of them more skilfully than others, but that all human conduct is determined by such a calculation as each human being is able to make for himself of the way in which he can get pleasure and avoid pain. In this respect all men are alike. We are all of us governed by "two sovereign masters, pain and pleasure," which control the chain of causes and effects. They are the things which rule us.

In drawing up the felicific calculus, Bentham regarded himself simply as showing what we do in deciding our course of conduct; what we do instinctively; without knowing it. Although he thought frequently about instinctive action, he seemed to think most of our actions the result of calculating choice and what we all do in proportion to our intellectual ability. This felicific calculus, then, gives us a functional sketch on the one hand, and on the other hand it gives us a criterion of what is right and what is wrong, for those things are right which maximize the greatest happiness of the greatest number,-- the greatest attainable amount of happiness for the community as a whole. Anything which jeopardizes the attainment of this maximum happiness is wrong and anything that permits it is right.

XVII

BENTHAM'S FELICIFIC CALCULUS

On Tuesday I was speaking about Bentham's felicific calculus, that curious scheme by applying which he hoped to turn the moral sciences -- what we now-a-days call the social sciences -- the moral disciplines, into real sciences. That calculus, as I said, dealt with pleasure and pain as the two sole motive forces of human conduct. But these two forces were found to have some seven different dimensions, all of which must be taken into account when one is dealing with problems of social behavior; intensity of feelings, their duration, their certainty, their propinquity, their fecundity, their purity, and finally their extent.

Now in working out this calculus and actually applying it there are certain obvious difficulties. Bentham wrestled with these difficulties as best he might. It is instructive to see what the difficulties were and how he dealt with them. In the first place, if one is going to apply this calculus in the social sciences, one must face the question whether the feelings of different people are really comparable. Whether this is the problem as it turns up in the work of an economist, whether a given sum of money, a dollar for instance, represents the same amount of enjoyment to different people -- that is a question upon which opinions differ considerably now-a-days. You find many economists who say that we have no justification for comparing the feelings of different men, that we have no means of knowing whether the same commodity when consumed by different individuals gives them the same measure of satisfaction. And there are other people who say, perhaps we cannot compare the feelings of different individuals, but at least we can with much confidence compare the feelings of considerable groups of individuals, providing the groups live under circumstances which are not dissimilar.

Bentham, in thinking about this matter, wavered a little bit from time to time; he was not always consistent. But the ground on which he seems to have rested his argument when he faces the difficulty most seriously was that we have to postulate the similarity of people's feelings. I will read you a passage from one of his unpublished manuscripts which has been printed in one of Professor Halevy's books:*

"'Tis in vain to talk of adding quantities which after the addition will continue distinct as they were before, one man's happiness will never be another man's happiness; a gain to one man is no gain to another: you might as well pretend to add 20 apples to 20 pears ... This addibility of the happiness of different subjects, however fictitious it may appear when considered rigorously, is a postulatum without the allowance of which all political reasoning is at a stand; nor is it more fictitious than that of the equality of chances to reality, on which that whole branch of the Mathematics which is called the doctrine of chances is established.'"

He came to the conclusion that we have to assume that the happiness of different people is alike if we are going to have any science of ethics or of politics.

A second difficulty came up when he considered carefully the question whether a man could count the intensity units in his own pleasures. Intensity is, of course, the first of the dimensions of pleasure and pain which he takes into consideration; and on thinking the matter over he saw that it was by no means a simple matter to say that you can tell how many units of intensity anyone of the pleasures and pains you experience contains. Here again Bentham wavered. In one passage he said:

"...the degree of intensity possessed by that pleasure which is the faintest of any that can be distinguished to be pleasure, may be represented by unity. Such a degree of intensity is in every day's experiences; according as any pleasures are perceived to be more and more intense, they may be represented by higher and higher numbers..."**

But in another passage Bentham frankly remarks that intensity is not "susceptible of measurement."***

The third question is whether a man can compare quantitatively his qualitatively unlike pleasures or pains -- whether you can compare what Bentham calls "pleasures of amity" with "pleasures of the palate." If you are really going to have a calculus of felicity you must find some way of considering all these different kinds of pleasure in terms of a common denominator, and also you must have a common denominator for all kinds of pains, and subtract your pains from your plea-

---

*Halevy, La Formation du Radicalisme Philosophique, 1901;vol. iii, p. 481
**Ibid., vol. iii, p. 481
***Works, vol. iv, p. 542.

sures; otherwise you cannot determine the purity of any given pleasure, provided it is, as commonly happens, a·pleasurable sensation mixed in with certain painful sensations: the pain you may experience in taking the subway downtown in order to get the pleasure of attending a theatrical performance. You must have some kind of denominator if you are going to calculate.

Bentham considered that problem in his later years, and came to the conclusion that the best hope we have of comparing different kinds of pleasure and pain is to represent each kind by its money equivalent. In the passage which I shall read, you will see a very interesting anticipation of Alfred Marshall's use of "money measures" in economic work. Marshall, we shall find, in his Principles of Economics says that economics centers upon money because money is the only means that we·have·of measuring the force of motives. Listen to Bentham's way of putting that idea:

> If of two pleasures a man, knowing what they are, would as lief enjoy the one as the other, they must be reputed equal . .If of two pains a man had as lief escape the one as the other, such two pains must be reputed equal. If of two sensations, a pain and a pleasure, a man had as lief enjoy the pleasure and suffer the pain, as not enjoy the first and not suffer the latter, such pleasure and pain must be reputed equal, or, as we may say in this case, equivalent.

> If then between two pleasures the one produced by the possession of money, the other not, a man had as lief enjoy the one as the other, such pleasures are to be reputed equal. But the pleasure produced by the possession of money, is as the quantity of money that produces it; money is therefore the measure of this pleasure. But the other pleasure is equal to this; the other pleasure therefore is as the money that produces this; therefore money is also the measure of that other pleasure. It is the same between pain and pain; as also between pain and pleasure.

> If then speaking of the respective quantities of various pains and pleasures and agreeing in the same propositions concerning them, we would annex the same ideas to these propositions, that is, if we would understand one another, we must make use of some common measure. The only common measure the nature of things affords is money.......

> I beg a truce here of our man of sentiment and feeling while from necessity; and it is only from necessity, I speak and prompt mankind to speak a mercenary language,......Money is the instrument for measuring the quantity of pain or pleasure. Those who are not satisfied with the accuracy of this statement must find out some other that shall be more accurate, or bid adieu to Politics and Morals.*

Then there is another difficulty in using the calculus, the difficulty we now-a-days call that of diminishing utility. Of course, this whole idea of measuring pleasures and pains was presently taken up by an economist, Jevons, and so made the basis of what we call the utility calculus. We shall find that Jevons used the ideas in more limited fashion and introduced an important change. Now Bentham saw that idea and it made him a lot of trouble. He said:

> The quantity of pleasure in the breast of the monarch will naturally be greater than the quantity in the breast of the labourer;

*Halevy, op.cit., vol. 1, pp.410, 412, 414.

...But...by how many times greater? Fifty thousand times? This is assuredly more than any man would take upon himself to say. A thousand times, then? - a hundred? - ten times? - five times? - twice? Which of all these shall be the number?....For the monarch's taking all purposes together, <u>five times</u> the labourer's seems a very large, not to say an excessive allowance: even <u>twice</u>, a liberal one.*

Now there you see is a very considerable difficulty. Bentham once, at least, thought he found a way of surmounting it. He argued as follows:

...money being the current instrument of pleasure, it is plain by uncontrovertible experience that the quantity of actual pleasure follows in every instance in some proportion or other the quantity of money. As to the law of that proportion nothing can be more indeterminate....For all this it is true enough for practice with respect to such proportions as ordinarily occur (viz.:small quantities), that <u>caeteris paribus</u> the proportion between pleasure and pleasure is the same as that between sum and sum. So much is strictly true that the ratios between the two pairs of quantities are nearer to that of equality than to any other ratio that can be assigned. Men will therefore stand a better chance of being right by supposing them equal than by supposing them to be any otherwise than equal. .....

Speaking then in general, we may therefore truly say, that in small quantities the pleasure produced by two sums are <u>as</u> the sums producing them.**

That is, Bentham in developing his felicific calculus got to the point of recognizing that it is easier to handle increments of small quantities of pleasure or pain and compare them, than it is to compare pleasures and pains as wholes. But he never grasped the possibility of thinking of pleasures and pains at some margin; and it is the idea of taking marginal increments for purposes of comparison that constitutes the important addition, to the felicific calculus which was made a generation after Bentham's death by writers like Jevons in England, Menger in Austria, and Leon Walras in France. Later on we are going to see exactly what Jevons did with this notion.

So much for the difficulties attending the application of the calculus. Now let us see what are the implications concerning human nature which it contain In the first place, it means that human beings are thoroughly hedonistic creature: That is, they are creatures whose motives are all in the character of desires to get pleasure or avoid pain. As Bentham put it, "Nothing but the expectation of th eventual enjoyment of pleasure in some shape, or the exemption from pain in some shape, can operate in the character of a motive...." That is, all human behavior is substantially guided by motives of getting pleasure and avoiding pain. Bentha: has a very curious and pretty passage explaining the way in which our minds work in this respect. He says that the idea of a pleasure or of an exemption from pai: applies itself in the first instance on our wills. Then if the idea is not perfectly clear, the will refers the problem to the understanding, and the understan ing has two jobs to perform: first, it must strike a balance between the value of this good and that of the pain or loss, if any, which present themselves as eventually to stand associated with it. That is, the understanding calculates the amount of pleasure that is in prospect. And second, if the balance appear to be :

* "Codification Proposal," Works, vol. iv, p. 541.
** Halevy, op.cit., vol. i, pp. 406, 408, 410.

favor of an act, then the understanding must choose the means by which that pleasure is to be obtained. These are the two offices of the understanding; to calculate the amount of the pleasure and then decide upon the proper means of ob-
taining it. Thereupon — that is, when these two offices of the understanding
have been performed — if action is to be the result, willingness is perfected
into volition, of which the correspondent action is the immediate consequence.
For the process that takes place, this description may serve alike in all cases:
time occupied by it may be of any length, from a minute fraction of a second, as
in ordinary cases, to any number of years.

Thus you see the whole process spread out before you. Your ideas of
pleasures appeal to your will. If the ideas are not clear and definite, the will
refers them to the understanding. Then the understanding determines whether the
act is worth while and goes on to select the proper means; and if the whole mental
operation of the understanding is favorable to the act, it then passes back to the
will and gets translated into action — that taking a fraction of a second, and
in some cases of elaborate deliberation occupying years. So, in the first place,
human nature is hedonistic in the most rigorous sense; and in the second place,
human nature is rational; we are calculating creatures.

And in another passage he says, answering an objection that passion does
not calculate:

> When matters of such importance as pain and pleasure are at
> stake, and these in the highest degree (the only matters, in short, that
> can be of importance) who is there that does not calculate? Men cal-
> culate, some with less exactness, indeed, some with more; but all men
> calculate. I would not say, that even a madman does not calculate.
> Passion calculates, more or less, in every man; in different men, accord-
> ing to the firmness or irritability of their minds: according to the
> nature of the motives by which they are acted upon. Happily, of all
> passions, that is the most given to calculation, from the excesses of
> which, by reason of its strength, constancy, and universality, society
> has most to apprehend: I mean that which corresponds to the motives of
> pecuniary interest...*

And here we see the reason why, from Bentham's point of view, economics
could be more nearly perfected as a science than any of the disciplines which we
associate with it. In economics you have the best chance to determine, to discuss human action on a scientific basis, because the motive of pecuniary interest
is the motive in following which we calculate most commonly and most accurately.

The third characteristic of human nature implied by this general view
is that it is essentially passive. That is, we do not have propensities to act,
but are pushed and pulled about by the pleasure-pain forces of our environments.
Conceptions which take human nature to be essentially active are quite foreign
to Bentham. As he puts it:

> ...on every occasion, conduct — the course taken by a man's conduct—
> is at the absolute command of — is the never failing result of — the
> motives, — and thence, in so far as the corresponding interests are
> perceived and understood, of the corresponding interests, — to the action
> of which, his mind — his will — has, on that same occasion, stood ex-
> posed.**

*Works, vol. i, pp. 90-91. Compare the similar passage in Principles of Penal Law
vol. i, p. 402.
**"A Table of the Springs of Action," Works, vol. i, p. 218.

Human nature is passive, not only in the sense that our actions are determined for us by pleasures and pains that have gone into the making of our minds and impinge upon us at any given moment, but also in the sense that we dislike exertion. In his Table of the Springs of Action, the most elaborate of his psychological discussions, Bentham includes both pleasures and pains of the palate, of sense, of wealth, of amity, of reputation, and so on through eleven heads until he comes to labor, and under that head he includes only pains. Enlarging on that subject he says:

> Aversion — not desire — is the emotion — the only emotion — which labour, taken by itself, is qualified to produce: of any such emotion as love or desire, ease, which is the negative or absence of labour — ease, not labour — is the object.*

Another characteristic is that the only defects which human nature is capable of are defects of the understanding. Of course, one cannot have a bad motive on Bentham's showing. There is not anything as a bad motive because the only motives are to get pleasure and avoid pain; and in so far as a person is obeying any motive he is to that extent obeying a good motive. But we may perform actions which are bad in the sense that they produce more pain than pleasure to ourselves, and particularly we may perform actions which are bad in the sense that they produce more pain than pleasure to others. We do the first particularly when we do not understand the consequences of our actions. To read again Bentham's formulation of the notion:

> Indigenous intellectual weakness — adoptive intellectual weakness — or, in one word, prejudice — sinister interest (understand self-conscious sinister interest) — lastly, interest-begotten (though not self-conscious) prejudice — by one or other of these denominations, may be designated (it is believed) the cause of whatever is on any occasion amiss, in the opinions or conduct of mankind.**

Similarly whatever lack of unity there is in people's actions must be due to differences in their intellectual ability in calculating pleasures and pains. If we were all on the same intellectual level and exposed to the same circumstances, we should all behave alike. The only reason for the gulf that separates civilized man from the savage is that the civilized man is a better calculator of pleasures and pains than the savage. In

> the variety and extent of the ideas with which they have been impressed ...may be seen the only cause of whatsoever difference there is between the mind of a well educated youth under the existing systems of education, and the mind of the Esquimaux, or the New Zealand savage at the same age.#

And in consequence of this fact that all our inequalities and all our mistakes are due to intellectual error, to the failure of our understandings as calculating machines, the consequence of that is that the sole and sufficient method of improving human conduct and raising human welfare is education. All that a man needs to make his conduct perfect is the kind of training which will make him a good calculator in the sense that he will see what pleasures are to be had by certain lines of conduct and what pains these lines of conduct render. Conse-

---

*Works, vol. i, p. 214.
**"Springs of Action," Works, vol. i, p. 217.
#"Chrestomathia," Works, vol. viii, p. 11.

quently, education is in a sense the sole object of every worthy social movement. The whole penal system should be conceived as an educational apparatus. As I said at the last hour, Bentham gave long years of his life and far more money than he could afford, to try to establish the prisons upon that basis, - to make them schools for the reformation of character, that is, schools in which the criminals would be taught how to associate properly the ideas of pleasures with certain acts, and the ideas of pains with certain acts.

So, too, his whole conception of the legislation of the country, the work of its rulers, was that that work should be done in such a fashion as to make men associate correctly among the pleasures and pains which their actions are likely to produce.

So, too, Bentham became one of the earliest reformers of the British school system. He devoted a good deal of time and attention to drawing up a scheme for a "chrestomathic school...for the use of the middling and higher ranks in life," which was designed to improve the ability of the students to make proper associations between pleasures and pains to make them into good calculating machines.

So, too, he was one of the people to help finance Robert Owen's scheme of industrial education at New Lanark, that interesting experiment that tried to surround the employees of an industrial establishment with conditions which would improve their moral character, and from Bentham's point of view with conditions which would make them better calculators than they otherwise would have been.

There was one particular difficulty in this connection which Bentham had to face, and that was the realization which did not dawn upon him until rather late in life, until after his bitter disappointment about his Panopticon scheme, the realization that men do not spontaneously desire the greatest happiness for the greatest number. In his earlier years, he seemed to take that for granted. But when he found that people were not really interested in this grand conception of "grinding rogues honest, and idle men industrious," he explained the fact by saying that men are necessarily selfish. They are so constructed on the basis of his own principle that they must prefer their own pleasure to that of other people.

Well, then, how can you arrange a satisfactory government? You will have to arrange a scheme under which people can get pleasure for themselves only by acts which will give pleasure to others. And the later years of Bentham's life were mainly devoted to drawing up an elaborate scheme of that sort, a constitutional code, in which all the laws were intended to inflict pain upon somebody whenever that person performed an act which would be the cause of pain to others; and to give pleasure to people when their acts were of a sort that gave pleasure to their fellows. This scheme is one with many modern democratic features: vote by secret ballot, for instance; choise of all officers of government by the people at large; very frequent elections so that any official that did not give pleasure to his constituency by his policy might be promptly repudiated; - a thoroughgoing republican scheme of government with a rather wide suffrage.

Now all this, you see, is just the logical working out of Bentham's fundamental conception that human conduct is controlled by two sovereign masters. It lays in Bentham's eyes, as I have said once or twice, the logical foundation upon which we can construct two structures; on the one hand, a system of morals; on the other hand, the social sciences. That is, the scheme tells us that our conduct is controlled by certain forces of pleasure and pain; and further it tells us that by studying the forces of pleasure and pain in a certain environment you can tell what people will do. It also gives us a criterion by which to judge what is right and wrong.

Bentham thought that of these two, it was far more important to show what is right and what is wrong with reference to social institutions than it is to develop the sciences. In fact, from his point of view the sciences had no value except their utilitarian value: what they could contribute toward our understanding of how to get pleasure and how to avoid pain. The development of the social sciences is just one of our processes of taking ourselves account of the way we can make successful calculations with reference to not merely ourselves but with reference to large communities.

As between these two matters, the passing of judgments upon institutions and their effects, is not only the more important but it is also the more certain operation. For from Bentham's own point of view there are only two ways in which to give a really scientific account of human behavior. Of course, you have to deal with the forces of pleasure and pain that are going to rule conduct, but if you are any observer you will note that since men are not good calculating machines you cannot expect that what you as an enlightened theorist presumably calculate concerning the promise of pleasure or pain to be held up by a certain act will be seen by all the other people. They will, many of them, be irrational in calculating any certain response; and so far as they are bad calculators your theories are based on your own theories of pleasures and pains and will not show exactly what they will do.

So you are forced to study the defects of the understanding of classes of men and allow for them in your theory. That is something that you will find the classical economists doing; that is practically what Malthus was doing when he said that the working classes, owing to their defective foresight, brought the most grievous of pains upon themselves by marrying too early and having too large families.

And that view of one of the standard defects of human nature was taken over by the classical economists; it made one of the corner-stones of their theory Ricardo, for instance, assumes that men are not perfectly rational in deciding upon the relative advantages of investments at home and abroad; they prefer investments at home and do not calculate with impartiality, and that makes it necessary to distinguish between the problem of value and prices in one country and values and prices in international trade. And then men think they understand business cycles by saying that in periods of prosperity people get too excited: they allow their feelings to bias their business calculations, and so we have had speculations which produce an unstable situation, ending in crisis.

So, at large, you can explain how people are going to act by making allowances for widely prevalent failures of the understanding. But, of course, that sort of operation is not any too certain; and there is only one other way you can do the thing, that is, actually observe what people do, – a procedure which neither Bentham nor anybody at his time thought of resorting to, a procedure we are just beginning to adopt now-a-days, and we have the advantage of very considerable mass observations of human behavior given us by statistics.

If you sum up the idea of the felicific calculus you see that after all Bentham's writings he did not get an instrument by means of which he could really put the moral branches upon anything like the same definite scientific basis as that on which the physical branches of knowledge rested in his day. His calculus at best was clumsy. It had to take account of at least seven aspects of pleasures and pains when it was applied to purposes of social sciences, for social sciences have to take account of the community and so its number and the tendencies of acts and so bring in the propinquity and fecundity and period of pleasures.

But more serious than this elaborateness of the calculus are the doubts
attending the application of its very fundamentals. There is that gross difficulty of trying to count intensity units. There is still the lurking difficulty that you have to suppose, without knowing if you are justified in so doing,
that similar pleasures enjoyed by different subjects are alike. And then you face
finally this great difficulty that even when a calculation is being made by an individual, he has corresponding difficulty in comparing his qualitatively unlike
pleasures, and finally, that he is troubled by the fact that pleasures keep varying
in their intensity as the acts of consumption proceed.

Needless to say, Bentham never did work it out in practice, so far as I
have been able to discover, and while I have not read by any means all the many
volumes of his work, I have read the most significant, and I do not think that I
could have overlooked the fact if he had done so. Bentham never did work up any
single problem of the felicific calculus; that is, he never does give figures which
will tell you how many pleasure units will be derived by an individual or society
from any given line of action. But he did accomplish something that was nevertheless of very considerable value: he held up before men the ideal of establishing the moral branches on a scientific basis. More than that, he worked out with
curious explicitness the logical implications of the notions of human behavior
which prevailed in his own generation and notions which we are very likely to take
up with if we do not make specific studies of psychology or if we are not unusually capable in the old art of self-examination.

XVIII

BENTHAM'S CONCEPTION OF HUMAN NATURE

I have set forth the general outline of Bentham's felicific calculus. Today I want to point out certain implications in that calculus concerning the
characteristics of human nature, the sort of notion about the fundamental nature
of man that Bentham entertained. This is the matter that concerns us most. It
is for the sake of this that I deal with Bentham for, as I pointed out before embarking on this discussion, the general character of any writer's opinions concerning human nature exercises a controlling influence over his speculations in the
social sciences. Whether he be dealing with problems of legislation, or education,
or criminology, or economics, or any aspects of human nature, that will hold true.

The first implication about human nature is the obvious one that men are
hedonistic creatures. That is, what controls their actions is a desire to get
pleasure. Bentham reiterates this statement in various forms. Nothing but the
expectation of the eventual enjoyment of pleasure in some shape, or exemption
from pain in some shape, can operate in the character of the motive. All our
motives, then, are fundamentally alike. There can be no such thing as a bad
motive, for the only thing that can possibly induce a man to commit any act is the
expectation of deriving pleasure from it or avoiding pain; and the minimizing of
pain is one of the necessary features of maximizing pleasure. There cannot be a
disinterested action. The only thing that can be wrong with your conduct is that
you act in such a way perhaps as to create more pain for others than you get for
yourself. But the motive by which you act is the desire for your own pleasure
and that is, of course, a good motive.

Just how the idea of pleasure acts upon us to lead us to do this, that,
or the other thing is a matter that Bentham sets forth in some detail. That is a
matter of very considerable interest to a psychologist. Later on we shall have

occasion to note the process by which this hedonistic view of human behavior broke down because later inquirers could not accept such an analysis as I am now going to read to you from Bentham as to the operations that go on in our consciousness: "Every operation of the mind then, every operation of the body is the result of the will or volitional faculty."

I want to emphasize the fact which I have also mentioned casually that this general conception of human nature, these implications that I have set forth, greatly facilitated the task of building up the social sciences on a speculative basis. It cut out all the puzzles about human nature that beset us today; it left out of account all the questions about differences between characteristics with which we are born and characteristics which we gradually acquire. It reduced differences among men primarily to differences of understanding. It enabled a person to give an account of conduct primarily in terms of the pain and pleasure forces of the environment. Bentham could set forth with this system of human nature in mind to build up with a high degree of confidence, discussions of economic behavior, as he did in his tract on usury, and then his later small tracts on political economy. He could, and did, on a much larger scale deduce from his notions of human behavior and his knowledge of what pleasures and pains a modern environment offers to people, schemes for educating children and re-educating adults, for human nature is passive if it is rational. Then, as I said before, all you have to know in order to explain what people do is how they can get pleasures and how they are likely to err in their own calculations.

It should also be observed that the social sciences that you can build up have a double aspect, a double aspect derived from the fact that on the one hand right and wrong and on the other hand the chain of cause and effect are "fastened to the thrones of pleasure and pain." Our social sciences tell what ought to be done; and at the same time they are capable of telling us what people will do. They give us what from the modern point of view is a scientific account of human behavior, explaining under favorable circumstances, predicting human action, and on the other hand they show us definitely what is the right way of arranging all social institutions.

From the modern viewpoint it is common to hold that these two questions of what is and what ought to be are separate questions. And many people would say they are questions that had best be handled by different people. There are a good many economists who take the ground that if an economist begins to think too much about what ought to be he will get enamored of his notions and that they will cloud his understanding; he will begin to indulge in wishful thinking and his science will cease to be objective, it will wander off from the strict path of veracity, putting a genuine colorless representation of how social processes work into the maze of the author's own desires. If, however, a person wants to attack the question of what ought to be, then he should proceed not on a scientific basis fundamentally but should proceed upon a basis of trying to show whatever way he likes, in the last resort by going back to what he conceives to be fundamental philosophical principles perhaps. What are the criteria by which we are to judge right and wrong in a certain case? It will be true that a scientific account of how things actually go should prove useful to this ethical investigator because the ethical investigator may well have criteria which take account of the actual consequences which different lines of action produce and in that case the scientific analysis of the results of action should be taken into account by the philosophic genius. But from this point of view certainly it is an error for the man who is trying to draw up a science to venture over into the other ground.

Another characteristic of many modern investigators is that they take

their science to be presumably far more certain in its deliveries than their
ethical speculations. Sometimes of course we find people who seem to think
upon questions of right and wrong in the last resort as matters of more or less
personal opinion. How can one individual set himself up as a judge of what is
good for others? But in contrast to such uncertainties it should be possible for
a clear-minded investigator to give a really reliable analysis of the interrelations among the processes that take place in nature at large; and despite their
complexity it should be possible for him to throw a good deal of light among the
processes which take place in human relations.

Well, of course, not all philosophers would accept that viewpoint, but of
the philosophers who feel that they are building upon a rock of certain knowledge
a great many modern inquirers hold a skeptical view. Certainly we are inclined to
think, broadly speaking, that our scientific analyses are more assured than most
of our ethical speculations.

In contrast to these modern viewpoints you see Bentham's position holds
that science and ethics march side by side; it also implies that of the two inquiries, what ought to be and what is, the inquirers of what ought to be can
attain the higher degree of certainty. For you see when you are talking about how
men ought to behave you can (presumably as a first-class calculating machine with
correct associations in your own mind of our own pleasures and different lines of
activity) deliver verdicts which are going to be much more correct than will be
the verdict of the mass of men who are presumably on the average not in your class
intellectually; for when a man sets himself up as an investigator of the social
sciences he is certainly supposed to be a person of superior intelligence. If he
is not of superior intelligence he has no real message to give to his fellow-men.
And if he does possess superior intelligence then the conclusions at which he
will arrive as to the best means of contributing toward the greatest happiness
of the greatest number will be better than the conclusions that most men will
arrive at as to how their happiness can be maximized.

If you really want to give a close and careful account of how people
actually behave, then you have to go into the rather difficult problem of investi-
gating the character and extent of whatever intellectual weaknesses, indigenous
and adopted, the men whose actions you are dealing with are subject to. And that
is a matter which cannot be avoided if you are really going to arrive at an understanding of departures of human behavior from the line marked out by the rules of
the felicific calculus.

So that, to repeat, the deliberations of an ethical character, the determination of what ought to be, is a simple and more certain undertaking from
this viewpoint than the allegedly scientific account of how people actually behave.
To make this matter a little clearer, let me anticipate and point out that the
classical economists in using Bentham's approach did, nevertheless, spend a considerable amount of time in considering what Bentham would have called the indigenous or adopted intellectual weakness of man. The weaknesses to which they paid
most attention was the failure of the working classes to understand that by im-
prudent ventures into matrimony they would bring upon themselves very severe pri-
vations and great pains to their families.

Then also we shall have occasion to observe that Ricardo saw certain characteristic errors of calculation among the business classes with whom he was so well
acquainted. And just as the economists based their theory of wages, their theories
of population in large part upon the indigenous or adopted weakness of the working
class in respect to marriage, so Ricardo based certain modifications of his general principles of profits upon the fact that the business men tend to make cer-

tain standard errors in their expectations from men in different lines of action. You were driven, if you advanced with conceptions of human nature of the sort that Bentham entertained, on to these investigations as to the standard ways in which mankind make errors of calculation. And that means that your scientific conclusions in economics are dependent in part upon the accuracy of your observations of human weaknesses, — observations which, needless to say, were of necessity somewhat broad and rough.

One final point I want to make about the general character of the social sciences that were built upon the basis Bentham provided is that these sciences were supposed by Bentham's own philosophy to lead to practical conclusions. The only justification for social sciences, from his viewpoint, is that they might contribute toward the happiness of the greatest number. Anything that did not do that was of little value except perhaps as it might give pleasure to individuals. That is, in so far as, let us say, the cultivation of economics gives the same pleasure as chess gives. But as an important factor in human life whatever value it really possesses is to be found in the guidance that it can give toward policies which will enhance the greatest happiness.

One might think then that this great aim of the social sciences was a straight matter of deducing the proper conclusions from the felicific calculus. But it turned out in practice that different people who used the felicific calculus often arrived at diametrically opposed positions. I want to illustrate that by reference to a concrete issue. That issue is provided by views regarding the institution of property. Bentham and all his school, though they were great radicals of their day, believed very firmly in the institution of private property. That meant that they thought that the institution of private property was necessary to assure the greatest happiness. You might think that there was some inconsistency between belief in an institution which resulted in great inequality of possession and Bentham's clear insight into the diminishing utility of wealth. Quite obviously from Bentham's own viewpoint a given amount of income will, other things equal, produce for more happiness if it is evenly distributed among the different members of the community than if it is unevenly distributed as income is in a modern society. So that it might seem that from Bentham's viewpoint the great means to enhance happiness in a modern society is to strive toward equality of income.

Well, Bentham did not attain that result. He had his escape from what seems to be an inevitable conclusion. And yet there were many people who used his methods who did argue in the most straightforward way that only in a communistic state of society where incomes are substantially equal can a given amount of wealt maximize happiness. How Bentham was able to escape this conclusion is a matter which I shall take up at the next meeting.

XIX

THE FELICIFIC CALCULUS
IN PRACTICE

At the last two meetings you will remember I have been discussing Bentham felicific calculus. First I undertook to set forth the general outline of the scheme as Bentham himself explains it, and then second I dealt at some lenght with the implications of Bentham's ideas about the general character of human nature: how we are hedonistic creatures; how we are tacit in the sense that we are moved to action by the forces of pleasure and pain; how calculating, that is, rational our behavior is supposed to be. And then I went on to consider the serviceability of the felicific calculus as an agency for developing the social sciences. Taken

on its own recognizances, I said, the felicific calculus purports to give us on
the one hand an actual account of how men do behave, that is, to give us explanations of behavior, in other words, social sciences; and, on the other hand,
the felicific calculus undertakes to show how men ought to behave, that is, it
sets up an ethical standard, tells the individual on the one side and the person
who is interested in social questions on the other side what it is that he should
aim to accomplish.

Finally, at the end of the hour I was remarking that despite its scientific pretensions the actual conclusions to which the felicific calculus leads
depends very largely upon the unreasoned preconceptions of the social sciences.
And I was beginning to illustrate that proposition by citing Bentham's own attitude toward the institution of property. He and his disciples, the whole group
of the philosophical radicals, were genuinely radical in the sense that they
wanted to make great and sweeping changes in the social institutions of their own
country and the other countries. They were not men who feared criticism. They
were all throughout their existence a decidedly unpopular minority. They attacked
powerful interests, the landed interests of the country, for instance, and the
established Church. They showed no fear or favor, but they were firm upholders
of the institution of property. They were themselves people who came from the
middle classes and they thought that the future welfare of the nation and of mankind depended upon maintaining the right of the individual to whatever he produced. Their ideas about what he produced were the ideas of the business man.

Well, now how was it that they advocated this deep-set conviction of
theirs that property was not only a wholesome but an indispensable institution for
maximizing the happiness of man? Well, Bentham admitted that one of the facts
brought out in his analysis of the felicific calculus counted very heavily against
the institution of private property: that the institution of private property
results in a gross inequality of the distribution of wealth and of income. Now
an unequal distribution of income, as Bentham saw things, was, other things equal,
detrimental to the great end of maximizing happiness because of the diminishing
utility of wealth, because of the fact that if you have an income of £10,000 you
cannot get anything like ten times the amount of pleasure out of that £10,000 that
another person can get out of £1,000. So that, other things equal, you could increase pleasure by equalizing the distribution of income between the rich on the
one side and the poor on the other side.

That might have seemed a good, logical, conclusive case against inequality
of income and therefore against the institution of private property which gives
rise to such marked inequalities. But no says Bentham, and this is his argument:
every code of laws that is to promote the greatest happiness must do so by promoting the four most comprehensive, broad, and subordinate ends, namely, subsistence, abundance, security, and equality. That, of course, seems clear and
simple. Your great end is to maximize happiness; but to do that you have to make
sure that people have subsistence. Their happiness will not amount to much unless
they have not only subsistence but abundance. They will not be happy unless they
have security. And equality, so far as it is attainable, is another requisite to
maximizing happiness. So these are four subordinate ends which are indispensable
in a public policy. But he goes on: "equality is not itself, as security, subsistence, and abundance are, an immediate instrument of felicity." It gets this
claim upon us only from the diminishing utility of wealth. It is true that, other
things being the same, the greater the equality of the distribution of wealth
the greater the happiness. But other things are by no means the same. Unless -
he argues at length - people had security in the possession of that which they produce they would not produce; the motive for production would fall away. And since
any lack of security meant diminished production, with security would vanish

abundance. Indeed, it is doubtful whether men would be left even with subsistence

Now to equalize wealth would mean taking away from some members of the community that which they had produced. You could get equality only by infringing upon security; and hence we can seek to establish only that degree of equality which is compatible with security in the ownership of that which one produces.

Let me read Bentham's conclusion in his own words:

> So far as is consistent with security the nearer to equality the distribution is which the law makes of the matter of property among the members of the community, the greater is the happiness of the greatest number.

Only in so far as it is consistent with security then can we insist upon the rule of equality. That is an argument that Bentham advances. You see the critical point concerning the proposition is that people would not produce unless they had security that they would obtain the goods which they produced. Bentham puts that proposition forth as a self-evident matter. It did not seem to him to be a problem. And yet, needless to say, from the modern viewpoint that proposition covers a host of problems. Later analysts set to ask the questions: Well, what about production? Who is it that really produces? Is it the business man? Is he really the producer of all that wealth which is made in the difference between that which he sells his product for and the amount that he pays out for materials and cost, particularly that which he pays out for wages?

Men presently arose, some of them Bentham's own disciples, notably the same Ricardian Socialist, William Thompson, who was at one time Bentham's secretary and accepted Bentham's felicific calculus, who argued that the men who really produced the wealth were the workers and the wages they got did not represent the value of their product. So that in the distribution - Thompson's book was named Of Distribution - in the distribution of wealth as matters go at the present time the people who produce it are not secured of that which they turn out.

And then you can argue the question: Well, what security is it that is important in modern society? Is it only the security of the profit-maker in his winnings? Or, on the basis of the rule of the greatest happiness of the greatest number, is the most important problem the security of the worker in his job? And then you can argue further questions: Is it or is it not true that we should take different specimens of humanity as substantially equal in their sensibility? Are there ways of supporting Bentham's contention that property, despite the inequality that it produces, is a necessary human institution? There are ways of supporting that contention other than those seen by Bentham and one was found presently by that very brilliant, much later disciple of Bentham, Professor F.Y. Edgeworth of Oxford.

Edgeworth contended that men are not equal as pleasure machines. Being a mathematician, he introduced his discussion of social arrangements by thinking of men as machines for manufacturing the raw material of consumers' goods into pleasure. And he assumed without argument that men differ in their capacity as pleasure machines. Broadly speaking, he contended that the members of the upper classes were better pleasure machines than members of the lower classes. They were more sensitive individulas, they were susceptible of more education. And he went on to contend that men, broadly speaking, are better pleasure machines than women, a contention that he supported by reciting the lines:

> Woman is the lesser man, and her passions unto mine
> Are as moonlight unto sunlight and as water unto wine.

And on that basis of assuming that the aristocracy are better pleasure machines than the common run of men, that men are better pleasure machines than women, he argued with perfect logic that to maximize happiness you should give larger incomes to the aristocracy than to the common run of men and you should give larger incomes to men than to women.

      I am citing these various matters at the present time to illustrate my point that the felicific calculus, despite its high scientific pretensions, really did not in fact lay a basis for a genuinely conclusive determination of the issues it was employed to discuss. When he came to working out any practical problem to maximize pleasure, like this problem of the institution of private property, the social scientist had in practice explicitly or implicitly to supplement the felicific calculus by further assumptions, assumptions such as Edgeworth's assumption that there are class and sex differences in the efficiency of human beings for turning commodities into pleasure, or assumptions like Bentham's that if there is any interference with the security of the profit maker in getting his profits for himself, production will fall off so greatly that abundance will disappear and subsistence may be compromised.

      And these assumptions, you see, are assumptions that you could test only if you could actually measure the pleasures that people get from certain commodities with the same certainty that you can measure the weights of human beings or measure their statures. Then you could decide these issues as to class and sex differences in the capacity of people for getting pleasure out of the consumption of a given amount of food. You could experiment. All you would have to do is to make measurements on a sufficient sample of the British aristocracy and members of British trade unions, both men and women, and you could tell definitely then whether Edgeworth was right or wrong in his assumptions.

      So, taking up Bentham's assumption, you could actually make experiments of the extent to which a diminution in the part of the product which profit makers were allowed to keep for themselves would have upon their activity as producers. But just because the felicific calculus could not be used in this plain literal fashion like simple measures of weight and length could be used, the people who operated with it always had to fall back in their use of it upon unproved assumptions. And the consequence was that different people who used this calculus could arrive at results as dissimilar as the people who made no pretense at utilizing scientific methods. And it presently appeared that over against the philosophical radicals in Great Britain with their staunch defense of property there arose a group of people, several of whom, not merely William Thompson alone, but two or three others who were professed exponents of Bentham's views on human nature, who agreed in a good many of his political conclusions -- there arose a group of people who at the time were commonly called the "labor writers" and in later years referred to as Ricardian Socialists -- people who represented the wage earner's view of social arrangements just as the philosophical radicals represented the middle class viewpoint.

      These labor writers were, in so far as their economic analysis was concerned, the intellectual forerunners of Karl Marx. They were people who started using Marx's terminology, the idea of the exploitation of labor through the capture of a part of the produce which was really due to the workingman's effort, capture of it by employers. And they argued that to maximize happiness it was necessary to give the product to the people who turned it out. That is, to give to the employer that portion which was a fair recompense for the labor he himself bestowed upon the production plus-- and this was a point about which they differed--

plus, some would say, an allowance for the use of his capital. Capital could be thought of as the stored up results of human labor; and any one who worked to produce things and get his reward might not consume them all himself but might accumulate some, put these things he accumulated at the service of the community by using them to produce other goods. And in that case he should have as part of his return not merely the reward of the labor that he himself devoted to organizing and possibly participating in the profits of manual production but also a proper return for the use of the past product of his labor which he was indeed employing—his capital. But these Ricardian Socialists came out to conclusions about the best way of maximizing happiness which were worlds apart from the conclusions arrived at by Bentham... .

All of which, to repeat, is by way of indicating how definitely the felicific calculus failed of accomplishing the high aims which Bentham had in mind when he drew it up. He cherished, I may remind you, the dream of becoming the Newton of the moral world, that is, of devising a calculus which could be employed in the study of human behavior, which corresponded in its conclusiveness and certainty to the calculus that Newton had employed in his studies of celestial mechanics. And the only trouble with the thing was that he really could not make the measurements that the calculus called for in any sober, simple, and direct sense. The consequence was that the dispositions which he and his bold and active and able disciples gradually excogitated ended by being about as uncertain as the current discussions of the day concerning what ought to be done.

Now all this was not clearly apparent to Bentham's generation. I think all this had to be found out by experience apparently because Bentham's own disciples in editing his manuscripts were not sufficiently keen or sufficiently bold to put in their master's own most penetrating critique of his method. And it was not until other people had attempted to use this method gradually that its deficiencies became clear. But to this day you find that there are plenty of people who do think that men's behavior is controlled by the two sovereign masters pain and pleasure, people who do think that our conduct is, at least in the majority of instances, calculated; that we are guided by the algebraic sums of pleasure and pain that we cast up in our heads. And among the people who take this view are not a few people who are interested in economics. Views of that sort, of course, are really of controlling importance in determining the type of economics that a person develops. It is because these notions about human nature have played so large a role in the building up of the kind of economic theory that we have had, and to a certain extent still have today, that it seems to me indispensable to dwell at such considerable length as I have done upon Bentham's work.

I will try to go back a little later to say something more about the practical activities of the philosophical radicals, the very great services that they rendered to their country in effecting reforms; and from time to time as we deal with later people I will have to refer to Bentham again when we see the sunlight or the shadow of his work shed upon the thinking of later writers on economics. But for the moment I am going to pass on and take up the work of the next master on our list. That master is Robert Malthus and the work which he did that had so profound an influence upon the later growth of economics was his discussion of what he called the "principle of population."

Now Malthus's problem of population was just as obviously an intellectual reflection of current events as was Adam Smith's "simple and obvious system of natural liverty." On the one hand the British population was growing rapidly. The poor rates—that is, the local taxes which were imposed very largely for the care of the sick and indigent—were becoming oppressive. The tax-paying people of England, that is, the people who read books and did the formal thinking, were

deeply concerned about this weight of taxation super-added to the very heavy
burdens of imperial taxation which the wars and the rapidly swelling debt imposed
upon it. Then there was an intellectual stimulus to thinking on the subject
that came to Malthus indirectly from the French Revolution.

XX

MALTHUS AND THE PRINCIPLE OF POPULATION

At the earlier meetings I have said that the French Revolution turned
speculation for a considerable time away from the field of the social sciences,
the field in which Adam Smith was working; and, as a consequence, during the
whole period of nearly half a century between the appearance of The Wealth of
Nations and Ricardo's Principles of Political Economy only two important contributions appeared; one, of no very great consequence by the Scotch economist,
the Earl of Lauderdale, a book on public wealth in which he pointed out that
Adam Smith's statement that the wealth of a nation is the aggregate of the wealth
of the individuals belonging to it overlooks the obvious and not unimportant fact
that there are considerable sums of wealth which belong, not to individuals, but
to the country as a whole, - a qualification of one of Adam Smith's leading
statements, but a qualification so obviously correct, so generally accepted as soon
as it was stated, that it cannot be said to have made any marked change in people's
thinking about economic problems.

The second contribution made in this period was, of course, Malthus's discussion of population, and needless to say that was a contribution of first rate
magnitude. Inasmuch as the view which Malthus took of what he called the "principle of population" was presently incorporated into the body of classical economic
theory and became one of the corner stones of the classical system. It is therefore appropriate that in our review of the social process by which political economy grew up in England and became a body of knowledge which might more or less
fairly aspire to the title of being a science, - it is appropriate that we should
review briefly what Malthus added to men's thinking about economic problems. As in
dealing with Adam Smith and his times, I shall likewise endeavor to consider the
other writers in relation to their times. In talking about Malthus, I shall
attempt to show how his work was related to current social developments. This
task is simpler in Malthus's case than it is in that of Adam Smith because his
discussion of population grew very obviously - as is recognized even in our general histories of economic theory - out of the conditions of the time.

I remarked at an earlier lecture that the first British reaction to the
French Revolution was one of jubilation. They thought that the French people were
throwing off that hated tyranny which was repressing freedom of thought and was
weighing so heavily upon the inspired in France. Among the people who were most
enthusiastic about the French Revolution was William Godwin, a pamphleteer, a man
of letters, of extraordinary imagination and very considerable facility in writing.
Godwin was one of the few people whose opinion of the French Revolution was not
reversed by the Reign of Terror. In 1792 he published, under the inspiration of
the French Revolution, one of the most remarkable English books of the late eighteenth century called Political Justice, in which he argued for the desirability of
what we should now call the communistic organization of society. He got his general conclusions very much as Bentham and Adam Smith did in large part from his
own uncritical ideas about human nature. Godwin had a strong natural tendency
toward virtue; the trouble with men as we see them in the modern world is that
their good natures have been corrupted by bad institutions. Sweep away these bad

institutions that so often impose penalties upon the practice of virtue and offer reward for selfishness and vice, and the crude beauty of man's own inherent qualities will come out. Sweeping away these bad institutions leaves one with a society in which there is a minimum of coercion, a society in which people will spontaneously cooperate with one another in the production of wealth, in which there will be a substantial equality in sharing the profits of labor, and in which felicity will attain its maximum.

This philosophy, anarchistic communism that Godwin argued for was one not to be imposed by the iron hand of a class government. It was one of spontaneous cooperation of individuals far more free than individuals are in any society that is known to history. This ideal of a free anarchistic communism was naturally open to attack; and Godwin the pamphleteer who had to live largely on the proceeds of his writing found plenty of openings for defending himself against critics. One of his later books was called The Enquirer and appeared in 1797. In that book he argued still more plainly and simply for a communistic order among men. His own language is as follows:

> ...a state of cultivated equality, is that state which in
> speculation and theory, appears most consonant to the nature of man,

of course, it is to be the nature of man as Godwin saw man —

> and most conducive to the extensive diffusion of felicity.

This book was widely read and commented upon in England. Among others, it fell into the hands of one Daniel Malthus. He was a somewhat eccentric country gentleman who enjoyed a competence sufficient to make him a man of leisure, but not a man of large wealth, and to enable him to educate his son. Daniel Malthus had been brought up at Oxford, had become deeply interested in botany, and was much given to social speculation. He had been one of the English friends of Jean Jacques Rousseau and indeed was one of Rousseau's executors, one of the few English friends whom that very difficult French genius did not alienate or quarrel with. He was a romanticist and he was inclined to accept with very little qualification the conclusion that Godwin drew that the state of cultivated equality would be most conducive to the extensive diffusion of felicity.

But Daniel Malthus had a son, Thomas Robert, whom he had sent to Cambridge where the young man had studied history and poetry and paid some attention to mathematics. I have said that Daniel Malthus was a somewhat eccentric country gentleman; he showed his eccentricity also by the fact that though himself an Oxford man he sent his son to Cambridge, an act that was even stranger at that time than it would now be for a Harvard man to send his son to Yale. Thomas Robert showed that he had good mathematical abilities by taking rank as the ninth wrangler at the time of his graduation in 1788. After he had taken his bachelor's degree, he studied on at Cambridge for nine years, devoting himself mostly to social studies. In 1797 he got a master's degree and became a fellow of Jesus College, a position which gave him a small stipend. At this time he was thirty-one years old. Thomas Robert had a temperament very different from that of his father, for although he was fond of poetry, nevertheless he was a man of fact, a person who was always inclined in confirming his opinion to fall back as far as possible upon historical experience as the safest guide on which to build expectations of the future. He always wanted to supplement his historical studies of the past by wide observation of current conditions.

Now this rather matter of fact young scholar from Cambridge differed radically from his father in his opinion about the validity of Godwin's conclusions.

The two seem to have debated the question in the most friendly fashion at very considerable length. Young Malthus formed the conclusion that the Utopia which Godwin cherished would be wrecked because if you could at any time establishhhhh a state of cultivated equality among men that state would presently be destroyed by an increase of the population so rapid that presently a large part of the people would be unable to get enough food to keep them alive.

This idea that the future prospects of mankind's improvements are in very large part negative, because of the danger of a rapid increase in population, is often thought of as Malthus's discovery. That is not by any means the case. That notion that if people were better off their improved condition would prove but temporary because of an increase in population so rapid that it would outrun the food supply had been a rather familiar one in England for some time. I had occasion casually to mention the fact in talking about Adam Smith that one of the questions among speculators on social matters in the eighteenth century was the increase in population. They debated very seriously the question as to whether the population was denser in the times of classical antiquity, in the great days of Greece and Rome, than it was in modern Europe,-- a controversy in which David Hume had joined. And, as we have noticed, they debated whether the British population had increased or diminished since the Restoration.

Among Adam Smith's Scotch friends was a Dr. Robert Wallace, who in 1761 published a book which he called Various Prospects of Mankind, Nature, and Providence. In that book Dr. Wallace had discussed the question whether community of goods--that was his phrase for communism--would not be a cure for most of the social ills from which man suffered. And he had come to the conclusion very reluctantly that if a community had been established there would presently ensue an excessive population. Men are always inclined, he argued, to marry and multiply their numbers till the good is barely enough to support them all.

So you see this objection that Malthus made to Godwin's argument if favor of a state of cultivated equality was an argument that had been made before The Wealth of Nations had appeared. And Godwin had not overlooked this reply to his argument for communism, for since Wallace's day this objection had been the stock argument advanced against all communistic speculations of the sort that Godwin had indulged in. It was indeed so much a stock answer to communistic ideals that Godwin had himself taken up the passage in which Wallace pointed out the danger of excessive population and endeavored to show that Wallace's fears were not well founded.

Godwin's argument ran to the effect that in fact anybody who observes society at large will see that population does not outrun food supply. Go to Switzerland; go to England; go to America, and you will find that really there is a pretty decent balance established between the food supply of these various populations and their rate of increase, that after all in every country of the world the food supply was sufficient to keep the population alive, -- a statement which though perfectly valid in a certain sense did not at all meet the point Wallace had in mind.

And then Godwin argued, secondly, that if there should be an excessive population in any one country that could readily be relieved by emigration. The world was wide; and in his time it seemed half empty. The European populations could settle the vast half-explored regions of the Americas. There was Africa; Asia was still largely unknown. It seemed silly to him to talk about the danger of excessive population for centuries to come while the world offered so many places for settlement in the practice of skilled agriculture. Myriads of centuries might pass without any grievous trouble, and in those myriads of centuries many things might happen in the way of finding solutions for the great problem of feeding mankind.

And, in the third place, he fell upon his favorite notion of the perfectibility of man. Just sweep away the bad institutions from which man suffers and his admirable character will reveal itself. He quoted one of Benjamin Franklin's sayings that mind will one day become omnipotent over matter. Godwin interpreted this to mean that man's intellectual capacities would one day become omnipotent over his passions, — that people would really learn self-control. And he went on with some perhaps airy speculations to the effect that possibly the need for marriage might be superseded by earthly immortality and desire for marriage be superseded by man's increasing addiction to intellectual pleasures.

What Malthus then did was not to invent the principle of population as an answer to Godwin; what he did was to undertake to refute Godwin's refutation of Robert Wallace. The line that he took is best shown by quoting briefly from the first edition of his Essay. This first edition was published in 1798.

XXI

THE ESSAY ON THE PRINCIPLE OF POPULATION

What Malthus did in answering his father was to rebut the answer which Godwin had made to Wallace. As he said himself in the preface of his first edition:

> The author at first sat down with an intention of merely stating his thoughts to his friend, upon paper, in a clearer manner than he thought he could do in conversation. But as the subject opened upon him, some ideas occurred, which he did not recollect to have met with before; and as he conceived, that every, the least light on a topic so generally interesting, might be received with candour, he determined to put his thoughts in a form for publication.

The result was the first edition of his book called An Essay on the Principle of Population as it Affects the Future Improvement of Society, with Remarks on the Speculations of Mr. Godwin, M. Condorcet, and Other Writers. That was a little loosely printed octavo of some 396 pages, published anonymously. It is a book that has become extremely rare, since it was presently superseded by the second edition, and since then a number of other editions were published even in Malthus's own lifetime. The first edition has long been one of the interestingly rare items, much sought by collectors of texts upon political economy and happily for the convenience of all of us who are interested in such matters the Royal Economic Society published a facsimile reprint in 1926.

Malthus begins his argument by saying:

> I think I may fairly make two postulata.
> First, That food is necessary to the existence of man.
>
> Secondly, That the passion between the sexes is necessary, and will remain nearly in its present state.

That is, he assumes that Godwin is wrong in his expectations that we are going gradually to master our passions and get more of our pleasures from the intellect.

Assuming, then, my postulata as granted

he goes on

I say, that the power of population is indefinitely greater than the power in the earth to produce subsistence for man.

And he goes on to develop that notion with the celebrated idea of the two ratios, the geometrical increase of population and the arithmetical increase of the food supply.

Population, when unchecked, increases in a geometrical ratio. Subsistence only increases in an arithmetical ratio. A slight acquaintance with numbers will show the immensity of the first power in comparison of the second.

By that law of our nature which makes food necessary to the life of man, the effects of these two unequal powers must be kept equal.

This implies a strong and constantly operating check on population from the difficulty of subsistence.

Well, now, of course the whole argument turns on this assumption, and so far it is no more than an assumption that food tends to grow only at an arithmetical ratio while population tends to increase in a geometrical ratio. How is it that Malthus justified this contrast between the rate at which population and the rate at which food increases? His statement concerning the rate at which food increases runs as follows:

Through the animal and vegetable kingdom, nature has scattered the seeds of life abroad with the most profuse and liberal hand. She has been comparatively sparing in the room, and the nourishment necessary to rear them........

If you take single plant species you will find very many that given an opportunity will increase at a vastly more rapid rate than the human race. But the limiting factor, says, Malthus, is the room which is available for the increase of food. The race of plants and animals shrink under this great restrictive law.

You will observe here that Malthus does not say anything about what presently came to be one of the great tenets of classical political economy, namely, the law of diminishing returns, - the proposition that given a piece of land it is possible to increase the produce raised on that land more or less indefinitely, but that after some certain point of intensity of cultivation has been reached the additions to the produce that can be made by further increments of capital and labor in cultivation will be at a diminishing rate. A long while after Malthus published his Essay, John Stuart Mill hitched together Malthus's proposition concerning the tendency of population to increase at a geometrical ratio and this proposition concerning the diminishing returns from the cultivation of land. And by making the junction between the law of diminishing returns and the supposedly geometrical ratio of population to increase he gave the Malthusian theory of population a better logical form, more convincing than Malthus makes it.

So far as I can see, Malthus does not come much closer to demonstrating

-118-

the fact that food supply increases only in arithmetic ratio than the passage—
that I have read in which you see the critical item is the limitation of room fo
plant growth. If it were possible on the room available to increase output at
a steady rate by the expenditure of human labor, then there would be no logical
reason why a geometrically growing population should not maintain itself with no
decline of comfort. And Malthus really just leaves this as a vague notion that
the limitations of room do set an insuperable bar in the way of indefinite increase of food supply as population increases. If there is any passage in which
he comes closer to the law of diminishing returns that the one I told you, it is
one that follows a few passages later:

> In the next twenty-five years, it is impossible to suppose
> that the produce could be quadrupled. It would be contrary to all our
> knowledge of the qualities of land. The very utmost that we can conceive,
> is, that the increase in the second twenty-five years might equal the pre-
> sent produce.

That is the view of the situation given by the law of diminishing returns. If
you take the produce of England as it stands at one moment and try to increase
it, you can do so but then a quadrupling of the effort expended could not be expected to accomplish more than a doubling of the output. To suppose more than
that is contrary to our knowledge of the qualities of land.

> Let us then take this for our rule, though certainly far beyond the
> truth; and allow that by great exertion, the whole produce of the
> Island might be increased every twenty-five years, by a quantity of
> subsistence equal to what it at present produces. The most enthusiastic
> speculator cannot suppose a greater increase than this. In a few cen-
> turies it would make every acre of land in the Island like a garden.

> Yet this ratio of increase is evidently arithmetical.

- because it just adds the same amount of produce every twenty-five years.

> The geometric increase of man he discusses as follows:

> I said that population, when unchecked, increases in a geo-
> metrical ratio; and subsistence for man in an arithmetical ratio.

> Let us examine whether this proportion be just.

> I think it will be allowed, that no state has hitherto
> existed(at least that we have any account of) where the manners were so
> pure and simple, and the means of subsistence so abundant, that no
> check whatever has existed to early marriages.....

> In the United States of America, where the means of subsistence
> have been more ample, the manners of the people more pure, and consequentl;
> the checks to early marriages fewer, than in any of the modern states of
> Europe, the population has been found to double itself in twenty-five year;

And there was some such rate of increase in the American population according t
our censuses for, let us say, the first half of the nineteenth century.

> This ratio of increase, though short of the utmost power of
> population, yet as the result of actual experience, we will take as our
> rule; and say,

That population, when unchecked, goes on doubling itself every twenty-five years, or increases in a geometrical ratio.

Let us now take

—he turns to the other side—

any spot of earth, this Island for instance, and see in what ratio the subsistence it affords can be supposed to increase. ...

Then he goes on to the discussion that I have just read, supposing that the population of England at the time he wrote was about seven million, that the produce of the given island was sufficient for the subsistence of these seven million, and then considering what would happen after a while if population in England should grow at the rate characteristic of population.

Then he goes on with the great disproportion which exists between geometric increase in numbers of humanity and the ratio of increase in the food supply.

Taking the population of the world at any number, a thousand millions, for instance, the human species would increase in the ratio of—1,2,4,8,16,32,64,128,256,512, etc., and subsistence as—1,2,3,4,5,6, 7,8,9,10, etc. In two centuries and a quarter the population would be to the means of subsistence as 512 to 10; in three centuries, as 4096 to 13; and in two thousand years the difference would be almost incalculable, though the produce in that time would have increased to an immense extent.

So it is clearly demostrated, from his point of view, that the increase of population is necessarily held in check by the deficient supply of food. He goes on to discuss in his temperate fashion what actually does happen. All this he says is simply speculation as to what might happen if there were some magical way of supporting people without food. In practice

...The constant effort towards population, which is found to act even in the most vicious societies, increases the number of people before the means of subsistence are increased. The food therefore which before supported seven millions, must now be divided among seven millions and a half, or eight millions. The poor consequently must live much worse, and many of them be reduced to severe distress. The number of labourers also being above the proportion of the work in the market, the price of labour must tend toward a decrease; while the price of provisions would at the same time tend to rise. The labourer therefore must work harder to earn the same as he did before. During this season of distress, the discouragements to marriage, and the difficulty of rearing a family are so great, that population is at a stand. In the meantime, the cheapness of labour, the plenty of labourers, and the necessity of an increased industry amongst them, encourage cultivators to employ more labour upon their land; to turn up fresh soil, and to manure and improve more completely what is already in tillage; till ultimately the means of subsistence become in the same proportion to the population as at the period from which we set out. The situation of the labourer being then again tolerably comfortable, the restraints to population are in some degree loosened; and the same retrograde and progressive movements with respect to happiness are repeated.

So population in practice he conceives of as growing in number. You have your periods of not too severe discomfort, population spurts a bit, then the numbers become larger and they cannot live according to their wonted fashion on the food supply. The result of that period of distress is a check to marriage and increase in the infant death rate. Population is held down. But that means that labor becomes cheap and so there is an increased inducement to spend labor upon improving good agriculture. And the consequence is now something of a spurt in the food supply and that increased abundance of food removes the severe distress of recent years and population begins to increase again. But that increase in population cannot go very far before it outruns the increase in food supply and you have another period of severe hardships for the mass of men. He goes on:

> This sort of oscillation will not be remarked by superficial observers; and it may be difficult even for the most penetrating mind to calculate its periods. Yet that in all old states some such vibration does exist; though from various transverse causes, in a much less marked, and in a much more irregular manner than I have described it, no reflecting man who considers the subject deeply can well doubt.

This is the fundamental argument; and to Malthus the whole proposition is nearly self-evident. I will read you the words in which he concludes his exposition of the principle of population:

> The theory on which the truth of this position depends appears to me so extremely clear, that I feel at a loss to conjecture what part of it can be denied.

> That population cannot increase without the means of subsistence, is a proposition so evident that it needs no illustration.

> That population does invariably increase where there are the means of subsistence, the history of every people that have ever existed will abundantly prove.

You see that is an appeal to human experience and is exactly the appeal in which history since Malthus's time has shown his fundamental argument to go wrong. Since his time there has been an increase in subsistence, a rise in the standards of living in most of western Europe and in those districts settled by the European population across the seas, and that increase has been accompanied not by more rapid growth in population but slower growth. But Malthus could not see this and he seems to feel content with the security of this position as something demonstrated by history, the proposition that men cannot live without food. And he goes on:

> And, that the superior power of population cannot be checked without producing misery or vice, the ample portion of these two bitter ingredients in the cup of human life, and the continuance of the physical causes that seem to have produced them, bear too convincing a testimony.

That is the principle of population as he founded it in his first endeavor. This exposition takes up only a small portion of his book, and the rest of the book is devoted to a survey of experience to show how thoroughly in accord with the principle of population are the teachings of history. In this survey Malthus takes up first the condition of men in a savage state and then he takes up their condition under civilization and endeavors to show on the basis of really rather slight and flimsy studies of population increase in different quarters of the world at different times how population has in fact been kept down to the level of food.

In this connection he developes somewhat his idea of what it is that keeps men in practice from multiplying in numbers as rapidly as they do under such favorable conditions as were presented in his time by the United States of America where fertile land was abundant. His development is to show that there are two general classes of checks which keep people from multiplying; one is what he calls the preventive check, and the other is what he calls the positive check.

> ...An intimate view of the state of society in any one country of Europe which may serve equally for all, will enable us to answer this question, and to say, that a foresight of the difficulties attending the rearing of a family, acts as a preventive check; and the actual distress of some of the lower classes, by which they are disabled from giving the proper food and attention to their children, acts as a positive check, to the natural increase of population.

Now this preventive check, he says, operates in some degree through all the ranks of society in England. He goes on to say that well educated men who do not have any considerable property are likely to hesitate very much before they plunge some woman they love into the distress which would ensue from a fruitful marriage when it has turned out that the husband was not able to earn sufficient to keep his wife and children in the social status to which the wife and he had been accustomed. Then he goes on to say that

> The sons of tradesmen and farmers are exhorted not to marry and generally find it necessary to pursue this advice, till they are settled in some business, or farm, that may enable them to support a family.....

So among classes of that sort the preventive check is fairly effective.

> The labourer who earns eighteen pence a day,

- that seems to have been the standard earnings in agricultural districts in Malthus's time -

> and lives with some degree of comfort as a single man, will hesitate a little before he divides that pittance among four or five, which seems to be just sufficient for one.........

And servants he thinks particularly are likely to be influenced by the preventive check.

> ...They possess the necessaries, and even the comforts of life, almost in as great plenty as their masters. Their work is easy, and their food luxurious, compared with the class of labourers. And their sense of dependence is weakened by the conscious power of changing their masters, if they feel themselves offended. Thus comfortably situated at present, what are their prospects in marrying. Without knowledge or capital either for business, or farming, and unused and therefore unable to earn a subsistence by daily labour, their only refuge seems to be a miserable alehouse, which certainly offers no very enchanting prospect of a happy evening to their lives. By much the greater part, therefore, deterred by this uninviting view of their future situation, content themselves with remaining single where they are.

So there is a preventive check to population which has some influence even upon members of the laboring classes, has more influence on servants, is more or less

generally regarded by the sons of farmers and small tradesmen, and still more
likely to control the minds of men of education.

> ...it will be allowed, that the preventive check to population in this
> country operates, though with varied force, through all the classes of the
> community. The same observation will hold true with regard to all old
> states. The effects, indeed, of these restraints upon marriage are but
> too conspicuous in the consequent vices that are produced in almost every
> part of the world; vices that are continually involving both sexes in
> inextricable unhappiness.

But the preventive check with accompaniment of vice is insufficient
to keep population down in practice to the level of the food supply. And the con
sequence is that the positive check comes into action.

> The positive check to population, by which I mean, the check
> which represses an increase which is already begun,

– does not prevent it, but represses an increase already begun –

> is confined chiefly, though not perhaps solely, to the lowest orders of
> society.......

And he goes on to tell how this works.

> ...it has been very generally remarked by those who have attended to
> bills of mortality,

– bills of mortality is the name given in England at that time to their vital
statistics, records of births, and of course in this case particularly, of deaths

> that of the number of children who die annually, much too great a pro-
> portion belongs to those, who may be supposed unable to give their offspring
> proper food and attention;

Even now we know that the death rates, particularly among very young children,
are very uneven between classes of people having different incomes. The lower
the income, the higher the infant mortality rate as a rule.

> exposed as they are occasionally to severe distress, and confined,
> perhaps, to unwholesome habitations and hard labour. This mortality
> among the children of the poor has been constantly taken notice of in all
> towns. It certainly does not prevail in an equal degree in the country;
> but the subject has not hitherto received sufficient attention to enable
> any one to say, that there are not more deaths in proportion, among the
> children of the poor, even in the country, than among those of the middling
> and higher classes.

So this survey of the actual increase of population under the conditions
of savagery and civilization seems in his eyes to confirm the speculative, theore
tical argument based upon his two ratios. And once more he sums up again. I will
read:

> Famine seems to be the last, the most dreadful resource of
> nature. The power of population is so superior to the power in the earth
> to produce subsistence for man, that premature death must in some shape
> or other visit the human race. The vices of mankind

--which he seems to think pretty regularly a preventive check--

are active and able ministers of depopulation. They are the precursors in the great army of destruction; and often finish the dreadful work themselves. But should they fail in this war of extermination, sickly seasons, epidemics, pestilence, and plague, advance in terrific array, and sweep off their thousands and ten thousands. Should success be still incomplete; gigantic inevitable famine stalks in the rear, and with one mighty blow, levels the population with the food of the world.

Now it was this view of Malthus, set forth in such uncompromising form, that led the sharp-tongued Carlyle to call political economy the dismal science. It does seem a dismal prospect that Malthus demostrated to be the fate of human kind. The great bulk of men must, according to his view, give up all hope of ever living in any higher degree of comfort than that in which they existed in his own day.

In his second edition Malthus found some escape from this dilemma, but here no escape is held out. A preventive check acts, to be sure, but it is inadequate; and what is worse when men delay their marriage they are very apt to plunge into vicious moral habits which have the same effect of retarding population increase.

Having demonstrated the principle, both theoretical and historical, Malthus then turns to discuss the errors concerning population which have been committed by earlier writers. He finds some fault with Mr. Wallace. Adam Smith, he holds, made a gross error in supposing that every increase of capital was an increase in the funds for subsistence. It is not true if you accummulate a greater amount of wealth in the nation that that means a proportionate fund for the means of subsistence. For it is patent on his researches that England has grown in wealth and yet that has not meant any sensible long-run amelioration in the condition of the lower classes. And in particular, he pays his respects to Mr. Godwin, telling us what is the fundamental cause of the error into which Godwin fell. And that cause is Godwin's mistaken ideas about human nature. Here is an economist coming to a realization that a difference between his own views and those of an authority from whom he differs is rooted in differences of psychological assumptions. He says:

Mr. Godwin considers man too much in the light of a being merely intellectual. This error, at least such I conceive it to be, pervades his whole work, and mixes itself with all his reasonings. The voluntary actions of men may originate in their opinions; but these opinions will be very differently modified in creatures compounded of a rational faculty and corporal propensities, from what they would be, in beings wholly intellectual. ...

... The cravings of hunger, the love of liquor, the desire of possessing a beautiful woman, will urge men to actions, of the fatal consequences of which, to the general interests of society, they are perfectly well convinced, even at the very time they commit them. Remove their bodily cravings, and they would not hesitate a moment in determining against such actions. Ask them their opinion of the same conduct in another person, and they would immediately reprobate it. But in their own case, and under all the circumstances of their situation with these bodily cravings, the decision of the compound being is different from the conviction of the rational being.

The superiority of the pleasures of intellect to those of sense, Mr.
Godwin considers as a fundamental truth. Taking all circumstances into
consideration, I should be disposed to agree with him; but how am I to
communicate this truth to a person who has scarcely ever felt intellectual
pleasure. I may as well attempt to explain the nature and beauty of
colours to a blind man.

So Godwin's notions about the perfectibility of man as an earthly vision
of a future in which felicity would be distributed among all members of society
that lived in a cultivated state of equality must be set down most reluctantly
but still most firmly as a fair delusion!

It is, undoubtedly, a most disheartening reflection, that the
great obstacle in the way to any extraordinary improvement in society, is
of a nature that we can never hope to overcome. The perpetual tendency
in the race of man to increase beyond the means of subsistence, is one
of the general laws of animated nature, which we can have no reason
to expect will change. Yet, discouraging as the contemplation of this
difficulty must be, to those whose exertions are laudably directed to the
improvement of the human species, it is evident, that no possible good can
arise from any endeavours to slur it over, or keep it in the background.
On the contrary, the most baleful mischiefs may be expected from the un-
manly conduct of not daring to face truth, because it is unpleasing. ...

Now having finished this demonstration and then come to such a dismal
prospect of the future, Malthus seems to have been a little troubled in his mind.
He had been trained for the Church; and it seemed to him, as he thought about the
principle of population, that it might be regarded by many people as a sad reflection upon the benevolence of the Creator. And he felt a poignant need of trying to justify the principle of population with the doctrine that the world is
controlled by a beneficent and omnipotent God. So he set forth to justify the
ways of God regarding the population to mankind. His argument is really very
interesting. It sounds to us quaint. And perhaps he did not feel so sure of
its validity, for in later editions he made less of this point. The general run
of his argument I should like to put before you. It is to the effect that despite his omnipotence the great Creator, almighty as he is, may find that it is
necessary to take a certain time, or at least what appears to us time, to accomplish his ends. The need that he seems to have in mind with reference to man is
to create spiritual happiness, — happiness that exalted qualities of mind. This
happiness is created out of the dust of the earth. And to accomplish this great
task God has found certain methods which from the human point of view seem to be
very slow-acting. This, Malthus goes on, is

not for the trial, but for the creation and formation of mind; a process
necessary, to awaken inert chaotic matter, into spirit; to sublimate the
dust of the earth into soul; to elicit an ethereal spark from the clod of
clay. ...

The process of accomplishing that is first of all to give man his senses.

The first great awakeners of the mind seem to be the wants of the
body. They are the first stimulants that rouse the brain of infant man into
sentient activity: and such seems to be the sluggishness of original matter,
that unless, by a peculiar course of excitements, other wants, equally powerful, are generated, these stimulants seem, even afterwards, to be necessary,
to continue that activity which they first awakened. The savage would
slumber for ever under his tree, unless he were roused from his torpor by the

cravings of hunger, or the pinchings of cold; and the exertions that he makes to avoid these evils, by procuring food, and building himself a covering, are the exercises which form and keep in motion his faculties, which otherwise would sink into listless inactivity................*.....
Necessity has been with great truth called the mother of invention. Some of the noblest exertions of the human mind have been set in motion by the necessity of satisfying the wants of the body.

Well, from that point of view you see the principle of population may be regarded as a part of God's design for mankind.

To furnish the most unremitted excitements of this kind, and to urge man to further the gracious designs of Providence, by the full cultivation of the earth, it has been ordained, that population should increase much faster than food. This general law,(as it has appeared in the former parts of the essay) undoubtedly produces much partial evil; but a little reflection may, perhaps, satisfy us, that it produces a great overbalance of good. Strong incentives seem necessary to create exertion; and to direct this exertion, and form the reasoning faculty, it seems absolutely necessary, that the Supreme Being should act always according to general laws. The constancy of the laws of nature, or the certainty, with which we may expect the same effect, from the same causes, is the foundation of the faculty of reason........

The principle, according to which population increases, prevents the vices of mankind, or the accidents of nature, the partial evils arising from   general laws, from obstructing the high purpose of the creation. It keeps the inhabitants of the earth always fully up to the level of the means of subsistence; and is constantly acting upon man as a powerful stimulus, urging him to the further cultivation of the earth, and to enable it, consequently, to support a more extended population.

That the difficulties of life, contribute to generate talents, every day's experience must convince us. The exertions that men find it necessary to make, in order to support themselves or families, frequently awaken faculties, that might otherwise have lain forever dormant; and it has been commonly remarked, that new and extraordinary situations generally create minds adequate to grapple with the difficulties in which they are involved.

So it seems that the idea of this harsh-seeming principle of population is no reflection upon the benevolence of the Creator. On the contrary, it is a necessary part of his general scheme for awakening our mental and spiritual faculties that if we lived in ease might remain forever dormant. But so long as we can be sure that indefinitely the race is going to tend to outrun the food supply, so long as we may be sure that we shall be forced through these exertions to the best mental and spiritual development.

XXII

THE EFFECT OF MALTHUS'S ESSAY; HIS LATER EDITIONS

The first edition of Malthus's Essay on the Principle of Population achieved a very great popular success. That was secured by its general character. It
was a book that dealt with a subject which was beginning to concern Englishmen
very closely, and it was on the popular side so far as poeple who were able to
buy books were concerned. They were, of course, the class of people who had to
pay the poor rate; and the rapidly increasing cost of these taxes for the support
of paupers was becoming a burden of rather rapidly increasing size. And then the
matter under discussion was interesting. Malthus laid out the problem in
a broad and clear fashion; he argued the case of his two ratios in a seemingly
convincing way. Anybody could understand his meaning. And finally the whole subject was made more attractive by controversy. Here was that brilliant cultivator
of Utopia, William Godwin, stating that mankind had illimitable prospects of
improvement before it, and here was the characteristically stolid Englishman,
Malthus, seeming to prove with certainty that the speculator's Utopias were vague.
Godwin himself testifies to the effect of Malthus's book upon public opinion. He
says sorrowfully that it converted friends of progress into reactionaries by the
hundreds.

Malthus's Essay had another notable success in that it was one of the two
influences which led William Pitt to drop a favorite scheme of his own. William
Pitt was still Prime Minister. In 1796 he had proposed a new plan of poor relief
in order to encourage the growth of population. Of course, now that England was
engaged in a very serious war, the thoughts of statesmen were turned, as they
always do under such circumstances, to the problem of maintaining an adequate
supply of man-power - not only an adequate number of soldiers to fill the ranks of
the armies, but also an adequate number of workers to provide the materials of
war for the armed forces and keep the civilian population in good morale. In
order to stimulate the increase of population, William Pitt had suggested that the
old English system of poor laws which, while they professed to grant relief to
people who could not really earn their living, had nevertheless granted relief
in such a grudging fashion as to make the penalty of inability to earn a living a
very severe one. For that old scheme he proposed to grant very liberal relief to
families that had numerous children. He said in the House of Commons in his
speech introducing the measure: "Let us make poor relief in such cases a matter
of right and honor instead of a ground of approbrium and contempt." That bill, as
I say, was introduced in 1796, but in 1800 - very early in 1800 - about a year and
a half after Malthus's first edition had appeared, Pitt withdrew the bill, telling
the House of Commons that he still thought his scheme good, but that he had
droppedit in deference to those whose opinions he was bound to respect. These
people were Malthus, on the one hand, and Jeremy Bentham on the other. His bill
from the point of view of Malthus, would have encouraged still more that rising
tide of population which threatened such dire results to the working classes.
Jeremy Bentham at the same time wrote one of the cogent papers on the subject
though it was not published until much later, and his paper came to the attention
of the Prime Minister.

The success of the first edition fixed Malthus's career. He became in his
generation the great English authority upon population and the poor laws. But he
was himself far less satisfied than most of his readers with his first edition.
The more he thought about the matter, the more he came to realize that he had comparatively little basis in experience to build upon, that his review of the way
population actually increased in a state of savagery and state of civilization was

after all a pretty superficial affair. While he had set up his arguments on the
basis of two ratios, he had argued from certain assumptions which he took for
granted. He never felt content in his own mind until he had tested his speculative opinions as well as he could by appeal to experience. As I have said,
Malthus was temperamentally a realist, and his first essay was a clever piece of
dialectics. He wanted to find out whether the real facts of the case sustained
the view he had put forward and argued rather than supported by evidence. As
he said in the preface to his second edition, he was determined to turn his
leisure reading "towards an historical examination of the effects of the principle of population on the past and present state of society."

Although he was a Fellow of Jesus College, Malthus had considerable
leisure and he turned that leisure to ransacking the literature directly bearing
upon the increase of population. He hunted through a variety of sources to learn
what he might about the size of populations in various countries of the world in
the past and in more recent periods, and upon the rates of increase. Then in
order to enlarge his observation of contemporary conditions, he went off in the
summer vacation of the year following his first publication with a party of
college friends to visit the continent. They went to Germany, Sweden, Norway,
Finland and Russia, - the only part of the continent that was then open to an Englishman, for at that time England was at war with France so English subjects did
not find ready access to France, Italy, or the western part of Europe. Everywhere
he studied, as well as a traveler could, the population problems which were presented in different countries; and particularly he tried to find out in some detail what it was that kept the population of old, thickly settled regions from becoming so numerous that the food would be inadequate.

Then in 1802, when the short peace of Amiens between England and France
was established, he went to the continent again, this time visiting France and
Switzerland. Altogether he devoted five years to a very careful survey of all
the evidence on the subject of population, and then in 1803   brought out his
second edition. It was again called An Essay on the Principle of Population, but
it had a more elaborate sub-title. This time he signed his book T.R. Malthus, A.M.,
Fellow of Jesus College, Cambridge. This second edition is the form in which
nowadays we commonly read the Essay, - or one of the later editions which were
subject to comparatively little further change.

This second edition was a very much more substantial performance than the
first. It contained four times the volume of material. Its survey of the historical and contemporary materials bearing on the numbers of the population and rates
of increase was far more thorough. And what was more to the purpose, the important difference between the first and second editions was that Malthus modified
his theory of the checks by which population is kept down to subsistence. This
modification consisted in introducing what he now called the moral check as one
of the means by which the numbers of mankind are limited. As he put it in the
preface of the second edition:

> Throughout the whole of the present work I have so far differed
> in principle from the former, as to suppose the action of another check
> to population which does not come under the head either of vice or misery;
> and, in the latter part I have endeavoured to soften some of the harshest
> conclusions of the first Essay.

To a modern reader who comes across the remarks in the first edition about
the preventive check, it might still seem that after all the moral check is merely
a new name for the preventive check. But seemingly Malthus himself thought of the
preventive check as hesitation on the part of people to marry because they could

forsee the misery they might bring upon themselves by acquiring families before their earning power was equal to maintaining them in the way in which they and their prospective wives were accustomed to live. And it was not this preliminary caution, it was misery and vice which was the effective check to population. But now on further reflection he came to the idea that it really is possible for people to treat the question of what they usually individually do about marrying and begetting children from the moral point of view, that the preventive check does not necessarily mean simply an increase of vice. What he recommended to all individuals and of course particularly to members of the working class was that they should postpone marriage until the time came when they had a reasonable prospect of earning incomes sufficient to support their families in the conditions to which they were accustomed and that in the meantime they should practice continence.

This moral check, that is, the idea that men would gradually learn to practice self-control in the matter of procreating their kind, dispenses with the necessity of the elaborate attempt in the first book to justify the ways of God to man in respect to the number of population, for here he made it clear that men can make the conditions which the number of population creates for them a means for acquiring moral virtues. The Lord is trying to give all a long process of education; there is no other reason in the nature of things why people should suffer any evils from the principle of population; vice and misery are not really necessary. And taking this view, Malthus could contemplate the future of mankind with much more hopeful eyes than he could do in the first edition when he was holding that population was everywhere kept from expanding beyond a certain rate either by misery or by vice. When one took into account the possibility of applying the moral check, that is, of postponing marriage and practicing continence before marriage, it seemed comparatively easy to supply every country with just that number of people who could be supported at the most desirable standard of living.

Malthus seems to have had, when he published this second Essay, no idea in his mind that there might be such a thing as we are becoming familiar with under the general popular phrase of birth control. Birth control doctrines, however, began to be preached toward the close of his own life by no less considerable public figures than Robert Owen, the great Utopian Socialist, and Francis Place, the celebrated radical tailor whose biography has been so charmingly written by the late Graham Wallas. And rather curiously these doctrines concerning the possibility of marriage without children were given the name of Neo-Malthusianism. Probably that name would have caused Malthus himself grave concern. He seems not to have approved of Neo-Malthusianism. The moral check to him to the end of his life apparently consisted of postponing marriage and during that period practicing a perfect continence. Perhaps he would have felt that this more or less technical and quasi-mechanical way of trying to fight the dangers of over-population was an unworthy one.

In this second edition, then Malthus's doctrine of population comes to its full form, so far as he was concerned, though, as I have remarked, it became a mor cogent piece of reasoning when John Stuart Mill at last related it organically to the law of diminishing returns from land. This new edition was much less adapted to popular reading than the first because it was a vastly more learned, more thorough, and necessarily more extensive book. But it reinforced Malthus's intellectual reputation and made him more than ever the great authority upon population. Replies to the argument in the newer form kept appearing pretty regularly and from time to time Malthus found occasion to issue new editions which differed from the second merely in that they contained replies to new adversaries. Thus he brought out a third edition in 1806, a fourth in 1807, a fifth in 1817, and a sixth in 1826, near the end of his life. That sixth edition is the best of all to read because it contains the very last teachings of the author.

Malthus not only became, by virtue of these studies of population, the great authority upon that special subject, but he also became what I think one might call the first professional economist in England. You could hardly call Adam Smith a professional economist. Economics was still in his day one of the moral branches and he thought of it as one of the subdivisions of moral philosophy. And after he had written a book, The Wealth of Nations, he became a public official. But Malthus in 1805 became a professor of political economy and history; the two chairs being combined, at Haileybury College, a little college which the East India Company set up in the south of England to train men who were going out to India in its service. And besides his teachings of economics he continued to think and write about many phases of the subject for the rest of his life. His pamphlets are numerous and celebrated. In one of them he appears as the co-discoverer with West and Ricardo of the differential theory of rent, that item in economic doctrine which presently played so great a role in the organization of what Malthus himself called the new political economy. He was the master to whom the proprietors of the Encyclopedia Britannica of that day turned to for articles on political economy. He was one of the authorities regularly called before royal commissions when economic questions were under discussion in Parliament. He became a close friend of David Ricardo. The two were very active correspondents; and though by temperament they differed radically, each exercised a very considerable influence over the opinions of the other.

Finally, as an outgrowth of his teaching in college, he published a treatise under the title Political Economy which came out in 1820 and of which a second edition with annotations by the author was published after his death in 1836; a book that, though better in many ways, from the modern standpoint, than Ricardo's Principles of Political Economy, has exercised considerably less influence upon the development of English economic theory.

Malthus was, as I have said, very distinctly a realist in temperament. His belief in basing opinions on economic problems, so far as possible, upon a close study of facts, had doubtless been confirmed by the fact that his chief attention had been given to the problem of population, a problem concerning which he could get, even in his day, rather abundant statistical information, a problem that could be treated largely upon a factual basis. And you find, if you look into his Political Economy that this realistic bent of his mind is evident on almost every page. You will also find, if you read his correspondence with Ricardo, how widely these two men differed in their general methods of attack upon any problem. Ricardo was a man exceptionally gifted in the art of speculation; he wanted to set all his questions in the most abstract and general form that was possible, and he had comparatively little faith in or fondness for factual investigation or for basing his argumentation upon anything less than supposititious cases. It is a method of work which can be and often has been gravely abused, but it is a method of speculation which, in the hands of a man who has sagacity in choosing the supposititious cases to be argued about, has very great advantages, - advantages which were far more striking in the days of Malthus and Ricardo than at present, because there were very many problems at that time concerning which men could hardly learn anything of a factual nature. It was almost necessary to argue about them, if you argued at all, on the basis of definite assumptions; and in that type of argumentation Ricardo was one of the most successful dialecticians.

One of the advantages of that method of developing economic theory is that it enables a man to work very fast. A person who does that type of work does not lose any time in gathering material; he formulates his supposititious cases upon the basis of his general observations, supplemented, no doubt, by more or less casual reading of statistical evidence. By working on cases which you make up in your own head, it is comparatively a quick and simple procedure in the hands of a person like Ricardo. It is capable of yielding brilliant results and of yielding them rapidly. On the other hand, Malthus based his work on factual information, and his discussion consisted very largely in dwelling on limitations of our knowledge thus lacking the sweeping conclusions of the sort which Ricardo could draw on the basis of supposititious cases which he believed applicable to the world in which we actually live. If they are applicable at all, they are applicable only with many exceptions and reservations; but a book that is a discussion of economi problems dwelling always on these reservations and exceptions and limitations is a book that is by no means likely to impress the minds of the mass of men with an thing like the firmness and promptness with which those minds can be impressed by a discussion of the kind that a Ricardo could produce. So it happened that Malthus, though he had established his reputation as the foremost living economis in England years before Ricardo published his first pamphlet, and though he alway continued to be looked upon as one of the great pillars of the classical school because of his contribution to the discussion of population, nevertheless was pre sently overshadowed by his more brilliant friend and contemporary. There are plent of people who still think of Malthus's most valuable contribution to the development of economic theory as having been the influence that he exercised upon Ricardo, for curiously enough these two men who differed so greatly in their methods of work and in their ways of approaching any kind of human problem became very close and admiring friends. They had continual differences of opinion about the several subjects which occupied them, but those differences of opinion were alway occasions for their writing long argumentative letters to each other, each man do ing his best to sustain his view, but by putting that view forcibly before the other doubtless contributing greatly to the development of the other man's opinio That sort of service Malthus certainly did render to Ricardo. Still I am incline to think that anyone nowadays who goes back and reads Malthus's own book on political economy cannot help feeling, as I have said, that it is a rather remarkable production, a book which on not a few, even of the technical questions of economi theory, occupies a position which in the light of later knowledge seems sounder than the position taken by Ricardo.

XXIII

DAVID RICARDO: HIS LIFE AND EARLY WRITINGS; THE BULLION CONTROVERSY

The new political economy which Ricardo and his circle developed in the first quarter of the nineteenth century was based very largely upon the work of Adam Smith. The classical political economists were not men much interested in the history of political economy. To them it seemed as though The Wealth of Nation summed up almost all that need be known about past thinking in this field. They looked upon not merely the Mercantilists but also the Physiocrats as people whose work was viciated by fundamental errors; and it was more a matter of curiosity tha of any desire to know what they thought that their works were read. Indeed, it is curious to read opinions in contemporary letters. For instance, Francis Horner stated in his diary that he found the French economists unintelligible.*

*"This afternoon I gave a second or third sitting to the doctrine of the French Economists, which I perceive will cost me many an hour before I comprehend their meaning in the first place, and in the next place form my opinion on the justness of their principles. I have not yet been able to procure Quesnai's original work I can understand Turgot's treatise on the formation and distribution of riches, but I see no reason to admit his doctrines; but as to Mirabeau's Philosophie

The whole generation was a generation intent upon constructive work, and what they valued in the past was simply that upon which they could build. But while they regarded <u>The Wealth of Nations</u> as summing up all that was important in past economic work, they were beginning to be rather critical of many of Adam Smith's doctrines. Arthur Young, for example, the great traveler through the rural districts of France and England wrote that no abler work had been published but none fuller of poisonous errors. Jeremy Bentham had, as he believed, set Adam Smith right on usury. Malthus had changed the whole perspective at which people looked at the problems of population. Lord Lauderdale had pointed out Adam Smith's errors in regarding the wealth of a nation as the sum total of the wealth of the individuals who composed it, omitting the considerable amount of public property in the country. J. B. Say, the leading Continental disciple of Smith, declared that <u>The Wealth of Nations</u> was destitute of method; and he introduced a new framework for the work published in his treatise: successive books which dealt in an orderly fashion with production, exchange, distribution, and consumption.

Francis Horner, when invited by a publisher to bring out an annotated edition of <u>The Wealth of Nations</u>, - that is, invited to supply notes which would correct what was amiss in the original work and bring certain matters down to date - he declined on the ground that he was reluctant to expose Smith's errors. But what Horner refused to do, others did. Before the turn of the century, annotated editions began to appear, editions in which the editors definitely set themselves to bring his discussions down to date. The first was published by W. Playfair in 1805, and the second appeared only nine years later, edited by D. Buchanan.

But, of course, corrections of detail in <u>The Wealth of Nations</u> would not have produced a new type of economic theory. For that there was required something far more fundamental; and this more fundamental thing came into English economic thinking because the economists centered upon a new problem, a problem which was brought to their attention by a change in social life. So in discussing the development of classical political economy, and the appearance of a new type of economic theory differing from that represented by Adam Smith, we shall again have to follow in large measure the same method we used in dealing with Adam Smith: we shall have to see what it was in the social life of the time that turned people's attention in another direction.

Before doing that, I ought to say a bit about the unusual preparation for his work which was enjoyed by the central figure in the group that produced this political economy, that is, about the earlier life of David Ricardo. Ricardo was born in London in 1772. He was the son of a Jewish family which had settled in London only comparatively few years before his birth, a family that had lived successively in Spain, Italy, and Holland, and then had moved to England. His father had opened in London a mercantile and brokerage house, but, as happened in the case of a good many such concerns, his father had gradually turned from dealing in commodities to dealing in bills of exchange and in public securities. David was put into this business at fourteen years of age, so that his schooling was cut short; and in that business he doubtless had a very thorough and excellent training in a type of work which required very close figuring and the continual exercise of good judgment.

A great change in his life came when he fell in love at the age of twenty-one (1793) with a Quakeress. Of course, from the point of view of an orthodox Jew

Rurale, of which I have read a few chapters, I can scarcely attach a meaning to his terms." - Memoirs and Correspondence of Francis Horner, M.P., edited by his brother Leonard Horner; vol. I, p. 160.

like his father, it was impossible that the family should ally itself with a family of gentiles, and the young man had to choose between the lady whom he loved and continuation in the family tradition. He decided upon a very bold course. He left his home, he left the synagogue, he left his father's business, and married the Quakeress when he was only twenty-one, and set up in business for himself – set up with a very small capital. Late in life he told one of his friends that at that time he had barely ₤800, – a very slender capital, even in those days, with which to set up a financial house in London. But he had the backing and support of some of his family friends, and what was far more important he had business genius. So that, despite his extremely slender capital at the beginning, he very rapidly made his way.

While he was doing so, he kept up a series of studies in which he felt a great inclination, though his schooling had been cut short, to work rather systematically at mathematics, at chemistry, at geology, and minerology. And then by accident in 1799, while he was staying in Bath for his wife's health for a short time, he came across a book that centered his intellectual interests in economics; that was The Wealth of Nations. He read it with the liveliest interest, not to say excitement. At that time he was twenty-seven years old. And from that time forward he devoted a large part of what leisure he could get from his business to further readings in this field. He read Malthus's Essay on the Principles of Population with an interest only second to that which he had felt in The Wealth of Nations. He followed the rather large and rapidly increasing pamphlet literature on economic questions of the day, and when the Edinburgh Review was presently established – the first of the great quarterlies that dealt, at least in a quasi-scientific manner with problems of current interest – he became a regular sub-scriber and close reader of the articles on economic subjects.

He continued to prosper in his business; between 1799, when he first read The Wealth of Nations, and 1809 he established for himself a strong position in the financial world of London. The strength of that position is shown by the fact that he became one of what were then called the loan brokers – nowadays we would say that he became a member of the underwriting syndicate – which handled the large government issues of loans made necessary by the wars with Napoleon.

In 1807, while England was carrying on the doubtful struggle against Napoleon, an economic controversy arose which particularly attracted his attention. A certain William Spence published a pamphlet called "Britain Independent of Commerce," – a pamphlet in which he sought to say that Napoleon's Continental policy could produce no serious consequences upon England. That is, the effort of Napoleon to cut off all English commerce with the Continent would not injure England vitally because after all there was just one source of national wealth and that was agriculture, – a recrudescence of Physiocratic ideas, though I do not know that William Spence got the notion from headquarters.

This pamphlet attracted the attention of James Mill who was at that time a struggling literary hack in London trying to keep a large and rapidly increasing family going while he spent all the time that was not required for making bread and butter upon the great history of British India, the book with which he expected to establish his position in life and make himself secure. Mill replied to Spence in a pamphlet called "Commerce Defended" in which he tried to explode the policy that agriculture is in any greater sense than manufacture or commerce a source of wealth. This pamphlet of Mill's came into the hands of David Ricardo. Ricardo read it with his customary avidity for economic analysis, and had a meeting with the writer; that meeting led to an intimacy that had a notable effect upon the whole course of Ricardo's life.

For one thing, James Mill was at this time the closest friend and associate of Jeremy Bentham, the central figure in that small group of Philosophical Radicals who were beginning to gather round the old sage in his London seclusion. And Mill promptly introduced his new friend to Mr. Bentham. Bentham and Ricardo seem never to have become very intimate, though they remained on very good terms with each other until Ricardo's death. Though Ricardo was a much younger man, he died some years before Bentham. In politics Ricardo always avowed himself a disciple of Jeremy Bentham; how much he owed to Bentham intellectually is hard to say.

But certainly the debt he owed to Mill was very heavy, not so much that Mill suggested ideas to him but that he was a born schoolmaster, a grand trainer in logical methods of developing arguments and of presenting them. Ricardo used to send his writings to Mill and ask for Mill's criticisms. To what Mill did for him may be attributed, I dare say, a large part of such success as he finally achieved in putting out his ideas in intelligible form, for to the end of his days Ricardo always suffered the handicap of inadequate schooling. He could put his ideas forward in singularly compact shape and in fairly good order when he was writing a letter or pamphlet, but for discussions of a more elaborate sort he felt himself deficient in organizing skill. Indeed, it is perhaps questionable whether Ricardo would ever have become a writer had it not been for the urging of his friend James Mill.

His first venture into print came as the result of his indulgence in the Englishman's habit of writing to newspapers. In 1809, when people were beginning to discuss the question whether the Bank of England notes were really depreciating, Ricardo sat down and wrote a brief and vigorous letter to the Morning Chronicle, pointing out that if Bank of England notes were really worth their face value in gold, then there could be no more than a trifling premium upon the foreign exchanges which were then on a gold basis. You remember that one of the first results of the series of wars with the French Republic and Napoleon had been the necessity of suspending specie payments at the Bank of England, and that left the Bank of England notes by far the most important form of money in circulation. As a consequence of that, we now saw prices had begun to rise, and fluctuated very violently. The country had an irredeemable paper standard. But there were people in Ricardo's days, as there are in every generation since, who hold that Bank of England notes had not depreciated, but gold had appreciated in value. And it was to explode that already ancient heresy that Ricardo first entered the lists as a newspaper writer.

Two or three people wrote some tart rejoinders, and Ricardo added two letters to his first one. And then he was persuaded in the spring of 1810 to publish a small pamphlet called The High Price of Bullion, a Proof of the Depreciation of Bank Notes. That pamphlet was republished a few years ago by Professor J.H. Hollander, and those of you who are interested in Ricardo's development may like to look at it. You will also find it in Ricardo's Works edited by McCulloch.

Now that pamphlet is interesting, particularly because it shows how Ricardo set about discussing an economic problem. Of course, as a man who had been brought up in a bill brokerage house, as a man who had long and extensive dealings in foreign trade, a man acquainted with all the intricacies of the market for bills and securities, he knew the facts which were under discussion at first hand. But when he set out to explain what was the real situation with regard to Bank of England notes, he began by expounding what he calls the laws that regulate the distribution of the precious metals throughout the world, that is, he started with a great generalization. Professor James Bonar says that, so far as he knows, — and he is one of the people who has read the literature of this time most intensively - that is the first occasion an economist is found using the word "laws" in this sense, the first time anyone is thinking of economic laws in the way Ricardo presently taught everyone to think of economic laws.

He started then with the laws which regulate the distribution of the precious metals throughout the world; and what few facts he cited in the course of his discussion he cited not as a demonstration of the laws but as illustrations of their working. And yet, to repeat, he was a man who knew the facts. Now that means that in the course of his intellectual operations he instinctively thought about a thing in terms of generalizations, - the generalization that it was interesting and important to recognize; and so far as one had any use for facts, it was as illustrations of generalizations.

This pamphlet of Ricardo's had a most gratifying effect. It promptly ran through four editions and it helped Francis Horner, who was then in the House of Commons, to get appointed that committee which soon became celebrated under the title of the Bullion Committee, a committee of the members of the House whose business it was to study and report upon the conditions of the currency. The Bullion Committee, under Francis Horner's skilful guidance - for he was included in the Committee - presently published the document which is always cited now-a-days as The Bullion Report, - a landmark in the development of monetary theory and a book of such importance that only four or five years ago Professor Edwin Cannan published an edition of it with copious introductory matter and explanatory notes. That is one of the volumes which any person who is interested in Ricardo's development does well to read.

It is true that the Bullion Committee took very great pains. They certainly did not mention Ricardo's name, but they did adopt substantially his theory of the currency situation, a view that the Bank of England notes were depreciated and that the measure of their depreciation was to be found in the premium upon bullion.

Even with the backing of the parliamentary committee, however, the view that the Bank of England notes were depreciated was not universally accepted; and presently one of the leading merchants in London, Charles Bosanquet, a man of large experience, challenged the views of the Bullion Committee and the opinions expounded in Ricardo's pamphlet. He put himself forward as a man of facts and said that Ricardo was a mere theorist. Among other things, he cited a table showing the rates of exchange between London and Paris and Hamburg, a table which he said proved that the phenomena in England were to be explained in differences in the price of international exchange, and all the talk about the consequence of the high price of bullion was beside the point. The fact was, of course, that the Bank of England notes had not fallen in value but that because of interference with foreign trade gold bullion had risen in value.

Ricardo answered these Practical Observations on the Report of the Bullion Committee, published by Bosanquet, in a new pamphlet,* and again he showed in a most interesting was his peculiar way of treating economic problems. Regarding those tables of Bosanquet showing the London exchange on Paris and Hamburg, he pointed out that if they were correct, a dealer would have made a profit of a hundred per cent per annum for four years by shipping gold from Hamburg to Paris, a fact that presumably a non-professional reader of this table would never note, but which Ricardo as an old hand at foreign exchanges saw on the face of the figures. And then he went on to say that "For any man to compare the account of the

*Reply to Mr. Bosanquet's Practical Observations on the Report of the Bullion Committee, 1811.

Hamburg exchange, and of the Parisian, and not to see that the accounts were incorrect, that the facts could not be as so stated, is very like a man who is all for fact and nothing for theory. Such men can hardly ever sift their facts. They are credulous, necessarily so, because they have no standard of reference."

Ricardo's share in the bullion controversy brought him before the public in a more prominent fashion than before; and, what was more important for his mental development, brought him into contact with Malthus. By this time Malthus, the most celebrated economist of the age, was teaching history and political economy in the East India College down at Haileybury. As a teacher he had to touch in his courses upon certain problems relating to the currency, and when Ricardo's pamphlet came out he naturally wrote to this obvious expert upon currency matters for advice. There followed an exchange of letters which gradually grew more frequent and intimate, – letters that formed the beginning of another friendship which was second only – if second in importance to Ricardo's intellectual development – to his friendship for James Mill.

Now Malthus and Ricardo, from a year or two after they had begun writing to each other, became regular correspondents. They differed on almost all the economic questions which they took up; but each one had a very high opinion of the other man's capacity, a very deep interest in his views, a very honest desire to get his criticisms; so that all the matters which they published during the rest of Ricardo's life were discussed in their letters before publication and continued to be discussed in their letters afterward. More than that, the two friends seized every opportunity to visit each other in the country, Ricardo even going down south to Haileybury and Malthus to the west of England where Ricardo presently set up a country estate and frequently staying with Ricardo on his trips to London. There are few cases on record where two men who differed from each other had so much to do in stimulating each other's development. They were peculiarly equipped to help each other just because they were intellectually different. Malthus was an empiricist; he was a person who trusted fact. He liked to deal with statistics, with history; and the only generalizations that he really cared about were generalizations which could be supported on the basis of facts that a man could gather for himself or get on a larger scale in statistical tables and history records. And Ricardo, as we have seen, was a rationalist; what he believed in were generalizations. And while all these generalizations were compatible with observations, he was very critical of facts when they ran counter to the opinions he entertained. That experience Ricardo had in proving that Bosanquet's tables were all wrong was of a sort that he frequently had. For him facts were important, but they ought always to be looked at in a critical fashion, and the man who was all for facts and nothing for theory could not even get his facts straight, in his eyes.

These two close friends, – one of them always trying to build upon fact, the other always trying in a subtle mind to set up a better world in which the real truth was shown by broad generalizations, – kept interchanging the most vigorous criticisms of their ideas in letters and supplementing those criticisms in their talk just as long as they both lived and, as I said, each man owed a great deal to his friend of opposite temperament for keeping him actively at work upon economic problems. Very likely it drove him to follow out the line of work which was native to his own mind in somewhat more extreme fashion than he otherwise would have done.

For the first four years of the acquaintance, the letters of Ricardo and Malthus deal mainly with the topic that first brought them together: discussion of the currency affairs. But presently they came to center their attention upon a new subject, and this was the problem which led to the development of a new orientation in economic theory. Ricardo explained what the new topic was in a letter to his friend Hutches Trower. He said that they had been discussing the circumstances which regulate profit.

> Nothing, I say, can increase the profits permanently on trade, with the same or an increased capital, but a really cheaper mode of obtaining food. A cheaper mode of obtaining food will undoubtedly increase profits, says Mr. Malthus, but there are many other circumstances which may also increase profits with an increase of Capital. The discovery of a new market where there will be a great demand for our manufactures is one.*

Now that sounds like a very abstract statement of a rather abstract problem, but the problem, as I shall proceed to show, was one that came to Malthus and Ricardo directly out of current politics, the current politics being an issue that had come to the fore as a result largely of the war.

In its political form the problem was the current phase of the corn law struggle. Before England had entered upon the wars with the French Republic, she had already become so thickly populated that she had to import in most years a part at least of her grain supply. That importation had, of course, led to opposition on the part of English landlords, who thought that foreign corn would lower the price in England, that lower grain prices in England would mean lower profits for farmers, and therefore lower rents for themselves. And since the agricultural interests dominated Parliament, they quite naturally resorted to protection in the corn law that was in force at the time Malthus and Ricardo began to debate their new issues, and that was the law of 1804. That law had imposed a sliding duty on the importation of grain. When the English price of wheat was less than 63s per quarter, the import duty was 24s3d, that is, it was the intent to keep the English price up to 87s. But when the English price rose above 63s, the import duty was scaled down until it reached 6d a quarter at the highest level of prices.

Now this law passed in 1804 had had no practical effect for the simple reason that the country had had a series of bad harvests, that it was at war, and that Napoleon's Continental policy had been aimed to cut off importations of anything into England from the Continent or exportation of anything from England to the Continent. The result was that the country had depended mainly upon food grown at home; and since the harvests on the whole had been bad the price of wheat had almost all the time been so high that on what came in only the 6d duty had been imposed. This import duty had given the English landlords a high price of grain.

In 1813 the price of grain had risen so high that the country as a whole was becoming uneasy over the situation. The price of wheat in that year was 118s. per quarter. That was the price at which it made it extremely difficult for the average English workman to buy bread. In the face of what seemed to be a grievous scarcity of food, Parliament appointed a select committee to inquire into the corn trade of the United Kingdom. This committee worked over the problem rather seriously and presently brought in a report which pointed out the national danger in depending upon a foreign food supply, lamented the high prices which the English populace were compelled to pay for wheat, and therefore for bread, and suggested as a remedy that agriculture be stimulated. The way to stimulate agriculture which they recommended was to raise the import duties. They proposed that the "regulated price", as they called it, on which the high duty should be imposed, should be

*Letters of David Ricardo to Hutches Trower and Others, 1811-1823, edited by James Bonar and J.H. Hollander; Oxford, 1899, p.6.

raised from 63s to 105s2d. The old law, you see, imposed the duty of 24s3d when the price in England was under 63d; they suggested that the duty be imposed whenever the price was under 105s.

The trouble they were trying to remedy was the high price of grain. They were going to impose an almost prohibitive duty on grain, and do it in the faith by getting grain permanently at a very high price they would encourage such an extension of British agriculture as would give the country an adequate supply from domestic sources. Of course, that was exactly the kind of proposition to arouse the attention of all economists, and particularly the economists who shared Adam Smith's faith in free trade.

This committee report was laid before the House of Commons in June 1813. The House took it up, but it presently appeared that there was going to be very severe opposition to raising the regulated price to any such figure as 105s. Accordingly the problem, after being debated for a brief while, was put over until the next session. It came up again in May 1814. In that year, however, the outside situation was very different. The harvest in the autumn of 1813 had been abundant in England. In the winter, the allies had invaded France. 1812 was the year of Napoleon's march to Russia. The winter of 1812-13 was the time of the burning of Moscow and the retreat of the Grand Army. Then later in the year came the European uprising against Napoleon; the decisive Battle of Leipzig was fought in October 1813; and in the winter of 1813-14 the army of the allies had marched through France, had taken Paris, and Napoleon had abdicated for the first time in April. So that when the bill came up for discussion in May 1814, Napoleon had been dethroned and commerce with all European ports was open once more.

The price of wheat which a year before had been 118s was now 73s, and the people who were indignant about the situation wanted it continued no longer. They said that the cost of bread was too high. But the agricultural interests said that the price was ruinously low; they were very much concerned, not only for the immediate present, but also for the future, because they thought that unless something was done, the English market would now be regularly flooded by grain raised by the cheap labor of Polish peasants, if not by grain from France.

The Committee, in bringing in the measure adopted in the spring of 1814, suggested as the regulated price to be adopted, not 105s as they had done the year before, but 84s; that is, they proceeded now to alter the old law of 1804 so that the high duty would be imposed, not when the British price was under 63s but when it was under 84s.

The debate on that question was long and animated. It developed into a conscious class struggle, - a class struggle between the landed interests which were preponderant in Parliament and the business interests of the country, which though but slenderly represented in Parliament were beginning to be exceedingly formidable debaters. The progress of the Industrial Revolution had led to the rise of thousands of merchants and particularly of manufacturers. Manufacturing had become a new element in the situation, leading to the rise of thousands of manufacturers from rather humble positions to positions where they were important dignitaries; they employed a good many people, and had become strong in politics as well as in business. The landed interests wanted a high price of grain, but the business interests were dead set in opposition because they entertained certain very definite opinions concerning the relation between the cost of food in England and their ability to compete in foreign markets with European merchants and manufacturers. They took it for granted that wages were determined by the cost of food. As one of their representatives, a great London banker Alexander Baring said in the House of Commons, "the laborer has no interest in this question; whether the

price be 84s or 105s a quarter, he will get dry bread in the one case and dry
bread in the other." He seemed to think the laborer was assured of his crust no
matter how high the price of grain. He had no interest, but his employer had a
very vital interest in the question; for if he had to pay wages based on 105s
per quarter, then he would have great difficulty in selling goods in competition
with men on the Continent whose wages were based on the low prices of wheat which
obtained in Russia, Poland, Austria, Germany, and France.

In order to represent their side successfully in Parliament, the business
interests of the country organized in very effective fashion and began to flood
the House with petitions. It has been said that the number of petitions was
greater than ever before in dealing with any issue; and the opposition became so
great that it appeared to the government inexpedient to push the amending bill
through without further inquiry. So in the spring of 1814 they again deferred
the matter. Both the House of Commons and the House of Lords appointed new special
committees for further study. These committees held a series of meetings in
London where they took evidence which was published, and their report was looked
over by everybody with the keenest insight; and naturally the economists were especially interested, and what share they took in the discussion I shall state at
our next meeting.

XXIV

THE ROLE OF THE ECONOMISTS IN THE CORN LAW STRUGGLE.
RICARDO'S LATER ESSAYS AND LATER LIFE

At the last meeting I recounted the current of events which brought the
corn law question to the fore in English politics at the close of the Napoleonic
Wars. As I said, that question turned into a class struggle between the employing
interests on the one side and the landed interests on the other side, - a class
struggle which dissolved that tacit partnership among all property owners which
had been temporarily produced by the French Revolution. The English reaction
against the French Revolution had produced the Anti-Combination Acts, measures
which were adopted with the fullest assent of the landed majority in Parliament to
check the organization of unions among men to get higher wages.

This corn law struggle turned, as I have pointed out, on the share in the
national income which might reasonably be expected to go to the landed interests
on the one side and the capitalist interests on the other side. The landed interests thought that their share in the national income was threatened by the fall
in the price of grain which would follow the resumption of commercial intercourse
with the Continent after Napoleon's power had been crushed; and to prevent that
fall in their income they wanted to raise the point in the price of grain at which
the high duty was imposed. so as to keep the price of grain, and thus keep up
the profits of farmers and the rents they could pay the landlords.

On the other side, the capitalist interests contended that high price of
grain meant high wages, high wages meant high cost of production in England, and
high cost of production in England would check the growth of English trade. That
was the ground that they adopted in parliamentary debates. Of course, to them as
individuals it meant a question of maintaining profits.

So the problem of distribution was brought to the fore in England in a
rather peculiar form. The point to which I brought the story at the end of the
hour on Tuesday was the summer of 1814, when both the House of Commons and the
House of Lords had appointed committees to consider the corn law problem, and

these committees were sitting in London during the summer, taking evidence and preparing the report which they should submit to Parliament at the spring session.

Now this episode, of course, interested the economists very deeply, and it led to the almost simultaneous publication of four most remarkable pamphlets:

(1) T. R. Malthus, An Inquiry Into the Nature and Progress of Rent, January 1815.
(2) Edward West, An Essay on the Application of Capital to Land, January 1815.
(3) David Ricardo, An Essay on the Influence of a Low Price of Corn on the Profits of Stock, February 1815.
(4) Robert Torrens, Essay on the External Corn Trade, March 1815.

in all of which what seemed to economists of the time a revolutionary discovery regarding the causes that determine rents was announced. The doctrines concerning rents laid down by Malthus, Ricardo, West, and Torrens were much the same though, of course, not identical.

The fact that four different men considering this problem could arrive at similar conclusions, though perhaps no two of them except Ricardo and Malthus were in close touch with each other, is an interesting example of how when times are ripe intellectual discovery seems to occur to different minds at about the same time.

Of these four pamphlets, all of which were published about the same time because the authors wanted to get their works out in time to influence the decision which the parliamentary committees would reach, much the most remarkable is Ricardo's. That was written in scarcely more than a week. It contained about twenty pages of text, but it not only expounded the new doctrines of rent but also sketched a general theory of distribution, -- sketched that theory of distribution which became the central feature of classical political economy.

We noticed in discussing The Wealth of Nations that Adam Smith laid very little stress upon the theory of distribution. We saw that seemingly that topic had not played any considerable part in his thinking about economics while he was teaching at Glasgow; that he had not discovered the importance of the problem until he went to France and became acquainted with the Physiocrats, and that on returning he worked in a theory of rent into his old framework, but worked it in, in a rather curious fashion -- in a fashion that may fairly be taken to indicate that he assigned it far less importance that it assumed in Ricardo's mind. You will remember that The Wealth of Nations begins with the division of labor, that this implies exchange, that exchange makes necessary the use of money, that the use of money means handling commodities on the basis of their prices, and that prices of commodities can be resolved into certain component parts, -- the component parts being rent, wages, and profits -- so that Smith does arrive at the theory of distribution through an analysis of the prices of commodities, which resulted from using money as a means of exchange, which in turn is a result of the division of labor.

In Ricardo's eyes, on the other hand, at least by the time he published his Principles of Political Economy, to determine the way in which the produce of the country is divided had become the principal problem of economic theory. That is the view which he lays down in the preface.

Well, now, what we have seen about the course of English politics in Parliament shows that Ricardo got this problem -- his appreciation of its import-

ance -- not in his study, but by following current events. We should also notice
that Ricardo got his peculiar conception of what the problem of distribution is,
directly from the parliamentary struggle. The word "distribution" is a word of
many meanings. You can take a problem of the distribution of wealth to refer to
the distribution of ownership; how the wealth of the country is divided. Or you
can take it to refer to the distribution of income. And if you are talking about
the distribution of income, you can talk about the distribution of money income
or of commodity income, -- income of goods or income in satisfactions. And when
you are talking about the distribution of income you can treat it as a problem of
the actual amount of income that different people get, assuming dollars or so much
goods per capita; or you can talk about the proportions in which the total income
of the country is divided up. And if you are talking about proportions of income
you can study the way in which income is divided among individuals, or you can
study the way in which income is divided among the factors of production. Or you
can study the way in which income is divided among certain classes of the population. You can also treat the problem of distribution, as some later writers have
done, as a problem of finding out why incomes have to be paid for the use of
certain factors. Why do we pay interest; why do we pay rent; why profits; why
wages?

Ricardo, in treating distribution, does not observe these various ways in
which the problem may be set up, but he just takes one of them. To him the problem
of distribution concerns the distribution of income; and in the study of the distribution of income he is concerned primarily with what we call real income, that
is, the amount of goods capable of satisfying wants. And in thinking about the
parties among whom the distribution takes place he proceeds in the simplest and
most straightforward fashion to assume that the question is about the classes, --
the recognized income classes of the country. He does not treat individuals, but
landlords as such, profit-makers as such, wage-earners as such. And finally in
talking about the distribution of real income among these classes he does not
think of trying to determine how much income each one of these classes gets, but
the proportions in which the total income is divided among them or rather how these
proportions, which he does not attempt to figure out on a percentage basis, are
going to be affected by certain changes.

Now this peculiar interpretation of the problem of distribution Ricardo
got just as directly from the corn law struggle as he got the problem itself. His
theory of distribution is an economist's analysis of the problem under debate in
Parliament in the form in which that problem appeared in Parliament. It was
there taken for granted that the important question was to see how a proposed
change in the duties -- the import duties--upon corn would affect the relative
shares of landlords and capitalists. In Parliament it was taken for granted that
wage earners had no interest in this struggle; to repeat the picturesque phrase
used by one of the debaters, Alexander Baring, "the laborer has no interest in this
question; whether the price be 84s or 105s a quarter, he will get dry bread in the
one case and dry bread in the other."

And so Ricardo took it for granted that real wages were substantially constant; that the variable factors were profits and rent. In Parliament they took
it for granted, of course, that society was divided into three classes, for as
yet the differentiation of the profit-making class into active business people and
investors had not proceeded far enough in practice to count for very much in men's
reflection on economic problems. And so too, Ricardo took it for granted that
there were three shares in distribution: rent, profits, and wages.

Now I want to call your attention to the way in which Ricardo treated the
problem which he had thus taken from current politics in his Essay. It is inter-

esting as another exemplification of his favorite methods of work, and exemplification that is a little clearer in outline than that offered by his Principles
of Political Economy, -- clearer because, as I said, the pamphlet is so short; it
covers some twenty pages in McCulloch's edition of Ricardo's works.

Ricardo begins by simplifying his problem. His problem is to show what
changes will be brought about in the share of income going to profits and to rent
by a growth of population and an increased accumulation of capital. To treat that
problem, he simplifies explicitly in part, implicitly in large part. The logical
important simplifications he makes are these:

(1) That the one important purpose of an increase of population and further
accumulation of capital is an extension of cultivation.

(2) That all the other important factors in the problem are going to remain constant. Particularly he assumes at the outset that there is no important
change taking place in methods of cultivation. He assumes also that real wages are
going to remain constant; that workers will get neither a larger or smaller amount
of commodities to consume. He assumes also that he can discuss the problem without
reference to the problem of imports from other sources.

(3) He simplifies by leaving money out of account and reducing capital
laid out by farmers, the wages that they pay to workers, and the rents that they
pay to landlords, all to quarters of wheat; that is, he carries on the whole discussion on a commodity basis.

Now let us see what he does with the problems thus simplified. He ana-
lyzes rents as follows: The increased number of the population and the increased
amount of capital accumulated, together with the constancy of real wages, make it
necessary to get lower food. The greater amount of food, combined with the unchanged methods of cultivation and the assumed unchanged amount of grain imported make
it necessary to use more land or to use the lands already under cultivation more
intensively. The additional lands that will be taken into cultivation must be
lands of a lower grade of fertility, otherwise they would already have been cultivated. And when you cultivate old farms more intensively your additional outlay
will result in lower return in grain for the amount of capital and labor that you
expend.

Now on the poorer lands that are taken into cultivation no rent is going
to be paid. On these lands, therefore, the produce that is obtained is divided
simply among two classes: the employing farmers and the laborers. And since real
wages remain constant, the reduction in the return which the land makes will fall
wholly upon profits. That is, the net effect of increasing population and accumulation of capital is to reduce the share of the product obtained, on what we have
since come to call marginal land, that goes to the capitalists, the employers.

But finally competition equalizes the return to capital in all employments.
Therefore, the lower rate of return to capital in agriculture, that is, the smaller
share of return which the capitalist employer receives, will be extended from marginal lands in agriculture to all other lands in agriculture and to all other industries. So that the conclusion can be stated in the form that increasing population and accumulation of capital lead to a reduction in the profits on stock,
and that reduction of the profits on stock is accompanied by an increase in rent
over the lower profits which people get on marginal lands; and the competition
which equalizes rent on all lands used means that the difference between the returns obtained on good lands and on the poorest lands in cultivation will grow
wider; and it is this difference which makes rent. So that with the fall in the
share of income that goes to capitalists there goes also an increase in the share

of income that goes to the landlords.

Having carried through the argument this way, Ricardo turned back and explicitly drops several of the simplifications. First, he says that this argument is borne out on the assumption that money is not used. Does that assumption really make any difference to the argument? Yes, he says, it makes one important difference: When you are thinking about this process in terms of money you have to admit that the resort to poorer lands will cause the price of agricultural products to rise in comparison with the prices of goods of other sorts. Now inasmuch as landlords are paid either in bushels of grain or some form of agricultural products, or are paid in money, they are going to get out of this privilege a double gain. First, they will get a larger share of the produce; and second, the rise of agricultural commodities in price, as compared with other commodities, means that the larger share of the profits which the landlords get will be worth more to them. And so Ricardo writes:"It follows then that the interest of the landlords is always opposed to the interest of every other class in the community." The situation which reduces profits, which makes it difficult for laborers to avoid a reduction of real wages redounds to the benefit of landlords, redounds to their benefit in a double way. That celebrated sentence is one of the sentences in Ricardo's writings that has exposed him since that time to a great deal of opprobrium. It was one of the sentences to which his friend Malthus took the strongest exception, -- one of the sentences which long made him exceedingly unpopular with the whole landlord class; and it is a sentence which he does not repeat in his Principles in the same sharp form in which he wrote it in this hasty pamphlet of 1815.

The second simplification Ricardo dropped was; he admitted that methods of cultivation had changed; and that just in so far as methods of cultivation improved, the whole line of analysis which he had developed required modification. In so far as people can increase the quantity of food which they produce by a given outlay of capital and labor on good land, to that extent they will not have to resort to the cultivation of poorer lands and the more intensive cultivation of old lands to get the food required by an increasing population. He makes that admission. He does not undertake to say how important the admission is. But it is frequently clear from the run of his exposition that he regarded this as a modification of comparatively secondary moment, -- a modification, but not a modification of such importance as to prevent the general conclusion-which he had derived from the assumption that methods of cultivation remained constant-from keeping its fundamental importance in all thoughts about economic policy.

Then, in the third place, Ricardo dropped the assumption that real wages remained always the same. He admitted that they changed. What he said was that real wages changed as population or capital grows faster. When population is growing faster than capital, wages fall; and when capital grows faster than population, wages rise. But he said nothing can be positively laid down on this head; and therefore there is no reason to modify the general conclusions that have been drawn.

The general analysis stands, then, in his eyes, that the effects of progress in a country, -- meaning by progress an increase of numbers and an accumulation of capital, -- are gradually to reduce the profits on stock and to give a double gain to the landlord classes, leaving the wage earners with a substantially fixed real income.

Now, of course, you see the bearing of this doctrine upon the corn law struggle. If Ricardo's analysis of the national situation is right, it was insanely foolish to bring on this chain of unfortunate circumstances by checking the further importation of corn into England. The way to prevent the necessity of resorting to poorer soils, reducing profits, and raising rents, was to get as large a proportion of the country's food supply -- the supply required by increasing numbers -- by importing from abroad and paying for those imports with manufactured goods.

Ricardo does not himself explicitly draw this conclusion. The bearing of his analysis was patent to any quasi-intelligent man. Ricardo had no very high notion of the intelligence of the majority of the landowners who sat on the parliamentary benches; but probably he felt that most of them were so dull and prejudiced that nothing he could say could make the point clear; and to anybody with sense his clarity was apparent.

We learn from Ricardo's letters soon after this pamphlet had been published that he felt very well pleased with his general arguments despite Malthus's criticism; he was confident that his conclusions were valid and vastly important. And he also found to his chagrin that his exposition had been far from successful. A great many people misunderstood him, and he said himself that he thought the misunderstandings were largely his fault. So that he became very eager to re-work this dicussion, go over the matter again on a larger scale, and see whether on a second trial he could not set his analysis in such fashion as to be more readily comprehensible. But almost exactly at the same time as his Essay on the Influence of a Low Price of Corn on the Profits of Stock was published, Napoleon returned from Elba.

Now when Napoleon had abdicated, Ricardo had begun retiring from business in London. Of course, Napoleon's abdication and the supposed ending of the war was followed by a very great rise of English government securities. Ricardo was a large holder of them, and he took the opportunity of hoarding for the bull market in British consols to begin selling out and investing his property in land. At his death he held some four or five hundred acres of land at Gatcomb Park in Gloucestershire, and several thousand acres also in the neighboring country of Hertfordshire. He had begun to make these purchases and retire from business, but Napoleon's return produced another set of very violent fluctuations in stock and he had to give very close and unremitting attention to his business again, and that prevented his getting at once to the task of expounding his views in a more adequate fashion.

The English Government, on Napoleon's return, acted with extraordinary energy. They got Wellington's force in Belgium brought up to a higher level of efficiency. The Battle of Waterloo was fought in June; and Ricardo, who had been following these events closely, wrote soon after Waterloo to his friend Malthus that he had apprehended as great a profit on the fluctuations as he had ever hoped to make upon any turn in the market.

When the war was over for the second time, he resumed his plan of retiring from business, closing out his securities and putting the bulk of his fortune into lands, -- a step which, on his own analysis, was a very wise step to take since the landlord stood to be the great beneficiary of economic progress. However, it is to be said in Ricardo's honor that after he had embarked a great part of his fortune in land he continued to be just as uncompromising an opponent of the corn laws as he had been before.

By the end of July he was free to work again. But then he was diverted a second time. One of his best friends was Pascoe Grenfell, a steady man who had a seat in Parliament. Grenfell asked his help for a broadside attack on the Bank of England. Now Ricardo wrote in his letters that he always enjoyed any attack on the bank of England. He was a stockholder in the Bank, and he thought that the officials of the Bank ought to divide up the enormous profits that he felt sure they had been making during the wars, that they should pay out larger dividends. As a stockholder he demanded an accounting; and then as citizen he felt that the bank was overcharging the government for its services as fiscal agent. And in the third place, as an economist Ricardo thought that the right of issuing paper money was a right that really belonged to the government; that the Bank of England was making for its proprietors, among whom he was one, an enormous profit through exercising a right that belonged to the people as a whole, and the revenue from which ought to go to the government.

So when this appeal came from Pascoe Grenfell, Ricardo turned to with a good will and prepared one of his most vigorous pamphlets, Proposals for an Economical and Secure Currency. That appeared in February, 1816; and when that pamphlet was off his hands, Ricardo "recurred," as he wrote to Malthus, "to rent, profits, and wages." He worked on his new book uninterruptedly all through 1816, his chief trouble being that at his fine estate in Gloucestershire he had that summer a superfluity of house guests, and the time that he devoted to their amusement as host interrupted rather sadly the time he had for writing. He also found that he got on with his writing less rapidly than he had expected. The difficulties that he encountered, according to his letters, arose from the difficulty of composition. To the end of his days he remained an unsuccessful writer, and what he got down on paper he got down by very strenuous effort. More than that, when he took the problem up in a more serious fashion he found that before he was in a position to discuss this simple problem of distribution he would have to clarify his ideas on the underlying concept of value. So in the Principles you find this in the first two or three chapters, and various other chapters scattered through the book are devoted to his attempt to work out a statement of value which is more clearly related than Ricardo's own exposition shows to his discussion of the laws of wages, profits, and rents.

He also judged it wise, while he was writing his book, to re-read Adam Smith, Malthus, and J.B. Say whose French treatise on political economy was then the leading Continental book upon the subject; also the notes which Buchanan had prepared for The Wealth of Nations in that annotated edition. But apparently, at least from his own letters, Ricardo did not think it necessary to gather any materials of any sort to make any additional observations of economic behavior, collect any statistics, or read any government reports. All that side of the matter was apparently clear in his mind. What he now sought to do was to elaborate his theoretical conceptions of value and to see what other theorists had said about his problems. By dint of hard work he finished the book in the early part of 1817, presumably; anyhow, it was published in 1817. Presently I shall want to deal a little more elaborately with the contents of Ricardo's Principles of Political Economy. Then I shall deal with the other things in that discussion. But in the meantime, let me add a few words about the latter part of his life.

As soon as that book was off his hands, he took his whole family over to the Continent for a tour. It was the first time in many years that the English people could visit France and the countries which had to be reached through France. Ricardo, his wife, and numerous children went over in a body and greatly enjoyed their travels.

When he got back he accepted membership upon a committee which had been asked to inquire into the feasibility of Robert Owen's scheme. Owen was the great English socialist who was most famous then as a man who had developed a scheme to improve industrial relations, and he believed his experiment in his own mill at New Lanark to be universally applicable. He was very eager to get attention directed to his scheme; and Ricardo, who was very benevolently disposed, was beginning to feel that some plan of this kind might work. He took his seat upon the committee invited to study the matter, but he had reluctantly to come to the conclusion that after all Robert Owen's plans could not be applied on any grand scale; and if they were, could not be expected to bring about such great results as he hoped from them.

Then in 1818 he was made sheriff of his county. In those days that was an appointment that brought with it a considerable social distinction. Ricardo had become one of the leading landowners in Gloucestershire. He had entered the class from which these honorable officers were chosen, and it was a decided personal tribute to him that despite his Jewish origin his station in the county was thus recognized.

You will remember he became eager to enter Parliament, and he consulted with Jeremy Bentham on ways and means. Of course, his only practical way to enter Parliament and maintain his independence was to buy a seat. We do not know definitely the terms on which he got a seat, but the best accredited account is that he made a loan of ₤20,000 free of interest to the proprietor of the borough of Portarlington in Ireland. He was returned from Portarlington and sat for that Irish constituency for the rest of his life. It is interesting to observe that apparently he never took the trouble to cross over and visit his constituency.

But in Parliament he discharged his duty with the greatest regularity and effectiveness. He was always in his seat when sessions were being held; he was a frequent and seemingly a rather effective speaker. We have various contemporary statements which show the attention with which he was listened to in a discussion of all economic problems. He also took a very liberal stand on all questions of a distinctly economic color. He was one of the most active proponents of Parliamentary reform; that is, one of the fighters for a change in the suffrage laws which would give votes to a larger part of the people. He stood for Catholic emancipation. (Catholics, of course, in those days were debarred from holding public office.) He was vigorously defending the freedom of the press and the right of public meeting; and perhaps he was most notable of all for the extraordinary vigor with which he urged the country to impose a levy upon capital in order to reduce the staggering war debt. He thought seriously that by a levy on capital the debt might be extinguished or greatly reduced although, of course, he would have been one of the people of the country hit by such a levy, but he defended that measure with great energy.

XXV

RICARDO'S LATER YEARS -- HIS PRINCIPLES OF
POLITICAL ECONOMY

I must say a few words more about the closing years of Ricardo's life. He entered Parliament, as I remarked on Thursday, and to his work in Parliament he devoted as much vigor as he had done to his business and to the development of economic theory. In Parliament he was a radical of the radicals, standing for all sorts of measures which in his day were extremely unpopular.

Nowadays we are wont to think of the classical economists as, on the whole, a rather conservative set of people, - people who believed so heartily in maintaining the security of property. We are accustomed to think that they could in no sense be called ardent reformers. But that is to judge the men by the standards of our time, not by the standards of their time. In comparison with the overwhelming majority in Parliament, Ricardo was a person who wanted to change all sorts of social institutions and he had the Englishman's fine disregard of opposition when it came to matters of numbers, being always ready to incur whatever odium would follow the championship of a course which he thought was right. Thus he was one of the most eager advocates for Parliamentary reform, for freedom of the press, for the right of public meeting, for Catholic emancipation, and for a levy on capital to pay the war debt.

Now during the closing years of Ricardo's life the favorite interests of his parliamentary career occupied his chief attention. His interest in economic theory was not lost, but it rested in a secondary place. He kept up his active correspondence with Malthus, and in some of his later letters to Malthus he made developments upon his fundamental economic notions that went beyond anything that got into the Principles. He presently began an equally active correspondence with a younger economist, John Ramsay McCulloch, a Scotchman who came down to London to push his fortunes and who became one of the most conspicuous economists in the generation between Ricardo and John Stuart Mill.

Ricardo also began, while he was in London, giving a series of breakfasts to people who were interested in the development of economic theory. Out of the breakfasts at his home there presently developed the Political Economy Club, an organization which has had a long history and which has played a really prominent role in the development of economics in England, though in the last generation or two it has been overshadowed in importance by the Royal Economic Society.

He also was induced by his publisher to bring out new editions of the Principles in 1819 and 1821; and in each of these editions he made certain changes. Very much to his honor, he disavowed a notion expressed in the first edition which he had come to believe untenable, a notion concerning the influence of the adoption of machinery upon the economic welfare of wage earners. But the changes that he made were only incidental. He would not take the time for any thoroughgoing recasting of his theory as a whole; so that he left the book at the end with the same impress of rather hasty work that it had at the beginning.

Finally, he continued to publish economic pamphlets from time to time. But these pamphlets all deal primarily with questions of the day, dealing with them in Ricardo's characteristically fundamental style. In 1820 he published an Essay on the Funding System, a phrase which at that time was equivalent to public debts in current terminology. In that essay Ricardo strongly recommended a pay as you go policy in handling the government finances. He took occasion to urge before the general public that plan for paying off the war debt by a levy on capital which he had expounded in Parliament.

In 1822 he published another pamphlet on protection to agriculture, a pamphlet in which he vigorously urged a repeal of the corn laws, admitting only that in carrying out the repeal of the corn laws care should be taken to reduce the duty by degrees in order that agriculture, the farming business, might have time to adjust itself with a comparatively little loss.

Finally, at the time of his death, he was writing another pamphlet which was later published, called a Plan for the Establishment of a National Bank; that is, the essay in which he recommended the separation of the issue department of the Bank of England from the banking department. He here suggests that fundamental scheme of changing the most important banking institution in England which was years afterward adopted by Sir Robert Peel and made the most important feature of the great Bank Act of 1844.

Ricardo died in September 1823 as the result, if I remember rightly, of an ulcer in the head. He was than only fifty-one years old. The warmth of the expressions of sympathy that his death called for is really remarkable when one is accustomed to find nothing but laudatory expressions used in obituaries; but it is quite clear that Ricardo's friends felt his loss to an exceptional degree; not only felt the loss to the country and to economics that was sustained by his taking off at this early age, but also felt a personal loss. He seems to have been exceptionally successful in his friendships, just as he was exceptionally successful in business, in economic theory, and in politics.

About that last matter I want to read you one or two passages from different sources to give you a livelier impression than I otherwise can of the role that this Jewish business man was able to play in a highly prejudiced House of Commons where he was the representative not only of the race that suffered under graver disabilities at that time than it does now, but also where he stood for so many radical reforms that most of the men felt a real antipathy for him.

The first of these passages I want to read to you is from William Smart's Economic Annals of the Nineteenth Century, 1821-1830, (p. 180):

His (Ricardo's) first prominent appearance was on 24th May, 1819, in the debate of Peel's resolutions respecting the resumption of cash payments, when he was loudly called upon from all parts of the House. Thereafter Ricardo was an acknowledged power. His voice, indeed, is described as 'harsh and screamy'; he used no arts of eloquence, said what he had to say in the fewest words and plainest way, and never abused his opponents. But his calm, serious exposition of principles, his severely independent tone, his habit of bringing everything to the test of economic theory, distinguished him from every man in the House. Behind it all was the respect commanded by a noble character and an unblemished record.

Another view of his position in Parliament is afforded by a very celebrated passage from one of the speeches of Henry Brougham who was one of the rising young liberals connected with the Edinburgh Review who in the great parliamentary reform cabinet of the 1830's became Lord Chancellor, a man who is also known as having given his own name to a new design for pleasure carriages. In a debate upon protection of agriculture in 1820 Brougham took occasion to say that the member for Portarlington (Ricardo) had argued:

as if he had dropped from another planet; as if this were a land of the most perfect liberty of trade - as if there were no taxes - no drawbacks - no bounties - no searchers - or any other branch of trade but agriculture; as if, in this Utopian world of his honourable friend's creation, the first measure of restriction ever thought of was that on the importation of corn - as if all trades were on an equal footing, and that, in this new state, we were called upon to decide the abstract question whether or not there should be a protecting price for corn. But we were not in this condition. We were in a state of society in which we had manufactures of almost every description protected in every way, even to criminal enactments, to protect the raw material from going out of the country, in order thereby to assist the native manufacturer.*

The passage is interesting because it indicates that in his speeches in Parliament

* Cf. Smart, William, Economic Annals of the Nineteenth Century, 1801-1820, p.733 note; also Hansard's Parliamentary Debates, N.S. i, 685.

he impressed some, even of the most intelligent of his fellow-members, as having
that somewhat high abstract character which is so notably a feature of his economic theory.

Finally, I will read an extract from Mr. J.L. Mallet's _Diaries_.* Mallet
was one of Ricardo's fellow-members in the Political Economy Club, and a very
intelligent English merchant; a person much more realistically minded than Ricardo,
but who had a very high regard for him.

> I doubt also whether his parliamentary career contributed to his happiness,
> as much as it did to his reputation: for when I alluded to any useful and
> sensible remarks he had made in the House, he often observed that he had no
> sort of influence there, and that few people were less attended to. It
> is said that his voice, although sweet and pleasing, was pitched extremely
> high, and his distinct articulation gave him an advantage in the House of
> Commons by fixing attention, which is not the case with monotonous tones.
> (Compare with Smart's description above!).

> I have already mentioned the pleasure with which I observed in my visit
> to Gloucestershire in 1817, the respect entertained for Mr. Ricardo by
> his country neighbors and the gentlemen of the County; but I am sorry
> to say, that an illiberal political feeling was subsequently generated by
> his exertions in the House, in favour of financial and political reform,
> and more particularly against all criminal proceedings for matters of op-
> inion and works of religious controversy. This feeling grew so strong
> that notwithstanding his station in the County, his large landed property,
> his endeavours to promote industry and true charity in his neighborhood,
> and the general esteem in which he was held, the Duke of Beaufort declined
> three years ago placing him in the Commission of the Peace for the country.
> And yet I believe that several members of the administration felt on many
> occasions the value of his disinterested and enlightened support; but his
> habitual cooperation with (Joseph) Hume, his steadiness in voting upon
> all questions involving the liberty of the subject and economic reform,
> and above all, his speeches on the confinement of Carlisle and his family
> for blasphemous publications, marred all his usefulness in their eyes.

All of which means that Ricardo was quite ready to sacrifice his standing and his
reputation whenever it became necessary to do so in supporting the causes that
commended themselves to his conscience.

So much for the man. Now let us turn to an examination of Ricardo's
theories. I am taking it for granted that you have read the _Principles of Poli-_ =
tical Economy with that close attention which the book demands; for it is only
as one reads closely and turns back and forth, compares what is said in one chapter
with what is said in other chapters, that one gets any adequate comprehension of
the character of Ricardo's theoretical accomplishment.I am taking it for granted,
then, that you know what is in the book; and what I think I can help you to do is
to consider some problems that the type of theory there presented raises in a
modern mind.

The subjects which he discusses are, of course, price in its relation to
value, distribution of income, the questions of taxation, and certain long-period
tendencies in the progress of wealth and population, or, to use more modern phraseology, the secular trends in the production of wealth and in the sharing of the
national income among wage earners, rent receivers, and profits receivers.Now that
is a much narrower range of topics than Adam Smith had discussed. Ricardo has substantially nothing to say about production as such, nothing to say about consump-
* In Political Economy Club, Minutes of Proceedings, etc.Vol.VI (Centenary Volume)
1921; pp. 212-213.

tion as such, hardly anything to say about the development of economic institutions. But with the topics which he selects as those of central theoretical interest he deals much more fully than Adam Smith had done. And it is a tribute to his sagacity that the topics in which he centered his interest are the topics which in the whole period since Ricardo's death have continued to seem to most economic theorists the central problems of the science.

When you compare what Ricardo had to say about value and price, distribution, the incidence of taxation, and the secular trends of the production of wealth,with what is said in modern treatises upon the same subjects, you may be struck by the fact that Ricardo's work shows a rather marked lack of continuity. A modern treatise which deals with these subjects, for instance Alfred Marshall's Principles of Economics, is an organic whole; every part of the discussion really bears upon every other part.

In contrast, Ricardo's Principles seems like an assembly of mechanically disconnected parts. Let me show what I mean in a little more detail. To begin with, Ricardo has three laws of value:(1) the law of supply and demand; (2) the law of cost of production; and (3) the law of comparative costs. Well, you can find in some modern treatises these three laws laid down, but if they are treated as distinct laws in modern treatises, it is shown that, after all, each one has its bearing upon the other; that they are very closely related. Now Ricardo did not see these inter-relations among those laws. In consequence, in his letters to Malthus he definitely contested the opinion that the law of the cost of production is closely related to the law of supply and demand. Malthus took the modern view that these two laws are connected because the law of cost of production bears upon the price by showing the conditions upon which the supply of freely reproducible commodities depend, and that the law of cost of production is simply an elaboration of the conditions on which the supply depends.

Ricardo, on the contrary, in answer to Malthus says:

Do you not suppose that in case there is a marked reduction in the cost of producing some article its price will fall off, making thereby no change whatever in its supply.

- clearly contrasting these two laws with each other. Nor did he see how his law of cost of production could be closely related to the law of comparative costs. He really seemed to believe that this law of comparative costs, which is used to explain exchanges in international trade, is quite different in its character from the law of cost of production which is the most important of the laws of value when you are considering exchanges within a country. Also note that these three laws of value are quite distinct from the laws of distribution, with one unimportant exception: Ricardo does point out that demand and supply regulate the market price of labor and the market rate of interest, - but that is all.

In our modern treatises the practice is to begin as Ricardo did by treating value and to show that all problems of value can be discussed in terms of supply and demand, usually with utility analysis to explain the conditions on which demand depends, and cost of production analysis to explain the conditions on which supply depends over periods of considerable length; and then to present this law of value as applicable to all economic values whatever. With that as a foundation, the modern theorist goes on to develop a discussion of distribution by showing that wages are the price of labor and therefore capable of being treated as a problem of value; that interest is the price paid for the use of loan funds, and therefore is capable of being treated as a value problem; that rent is the price paid for the use of land, and therefore capable of being treated as a value problem; and that profits is the price which a community has to pay for the services of business organizers and risk takers, and therefore, once more, capable of treatment as a problem of value.

That scheme, you see, integrates a modern book on economic theory in high degree. You do not get such an integration in Ricardo. There stand his three laws of value independent of one another, and then there come three laws of distribution independent of the laws of value. Moreover, these laws of distribution are unlike each other. His law of rent is drawn in terms of differences in the yield which different pieces of land will make with different outlays of capital and labor; it rests on differences in the fertility of soils. His law of wages is substantially that wages are controlled by standards of living; and in his view these standards of living are not very elastic. And his law of profits is that profits follow inversely as th cost of labor. He has, therefore, three laws of distribution, unlike in form, and all of them independent of the laws of value.

Moreover, these three laws of distribution at a given time have to be supplemented in Ricardo's system by three other laws concerning the secular trends of wages, rent, and interest. In the long run, wages tend to remain constant, or perhaps to shrink slightly. Profits tend to fall, and rents tend to rise. And the three laws of distribution, at the present time, are supplemented not only by these laws concerning secular trends, but also by certain supplementary propositions intended to account for the differences in wage rates and profit rates in different branches of employment. Ricardo takes over Adam Smith's view that differences in the rates paid for different kinds of labor must be accounted for by differences in the amount of skill or training or responsibility, or agreeableness of different trades, and to hold apparently that the like is true of profits; also bringing in there the element of the risk involved. Lines of business which are disagreeable, or require an exceptional amount of training, or are hazardous, bring current rates of profit which are higher than those trades of a different sort.

In just one respect Ricardo's treatise is highly integrated. His views concerning the incidence of taxation are closely reasoned corollaries from his theories of distribution. From the technical point of view, Ricardo's discussion of the incidence of certain taxes is perhaps the most remarkable part of all his speculations. He can tell you definitely wherein taxes on wages are going to be shifted, - taxes on rent, taxes on profits. He can tell you those things because he is so sure about his underlying propositions concerning the laws of wages, rent, and profits. Wages have to be shifted simply because the wage earner, controlled by an inflexible standard of living is such that if you impose a tax on laborers which would have to be paid by them, it would reduce the real wage that they receive. That would lead to a check in their numbers, and consequently to a diminution in their supply, and so to an increase in their money wage, an increase just sufficient to enable them to pay the tax; but that increase in their money wages of course, would transfer the burden of the tax on wages from the working class to the employing class. That is just an example of the way in which Ricardo uses his theories of distribution to give him a whole set of very interesting propositions about the shifting and incidence of taxes levied in various ways.

One matter of peculiar interest in thinking about Ricardo's work is the role that is played in it by speculation as such and by knowledge of facts, by observation. Ricardo was, as I have on several occasions remarked, a born reasoner, a man who wanted to solve problems by a process of excogitation, a process analogous to that by which we handle geometrical problems. At the same time, he was a man who lived a very active life; first, as a business man, and later as a combined country gentleman and member of Parliament. He had been eminently successful in conducting his affairs and had unusual opportunities of observing how people behave, so that his knowledge of fact concerning economic life of the England of his time was very considerable. The question is, what bearing had his observations on how things go, upon his theoretical work? How did his knowledge of fact and his predilection for reasoning on the basis of assumed premises get reconciled in his system as a whole?

Perhaps you will recall in discussing Ricardo's life I mentioned his first pamphlet on The High Price of Bullion and mentioned also the fact that in this pamphlet Ricardo starts by laying down the general proposition that gold and silver obey the law which regulates all other commodities; that they obey a certain law. Finally, I mentioned the fact that according to Professor James Bonar this seems to be the first occasion in which anyone had used the word "law" in just this sense in economic discussions. Now what did Ricardo really mean when he laid down a law concerning the movements of gold and silver? Quite obviously, he did not mean anything peculiar to gold and silver as such, and quite obviously he did not mean any laws that are passed by a governmental authority. He points out that in obeying economic laws gold and silver frequently violate governmental laws. What he really meant was that the gold and silver merchants, the people who are shipping gold and silver from one country to another, did so under the control of certain very definite incentives. That is, his law about the movements of gold and silver is really a law concerning the behavior of a set of business men. He puts it, how such men make their remittances "resolves itself entirely into a question of interest," that is, it resolves itself entirely into a question as to how they can make the most money.

Now that point to us, I think, is the crucial characteristic of Ricardo's whole type of economic theory. His whole theory is derived from reasoning about what it is to the interest of people to do. It is a statement of men's interests set up on the basis of a theorist's reasoning, and supplemented by a tacit assumption that as a rule people are going to follow their interests. Well, if that is the way in which a man is going to work, it is quite clear that this is the method he must employ in excogitating theories; it is what has commonly been called the deductive method. He has got to consider what people's interests are and from a consideration of these interests deduce what follows under given circumstances.

Ricardo, as I pointed out, began his work in economic theory by dealing with a highly technical problem: the problem which centered in the behavior of gold and silver merchants. Now the gold and silver merchants, -- the people of his day who played the same role in life that our dealers in foreign exchange play nowadays -- were one of the most expert bodies of business men you could find in England. The business was so difficult that no untrained man could be allowed any share in it. It was also a business in which nothing but pecuniary motives played any role to speak of. There was hardly any question of good feeling or adherence to honored traditions, except in the most minor methods of keeping books or something of that sort. There was nothing to interfere with the play of the most businesslike considerations. In other words, Ricardo started his economic work with the assumption that people are guided by the consideration of their interests; and his success in working on that supposition with the first problems he took up doubtless had much to do in emboldening him to adopt a similar procedure when he came later on to talk about the behavior of people who have very little of the business expertness, the freedom from prejudice, the freedom from emotional aberration which is characteristic of dealers in foreign exchange.

Ricardo apparently could overlook the fact on most occasions that the average investor and business man is in a very different position from the average dealer in foreign exchange. He did, as we shall find, make a few allowances on

this score. He did admit that business men have prejudices against embarking
their fortunes in foreign investments, and it is on the basis of that difference
that he thought it necessary to set up the law of comparative costs to cover
international exchanges and contrast that law with the law of cost of production
which accounted adequately, as he saw things, for prices inside the country where
competition suffered no bar.

We shall find he had certain definite views about the psychological
characteristics of working people, views that he standardized into his conception
that people have a more or less inflexible standard of living which regulates
wages. But aside from these exceptions and one or two others of less consequence,
Ricardo worked by imputing to his economic subjects at large the same type of
mind that he imputed to gold and silver merchants.

That, you will see, led him to build up in economics a type of economic
theory answering accurately to the logical specifications of the social theorist.
Bentham proposed to work on the basis of the felicific calculus; he supposed all
men to be guided by the search for pleasure. Ricardo supposes all men to be guided by the search for their economic interest. Just translate pleasure into
economic interest, and you have Ricardo and Bentham treating human nature from this
aspect on the same basis.

Also you will recall that Bentham got two parallel discussions out of his
consideration of what men do in the pursuit of pleasure. A theorist who ascribes this characteristic to mankind can discuss both what men ought to do to
get the most pleasure, and to a certain extent what they actually do to get the
most pleasure. Of these two discussions, I pointed out that from Bentham's point
of view the discussion of what people ought to do is one that a theorist can carry
on with the greatest certainty. It is also in Bentham's eyes the most important.

So too, Ricardo in considering economic behavior can discuss what it is in
men's interest to do and can also at need discuss how men occasionally depart
from the pursuit of their interests. Of the two discussions, however, interest
to do seemed to him the more important, the more scientific. I want to bring that
home to you by reading a passage from one of Ricardo's early letters to Malthus,
a letter written in 1811, where he says:

> I assume indeed that nations in their commercial transactions are so
> alive to their advantage and profit, particularly in the present im-
> proved state of the division of employments and abundance of capital,
> that in point of fact money never does move but when it is advantageous
> both to the country which sends and the country that receives that it
> should do so. The first point to be considered is, what is the interest
> of countries in the case supposed? The second what is their practice?
> Now it is obvious that I need not be greatly solicitous about this latter
> point; it is sufficient for my purpose if I can clearly demostrate that
> the interest of the public is as I have stated it. It would be no
> answer to me to say that men were ignorant of the best and cheapest
> mode of conducting their business and paying their debts, because that
> is a question of fact not of science, and might be urged against almost
> every proposition in Political Economy.*

Well, here you see how very definitely Ricardo came out with the statement that
the scientific part of economic science is a discussion as to what it is to the
interest of people to do; that the theorist is less concerned with actual be-

*Letters of David Ricardo to Thomas Robert Malthus, 1810-1823. ed. by James Bonar;
Oxford, 1887; p. 18.

havior and that if there is a discrepancy between the facts of actual behavior and the laws of the theorist concerning what is in the interest of people, there is a discrepancy between facts and science. It need not disturb the scientific inquiry, for, on this basis, the theory is not really concerned with facts; it is concerned with an analysis of economic interests...

Of course, all that looks as if we had to say that in the issue between fact and reasoning in Ricardo's work, reasoning on the basis of certain assumptions concerning men's interest kept the upper hand, and yet to think so would be a very great mistake because Ricardo was, after all, from start to finish, an eminently successful practical man. He was in fact a utilitarian of the Jeremy Bentham sort and believed just as Bentham believed that the value of science lay altogether in what it could contribute to human happiness. The only point in this -- and while it is the only point it is significant -- Ricardo thought that he could promote practical interests much more effectively by setting up abstract intellectual analyses of what people's interests are than he could by messing around and inquiring into actual human behavior.

I want to illustrate that a bit by reference to specific examples of Ricardo's theorizing. The first is afforded by his controversy with Charles Bosanquet, the British merchant who challenged Ricardo's conclusion that the Bank of England notes had depreciated because there was a premium on bullion. Mr. Bosanquet relied to prove this contention against Ricardo upon certain statistical tables which seemed to show that after all the fluctuations in the prices of the exchanges in London had not run parallel, as on Ricardo's theory they should do, with fluctuations in the local price of bullion; and Ricardo not only pointed out, as I remarked before that if the Bosanquet tables were correct the dealer in these matters could have made high profits in a series of years by shipping gold between Hamburg and Paris, but he also went on to say:

> If the facts had been as here stated by Mr. Bosanquet, I should have found it difficult to reconcile them with my theory. That theory takes for granted, that whenever enormous profits can be made in any particular trade, a sufficient number of capitalists will be induced to engage in it, who will, by their competition, reduce the profits to the general rate of mercantile gains. It assumes that in the trade of exchange does this principle more especially operate; it not being confined to English merchants alone; but being perfectly understood, and profitably followed, by the exchange and bullion merchants of Holland, France, and Hamburgh; and competition in this trade being well known to be carried to its greatest height. Does Mr. Bosanquet suppose that a theory which rests on so firm a basis of experience as this can be shaken by one or two solitary facts not perfectly known to us?*

Now the significance of that is that Ricardo, when challenged, went back to his theories for a justification of this general law that in dealing with the precious metals men are operating on the basis of their interests. His general law has here a foundation in the facts of his business experience.

---

*Reply to Mr. Bosanquet's Practical Observations on the Report of the Bullion Committee; Ch. II, p. 9.

XXVI

RICARDO'S METHOD OF WORK

You may recall that at the end of our deliberations of a week ago I was discussing the relations of fact and theory in Ricardo's type of economics. On the face of the returns you find Ricardo saying in so many words to Malthus that he is not concerned with matters of fact, in matters in which a science as such is concerned; he is arguing on the basis of certain assumptions. And as you read the Principles you feel as though that letter to Malthus, written in defense of certain speculations in other preceding letters to the same friend, was a statement of the methodological position of the writer of that general system of economic theory. You get from reading the book the impression that Ricardo is, after all, concerned, as some of his friends and fellow-members of the House of Commons charged him, as being concerned with an abstract world, as though he had no very deep interest in observing what was going on about him in discussing problems of deep human interest.

I was arguing that that conception is a quite superficial one; first and foremost because, as we have already seen, Ricardo got his problems direct from practical life. He was always the man who was trying to throw light upon questions which were important to Englishmen in his day. And then I went on to say that that view appears to be superficial when you examine some of Ricardo's detailed positions; and in support of that reaction I first drew your attention to the fact that in his discussions arising from that first publication of his on The High Price of Bullion, his discussions with Charles Bosanquet, he defended his assumption that men, in dealing with bullion follow their economic interests, by pointing to experience. Let me read the passage again:

That theory (Ricardo's) takes for granted, that whenever enormous profits can be made in any particular trade, a sufficient number of capitalists will be induced to engage in it, who will, by their competition, reduce the profits to the general rate of mercantile gains.

You see he appeals to the experience of people who, like himself, knew a great deal about the business in hand to justify the assumption on the basis of which he is reasoning - the assumption that it is economic interest that controls the movement of the precious metals.

The second illustration is, I think, of even more interest because it concerns a problem of large theoretical importance. It relates to Ricardo's discussions of rent. In order to illustrate Ricardo's position, I want to begin by referring to the treatment which was given to this problem of rent by Karl Marx in Das Kapital. If you want to find a person who is interested in developing the logical possibilities of economic analysis, do not go to Ricardo but go to Karl Marx. Marx, when writing his Das Kapital, observed that tables of the sort that Ricardo employs to illustrate his discussions should be made on the basis of a number of different suppositions. First, we can make tables on the assumption that the price of agricultural produce remains constant; then that it falls, or that it rises. And this gives us three main cases. Under each one of these main cases we may assume that the return on the second investment of capital in agriculture gives returns which are just equal to, or are less than, or are greater than the returns to the preceding investment. Here then are three variants of each one of the three main cases, so that you get nine cases to discuss. And then Marx goes on to show that there are three eventualities arising from the possibility that after the changes postulated, the former no-rent land may continue to regulate the price, or may be displaced by poorer land, or may drop out of cultivation.

There is a logician's layout of the theory of rent, of a man who does take hold of the problem as a speculative problem and inquires how it may be analyzed into different forms, and when he does this he gets nine variants.

Now when you read Ricardo, you find that instead of discussing nine cases and an indefinite number of other possibilities, he confines himself to four different sets of suppositions. First, he discusses rent on the basis of a rising price of agricultural products caused by increasing demand and diminishing returns. That is the kind of situation which he supposed existed in England during the Continental wars when the country had to raise the greater part of its food supply because it was cut off from the possibility of importing adequately and with certainty a large supply of grain. The second case he discusses is that of a falling price caused by decreasing demand. And the third case is that of falling price caused by improvements in agriculture. But it is the third case, he points out, that is capable of being subdivided, for the improvements in agriculture may either increase the productive powers of the land or may enable us to obtain the produce of land with less labor. That is, your improvements may have one of two effects; either they may reduce the amount of labor you have to expend or they may require the same amount of labor and give you more produce; Ricardo sees certain differences.

Now these cases, Ricardo says, are the cases which seem to him important to understand in order to throw light upon the conditions of his time and country. He was not interested in exploring possible problems that you can get out of the elements of the theory of rent in the way that Karl Marx was interested in discussing the logical permutations of the problem. Here, as in other cases, Ricardo, despite the fact that he was so much addicted to handling things on an imaginative, speculative basis, nevertheless confines himself to dealing with problems of great social importance.

What is true of rent is true of the other problems Ricardo discusses. If you like to play the kind of logical game Karl Marx played with rent, you can take the problem of wages as Marx treated it, or the problem of profits, and build it up in some similar fashion. Ricardo did not do it. To him this highly abstract method was designed to throw light on what was important for men to understand.

It appears, however, - and this I think is well worth stating because it is characteristic not only of Ricardo's type of theory but also of similar kinds of work done by economists since his day - that after all in Ricardo's type of theory facts and logic are sometimes, so to speak, at civil war with each other inside the system. The sharpest illustration of this conflict between what Ricardo knows to be fact and how he has to treat matters in reasoning about economic behavior on his basis is afforded by what he has to say concerning wages. Perhaps you know there has been much discussion of the problem as to whether Ricardo did or did not believe in the "iron law of wages." I want to read you a few excerpts from different parts of the Principles; and as I read them, please think of the question whether Ricardo did or did not believe in the "iron law." His general law of wages runs as follows:

> The natural price of labour is that price which is necessary to enable the labourers, one with another, to subsist and to perpetuate their race, without either increase or diminution.*

*Principles, Ch. V, Gonner ed. p. 70.

Which means, without either increase or diminution in numbers.

Now Ricardo goes on to point out that the market price of labor, the price which is really paid, has a tendency to conform to this natural price. But the market price may, in an improving society, for an indefinite period, be constantly above tha natural rate; for no sooner may the impulse which an increased capital gives to a new demand for labor be obeyed than another increase of capital may produce the same effect. The natural price itself is not fixed; estimated even in food and necessaries, it varies at different times in the same country, and very materially differs in different countires. It essentially depends on the habits and customs of the people. And Ricardo reinforces this statement, that the natural price of labor is itself a variable, by pointing out the difference between the English and Irish standards of living, between the English standards of his own day and earlier times, and between the standards of living in Hindustan and Russia. He even diverts attention, for a moment, to the advisability of trying to raise the standard of living, remarking:

> The friends of humanity cannot but wish that in all countries the labouring classes should have a taste for comforts and enjoyments, and that they should be stimulated by all legal means in their exertions to procure them. There cannot be a better security against a superabundant population.*

Now, of course, all that sounds realistic enough, - sounds as if Ricardo could not be classed as a believer in any "iron law of wages." The man who admits that the market rate may for an indefinite time be above the natural rate, and the natural rate itself differs somewhat from country to country and may be increased, a man who thinks it should be increased does not seem to be a person whom you can fairly charge with thinking that the laborer is never going to better his condition, that he is always to be bound down to some subsistence wage.

Well, now let me read you some other passages. Ricardo argues that if improvements in machinery greatly reducing the cost of production be

> extended to all the objects of the labourer's consumption, we should find him probably at the end of a very few years, in possession of only a small, if any, addition to his enjoyments, although the exchangeable value of those commodities, compared with any other commodity, in the e manufacture of which no such improvement were made, had sustained a very considerable reduction; and though they were the produce of a very considerably diminished quantity of labour.**

That is, if by the introduction of machinery you did increase real wages, that increase would last only a few years at most; and if the laborer did keep any part of the gain, it would be only a slight part. Again he asks what would be the effect on profits and manufactures of an increased cost of raising food, and in answering that question he writes:

> If, then, wages continued the same, the profits of manufacturers would remain the same; but if, as is absolutely certain, wages should rise with the rise of corn, then their profits would necessarily fall.***

---

* Ibid.,Ch. V, Gonner ed. p. 77.
** Ibid.,Ch. I, sec. i, Gonner ed. p. 11.
***Ibid.,Ch. VI, Gonner ed. p. 88.

He is absolutely certain that wages would rise with the rise of corn, which seems to imply that the laborer does get so much corn and if the money return is not adequate his money wages are going to rise. It seems to be an iron law.

Again, in another passage he says:

Diminish the cost of subsistence of men, by diminishing the natural price of the food and clothing, by which life is sustained, and wages will ultimately fall, notwithsatnding that the demand for labourers may very greatly increase.*

That is, cut down the cost of procuring the standard of living, and wages are going to fall because the population is going to multiply itself so as to force its money return back to the old level which custom has established.

Another passage:

Population regulates itself by the funds which are to employ it, and therefore always increases or diminishes with the increase or diminution of capital.**

The amount of capital which is used for employing labor is the thing which regulates population because if a little more money is spent in paying wages at any time, the market price of labor will temporarily rise above the natural price, and then an increase of population will send wages back. And he tells you that if the amount devoted to paying wages falls off, then for the time being the market price of labor will be below the natural price; laborers will not be getting their fixed standard of living and so their rate of increase will be diminished.

Once again:

A tax on wages is wholly a tax on profits.***

This is perhaps the most remarkable of all this dicta. You see, that means simply that if you do lay taxes upon the working people, those taxes are going to reduce their standard of living by taking away part of the money with which they buy food, lodging, and clothing; and that is going to diminish the increase of population. That will raise wages – raise wages only to pay the taxes, when this rise of wages will fall on the employers so that a tax laid on wages is transferred to the employers – to profits.

. . . in practice it is invariably found that an increase of population follows the amended condition of the labourer.****

In these latter passages it does seem that Ricardo accepted the "iron law of wages" in the most rigid form. What is the explanation? Is it that Ricardo is inconsistent? Not at all. You do not get a glimpse of the real explanation of his seemingly contradictory views until you think of their relation to Ricardo's type of theory, – the logical shifts which a man who tries to build up a theory of economic behavior by Ricardo's method is compelled to resort to.

*   Ibid., Ch. XXX, Gonner ed. p. 373.
**   Ibid., Ch. II, Gonner ed. p. 55.
***   Ibid., Ch. XVI, Gonner ed. p. 198.
**** Ibid., Ch. XXXII Gonner ed. p. 400.

The two sets of passages I read to you come from two different parts of the book. The first passage in which Ricardo is admitting that the market price of labor may be for an indefinite period above the natural price, and that this natural price is different in different countries;that it is different in different times for the same country;that it is capable of being raised and should be raised is one of the great objects of all well-wishing citizens, - all these things which indicate that wages are variable and not a constant come from the chapter on wages. Now in this chapter, wages was the one subject that Ricardo was discussing and when he was discussing wages by itself as a sole problem he could use his eyes, he could recognize the facts of this problem to the full.

The other passages I read to you come from the various chapters in which Ricardo is discussing other matters such as the effects of machinery, such as profits, such as the incidence of taxation. They come from chapters in which Ricardo is primarily interested in some other variable,and in which wages is a matter that has to be taken account of in order to get a clear light on problems involving the second variable in question: the effects of machinery, or profits, or the incidence of taxation, etc.

A person who is working with Ricardo's analytical methods cannot successfully handle a problem with two variables. When he is discussing problems in which there are two quantities present, he has to dispose of one of these quantities as a constant. And that he does when he is talking about wages in relation to something else.

Turn again to the simplest of these cases, the incidence of a tax that is laid upon wages. The variable that he is talking about here is the tax, and he wants to see where that tax is finally going to fall. He is pretty sure that in practice it falls on profits and he wants to give a clear decision on the matter. He was never patient with any position that was surrounded by a lot of "if's" and "but's" and "to a degree's". He wanted a clear-cut view. All right. Now, if you are going to suppose that a tax was laid on wages, you could tell nothing about the shifting of the incidence of the tax so long as you keep thinking about the variability of the natural rate of wages. If you say, "Yes, the natural rate of wages is after all a quantity that varies somewhat," it is quite possible that natural price itself may rise, and you have come to the conclusion that while part of a tax laid on wages is shifted to the employers, the rest goes to the working people. There is nothing clear-cut and nice about that. But if you suppose for the purpose of this argument that wages is a constant, accepting the "iron law of wages",then you can carry through your discussion of a fixed rate of wages with perfect logical precision.

And so, too, if you think about the effects of introducing machinery in industry, machinery, which reduces the cost of making and distributing goods to consumers. Now if, for purposes of this discussion, and in order to get a clear-cut decision, you assume again that wages are fixed, that they are a constant in the problem, then you can argue as to what the effect of introducing that machinery is going to be, that, the machinery will reduce the cost of getting the laborer's standard of living. For the time being, that is going to give laborers with their present money wages a higher real income, but since wages are fixed, a constant, that higher real wage is going to lead to an increase in their numbers and force wages down again until they get to the old standard of living, and that will mean that the advantages of the introduction goes to the employing class.

That is true about Ricardo's method of work at large. He is able, by operating as he does, to discuss his problems by taking up a series of cases, always confining his analysis to those situations in which one single factor is allowed to vary at a time. It is very much like the process of experimentation conducted in our physical and chemical laboratories now-a-days. If you really want to test experimentally some hypothesis concerning the rate two bodies fall, you arrange an experimental situation in which all the factors involved but one are constant. And so you put your feather and your penny in a glass and pump out the air and you let the two fall in a vacuum: and you find the light body and the heavy body fall at almost the same time - not quite, because you cannot get all the air out. You perform your experiment by creating an artificial situation...

Ricardo was forced into that sort of operation. He would take quantities he well knew to be variables, quantities which in other passages, when he was treating them at length, he pointed out at considerable trouble, did as a matter of fact change in value from period to period and country to country. He would take these quantities, and for the time being, without giving you any warning, assume their constancy just in order to get a situation about which he could reason simply and clearly. And that situation about which he reasons simply and clearly may have as little direct resemblance to the conditions of the world in which we live as the conditions under that glass in the laboratory from which you pumped out the air to drop your penny and feather at the same time.

The only trouble with the operation is that Ricardo as a rule did not take any pains to warn his readers of what he was doing. Probably he went ahead with this operation without thinking much about what he was doing himself; until having it called to his attention he was quite unaware of it. He was paying too high a compliment to the intelligence of his readers.

There is, then, involved in his method of analysis, of building up economic theory, the very considerable difficulty that without resort to a more elaborate scheme of analysis which will enable one to treat two or more variables at the same time, he is forced to assume facts which he well knows are not true, to argue on the basis of assumptions he knows well distort the facts of life. That is, of course, a limitation on the value of this method of work. It shows that in order to get a clear set of conclusions about economic problems, no matter how deeply and vitally interested you are in the practical issues of the day as was Ricardo, you are forced, if you adopt this way of working, to build up your discussion as a whole into a series of very artificial problems. And, once more, you arrive at conclusions which are logically valid only with reference to conditions contrary to fact from which they are drawn.

But if you really remember what you have done all the time, if you do not forget the limitations set upon the validity of the conclusions you have drawn, you are in a perfectly secure logical position and you may, if you have the insight of Ricardo, arrive at results which are practically of very great significance. The real danger is that you are going to forget that you have drawn conclusions on the basis of certain conditions contrary to fact, and then you will begin to think of these conclusions elsewhere as if they applied to the world at large; and that is a failing into which Ricardo's followers very commonly fell. In the generation that succeeded his death, you find that many and many a man, parading with the garments of the science of political economy, tried to teach the working classes of England, for instance, the lessons which Ricardo had drawn, putting even Ricardo's conclusions as if they were really based upon a study of actual England, trying to lead his hearers to believe that everything which Ricardo argued on the basis of certain assumptions, which he well knew to be assumptions contrary to fact, was immediately applicable to the affairs of life. And in that way they brought the science of political economy into very considerable disrepute, and a disrepute that was fairly earned if economics was fairly represented by these people who took conclusions reasoned out on the basis of certain assumptions and then applied them incautiously to the world as it exists.

The generation or two of English political economists, for instance, who tried to persuade the working classes that they could nɔt benefit themselves at all by trade unions, were basing their arguments fundamentally upon propositions concerning the relation between the natural price of labor and the amount of capital that was devoted to paying workers. Well, those propositions are found playing their role in Ricardo's political economy, and the arguments that were made by the opponents of trade unions could be validated by references to the sacred book, a book which in the generation played much the same role among the exponents of the capital side in social controversies that Marx's Das Kapital a generation or two later played among the worker's side in the later stages of the same controversy, and a book that was about as well adapted to such performances because it was a book almost as hard to read and understand!

You see, that is a very dangerous type of argumentation to play with. It is a safe method of procedure in the hands of a person who is as honest as Ricardo was and a person who had his skill in choosing the special cases to be set up in imagination for analysis. Ricardo was like a physicist or a chemist in insight, one who really knew how to arrange in his imaginary experiments, to arrange in the laboratory of his mind, those conditions contrary to ordinary fact which would throw light upon matters of great practical moment. His followers were many of those people who when they tried at all to carry further Ricardo's processes of investigation were fumblers in the laboratory, people who had no intuition concerning experiments which when tried would produce results of considerable significance. It takes a man who is honest and has extraordinary capacity to work by this method and achieve results of considerable value.

It was a method that doubtless Ricardo would have practiced in whatever generation he had been born into, because of the particular bent of his own mind. But it was a method that was particularly successful in his generation because it was almost the only method by which many of the problems on which it was necessary to get light could be successfully handled. Ricardo's contemporary, Malthus, as we have seen, was a person who had a native bent of a very different sort. He was a man who wanted actually to observe what went on the the real world, and to argue about these observations. He was a man who would have flourished greatly in a generation where it was really possible to collect an enormous quantity of measured observations about human behavior and then try and draw conclusions from them by applying the method of methodical analysis. Now Malthus could do that sort of thing very successfully with reference to one problem, the problem of population. Even in the first generation of the nineteenth century, the world had a considerable supply of vital statistics. They had all the mathematical tools of analysis which were required for handling what materials they had. But they had very few materials in the shape of measured observations - of statistics bearing upon the distribution of income. The great central problem of Ricardo's later life could not be handled by anyone at that time by the methods of the sort that Malthus liked to use. And when Malthus was facing the problem of rent, you remember he was one of the co-discoverers of the theory we now call Ricardian, he reasoned after Ricardo's fashion. He did so because he had to; because there was no other way of treating the question as to what determines the various sums paid for rights to use various pieces of farm land.

There was, of course, a strong beginning made even while Ricardo was living, in the direction of collecting statistical materials; some of the foundations on which later statistical technique was built up were being laid by the people who were working on the theory of probabilities. One of Ricardo's young contemporaries was the first man in England to suggest making index numbers of prices. But broadly speaking, the time was one comparatively destitute of statistical data, comparatively ignorant of methods of utilizing effectively what statistical data they had. And so, if one wanted to get any real light upon the economic problems of most general consequence of that day he was practically forced to resort to

Ricardo's method of thinking about how people would behave under certain conditions. And for that kind of argument Ricardo had very rare gifts, - gifts which enabled him with extraordinary rapidity to work out pretty much all of what became for the several generations following him the central problem of economics. His method was quick and easy, and it did after all lead him to a number of very significant results.

The time may be coming when we shall be able to attack problems of this order by methods which are more akin to those which Malthus instinctively liked, methods which depend not so much upon making imaginary experiments under conditions contrary to fact, but depend far more upon observing what people do, observing very widely and freely through the artificial aid of statistical data. And then we shall make the scientific part of the discussion consist in a quasi-mathematical analysis of these statistical results. But anyone who has tried to apply these methods of measured observation and analysis to economic problems realizes that the materials which even this generation possesses are far from being satisfactory for that type of work. And so we are continually falling back upon the general type of speculative discussion which Ricardo managed with such brilliant success. And we are therefore still exposed to the kind of dangers which Ricardo ran into, sometimes succumbed to in minor degree; the kind of dangers which some of his successors fell into far more disastrously, if they did not as a matter of fact, as I am sometimes inclined to suspect them of doing more or less consciously, tried to deceive themselves as well as others concerning the practical significance of results which are really argued out on the basis of assumptions which did not correspond to the conditions under which we really live.

And it is just because we are all of us still compelled when we try to do considerable work on economic problems, to make large use of the method of imaginary experimentation which Ricardo handled that it is desirable that we should ourselves appreciate not only the possibilities but also the dangers of that way of working, that we should try to cultivate in ourselves a very careful attention to the logical limitations to which any conclusions that we may draw are really subject, and we should have a very stern conscience about exaggerating the practical importance of the conclusions that we draw.

The later generations of people who have cultivated what is now often called "pure economics" are usually above reproach in this respect. They are very likely to draw their garments closely about them and to explain that after all the problems that they are discussing are problems of a highly special character, that the conclusions which they draw are, after all, conclusions of a very limited application; that their science makes but slight pretensions to offering advice to the man in the street or the man in the legislative chamber. In so far as they take that position they are, of course, above reproach, above suspicion. But from Ricardo's point of view, I fancy that people of this sort would have seemed rather disappointing; for a man so warmly concerned as was he with the questions of the day, so energetically eager to improve the lot of struggling mankind, would have thought them a set of people who were cultivating a rather idle science, a science that made no pretense to giving guidance to the citizen or statesman; and that such men, judged by sound utilitarian standards were of no great account.

To him, at least, the value of this whole method of imaginary experimentation was that, despite its limitations, it does enable us to arrive at practical conclusions of great moment, and it was in these practical conclusions that his interests centered.

XXVII

THE "POSTULATES" AND "PRECONCEPTIONS" OF ECONOMIC THEORY.
RICARDO'S PRECONCEPTIONS.

I have spent our last two meetings mainly in trying to make clear the general
logical character of Ricardo's type of economic theorizing. It is usually characterized as deductive theory. That is, however, a rather indefinite expression because
the logicians have no difficulty in showing that in all processes of human reasoning there is a constant shifting from deduction to induction and back again. I
think we get a clearer and livelier view of what Ricardo is doing if we characterize his operations as a series of imaginary experiemnts. He is like a man who is
trying to discover new facts concerning materials which cannot be manipulated by
the hands. His viewpoint is like that of a theoretical physicist, but a man who cannot use a laboratory, cannot invent apparatus and try different experiments. So he
takes these unintelligible materials of his and sets up ordinary cases in his mind
and proceeds to argue what will necessarily happen under these circumstances. It is
a process of trying imaginary experiments upon the economic behavior of man.

Now, of course, that method of work proceeds on the basis of various assumptions. In part these assumptions are explicitly made for every imaginary experiment;
but in part Ricardo is also working with certain broad and general notions which he
entertained, some of which he entertained consciously, others of which were implicitly present in his reasoning.

When political economy began to get self-conscious in the generation following Ricardo, when his followers were contriving to explain what precisely their great
masters had done, with what limitations their conclusions should be accepted, then
men began to discuss what they called the "postulates" of English political economy.
That type of inquiry was carried on most effectively by Walter Bagehot, whom most
of you must know as the author of Lombard Street (1873), one of the most brilliant
essays in monetary theory that has ever been composed.

Bagehot, was a man of extraordinary cultural range and a well-informed writer.
In his essay on The Postulates of English Political Economy, which you can find now-
a-days in a volume of his essays that has been edited by Richard Holt Hutton called
Economic Studies, he tried to show what were the general assumptions on the basis of
which economists worked. That was a lead in economics which at the beginning yielded
large returns, but which soon ran out, and which ran out for two good and sufficient
reasons.

You can no more — to give the first of these reasons - state what are the
logical postulates upon which an economic theory rests than you can state all the
causes of any physical event. Of course, our textbooks of logic have familiarized
us with the latter proposition. When we see the falling of a shot when fired from
a cannon and say that it is drawn down because of the attraction of the earth, it is
obvious we are giving a very inadequate account of the phenomenon. It may be an
account that is quite sufficient for the average mind, but when you try to give a
casual explanation of any single event in the world's history, it is not complete
until you carry it back to cosmography. Everything gets involved directly and indirectly in any attempt to assign a cause for anything that has happened.

The same is true of this effort to assign the logical postulates upon which
an economic theory rests. Let me illustrate with reference to the theory of rent.
In expounding the theory of rent itself, Ricardo was content to say that it presup-
poses, first that land is limited in quantity and variable in quality; and second

that the more fertile land is relatively scarce. It is quite obvious that you
could not have rents paid, according to the Ricardian law, unless both these suppositions were valid, — unless land were limited in quantity and variable in quality, — and unless land of the highest quality were relatively scarce. Now Malthus
was not satisfied with that statement of the postulates but added a third which he
thought still more fundamental. He said that rent could not be paid unless land
yielded a produce more than sufficient to sustain the cultivators; and, quite obviously, that also is true. Then came Senior, somewhat later, and he said that the
important postulate of the theory of rent is the law of diminishing returns. If
you could increase the quantity of produce that you can get from a given piece of
land by the simple process of increasing the labor and the capital you spend cultivating it and you increase profits proportionately to the increase of labor and
capital, then the Ricardian theory of rent would not hold.

Another one of Ricardo's slightly younger contemporaries, Richard Jones,
pointed out a postulate to him that the important thing about the theory of rent
was that it presupposed a certain definite form of economic organization in which
land was held by the class of landlords, in which it was cultivated by a set of
capitalist farmers, and in which the farmers got at least the large part of their
work done by a class of wage-earning laborers. And that with this situation as
presented in England there contrasted a widely different situation that existed in
India where there were no such classes and where rents of the Ricardian type were
not paid; and in his review of rent in different parts of the earth he found four
or five decidedly different forms of economic organization, one of which led to a
distinct type of argument about the use of land.

Bagehot, when he was writing his Postulates of English Political Economy,
suggested incidentally another postulate of this doctrine, a postulate which was
presently argued out more elaborately by Karl Marx. As Marx put it, the theory of
rent assumes that the state of the productivity of labor is a factor of very great
importance. The amount that you can get out of a given field depends quite as much,
argues Marx, on your knowledge of how to cultivate as it does upon the fertility of
the soil. And for illustration he could point to such facts as the difference of
yield of Indian corn in the United States when Indian corn was cultivated by real
Indians and when it was cultivated by American farmers on the same lands. The
yields were altogether different; the rents that could be paid were altogether
different. And still more recently at the centenary celebration of Ricardo's first
publication Professor Henry C. Taylor pointed out still another postulate: The
Ricardian theory of rent, rigidly interpreted, implies that all men who are competing for farms to cultivate possess essentially the same degree of economic
productivity. For if all farmers are not on a par in skill of cultivation, then it
cannot happen that competition will adjust the sums paid for the use of different
farms accurately to what Ricardo called differences in "the original and indestruc-
tible properties of the soil." If one man's capacity for cultivation gives him a
particular advantage in handling land of a certain grade and location as compared
with others, then he is likely to bid higher for that land, in comparison with other
grades, than any other competitor whose differential advantages as a farmer are
unlike his own.

Now all that is just by way of illustrating how far you will have to go a-
field if you really tried to list all the logical postulates involved in any economic doctrine. Anyone who is interested in these logical exercises should try to
state to himself exhaustively the postulates upon which other Ricardian doctrine,
aside from that of rent rests; and if he has considerable ingenuity he will rapidly
accumulate a long list of postulates and he will see that the list may be as interminable as the list of causes which are involved in the production of any physical
phenomenon.

There is a second difficulty with this way of trying to put the logic of classical political economy into perfect order, namely that the postulates on which a given economic doctrine rest will follow according to the precision which you ascribe to the doctrine itself. It is only when you take the doctrines in their most rigid form that you can proceed with any confidence to say what the postulates are; and taking these doctrines in the most rigid form is usually a distortion of the writer's meaning. For example, that theory of Ricardo's on which I was speaking on Tuesday that a tax on wages is a tax on profits; that is, a tax levied on wages will altogether be shifted to the employers of labor, and so paid out of profits. Now to accept that proposition literally we have to suppose an incompressible standard of living -- perfectly incompressible -- we have to suppose human nature of extraordinary rigidity in order to have an incompressible standard of living; and we have also to suppose that the commercial system possesses an almost incomprehensible degree of elasticity; so that a change produced in the standard of living will be transferred exactly -- "wholly" is Ricardo's phrase -- to profits.

Well, of course, we all realize that these logical postulates land us in absurdities, and so we are rather inclined to lose patience with the attempt to put our economic theory upon a logical foundation by this game of seeing what postulates are implied and what are ample for practical purposes, regardless of the problem in mind, in order to interpret the doctrine into whose postulates we are inquiring. And the purposes for which we use these formulas of economic theory are extremely varied; since they are varied, the postulates that we ascribe to the doctrines must be equally varied.

The subtle critics of a later generation have dealt not so much with the postulates of economic theory as with preconceptions with which the theorists worked; that is, those unreasoned convictions which they carried in their minds and which had much to do with determining the larger issues of their theorizing, with the solution of the problems they thought worth studying and with the general conclusions at which they arrived. Just as Walter Bagehot is the foremost exponent of the inquiries into the postulates of political economy, so Thorstein Veblen is the chief exponent of this other form of critical inquiry. If you are seriously interested in the general logical character of economic theory from Adam Smith to John Stuart Mill, you will find his papers on the preconceptions of economic theory among the most fascinating references to read. They appeared first in the Quarterly Journal of Economics as a series of three papers, published in 1899 and 1900, and since then they have been reprinted in a volume of Veblen's collected essays, a volume that is called The Place of Science in Modern Civilization.

With certain of Ricardo's preconceptions it is desirable for us to deal if we want to get what light we can upon the range of his interests and the peculiarities of his results. I think that for our purposes his most important preconceptions can be summed up in what he thought about the physical world at large, about social organization, and about human nature.

I will begin with the physical world. That appears in Ricardo's theory under the guise of natural resources. And there to his mind the important proposition was that the population will find it ever harder to wring a living for its increasing numbers from the soil. That is the most fundamental fact about the physical world for the economists and one of the most fundamental facts for anyone interested in the doubtful fate of human kind. Again, this law of diminishing returns; Ricardo thought that the accumulation of capital to improve methods of cultivation, of transportation, of importation of food from foreign countries, would in the long run wage a losing fight. He was ready to admit that for comparatively short periods it would be possible for an increasing population to live in a certain quarter of the globe without diminishing their standard of living, provided that they were rapidly growing in wealth, so that they would have more capital to employ, and that they were rapidly improving their agricultural technique; that they were able to draw food from other countries by exporting produce of non-agrigultural sorts. But when you looked at the problem seriously you had to admit that mankind would find it ever harder to get a living for its inevitably increasing numbers from the soil. It seems to us rather curious that Ricardo, living as he did in an age when agricultural technique was being improved very rapidly, and particularly in an age when the Industrial Revolution, as we now call it, was making rapid strides, should have attached so little importance, as he seems to have done, to the possibility of counteracting what he sometimes called "the niggardliness of nature" by the results of man's increasing intelligence. It is a question that he did not go into. He never argued it out, but simply took it for granted that however much we may learn about getting a living we will never get to the point where the spectre of overpopulation will cease to be a spectre of the most terrifying sort.

On the other hand, Ricardo was not troubled by the fear of soil exhaustion, by depletion of natural resources such as coal and iron mines, and by the destruction of forests. To him, in his type of theory, natural resources were a constant, and,because the land yielded returns that decreased proportionately as man increased the efforts spent upon it,--just for that reason, when he looked toward the future he looked with grave misgivings.It is that fact more than any other that gave Ricardo the reputation of being rather pessimistic.

Second, his preconceptions about social organization: Now Ricardo thought that the social organization of the country and the age in which he lived was something that had developed from a long past. You could look back upon that early and rude state of society which precedes both the accumulation of stock and the appropriation of land, the state of society which was exemplified to his mind by the tales that travelers and missionaries brought back from the Americas, from the islands of the South Pasific, or from Africa, from lands still imhabited by savages. But of that early and rude state of society which precedes both the accumulation of stock and the appropriation of land he had a most capitalistic point of view. He spoke of a weapon necessary to kill a beaver as capital. He implied in what he said about the exchanges of savages that they kept account of the average length of time it would take to kill a deer in comparison with what it would take to capture a fish. He implied that savages carry on their trade for commercial advantages,-- all of which notions, of course, are quite different from the notions that modern anthropologists who studied the lives and the efforts of savage men have come to entertain. It was precisely the notion a business man would have when he thought about a group of people with whom he had come in contact. They were just a business man's reflections, carrying over the categories with which he was familiar into the lives of people who live under circumstances altogether different,and just because Ricardo had this curiously capitalistic view of savage life he failed to see the great significance of the problem of how capitalism evolved--one of those problems which in the latter part of the nineteenth century came to occupy a prominent place in economic work.

Ricardo, in failing to see that there was a fundamental difference in character between the economic thoughts and behavior of savages and so-called civilized men, was in perfectly good contemporary company, for even in his days the professed ethnologists read their own thoughts into the minds of savages.It was only as people tried time and time again with repeated attempts to identify themselves as closely as possible with the viewpoint of the savage that even the ethnologists came to see how altogether distorting is the interpretation that we put upon the objective behavior of savages when we think of what they are doing in terms of what seems natural to us; and, of course, Ricardo, not being an anthropologist, quite naturally enough fell into errors which indeed the best ethnologists of his time and some even eminent

enthologists of our time find difficult to avoid. While social organization had
evolved out of an earlier and ruder state, Ricardo took it for granted that it had
reached maturity and was not going to change materially in the future. When he
looked forward, it was with the expectation that the progressive state in which he
then lived was going to run down like a clock into the stationary state. That is
another of his phrases:"the stationary state of society". But in that stationary
state he expected to see the same three classes of capitalists, landowners, and
laborers earning incomes of the same types:profits, rents, and wages, but dividing
them in slightly different proportions. From his viewpoint, the important difference between the progressive state and the stationary state was that in the transi-
tion from the former to the latter you are going to have a decline of profits; possibly some slight decline of wages,- certainly no increase;and certainly a marked
increase in rents.

In his opinion, Robert Owen and other reformers of the time who were specu-
lating about the possibility of making rather fundamental changes in human institutions were a set of visionaries, - visionaries in whose opinion no sane man could
put much trust. Why was it that the social organization, as Ricardo saw it, must
persist? It certainly was not because Ricardo had a high opinion of it. On the
contrary, as I have said several times, he was a radical reformer, a man who saw so
much amiss with social organization, and a man who did the best that he could to
remedy the remediable faults, of which there were many, but among which the most
important faults could not be counted. For Ricardo thought that aside from various
matters that we might hope to set straight if we thought hard and clearly enough,
social organization presents certain ineradicable conflicts of interests. The interest of the landlord is always opposed to that of the manufacturer, and to that
of the consumer. There is no way of keeping profits up but by keeping wages down.Of
course,Ricardo is here talking about proportions; but when he is looking into the
future, the pie to be divided between the three classes was to be similar in proportion to the number of mankind, so keeping profits up by keeping wages down is
keeping up the share of a larger piece. It is not merely proportionate wages but
actual real income on his logic that must be kept down in order to keep up profits.

Ricardo thought there was nothing to be done about this irreconcilable conflict because it is the effect of the natural course of things against which no man
can struggle with any hope of success. He further said that nothing contributes so
much to the prosperity and happiness of a country as high profits. But his whole
argument shows that the inevitable development of prosperity by high profits is to
stimulate the accumulation of capital, and the accumulation of capital tends to
drive profits down; and so this condition which contributes most to the prosperity
and happiness of the country is a condition which destroys itself whenever it exists.
If profits are temporarily high, it means rapid accumulation; and rapid accumulation
means a fall of profits; in other words, it leads to a situation which is not conducive to the happiness of the community.

It was not, then, because Ricardo thought that the social organization of
his day was one well adapted to insure human felicity when he thought it must be permanent. It was rather because he thought no change could be brought about without
landing mankind in a still worse predicament. And that conviction of his rested upon ideas of the same sort that Jeremy Bentham held that the attempt to increase man's
pleasures by dividing wealth more equally would necessarily be brought by interference with the property rights of owners.For if there were any interference with the
natural competition among man for the fruits of their property, - any danger that
a person would not be allowed to enjoy gains, the result of his industry, or to
have them bebefit his family, - then the total amount of wealth in the community
would fall off. That, of course, is still a conviction that is widely held.

The quantity of employment in a country must depend not only upon the quantity of capital but upon its advantageous distribution; upon the conviction of the capitalist that he will be allowed to enjoy unmolested the fruits of his capital, his skill and his enterprise. To take from him this conviction would at once diminish the productive industry of the country, and would be more fatal to the poor laborer than to the rich capitalist himself. This was a self-evident proposition.

Well, if the institution of property must be left in its present stage for fear of landing men in a situation where there would be no incentive to accumulate and therefore no employment, then, of course, the social organization can undergo no very far-reaching changes, and we must come forward to such a measure of effort as we can secure under a system that does set the different classes that share income in conflict with each other, a situation in which the interest of the landlords will always be opposite to that of the manufacturers and the consumers, a situation in which profits can be kept up only by keeping wages down.

Ricardo's preconceptions concerning human nature: On this head also Ricardo's general views were very similar to those of Jeremy Bentham's. Like Bentham, Ricardo conceived behavior as a calculating pursuit of self-interest, in business, in politics, in morals. And he conceived that all human beings were substantially alike so far as the grounds of their conduct were concerned. Hence, in thinking about problems in the social sciences, whether presented in economics, politics, or ethics, it behooves a man to think about the personal character of people; of goodness or badness. The institutions, then, moulded their minds; so Ricardo thought much more about the institutions which bear upon their interests. Let me read a passage or two:

> It is self-interest which regulates all the speculations of trade, and where that can be clearly and satisfactorily asserted, we should not know where to seek if we admitted any other rule of action.

Self-interest also regulates politics:

> Let me know what the state of their (the electors!) interests is, and I will tell you what measures they will recommend.*

You see, that good, stiff economic determinism applied to politics; and the same proposition held for morals:

> To keep men good, you must as much as possible withdraw from them all temptations to be otherwise.*

Of course, man is going to follow his interests; and if it is his interest to be bad, he will be.

> The sanctions of religion, of public opinion, and of law, all proceed on this principle, and that State is most perfect in which all these sanctions concur to make it the interest of all men to be virtuous, which is the same thing as to say, to use their best endeavour to promote the general happiness.*

All of this is perfectly good, sound Benthamite doctrine; and I may add, it is perfectly good, sound moral doctrine, according to William Paley, Bentham's great contemporary in theology.

---

*Observations on Parliamentary Reform, (McCulloch ed. 1852) p.554.

This being the case, our concern in all social matters should be not so much with individuals as with the large impersonal factors that shape men's conceptions of their self-interest. Ricardo was convinced that:

> our security for good government must rest on the institutions themselves, and the influence under which those who govern us act, and not on the more or less virtue in the characters of our government. The conduct of two different sets of men educated nearly in the same manner, acting under the same checks, and with the same objects in view, as far as our personal interests are concerned, cannot be materially different.*

All of which means, of course, that in the economics which the Philosophical Radicals developed through Ricardo, you have the same fundamental principles of human nature applied that you have applied by Jeremy Bentham when he is talking about ethical problems, problems of jurisprudence, problems of education, problems of constitutional law, problems of the treatment of criminals, problems of whatever sort touching upon mankind.

But while in general Ricardo accepted Bentham's viewpoint, he was very much less of a formulist than Bentham was. Now you recall that Bentham lived the life of a secluded philosopher; he was a man temperamentally unfitted for the rough and tumble of active life, and so he could very readily think of human nature in terms of a preconceived scheme, - a great classifier of logically related ideas. Ricardo, on the other hand, as we have seen, was a man eminently successful, a practical man in business, in his personal relations with his friends, and in politics. And that means, of course, that he was a man who knew people - who knew what to expect that they would do under given circumstances. He looked at human behavior not as it can be seen through the distorting windows of an academic study, but as it is seen by a man who is himself a successful actor in a variety of more or less competitive struggles.

And so, quite naturally, he qualifies the conception of human nature which Jeremy Bentham entertains by various realistic objections. He is quite ready to admit a whole series of lapses from perfect rationality, and lapses, some of which, at least, it would be really difficult to explain on Bentham's sole ground of accounting for lapses from rationality, namely the lapses due to defects of the understanding. For example, Ricardo points out that the chances of a reverse of fortune are always considerably underestimated by all of us. Now there is a lapse from economic rationality, and he thinks it is characteristic of men at large. We are always inclined to underestimate our chances of failure in an undertaking. He even points out that statesmen are subject to lapses from rationality, such, for instance, as a whole generation suffered from in the matter of Dr. Price's sinking fund, that grand scheme for paying off the public debt through the mystery of compound interest, a mathematical delusion from which they ought to have been exempt, and would have been had they really reasoned accurately.

Much more important is the fact that investors underrate the value of annuities. And more important still is the prejudice and obstinacy which makes business men cling to a declining trade. They always expect a change for the better, and therefore continue to produce commodities for which there is no adequate demand. And, of course, most important of all is what Ricardo calls the imprudence of the lower classes: that inability to understand their interests which leads them to marry early and to have large families of children.

*Letters to John Ramsay McCulloch, (Pub. of the American Economic Assn. vol, X, No. 3-6) p. 723.

Ricardo seeing these lapses from rationality, stresses habit as a factor in behavior much more than does Bentham. And, of course, it is habit that is responsible for keeping wages a constant, that is, the idea of a fixed standard of living as the most important regulator of wages; an idea that rests upon the conception that the habits of the working class in regard to consumption are singularly rigid. And also he says that the habits of business men check the migration of capital; and this presents, when we are thinking about the foreign trade, a problem quite different from that which we find when we are talking about domestic trade. It is this habitual preference of business men which makes it necessary to supplement the laws of value that prevail within a country with an additional law of production cost which regulates exchanges between two different countries. Once again, Ricardo points out incidentally that habit leads taxes to be paid out of income. Thus, when they are levied on capital, his favorite remedy for paying off the national debt, they will be paid out of income and the national capital will remain unimpaired.

And beside this emphasis upon habit, Ricardo laid very heavy stress upon at least one: instinct - if I may use the psychological category that continued to play a large role for two or three generations after his time. Instincts are hardly apparent in Bentham's psychology; but one of the foundations upon which Ricardo built was what we would be inclined to call the instincts of sex, what he called the delights of domestic society. When Ricardo attributed the danger of overpopulation not to the instinct of sex but to the delights of domestic society, he was not merely using a familiar euphemism; the real danger to be feared, the thing as economist was interested in, was the number of children born. Well, in his day birth control was just beginning to be discussed as a possible remedy, , a possible way of averting the dangers; but he took it for granted that when people married they would proceed to have children in such numbers as the Lord appointed. On the other hand, he took it for granted, apparently, that children in considerable numbers are not to be feared out of wedlock. It was the delights of domestic society that was the weakness - intellectual, moral, if you like, - of the wage-earning classes. It was this defect which was primarily responsible for the drab prospects that mankind faced, as Ricardo looked into the future. For if the mass of the wage earners did not succumb to these delights of domestic society, then population would not keep increasing and the terrible law of diminishing returns would not be brought into effective operation, profits need not fall, wages might even rise, and the day when the landowners and the receivers of tithes would become masters of a very large proportion of the total output of society might be indefinitely postponed. But Ricardo was a man who was always ready to face the logical consequences of his conceptions. He seemed to have taken it for granted that there was no particular use in trying to remedy this defect of human nature. The wage-earning classes were subject to undue influence when they contemplated the delights of domestic society, and so we must expect they would continue to be for an indefinite time.

Now with this conception of human nature, Ricardo had no need to set up a special economic man. All human nature, as he saw it, was fit material for the theorizing of an economist. But that is a matter upon which I shall have to elaborate a little further at our next meeting.

XXVIII

RICARDO'S CONCEPTIONS OF HUMAN NATURE, HIS
FOUR LEVELS OF ANALYSIS

I was speaking at the end of our last meeting about Ricardo's conception of human nature, his working idea about man's general equipment for directing his behavior. The fundamental fact to observe is that, like Jeremy Bentham, he conceived men to be essentially calculating animals; the most important element in directing what they shall do is an effort to find out where their interests lay. They are primarily creatures that are thinking about their interests and using their ideas of their interests to determine the course of their actions.

But I want to say that while this is a general broad proposition which it is most important to realize clearly if you want to understand Ricardo's general type of economic theory, it is also true, by way of qualification, that he did not have as rigid a conception of men as calculating animals as Bentham had. On the one hand, he admitted that even in solving certain technical problems like the value of annuities, men often calculate wrong. Of course, Bentham thought that they sometimes calculated wrong, but Ricardo takes occasion to point that out more than once. And thus Ricardo also lays occasional stress upon the fact that in their calculations men are warped by certain emotional attitudes such as the obstinacy which prevents men from deserting a declining employment when it would be to their interest to do so, - the emotional attitudes that make men prefer home to foreign investments, though foreign investments might yield much larger returns.

And then, also, he lays more stress upon the factor of habit, that playing a great role in his theory by virtue of the fact that it is substantially habit which fixes standards of living, and thus standards of living are the most important factor in determining wages in the long run.

And, finally, he lays great stress upon one element in human nature which since his time has usually been called "instinct" - men's longing to get married and have children.

Now in discussing Bentham I pointed out that his very simple conception of man as a calculating machine did much to facilitate the construction of social sciences by speculative methods. If you can suppose that what men do is going to be determined by their interests, and if you, as a human being with a wide outlook, can see broadly where men's interests lie, then you can tell what they will do. Along that line you can speculate freely, elaborately, subtly, comprehensively, concerning all sorts of problems of human behavior; not in economics alone, but in all the other social sciences: in jurisprudence, in education, in ethics, and law, and sociology.

You might expect that Ricardo's qualification of that general proposition that men are calculating animals would get in the way of his easy theorizing. These qualifications would indeed make him a lot of trouble if it were not for the fact that he treats these qualifications in a rather curious way. He, in his thinking about mankind, standardized these defections from rationality, so that he was able to treat them as constant elements in his problem; they were not variables, but they were constants. And the introduction of a constant into your problem causes less trouble than the attempt to handle variables.

Let me point out a little more clearly just what that means. Take first Ricardo's emphasis upon the factor of habit in giving us definitely crystallized standards of living, and his emphasis upon men's longing to get married and raise children. These two factors together: men's insistence upon having a certain standard of living and their eagerness to get married and raise children - keep real wages a constant, a fixed quantity, which may perhaps have a tendency over long periods of time of shrinking a little but which for the most purposes of economic theory can be treated as a factor in the situation which does not itself vary.

We have already had occasion to observe how this conception of a fixed real wage enables Ricardo to draw broad and sweeping conclusions about the future course of profits, but that he knew that in the long run profits, as the classical economists were accustomed to phrase it, tended to a minimum. They tended to a minimum because wages were going to be constant, and as the population increased it would be necessary to resort to poorer land or to cultivate old lands more intensively. The yield to the last increment in cultivation would be smaller, and if wages remained a constant then that last increment divided between wages and capital would of course, give a smaller share to capital, and competition would standardize profits in all different lines, for this reduction of profits in agriculture would be extended to reduction of profits in any kind of investment.

Well, now you see there how your psychological qualifications upon man's reasoning capacity help to simplify your problem of analysis by making this very important economic category of real wages a constant factor. And because it is a constant factor it is one that you can use in treating other variables. It causes you no trouble.

Another illustration: That matter of the patriotic prejudices which Ricardo says lead men to prefer home to foreign investments even though the home investments yield them a smaller rate of return than they might expect if they sent their money overseas. In Ricardo's way of treating this problem, that difference between the standard rate of profit achieved in home and in foreign investments makes no trouble at all. What Ricardo says is that this difference establishes a hard and fast line between two problems, namely, the problem of values inside a country, and the problem of values in international exchange. So he builds up two theories of value; one on the assumption that there is free competition among the people for investment capital in different lines, - that applies inside a country; - the other theory on the assumption that such free competition does not exist, and there values, instead of being regulated by cost of production, are regulated by what later writers called comparative costs - giving a technical term to Ricardo's ideas.

Once again, Ricardo sees that men rate the advantages of different trades in different ways, paying attention not simply to the money returns that they can get by going in for different occupations, but also paying attention to certain nonpecuniary advantages such as the honor that attaches to certain trades, and the social disfavor in which others are held. Now that you might expect would make it difficult to reason about a system in which you are supposing that competition is going to equalize rates of profits and rates of wages in all occupations. And it would unless you supposed that these prejudices which people have, these social prejudices of one sort or another in favor of certain occupations and against other occupations, were a constant factor in the situation. Ricardo does suppose them to be fixed - constant. And on that basis he supposed that there are certain differentials between the returns in money received in different occupations. These returns do not vary. He does not go into any effort to find out exactly what these differences in returns are, but supposes that they are a permanent part of our economic situation; and having made that remark he passes on. And when he says that competition tends to equalize the profits in all different trades, if he were thinking of this point he would say, instead, competition adjusts the profits in all the different lines of trade, so that the total attractiveness of all different lines of trades in the eyes of men remains the same, but in order that the total attractiveness may remain the same it is necessary that the money return in certain lines should be greater than others.

Thus you can qualify your general proposition that men are calculating animals, and still if you are willing to suppose that these qualifications once made simply give rise to a set of permanent differentials you may go ahead with your speculative account of what men will do, based on your analysis of their interest, and succeed almost as well as if you made no qualifications at all to the proposition that man are always seeking pleasure and avoiding pain.

It is rather curious to a modern reader to find how content Ricardo seems to have been with his qualifications upon human nature to say that some factor in the situation was fixed by habit. He does not go on to inquire what fixes habits. How is it that a certain standard of living gets established in a certain country at a certain time? What are the factors which may raise or lower that standard over a long period of time? That question, what fixes a habit, is a modern question, and one which Ricardo's generation had not gotten round to asking. If you are reading John Stuart Mill, you may have noticed even he, writing a generation later than Ricardo, very often has recourse to the same simplifying device. He ascribes certain factors in the situation to a social custom and leaves the matter there. That is, from the modern point of view, the statement of a new problem rather than the solution of an old one, and a problem which requires a type of approach very different from that which Ricardo or John Stuart Mill or anyone who is working with their conceptions of human nature could adequately handle.

I want to conclude what I have to say about Ricardo's conception of human nature by pointing out that he did not have any economic man in mind as a creature that was constructed for theoretical purposes and differed from the men that he knew. He did not need a separate economic man for the mere reason that Bentham did not need an artificial human being as the subject or hero of his whole group of social sciences. Bentham did not need an artificial man simply because his conception of human nature was itself sufficiently artificial, and was already fit material for spinning theories. And the same remark applies, with about the same degree of qualification that I have suggested we must make when we think of the differences between Ricardo's and Bentham's conception of rationality at large, to Ricardo's conception of human nature. I do not doubt that he believed his account of how men behave in pursuit of their economic interests was an account that applied to real men, and he could do so because he had a highly standardized conception of what human nature is. Anyone who has that conception of human nature may quite honestly deny that he is talking about an artificial economic man.

I think we may go a little further and say that Ricardo implies - and I do not believe he ever gave the matter very much thought - that in the matter of economic behavior, all mankind are divided into three classes and that they differ somewhat in their native constitutions. The capitalists, the laborers, and the landowners, if they do not differ in their native constitutions they at least differ in the qualities which they reveal in economic theory. The capitalists are presented as creatures who are animated chiefly by a restless desire to find the most profitable investments, a restless desire that is modified by an eye for the non-pecuniary advantages of certain trades and by a not insuperable preference for home over foreign investments.

The working classes, so far as human nature is concerned, are creatures who are dominated by habit and by a tropismatic longing to marry. And as for the landlords in Ricardo's system, they are people who are raised by their position over economic production to reap their gains in idleness and honor. As Ricardo wrote to McCulloch, "their rent is the effect of circumstances over which they have no control excepting indeed if they are the law makers and lay restrictions on the importation of corn." For the rest, he did not think of the landlord as a business man; he was just a person who owned land, and the competition of the farmers could be relied upon to give him certain rents. Those rents were determined by economic laws, and the landlords could not raise them. If they would just have that degree of activity which is necessary to make sure that their farms were offered to the best bidder, that was all that was necessary to enable them to get all the revenue, all the income that economic circumstances prompted. That was, needless to say, a rather grave caricature upon the landed interest of Ricardo's time. A great many of Ricardo's own contemporaries who were landowners were extremely intellectual people, - people who were improving the character of their lands, and oftentimes very active in Parliament in their own interests, not merely trying to get corn laws imposed which would raise the price of wheat and increase their rents, but very active in trying to get open fields or old pasture lands inclosed so that they could obtain a larger revenue from their farms. In supposing that they really had no control, exercised no influence over the conditions which determine rent except to vote for corn laws in Parliament, Ricardo was doing injustice to their rationality.

Well, now let me pass on to another and final topic which I think is of very considerable importance in understanding not only the classical type of theory but also several variants into which the classical type after a time split up. I call this topic THE FOUR LEVELS OF ANALYSIS.

To show what that means I begin again with Bentham. On the basis of human nature as conceived by Bentham or Ricardo, the real forces which control human conduct are pleasure and pain. Commodities are important because they are sources of pleasures and pains to us, - having them as a source of pleasure, doing without them as a source of pain. Money is important as a means of getting commodities. And finally, welfare or happiness - a hundred years ago the English used the word "happiness" far more than "welfare" - is a net balance of pleasurable feeling experienced in the long run.

Now you can treat human behavior from Bentham's or Ricardo's point of view - you can give an account of it in terms of pleasure and pain; or in terms of what men do about commodities; or in terms of what men do about money; or with reference to the happiness that they get in the long run.

Bentham, the great simplifier in all his discussions of social problems, tried to penetrate at once to the fundamental level of pleasure and pain. He tried to deal with the real forces that control our conduct. Ricardo, on the contrary, keeps passing from one level of analysis to another, talking about conduct sometimes in terms of sacrifices and satisfactions which are equivalent to pleasures and pains; sometimes in terms of commodities as, for instance, when he talks about real wages which are made of a mass of commodities; sometimes in terms of money; and every now and then he will pass some remarks concerning welfare.

And that example of Ricardo's of conducting his analysis sometimes in terms of real forces and sometimes of commodities, sometimes of money, and then mixing with this references to welfare, is an example that has been followed in later discussions and has given rise, I think, to not a little confusion of thought. It certainly has given us some very puzzling problems of interpretation, some very puzzling problems of analysis that we are only beginning to face very seriously in our own generation.

Let me show how the four levels of analysis appear in Ricardo's Principles. The most superficial of analyses, from his viewpoint, is the monetary level; and Ricardo was acutely conscious of the complications which the use of money introduces into economic theory. His very first essay - you remember that was on The High Price of Bullion, - was an effort to prove that the currency and its purchasing power was variable, that it was not a constant factor in business. And then because it was a highly variable factor, it made a great deal of trouble to a person who was interested in arriving at the broad type of conclusions of Ricardo that economic laws should represent. Well, now because money was a variable, in his Essay on the Influence of a Low Price of Corn on the Profits of Stock the pamphlet which preceded the Principles, Ricardo at the beginning of his analysis sets money aside and carries on his story in terms of quarters of wheat, supposing that the investment of the farmer consisted in so many quarters of wheat, that the wages he pays are paid in quarters of wheat, that the landlord gets a certain number of quarters of wheat, and that the farmer regains his profits in quarters of wheat. That is, the analysis is carried on in terms of the commodity wheat; and only after the analysis of the problem of distribution on the commodity level has been completed, does Ricardo say, now what difference will it make if we suppose, what is the fact, that men do not carry on their business transactions in terms of wheat, - they carry on their transactions in terms of money; and the answer is that in the long run it makes just one difference, namely, that agricultural prices tend to rise as compared with the manufactured products, and hence landlords get a double gain. They not only get a larger share of agricultural products in terms of wheat or any other agricultural product, but also these agricultural products of which they get a larger share bear a relatively higher money price.

When he came to write the Principles of Political Economy, he did not follow that precedent of his essay of 1815; he did not set money aside because it is a variable. Instead, he talked for the most part about people who were laying out money in their investments, paying wages, rents, and profits in money; but he avoided confusion on that score by supposing - and this is one of the few suppositions which he makes explicitly, not only makes explicitly but repeats two or three times in the course of his book - by supposing that the price level is not going to vary; by making money - the purchasing power of money - a constant in his analysis. Again driven to a simplification of the problem as indispensably necessary if he was going to carry on the kind of analysis which really interested him, he treated money as having a constant purchasing power. That simplifying device made it possible for him to carry on a large part of his analysis in terms of money. He says, for instance, that what all producers look steadily at is market price which may differ from natural or normal price. Well, of course, price means money level of analysis. He says that when the market price of labor is greater than the natural price men multiply rapidly, - again carrying on this analysis in terms of money. Or, once more, he explains the mechanism of the market for loan funds, the bill brokers and their work, all of which work is done in terms of money. And this discussion of what men do in terms of money has the advantage of keeping Ricardo's Principles more realistic in form than his analysis of the greater part of his Essay on the Profits of Stock.

But very frequently Ricardo passes over from this money level of analysis to the commodity level. For instance, he says profits are always paid by produce or by services. Well, produce and services, of course, do represent a commodity level of analysis. He defines capital in these terms: capital consists of food, clothing, tools, raw materials, machinery, etc. necessary to give effect to labor. That fundamental conception there is defined in terms of commodities. Real wages, the standard of living, which plays so large a part in his whole system of theory, is a certain variegated bill of commodities.

Once more, Ricardo points out that computations of money value may in some cases be very deceptive as, for example, when a small crop sells for more money than a large one. He had in mind exactly the sort of case which turns up rather frequently in our experience with reference to cotton. When the American cotton yield is very small the crop is very apt to bring in to the cotton planters - to the best of the knowledge which our statisticians are able to get for us - actually a much larger money return than they get when they have the misfortune to harvest an abundant crop.

Sometimes, of course, Ricardo, not content with the money level of analysis or the commodity level, goes deeper, as he supposes, and deals with the psychic level, the level of real forces. But apparently Ricardo felt much less at home when he was talking in terms of feeling of pleasures and pains than when he was talking about objective things like commodities or money. He did admit the fundamental importance of feeling, pointing out that desire lies at the basis of demand. But he did not go any distance at all in the direction of developing the theory of utility although, as we saw in dealing with Bentham, that theory of utility would seem to be the natural part of the utilitarian scheme for an economist to take up. What you would expect if you had been supposing that one theorist was intellectually influenced by another would be that the first great theoretical economist after Bentham would be a man who would say: Now these real forces that control our conduct are pleasure and pain, and we have got to see what we can do in explaining economic conduct in terms of these fundamental forces. And then the natural thing would be to take Bentham's analysis of utility and just add to it the one final notion about the importance of marginal pleasures and get that whole scheme of utility analysis which was, as a matter of fact, developed in the 1850's by the German writer Gossen, and then in the 1870's was developed almost at the same time by Jevons in England, Menger in Austria, and Walras in France.

Ricardo did not do that; and he did not do it because he ran into one of the difficulties which Bentham himself had raised and then set aside. You remember in discussing Bentham that I pointed out that he thought it was very questionable to institute comparisons among feelings of different men:

'Tis in vain to talk of adding quantities which after the addition will continue distinct as they were before. One man's happiness will never be another man's happiness: a gain to one man is no gain to another: you might as well pretend to add 20 apples to 20 pears...

Now that is the difficulty that Ricardo saw. He put it this way:

Every man has some standard in his own mind by which he estimates the value of his enjoyments. But that standard is as various as the human character.

Again:

From the same commodity two persons may derive very different degrees of enjoyment.

And still again:

Value in use (that, of course, is equivalent to Bentham's conception) you get from commodities cannot be measured by any one standard. It is differently estimated by different persons.

Now we saw that after representing this difficulty of comparing the feelings of different people in such a strong light, Benthem had gone on:

This addibility of the happiness of different subjects, however fictitious it may appear when considered rigorously, is a postulatum without the allowance of which all political reasoning is at a stand......

And just because it seemed necessary, if you were going to have political reasoning, to make comparisons among the feelings of different people, Bentham had proceeded to indulge in such comparisons.

Perhaps Ricardo would have gone with Bentham to this extreme if he had felt that this is a postulatum without allowance of which all economic reasoning is at a stand. But he did feel that he found a basis for economic reasoning just where the business man finds a basis for economic work: in money prices. And because the existence of money prices enabled him to give an account for economic behavior which seemed rational and satisfying, he was not forced, - as was Bentham whose interests were in matters like politics and law, - to make this assumption about which even Bentham seems to be very dubious in comparing the feelings of different people.

Ricardo's feelings were apparently that one can compare the shilling of one man with the shilling of another. Why should you pretend to compare their feelings? After all, it is the shilling which a man is willing to pay for something that counts in economic behavior. No matter how intense your desire for a commodity will be, you cannot influence the market price of it unless you have some money to offer for it. It is the quantities of money, not at all the intensity of your desire which is the force that actually counts. And to go back of the feeling, Ricardo seemed to feel, tended to recognize that wants are standardized and made dependable for business purposes by habits and customs; and so Ricardo steers clear of Bentham's subjective muddle and though a good utilitarian, he erects a system of economic theory in which utility itself plays a very modest role. Though a good Utilitarian, he erects an economic theory holding fast to the common sense assumption that we know almost nothing about the relative intensity of the feelings of different people and are not justified in comparing one man's sensations with another man's.

But in just one point, not a fundamental one, Ricardo did find himself driven to deal with these ultimate quantities. You find that in Ricardo's treatment of value. From his viewpoint, the important task of the economist is to give an account of relative values. But in trying to give account for variation in relative value, Ricardo found it necessary to contrast relative values with what he sometimes called absolute values, what he sometimes called real values, what he sometimes called positive values, and what he sometimes called natural values. As nearly as I can make out, all these four: absolute, real, positive, and natural are synonyms for one another in Ricardo's mind. There did hover in his mind a conviction that down underneath all these relative values expressed in price in which the economist is mainly concerned there is some fundamental form of value which is what we would like to get at if we could. Exactly what he meant by absolute value, or real value, or positive value, or natural value, I suppose, no man can be sure. He does not say. It seems to me that the implication by his discussion is that this absolute value is the importance that attaches to goods in terms of economic pains. That is just one man's interpretation, and it may be wrong. In the case of freely reproduceable goods, for example, Ricardo's logic is clearly that their practical importance lies in the sacrifice of production. That is done when we lose a good that can be reproduced. What we lose is not the use of the good itself, but the toil and trouble of making another good of that sort to take its place. Whatever determines the practical importance of a good, seems to be that which constitutes its absolute value. But, to repeat, that is a construction which I put upon the passages of Ricardo, not something that Ricardo himself has said.

So Ricardo's ultimate foundation for economic theory was the toil and trouble of production. But, on his showing, feelings have no importance until they get embodied in money costs. Men charge for undergoing toil and trouble. And while, on the other hand, demand rests upon desires for goods, our desires for goods do not count in the market place unless they lead us to apply money prices. And Ricardo makes no serious attempt to analyze money costs into subjective sacrifices, or demand prices into feelings of gratification which we anticipate from the consumption of commodities.

Finally a word about welfare. While Ricardo made little of hedonistic psychology, he definitely accepted the Utilitarian criterion of welfare. For example, he wrote to Maria Edgeworth:"My motto, after Mr. Bentham, is the greatest happiness to the greatest number," introducing an English solecism into Mr. Bentham's beautifully phrased motto. Every now and then he would test some economic situations by asking, does this way of running affairs contribute to the happiness of the community in the long run? But he did not undertake to use "happiness" as a way of explaining how and why men act. All the explanatory part of his discussion runs in terms of money or commodities, or occasionally of feelings and satisfactions, but he refers to welfare itself to create a basis for passing judgment upon a situation as a whole.

I will read you one amusing passage to conclude with. Ricardo came across a passage in Alexander von Humboldt's book on travels through South America, a book published in his time and which attracted a great deal of interest, telling about the lazy life of savages in South America and how happy they were. That was something that would naturally interest an economist, and Ricardo commented on it in a letter to Malthus:

> Happiness (says he) is the object to be desired, and we cannot be quite sure that, provided he is equally well-fed, a man may not be happier in the enjoyment of the luxury of idleness than in the enjoyment of the luxuries of a neat cottage and good clothes. And after all we do not know if these would fall to his share. His labour might only increase the enjoyment of his employer.*

XXIX

REASONS FOR THE POPULARITY OF RICARDO'S ANALYSIS

The Ricardian type of classical economics remained dominant in England for certainly a generation after its chief author had passed away. It remained dominant to such an extent that it prevented much attention from being paid to a considerable number of new lines of inquiry which in the eyes of later comers have seemed highly significant. So much did Ricardo obscure by his brilliancy the work of his contemporaries and those who came immediately after him that even the discoveries of that later period were substantially forgotten, forgotten to such an extent that it remained for Professor Seligman, a hundred years or so afterward, to call attention of the English themselves to such writers as Longfield, Lloyd, Jenkin, and Ravenstone.

It is interesting to inquire why orthodox Ricardian theory attained this prominent position. I do not suppose that we can claim that it was because of the surpassing merits of Ricardian analysis. Needless to say, the merits of Ricardo's work were very great, but certainly as a mere intellectual product the neo-classical analysis of Alfred Marshall is more thoroughly integrated, a more useful body of economics. And yet the generation that valued Marshall very highly put also

---

*Letters to Malthus, No. IXI, pp. 138-139.

high rating upon types of inquiries that were represented by the folk who followed Ricardo and attracted very slight attention from their contemporaries. I think the reason has to be found not in the sheer scientific merits of Ricardo's work but because of the practical usefulness of Ricardo's analysis to that class in the community which had, because of peculiar circumstances, the deepest interest in economic theory, and to promote whose interest the Ricardian theory was perfectly adapted.

Ricardo's world, on his showing, was one that was filled by three classes of people: landlords, laborers, and capitalists. Ricardo, of course, was anything but a satisfactory spokesman for the landlord class. They were supposed to be, so far as governmental matters were concerned, unquestionably the predominant class in the community. Ricardo had held the landlord to be a man whose interests were opposed to those of all other classes in the community and one would not expect that any fair representative of that economic class would regard Ricardo's speculations with favor. But the landlords were not a class of people that had any particular use for economic theory of any sort. They were people who were living on tradition. They objected to theory on principle. The problem that lay before them was the problem of preserving their peculiar privileges with as little pruning as possible. And so the fact that Ricardo as an economist was more unacceptable, let us say, than a man like Malthus to the landed interest counted very little to the landlords for they did not read even Malthus for the most part.

As for the laboring classes, they contained but a small proportion of people who read books, of people who could be expected to take an interest in an analytic treatment of social problems. Needless to say, though the proportion of workers that took an intellectual attitude toward the problems in life was small, that small proportion did, nevertheless, amount to not a few figures of able, energetic men. But these relatively few working class representatives who were concerned with the effort to understand intellectually the structure of society and how it bore upon the fortunes of their class had spokesmen of their own. They had that learned group of people who were called by their contemporaries the labor writers, William Thompson, Hodgkin, and Gray being perhaps the most conspicuous. These men in good part made use of Ricardian ideas but they gave these Ricardian ideas a twist that made them serve the interest of people who were trying to represent the claims of the working-man to a larger share of the national profit far more effectively than those claims were presented by Ricardo. They thought in so far as the working class wanted economic theory they did not have to go to Ricardo for it but could find the brand more peculiarly suited to their purpose in the writing of several other individuals.

On the whole, however, the more thoughtful working class of the period seemed to have come to the conclusion in the days when Ricardo was writing that after all the most important thing for them to push for was fuller representation of their class in Parliament. The great social movement that enlisted the loyalties and sympathies of the English working-men from, let us say, the early 1820's on to the 1840's, maybe the 1850's, was a political movement. First the movement to secure reform of the old House of Commons, to sweep away the rotten boroughs, to redistrict the country in such a fashion that the new industrial centers of the North might have representation proportionate to their numbers and then to alter the qualifications for the electorate. The first of these demands, the abolition of the rotten boroughs and redistricting of the country were carried through in the Great Reform Bill of 1832. But that measure left a property qualification upon the suffrage, and a property qualification which was high enough to bar the great mass of the working people from casting a vote. So that even after the Great Reform Bill had been passed, the working classes still had a grand political grievance. They argued that the Reform Bill had practically given the suffrage to the great mass of their employers, little as well as big, and by so doing had, if anything, provided a legislature which was less responsive than the old unreformed House of Commons to the views and needs of the working classes.

So what took hold on their fancy after the Great Reform was the Charter, that scheme for a thoroughgoing political reorganization of the country on the basis of "one man, one vote," a measure which, if they could have attained it, would have given them, in view of their predominant numbers, at least a theoretical opportunity to control the government. And until they had this power the majority of their spokesmen felt that it was not worth while fussing much over economic problems. Get the Charter; through the Charter get control of the House of Commons; and then use the legislature to right the wrongs of labor. That was the program - political rather than economic.

There remains then only the class that was represented by Ricardo as capital that had an extremely lively interest in economics. And Ricardian economics was, as I have already remarked, admirably fitted to their uses. Let me point out in what ways the Ricardian analysis aided the avowed and unavowed purposes of the capitalist class, distinguishing sharply between the capitalist class and people who belonged primarily to the great landed interest.

In the first place, Ricardo inculcated the paramount necessity of maintaining the security of property. I have read you some of the strong language that he used upon that head. He was firmly convinced that if anything were done to weaken the right of a man to obtain for himself the proceeds of his investment, that would weaken the inducement to save, it would check the accumulation of capital, and thus would have a most adverse influence upon the fortunes of the working classes. Needless to say, this doctrine of the paramount necessity of maintaining the security of property was a doctrine that was most welcome to capitalists. They knew it was right; Ricardo need not prove it to them. But the fact that Ricardo knew it was right, that to him it scarcely needed demonstration, made Ricardo thoroughly acceptable as an economist.

Ricardo's theory also had this comforting aspect, that taking over the Malthusian theory of population it proved that the working-man was responsible for his own poverty. Now poor relief was a heavy burden in those days, a heavy burden which the owners of property felt was forced upon them, for they had to pay the taxes out of which came funds for poor relief. And the misery in which a good part of the English population had long lived was being in some degree increased, and in many cases made more manifest, by the rapid growth of the new industrial towns. Misery and squalor are far less conspicuous when they are scattered around in delapidated but picturesque stone cottages over a wide countryside than when they are assembled in rotten masses of humanity in jerry-built slums of a new town that has no sewers. And there must have been a large proportion of the more intelligent people in the country who, whatever their economic interests, were shocked by the misery of the conditions under which a large proportion of the working people lived, who must have felt that there was something inhuman about these conditions, who must have felt sorry for children fated to grow up under such circumstances. And they very likely felt rather strong promptings to do what they could to relieve these sufferings. Well, people who were subject to these attacks upon their sympathetic emotions probably felt not a little comfort when they turned to the economist of the day and found that they and their class were guiltless, that all these miseries which they saw resulted primarily from what Ricardo called a too redundant population. When they realized that if anything were done by themselves or their associates to relieve this misery, to provide better living conditions, it would be futile because any mitigation of the hardships of the workers by raising their standard of living would inevitably have achieved one result: an acceleration in the growth of the population and so a return to the old standards of living or standards of misery - you get to talking in those terms - caused by a larger number of human beings.

It is, you see, a really rather comfortable doctrine from the point of view of people of property. Both these points that I have been speaking of: Ricardo's insistence upon the necessity of keeping the security of property untouched, and his concurrence with Malthus in the view that working people were responsible for their own suffering - both of these points would have been as agreeable to the landed class who were also property owners, and who likewise had to pay poor rates, as to capitalists as such. But then, in addition, Ricardo had another point of doctrine which of course was most acceptable to the capitalists and most unacceptable to the bulk of the landed gentry, and that was his doctrine of free trade, and more particularly his doctrine of free trade in grain. For he presents in his pamphlets as well as in his _Principles_ very strongly the view which the capitalists had presented in the great Corn Law debate of 1815 in Parliament, the view that the Corn Laws injured the country's economic development by keeping up the price of the grain, thereby keeping up the price of foods, therefore keeping up wages, and hence keeping up cost of production, and so finally limiting the export market for British manufacturers.

Now when Ricardo argued for abolishing the Corn Laws and extending British trade, he was arguing for that which the capitalist class desired and just as definitely was working for that which the landlord class felt might be its ruin. For to abolish the Corn Laws, to admit grain from France or Poland where the grain could be grown more cheaply than at home would undoubtedly bring down prices of the grains in the British market, and a reduction of the prices of grain would probably cause some land to go out of cultivation altogether, would certainly reduce the rent which British farmers could afford to pay, and so would cut off the great source of income for the landed classes.

There was another feature of Ricardo's analysis which was agreeable to the capitalists, and a matter not of much consequence one way or another to the landed interests. This was not so much a matter of Ricardo's own analysis as of conclusions which his disciples sought to build upon Ricardo's analysis - namely that attempts to interfere with the proper conduct of business on the part of government were to be objected to in principle. Now that of course is the general _laissez faire_ principle which has been argued much more strongly by Adam Smith than Ricardo. It had not been necessary for Ricardo really to develop that theme at any great length, but in the days that followed Ricardo all the really shocking abuses of the early Industrial Revolution began to attract wide attention and bills were introduced in increasing numbers into Parliament to control the manufacturing enterprises of the country, to check if possible the way in which they were exploiting labor. The first bills of this type, certainly the first law of this type which was passed, was enacted in 1815 at the insistence of one of the great cotton spinners themselves, Sir Robert Peel, to prevent the practical enslavement of pauper apprentices as they were called - young children from the poor houses shipped off to mills and frequently treated with the utmost brutality. But starting from that measure which was very restricted in its application, the reformers gradually became bolder and began to argue that not only young children but also young persons - which is a more or less technical legal term covering say fifteen to eighteen years of age - and finally, women ought to be prevented by law from working at night, ought to have their maximum weekly hours of labor limited. Also bills came in for requiring the betterment of working conditions, making unsanitary factories safe, to help the proper ventilation of coal mines, insisting upon the fencing of dangerous machinery.

There were not a few of the economists who were fundamentally ready to
argue that these arbitrary interferences by government with the conduct of business were going to ruin British industry. That fine start they had gotten in
sweeping the markets of the world by the adoption of machinery somewhat earlier
than any of their neighbors would presently be lost because it would be possible
to install similar machinery in countries where the government was too wise to
check enterprise, countires where manufacturers who could deal contractually
with every individual worker would get their labor on much more reasonable terms,
at much less cost than in a country where the government was imposing ghastly
conditions upon employers,limiting the return they might get out of their investment by refusing to let them run their factories at night, by preventing willing
workers from earning as much as they could by accepting any hours that were
mutually satisfactory to them, the workers, and their employers. Not all of the
disciples of Ricardo opposed the Factory Act and corresponding legislation regarding mines, but not a few of them did. And in so far as they took this line
they were once again developing an analysis of what purported to be in the interest of the country as a whole. That was particularly useful to these members
of the capitalist class and to their honor be it said that not all took this
view. Those members of the capitalist class objected to what seemed in the light
of later experience to be an imperative human demand for safeguarding the weaker
classes of society.

And finally the doctrine of wages that was espoused by Ricardo and put in
more definite form by his successors suited the ideas of the capitalist class
very thoroughly, the doctrine of the wages fund, the doctrine that the general
level of wages in any country is determined by two factors: on the one side the
capital of the country, on the other side by the population. Or, to express the
thing somewhat more accurately, is determined on the one side by the number of
people who want to work for wages and on the other side by that part of the
total capital of the country which technological conditions make it necessary to
utilize for employing labor. Well, if that is what determines wages, it is perfectly obvious that nothing which the wage earning classes themselves can do can
get them larger wages on the whole except of course the measure that was being
continually recommended by the economists, namely, the limitation of their numbers.

In particular it was obvious on this logic that trade unions were worse
than futile in attempting to get better wages for their members. A trade union
might, to be sure, by pursuing monopolistic practices deflect more than its fair
share of the country's total wages fund into the pockets of its members, but
any addition to its income that one trade union got for its members was definitely made at the expense of other members of the working classes. As a whole,
trade unions quite obviously could not benefit the working classes because they
could not reduce the number of people who needed wages to sustain them and they
could not add to the capital fund of the country or alter the technological conditions which determined that a certain part of the total capital fund should
be devoted to paying wages. So, to repeat, the trade union was useless or worse
than useless to the working people -- rather worse than useless because it gave
them notions bound to be dissipated and they paid part of their scanty incomes
to agitators who could do nothing for them.

So, broadly speaking, the analysis of economic conditions which Ricardo,
and still more Ricardo's followers, set up was an analysis that played rather
definitely into the hands of the capitalist class.When one says that, of course,
one is not bringing in an indictment against the honesty of Ricardo or of his
followers. They were not paid agents of capitalism. Ricardo was a great capitalist. He spoke what he thought were the lessons of his life. As we know from his

own record he was an extraordinarily generous and honest man and where he thought the interest of the country called for it he was quite ready to sacrifice his personal ambitions and those of his fellow-capitalists as when, for instance, he demanded a levy upon capital to reduce the dangerously large national debt that existed at the end of the war. It was a perfectly honest view of the way in which things ran in a modern world that Ricardo presented, only since it happened to be a view that agreed with the notions of the capitalists at large it was perfectly natural that political economy as Ricardo knew it, as his disciples standardized it, should be taken up primarily by this class, the one class that in England at that time had real use for some intellectual inquiry into the ways in which social organization worked. That class in the England of Ricardo's day was very much on the make. When Ricardo wrote, the government of the country was very definitely in the hands of the landed interest. I talked a great deal about the great struggle over the Corn Laws that led to the formulation of Riccardo's new theory of distribution. Well, consider this interesting commentary on the situation, that despite the brilliance of the case made by Ricardo and by the representatives of the manufacturing and commercial interests in Parliament, the Corn Law was not swept away. The Corn Law was kept after the wars were over at a point which was believed to guarantee the maintenance of a high price of grain. That meant, of course, to maintain landlord rent.

These people (manufacturing and commercial interests) felt themselves being excluded from their due influence in the country, an influence which they thought ought to be far larger in view of the great creative task that they were performing in increasing England's wealth, England's might. The advance of England that was being secured in such a notable way in the early part of the nineteenth century was due in comparatively slight measure to the landlords. True, they had been enclosing farms, they were improving the breeds of cattle, they were trying to force their tenants to adopt better methods of husbandry, but in comparison with the technical achievements secured by agriculture, the advances made by the introduction of machines, by the building of factories, by the building of canals, and then a little later by the far more spectacular building of railroads, by the introduction of steam into shipping, by the organization of trade on a wider basis, these changes were quite obviously the things that were making England a vastly greater power in the world. And the men who were themselves responsible for these great tasks of reorganization were legitimately the capitalists of the country. They were growing in wealth themselves as this reorganization proceeded. With their growth in wealth there went an increase in power, in the influence that they could exercise over the minds of other people. Being in this position of having to argue for the demands that they felt to be just, they needed a formal analysis of social organization in a way in which the landed classes did not.

I said a while ago that the landlords were standing on tradition. They defended themselves by pointing to English precedent. It is not the kind of thing that required a rationalization of a particularly rigid sort. But if you are in the position of challenging tradition, of trying to persuade your fellow-countrymen to alter their ways, then you have strong need for a logical presentation of your case. You probably realize that the logic by itself probably will not get you very far. In a political argument it is necessary to be backed up by clever organization, by emotional appeal. But unless you have got something to argue for that is clear in your own mind, that will withstand criticisms that may be brought against it in talking with other people, then you have not got a start upon the organization of your society, you have got very slender basis on which to rest your appeal.

The capitalist classes were the people who were performing the huge task

of carrying England's wealth and power forward on a grand scale.They realized in
considerable measure what they were doing. They wanted recognition from their
fellowmen, and most particularly did they want the proper share in that power
which was still largely in the hands of the landlords.They were the people who
found that they had need for a formal explanation of their place in society, of
the beneficence of their work;and full explanation could be made to show also
that they were opposed to the landlords who were necessarily in their economic
interest opposed to the community as a whole.So much the better.And that could
be made to show further that any interference by government with their operations
was a sin against common sense;that any effort on the part of the working-men to
get higher wages through organization was a fundamental error. Again, so much
the better. It was natural that these people should fall for economics, magnify
its scientific merits, should present it really not as a science but as doctrine.
And that was in large part the fate that overtook economics in the days that
followed Ricardo. He himself, I think we can justly say, had a scientific temper.
He was a man searching after the truth. He was ready to admit criticism. The way
in which he modified his earlier views about the impossibility of injuring working class interests by introducing labor saving devices into factories very
rapidly, shows how open and candid was his mind.

It is only as science remains subject to continual criticism, only in so
far as scientific men are always most interested in finding out what is wrong
with their views that knowledge can really grow. But, needless to say, if you
begin to use scientific doctrine for practical purposes, if you put it to propagandist uses, then the critic is a very troublesome person. You want a gospel
that you can preach, a gospel which will be far more effective if represented
as invulnerable. Such a gospel is perhaps best of all when it is contained in a
book so difficult that very few people can read it; so that any disciple can
take the opportunity of giving you his interpretation, and in taking that opportunity give his interpretation of the gospel any particular slant that the immediate occasion may call for.

Well, now Ricardian economics fell into the hands of popular writers,
people who represented primarily the outlook of the capitalist class, people who
wanted to discourage trade unions, people who wanted to oppose factory legislation or any other interference of government with private affairs, people who
wanted to abolish the Corn Laws. And they made the economic theory serve these
various uses. In the pamphlets of the day you find a vulgarized evolution of
Ricardianism made stiff and formal, the free play of that eager search after
truth characteristic of Ricardo and his friend Malthus disappearing and giving
place to a hard and fast dogmatism molded by small unscientific minds for immediate practical use. It was this brand of economics that became the reigning
representative of political economy in the days that followed Ricardo. When you
come to read John Stuart Mill you will find him speaking every here and there
about the "old political economy" as something that he wanted to get rid of,
something that seemed a burden upon the heads of mankind, that held in it no
promise for a finer life for the masses of humanity. Unless you know something
of this practical brand that had been made out of Ricardian economics, you find
it a little difficult to understand the dislike with which that generous soul,
John Stuart Mill, speaks of the "old political economy." But if you do realize
how far what had been a very rapidly developing piece of intellectual inquiry
was turned into a supposedly impeccable dogma and put to the practical uses of
one class in the community, then you will be convinced that he was another great
apostle, a man who once more opened the eyes of his fellow-beings to the possibilities of social organization of the future, another real emancipator, and
with him, in a very genuine sense, economics as a social science got a fresh
start.

XXX

THE PHILOSOPHICAL RADICALS: THEIR ACTIVITIES AND
POLITICAL POSITION

We spent the last two weeks or so in trying to get that general impression of the logical characteristics of the type of Ricardo's economic theory. Now there are certain other aspects of that work besides its logical characteristics to which we must pay attention if we want to understand its spirit, its character, its effectiveness in life.

This type of theory, seemingly so abstract in character, was intensely practical in its age. It was written by men who were Utilitarians and who believed that science itself had value only in so far as it might contribute to human happiness. These men devoted a great deal of very hard work to thinking abstractly about social problems because they thought that by so doing they were rendering the best possible service to the happiness of mankind.

In the second place, this political economy which seems to us now-a-days conservative in temper was, in its own day, a very radical body of doctrines. The men who produced it were reformers, and reformers of no mild type, but reformers who were calling for changes which seemed to the great body of their contemporaries of a dangerously revolutionary sort. They were men who had great moral courage, who did not hesitate to shock the "common sense," the inherited traditions of the bulk of intelligent Englishmen of their generation.

And, in the third place, this political economy which seems, as we read it in the old classical works, so strictly devoted to a discussion of its own problems, was in practical life much less sharply divided off from other social sciences than economics has come in later times to be. It was cultivated by men who were more than economists, by men who were very much interested in other intellectual problems, who as practical reformers were concerned not merely with questions like corn laws, sound money, trade unions, and so on, but men who were concerned with efforts to give England that form of political and social organization which would conduce to her happiness.

Now none of these aspects of classical political economy are dwelt on in the histories of economic doctrines. Those books are devoted to tracing the letter of the economic law from one writer to another. But you never will have any adequate appreciation of what classical political economy was, you will never I think, have any adequate appreciation of what role the social sciences can play in life unless you look at the thing as something broader, something more active, than a discussion of a set of varied, abstract problems conducted on the basis of an analysis of imaginary conditions. So I am going to spend today and our next meeting, at least, in trying to give you what impression I can of economics as offering a practical program of the reforms which the economists set to accomplish, and the way in which they worked toward the accomplishment of these reforms, and of the relations which economics had in those days to the other social sciences.

I can best begin that account by telling you something of the group of men with whom Ricardo was allied, both as a thinker and as a reformer, - the group that has been called the Philosophical Radicals. The center of this group was Jeremy Bentham. He provided the general outlook on life, the fundamental psychology which all the Philosophical Radicals accepted. He was their great teacher and prophet to whom they all looked up with a certain quizzical humor.

During the period when Ricardo was most active, Bentham's chief disciple was James Mill. Mill had come down from Scotland as a most vigorous, hardheaded youngster, who after getting trained for the ministry had found that his con-scientious scruples would not allow him to take Holy Orders, and he had, quite contrary to sound economic principles, married and begun to rear a family which had a new increment added to it every other year or so, at a time when he had no regular means of support. He was a man of most untamable temper and consider-able versatility, and he set himself to support his family by hack writing at a time when he was working upon a magnum opus, a great History of British India, the book to which he devoted years of toil in hours after he had finished what almost any other man would have considered a heavy day's work. And he added to all these literary labors the work of teaching his children himself and becoming the schoolmaster in his own family.

James Mill, not long after coming to London, became acquainted with Jeremy Bentham, and the two people struck up a great friendship. Mill was a man who had all the practical arts in which Jeremy Bentham was so deficient. He was a born organizer of movements. He was a born propagandist. He used even the opportunity of writing articles for the Encyclopedia Britannica. He put the practical con-sequences of Bentham's philosophical doctrines into a shape and into a place where they would be read by large numbers of the most intelligent of his contem-poraries. And James Mill was also a man who had great skill in directing a small bu skilful band of disciples. He was clearly a man of very striking personality, a man whom it was perhaps a little difficult to reform because of his austerity, but a man who, despite that common Scotch quality, attracted people toward him, held them, dominated them intellectually in a very remarkable degree.

It was through James Mill that Ricardo made his contact with Bentham and was brought into the circle of the Philosophical Radicals. It would seem, as I remarked in speaking about Ricardo's own life, that he never became closely in-timate with the closet philosopher himself; but he was, his (Mill's) son tells us, his father's dearest and most intimate friend, and no one could be a close friend of James Mill without being an ardent Philosophical Radical. And when-ever Ricardo had occasion to touch upon general political issues he avowed him-self, without scruple, a disciple of Bentham. It was from Bentham that he got his general conceptions of human nature. I do not suppose that is quite true, it is truer to say that he found that Bentham's philosophy explained in systematic fashion the conceptions of human nature which were based upon his own temper and observations of business conduct.

Other notable members of the group were Joseph Hume, a leading parliamen-tary light, Francis Place, that great radical tailor and political boss who did so much to organize the practical side of many of the campaigns carried on by the Philosophical Radicals, the man of whom Graham Wallas has written a most fascinating biography. And then there were various allies in Parliament and in journalism; in Parliament, for a long while, Sir Samuel Romilly, perhaps the most distinguished barrister of the day; the Whig philosopher Sir James Mackin-tosh; and that extraordinarily versatile Scotchman, Henry Brougham, who finally became Lord Chancellor; and, curiously enough, later, the second Sir Robert Peel became a defender of measures which Bentham and his group were arguing in favor of. On the journalistic side they had allies in John Black of the Morning Chron-icle, in Charles Maclaren of the Scotsman; so that they were operating both in England and in Edinburgh; and Fonblanque, the proprietor of the Examiner. A little younger than these men was George Grote, the son of a great London banker, who became deeply interested in the philosophical type of politics, almost as much interested in that as he was in Greek history. He is famous nowadays chief-ly because of the most erudite history of Greece which he published somewhat later in life.

Then there was John Austin, the author of the books on jurisprudence which served as the great text-books for English and American law schools for two generations. There was Edwin Chadwick, one of Bentham's amanuenses, who became a power in the demonstration for the Poor Law Bill drawn on Malthusian lines and vigorously defended by the Philosophical Radicals. And he somewhat later became the great leader of the movement for public hygiene, the first of the great champions of methods of reorganizing city life in such a fashion as to counteract the health hazards which were produced by the rapid growth of cities that had no adequate sewer systems, no adequate parks, or any other provision for disposing of the by-products of urban life which are inimical to health.

Then there was a still younger group, in which the most conspicuous figure, of course, was John Stuart Mill; and with him were associated a variety of men who cut a considerable figure in the London of their day, although to us their names are rather tame: Charles Austin; William Eyton Tooke, son of Thomas Tooke, the economist who wrote the great History of Prices and of the State of the Circulation during the Years 1793-1856; William Ellis, who did a great deal in the cause of improving religious, moral, and social conditions in the South Sea Islands; George Graham, afterwards an official of the Bankruptcy Court; John Arthur Roebuck, a vigorous member of Parliament; George Villiers, afterwards Earl of Clarendon, a great diplomat of the eighteenth century; Charles Buller, a barrister who became judge-advocate-general and later chief commissioner of the poor law. And somewhat later still, the tradition was carried on by Henry Thomas Buckle, the author of the History of Civilization in England; Alexander Bain, the Scotch psychologist whose books on the emotion and the will you may have had occasion to look at; from one point of view by Herbert Spencer; very distinctly by Henry Sidgwick, a man who taught a whole generation of social scientists at Cambridge; and, in a looser sense, the majority of the Englishmen of the latter part of the eighteenth century and early nineteenth century who became interested in the social sciences.

It was indeed a most remarkable group of men, remarkable for their several personal abilities and for the way in which they could cooperate, not only with themselves but also with groups who would accept some part of their general program. John Stuart Mill in his Autobiography tries to give us a definite conception of what the Philosophical Radicals stood for. He says their mode of thinking was characterized "by a combination of Bentham's point of view with that of the modern political economy, and with the Hartleian metaphysics."* David Hartley was a psychologist and philosopher of the middle of the eighteenth century whose system of thought has been summed up by Sir Leslie Stephen in the remark that he believed the world to be made up of ideas sticking together. That is, Hartley was the English philosopher who had most definitely formulated that metaphysical system which is based on the association of ideas and which was presently worked out in more mature form by James Mill and elaborated on certain sides by Alexander Bain. Mill, then, developed his theories by a combination of Bentham's point of view, of the Malthusian theory of population, of Ricardian economics, and of Hartley's metaphysics, that general principle of the association of ideas.

Now, from the modern point of view, the chief intellectual characteristic of this group of men was the wide range and the efficient working out of their knowledge. They were interested, like their master, Bentham, in the whole round of social sciences. To them psychology was basic; and the psychology on which

*Autobiography of John Stuart Mill. Published for the First Time without Alterations or Omissions from the Original Manuscript in the Possession of Columbia University; New York, Columbia University Press, 1924; p. 73.

they built had two leading ideas: from the functional point of view, it was hedonistic; from the structural point of view it was associational. That is, these men accepted Bentham's point of view that all our behavior is controlled by the attempt to get pleasure or avoid pain; and they held that the structure of our intelligence, our consciousness, is determined by associations among ideas. So that a properly skilled analyst who knows the experiences of any individual's past life should be able to tell exactly what notions a man's mind will contain. Our minds are made for us by associations of the ideas which have entered into our minds through the varied contacts of our day to day life. This psychological basis was worked out first by Bentham, then it was elaborated by James Mill in his classical book called An Analysis of the Phenomena of the Human Mind. It was substantially the same idea that dominated Herbert Spencer's psychology. And, as I have said already, was on certain sides elaborated further by Alexander Bain.

Perhaps second in importance to the Philosophical Radicals to this fundamental attempt to explain the human mind, second to psychology, was jurisprudence and its several branches: criminal law, procedure, evidence, constitutional law, theory of the state. It was chiefly in this field, that is, more than in any other, that Bentham worked, particularly in his later years, devoting such practical activity as he developed largely to criminal law. I had occasion to observe the great amount of energy he put into getting his Panoptican scheme adopted. And then after that proved a practical impossibility, he spent a good deal of time in trying to secure amendments of the criminal law which in the early part of the nineteenth century was still almost incredibly barbarous. A person might be hanged for stealing five shillings; - the laws were so barbarous in their terms that one of the great arguments against them was that no jury of honest men would convict people for petty crimes and expose them to the severe penalties which a judge was in duty bound to inflict, so that the law was in practice extremely ineffective, save as applying to crimes for which a jury thought a man ought to be hanged or transported.

Then Bentham also spent a great deal of his energy in later years in working out a constitutional code, not only for England but for the world at large- a code that was thoroughly democratic in all its features. It provided for the disestablishment of the Church, annual Parliaments, secret ballots, a law which set up a republican form of government in place of the monarchy, - proceeded to dispose altogether with the ancient British crown and to give the country a set of civil magistrates who should reach their office on the basis of the suffrage of all grown men. Bentham, if I remember rightly, never got quite to the point of seeing the necessity of granting the vote to women, but he did advocate in principle universal manhood suffrage. This line of work was carried on, particularly later, by John Austin.

In education, the chief workers were Bentham on the theoretical side; James Mill and Francis Place on the practical side. One of the great and solid achievements of the Philosophical Radicals was the indispensable part they took in organizing the University of London. That huge institution which it now is with its many branches was chiefly the outcome of the interest that Bentham had in setting up an institution which would be free from the defects of his own alma mater, Oxford, and which would provide a far more useful kind of education than either of the older universities. And his theoretical interest in the matter was very ably seconded by the active organizing efforts of James Mill and of Francis Place.

On the side of economics, which was, from the Utilitarian point of view, just one of several lines of work, all more or less on a par in interest, the chief workers among the Philosophical Radicals were Ricardo, and presently James Mill, and than in the next generation John Stuart Mill, and Henry Sidgwick, and Francis Edgeworth.

In ethics the leading names are, again, Bentham and John Stuart Mill, and Henry Sidgwick, and Herbert Spencer.

Logic and metaphysics: Bentham, and both the Mills and Herbert Spencer.

Then history, and philosophy, and philosophy of history came into the scope of their interests. We find them, all the Philosophical Radicals, as people who were deficient in historical outlook, and certainly they did every now and then betray themselves into positions which seemed to show that they had not learned what we regard as certain of the fundamental lessons of history, but they were themselves, nevertheless, very active workers in this field. As I have said, James Mill devoted an enormous amount of time to his History of British India, George Grote even more time to his History of Greece, and Buckle, the most philosophical in his way of writing history among the Philosophical Radicals, experimented on a considerable scale with a new type of history.

There is no such group of men in the world today as the Philosophical Radicals formed in early nineteenth century England. Their nearest counterpart in our times, I suppose, was supplied by the group of Fabian socialists in the days when Sidney and Beatrice Webb, George Bernard Shaw, Graham Wallas, and a few of their friends were in the heyday of their youth and intellectual vigor. But even they never undertook so ambitious a program of excogitating social problems on the one hand and putting over a series of practical reforms on the other hand as the program which filled the imagination of Bentham and his friends.

It is characteristic of these men that the very width, the very breadth of their program caused them difficulties. They dipped into the broad field of the social sciences at certain specific points, but they did not succeed in working out the problems, let us say, of jurisprudence, of ethics, and of economics, and of pedagogy so far that the edges of these several disciplines overlapped. Their work is all of a piece in a sense that it is all inspired by the same fundamental notions concerning human nature, but to a considerable degree their several disciplines to the end stayed more or less independent of each other. For example, James Mill covered a range of investigation almost as wide as Bentham himself. He wrote definitely on history, on politics, on economics, on ethics, on education, on psychology and metaphysics. If you read his different books, however, you do not feel that the historian has really absorbed and learned to apply in his historical work the lessons which you find him teaching as an economist.

I think it is largely this fact that members of the group did not really fuse their discoveries in the different fields in which they entered with each other, which has been at least partly responsible for the fact that our historians of economic theory have so egregiously failed to see the real interconnection which exists between classical political economy and the other thoughts that were teeming in the breasts of the economists in the early nineteenth century. If you read our histories of economic theory you get the impression that their authors record political economy from the beginning as having been an independent field of knowledge. To them Bentham's felicific calculus has nothing to do with political economy. James Mill to them is merely the author of the first school-book on economics; the History of British India is something they think they need not go into, and as for his Analysis of the Human Mind, that is merely a piece of psychology or psychological metaphysics. They even usually ignore

Ricardo's political career and fail to see how that economist was deeply concerned with such social problems as the rights of free speech. They write as if Francis Place had never lived, and that the movements, the practical movements, that he was organizing with his friends Mill and Ricardo, were matters of no economic concern. To them the Great Reform Bill of 1832 is political history, and something that a writer of economic theory can pass over. And when they come to treat of John Stuart Mill they often talk as if it were a fact that Mill tried to lug certain aspects of social philosophy into his economic system, as if he might perhaps have avoided certain logical inconsistencies in his economic theory if he had only stuck to his proper last.

That is quite a misrepresentation of what the greatest economists in England in the early or middle of the nineteenth century felt, quite a misconception. If you want to get a clearer view, a juster view of their economics you had better go not to the books on the history of political economy itself, but to such books as Sir Leslie Stephen's three volumes on the English Utilitarians, or Professor A.V. Dicey's book on Law and Opinion in England, or Graham Wallas's Life of Francis Place in which you have a vivid sketch of the Philosophical Radicals as a set of practical organizers in the midst of very exacting political problems. Or perhaps best of all to the three volumes on the Philosophical Radicals written by Elie Halevy, the French historian and philosopher.

The practical schemes that these men were pushing most of their time included law reforms, educational reforms, birth control, a cause very actively taken up by Francis Place and approved very cautiously even in his Encyclopaedia Articles by James Mill. It seems a curious place to get in birth control in the prudish nineteenth century, but James Mill was equal even to that; - sound money, free trade, governmental economy, abolition of all sinecures, the right of all working men to organize in unions - there the most active worker was Francis Place; - Church disestablishment - a cause that was very dear, particularly to the hearts of Bentham and Grote, but the one great cause of the Philosophical Radicals which they and their followers did not succeed in getting accomplished; - perhaps most of all parliamentary reform, that is, reorganization of the fundamental political institution such as would give at least a far larger part of the English population a share in choosing the legislature, and through the legislature the administration of the country.

Now when these people were living there were plenty of other reformers in England; the Whigs professed to be advocates of parliamentary reform, although they were very lukewarm advocates until the movement had gained such momentum that they were practically forced to take hold of it or disavow their nominal principles. There was the Clapham Sect, that great body of religious reformers centering around Charles Simeon, including Zachary Macaulay, Lord Macaulay's father, William Wilberforce, and many others. There were a few radical politicians like Durham the great owner of collieries in the north of England; Sir Francis Burdett, the man of large wealth who curiously took the popular side in most disputes. There were also a lot of people with panaceas, ranging from Robert Owen with his scheme for making over human nature, to the so-called Ricardian Socialists, the men who accepted Ricardo's doctrine of value, taking it far more literally and with less qualification than the author did, and who united with that Bentham's principles of utility and tried to develop with impeccable logic an organization of industrial economics such as would give the worker the full product, all that which he himself produces.

The Philosophical Radicals differed from all these people in the sense that they were more philosophical. They had a theory which underlay and which guided the reforms that they advocated. Of course, ardent church people like the Clapham

-190-

Sect needed no intellectual theory;they based their organization on the will of
the Lord, on religious grounds. Radical reformers like Durham or Burdett were
men who simply had a radical temper and a liking for political activity; men who
happened to be born in a curious mode and who liked to express their individual-
ity, but men who were not at all adapted to the cold calculating, abstract way
of attacking social problems in an analytical fashion. And the people with panaceas like Robert Owen or like the labor writers themselves, were men who borrowed a philosophy from others, as did the Ricardian Socialists, and simply turned
it to justify their own program, or they were people who worked up quite obviously a special analysis of human nature, a special analysis of some broad problems
to show that the broad panacea they advocated was that which mankind most needed.
None of these other groups of reformers tried systematically to determine from
a study of man's nature what social arrangements are most conducive to his happiness; and as Bentham's group did that, they deserved the name "philosophical."
They differed from most of the other groups also in that they occupied a position more or less in the middle, between the great bulk of intelligent Englishmen and the people who were most violent in demanding revolutionary measures
like the Ricardian Socialists.

    I want to illustrate that a bit by a quotation or two. James Mill under-
took to formulate the political program of the Philosophical Radicals in a pair
of articles that he published in the Westminster Review, a journal that they
issued as a sort of party organ.In the first number he reviewed the policies of
the Whigs, and then in a later number he reviewed the policies of the Tories.
The Whigs, he said, were "trimmers;" their game was "seesaw;" they were ever
promising to promote the interests of the people, and ever performing in the
interests of the aristocracy. The Tories, on the other hand, were even worse;
they were stupid and malignant upholders of abuses. And, of course, these people
whom he assailed so vigorously had no very pleasant feeling toward the Philosophical Radicals. The attitude of the Whigs can be judged from one of the essays
that Macaulay wrote and then suppressed when he sought to get an appointment
from the East India Company. For James Mill, after publishing his great History
of British India had become one of the most prominent officials of that concern,
and it would have been very difficult to get the appointment if James Mill had
taken an unfriendly attitude toward him. But in the full flow of his fighting
spirits, Macaulay had written:*

        We entertain no apprehensions of danger to the institutions
    of this country from the Utilitarians. Our fears are of a different
    kind. We dread the odium and discredit of their alliance. We wish to
    see a broad and clear line drawn between the judicious friends of practical
    reform and the sect which, having derived all its influence from the
    countenance which they have imprudently bestowed upon it, hates them
    with the deadly hatred of ingratitude. There is not, and we firmly be-
    lieve that there never was, in this country, a party so unpopular. They
    have already made the science of political economy - a science of vast im-
    portance to the welfare of nations - an object of disgust to the majority
    of the community. The question of parliamentary reform will share the
    same fate, if once an association be formed in the public mind between
    Reform and Utilitarianism.

*The above was published in the Edinburgh Review, June, 1829, in a reply to an
article by Bentham in the Westminster Review, No. XXI, Article XVI, defending
Mill against an attack made by Macaulay in the Edinburgh Review, March, 1829,
reviewing Mill's Essays on Government in the Encyclopaedia Britannica. It is now
to be found among Macaulay's Essays under the title Bentham's Defence of Mill.

And while they had this attitude of mind toward the position of the Whigs and Tories, the Philosophical Radicals, on the other side, opposed the popular representatives of the working classes. Bentham said that Cobbett was a "vile rascal."[*] He was the great spokesman of the agricultural interests, of whom, curiously enough, a biography is published every year or so. And Bentham said that Robert Owen "began in vapour and ended in smoke."[**] Place said that most of the Rotundardists, a group of men who met at the Rotunda in Blackfriars Bridge Road, London "were loud and long talkers, vehement, resolute, reckless rascals. Among these men were some who were perfectly atrocious, whose purpose was riot, as providing an opportunity for plundering."[#]

And as for the economic theory of the Ricardian Socialists, James Mill wrote to Brougham (3 Sept. 1832):

> The nonsense to which your Lordship alludes about the rights of the labourer to the whole produce of the country, wages, profits, and rent, all included, is the mad nonsense of our friend Hodgskin, which he has published as a system and propagates with the zeal of perfect fanaticism.[##]

Naturally, of course, these working-class people had as poor an opinion of the Philosophical Radicals as the spokesmen of the Whigs and Tories. Cobbett abused them with his unrivalled current of epithets, talking about Ricardo as a Jew stock-jobber, sneering at Parson Malthus, scarcely ever speaking of an economist without applying to him some stinging epithet. Even Robert Owen could find nothing to say in favor of the economists other than that they were liberal men and friends to the education of the people, but that there was not one sound, practical man among them.

This campaign which the Philosophical Radicals carried on is what Graham Wallas calls "the war on two fronts" - fighting the established powers in English social and political life on the one side, and abusing the rising group of working-class agitators on the other side. But it is very characteristic of them that they put through a long series of reforms which they had in their hearts. How they managed to get these reforms through is the matter of which I shall speak at the next meeting.

XXXI

POLITICAL EVENTS AND HOW THEY AIDED IN BRINGING ABOUT THE REFORMS WHICH THE PHILOSOPHICAL RADICALS ADVOCATED

At our last meeting I was speaking of the Philosophical Radicals and their various activities, - activities which, as I was pointing out at the end of the hour, brought them into very sharp opposition on the one side to the two great political parties of the time, the Whigs and the Tories, and on the other side brought them into opposition with the working-class radicals. They occupied in this respect a middle position. I suppose there is no reason to doubt the thoroughgoing sincerity of the abuse which the Philosophical Radicals and the respective parties and also the working-class radicals heaped upon each other.

---

[*] Works, X, 471, 570.
[**] Ibid., X, 495-97.
[#] Life of Francis Place, by Graham Wallas, p. 273.
[##] James Mill, by Alexander Bain; London, 1882, -. 364.

But this abuse did not prevent the Philosophical Radicals from cooperating in a very effective fashion with both parties whom they were ready at times, when they were laying down their program, to abuse so heartily.

It is interesting to follow the practical interests of this group to see that in practically all the causes which they espoused they found colleagues, associates who did not belong to their group. Their program for reform of the criminal law, for instance, was carried on in Parliament primarily with the assistance, first of Sir Samuel Romilly, one of the great Whigs, and then with the assistance of Sir James Mackintosh, a Whig; and after Mackintosh had died, with the aid of the second Sir Robert Peel, who was rapidly becoming a power among the Tories.

In their various aims to improve the condition of the lower classes, they cooperated very actively with men like the great Quaker of the time, William Allen, despite the fact that James Mill, according to his son's Autobiography,* was accustomed to say that the "ne plus ultra of wickedness he considered to be embodied in what is commonly presented to mankind as the creed of Christianity," James Mill held that view primarily because what was presented to the world at that time as the orthodox creed of Christianity included a firm belief in the doctrine of Hell. James Mill used to say, "think of a being who would make a Hell – who would create a human race with the infallible foreknowledge, and therefore with the intention that the great majority of them were to be consigned to horrible and everlasting torment."*

So too, the Philosophical Radicals in Parliament, Ricardo and Joseph Hume, were usually in the minority when they voted, but the minority to which they belonged was made up in ways which fluctuated with almost every issue presented to them. Sometimes the minority was composed mainly of Whigs, sometimes of Tories who differed from the dominant element in their party. And, on the other hand, the Philosophical Radicals were often able to use working-class movements and leaders to bring pressure to bear upon the government of the time. Their whole policy was one of trying to get their resolutions accomplished and they were not very scrupulous about the people with whom they collaborated. Anyone who would help them to accomplish some one of their aims was, for the time being, a good and faithful friend, however seriously they might differ from that man on other points, however heartily they might protest his other views on social matters, and however low an opinion their colleague had concerning their own philosophical and social viewpoints.

Thus the Philosophical Radicals were a very curious and interesting group of people. On the one side, they worked out in the most mature form of the day a whole group of social sciences. And these social sciences, as they worked them out, from economics to phrenology and education, called for a whole series of social reforms, – for reforms in law, reforms in education, reforms in the economic policy of the government, reforms in general, that is; also they wanted to remove all disabilities upon dissenters and to disestablish the Church.

This whole series of reforms for which they labored so heartily, they had no prospect of putting over because, as a group, they always remained small in numbers, a little band of rather hard-boiled, intellectual high-brows. They were a little band of intellectuals with a minimum of emotional driving power, of appeal; and they were very heartily disliked, not to say detested, by a large proportion of the people who were living at the time. And yet, somehow, this

* C.U. Press ed. p. 29.

group of people managed to put over a very large part of their whole program.
In fact, within two generations of the death of Jeremy Bentham, almost all the
great reforms for which he labored, saving the disestablishment of the Church,
almost everything except that, had been accepted by England; the changes in the
English constitution, and in English social and economic legislation, in English
education which occurred between, let us say, the 1820's and the 1870's, were almost all of them reforms of the sort for which the Philosophical Radicals had
fought and had acted.

How did these reforms come about? That is the next subject that I want to
discuss. And to discuss it, I must go back for a moment to the point where I
left the story of practical economic and social movements in England.

You recall my somewhat lengthy analysis of the reaction of the French
Revolution upon that current of reforms which had gotten under way in such a
promising fashion in the early days of William Pitt's ministry, - how the war,
and still more than the war itself, the English fear of a reign of terror in
their own land had converted the prime minister himself and almost all of the
propertied classes in England to a policy of extreme conservatism, a policy of
opposition to any, even the slightest, change which could possibly be avoided in
the political and social fabric of the country.

Now so long as the war lasted it was not likely that any change would come
about. But when peace was made after Waterloo, the English reformers in general,
the Philosophical Radicals in particular, thought that their day was dawning.
They hoped - the Philosophical Radicals at least - that by their logical appeal
to the minds of the nation they would be able rather rapidly to convert a large
proportion of their fellow-countrymen to the plans which they had in view. But
things did not work out in that way at all. Naturally the Tory party, which had
been in power during the war with the French Republic and with Napoleon, reaped
the benefit that usually comes to an administration that has carried on a
successful military contest. The party was established more strongly than ever
in public favor by the prestige of their great successes. So that the country
continued to be governed by the same set of statesmen supported by parliamentary
representatives of the same sort that had controlled the country's policy during
the war itself.

The policy of the Liverpool ministry - the Earl of Liverpool was the head
of the British government at the close of the war - in foreign affairs was to
support the Holy Alliance, that diplomatic organization which had grown up among
the members of the coalition which had won the great victory over Napoleon, and,
needless to say, the Holy Alliance was very far from an organization which Bentham could approve, with its insistence upon the principle of legitimacy, its opposition to democratic movements of any kind and every sort, its belief that the
Lord had appointed a chosen set of rulers to guide the destinies of mankind, and
that people who wished to take the guidance of their own affairs into their own
hands were misguided. Of course, notions of that sort were at the opposite pole
of social ideas from those of the Philosophical Radicals.

In domestic matters the policy of the Liverpool ministry was to maintain
law and order; and, of course, maintaining law and order in those days meant
seeing that the existing rules and regulations of the British government were observed as fully as possible. That task of maintaining law and order presently became a very hard one. It was made more difficult by the rapid rise to prominence
of two great economic issues. The first, and I am inclined to think the less important of the two so far as immediate conditions were concerned, was the battle
over the corn laws which we have already had occasions to observe, - that contest

in Parliament which resulted in directing the attention of economists to the problem of distribution, and which led to the formulation of the theory of rent,and then presently to the formulation of Ricardo's whole scheme of distribution.

Another important result of that contest in Parliament was that it dissolved the tacit working alliance which had existed since the days of the French terror between the landed classes in England and the other propertied classes. Of course,that contest was a fight, a class struggle, between those who were interested in agriculture on the one side, and those who were interested primarily in manufactures and trading on the other side. The latter were rapidly increasing in wealth and therefore in weight in the country, and this had led them, at least many of them, to believe with Ricardo that the interests of the landlord are necessarily always opposed to the interests of the rest of the nation. And that meant that in the future the British government which rested primarily upon the votes of the landlords who crowded the benches of Parliament could not also count upon the systematic support of the manufacturing and commercial classes.

The ministry then found its position in the country diminished by the fact that instead of having practically all the people of property behind it on fundamental issues of law and order it had, whenever it touched issues that led to a differentiation of interest between the farmers and the manufacturers and merchants, whenever it touched such questions it would have to choose between catering to one set of propertied interests or catering to another set of propertied interests. And while for the time being the agricultural interests in politics unquestionably predominated, it was also clear to thinking men that the manufacturing and commercial interests were increasing in power very rapidly.

The second economic circumstance which, as I said, made more immediate difficulty for the government was the state of trade which followed the close of the war. When the war was over, the British commercial classes and the business public at large thought that they would find a very ready market for the goods which they had been learning to manufacture in such large quantities, at such relatively cheap prices, in those countries which had until recently been controlled by Napoleon's armies; and they therefore began to ship goods to the Continent in very large quantities just as soon as Napoleon's fall was assured by the Battle of Waterloo. It turned out, however, that these European markets did not possess the wherewithal to buy. Europe was left, for the time being, poverty-stricken by the enormous series of struggles that had wasted the substance of her peoples, and the results in England were a series of serious bankruptcies and a great business smash at the end of 1815. Then there followed two or three years of extraordinary depression; 1816 and 1817 were very bad years. In 1818 business picked up, and the country enjoyed a rather brief period of mild prosperity. But that scarcely outlasted the year; in 1819 there was a relapse; and in 1820 times were bad. Business did not begin to pick up and employment begin to become active until perhaps 1820 or 1821. And then the country entered upon a period of active trade which in 1825 ended in another grievous crisis.

Now this general depression of trade and lack of employment would under the most popular of governments have doubtless caused much dissatisfaction. The government which was anything but popular in its attitude had caused grave discontent; and so the Liverpool ministry was faced in the late 18-teens and the early 1820's with a whole series of domestic brawls and disorders which it had to combat as best it might. In 1815 there were serious riots by the bargemen and sailors in the northern coal ports,and a bad disturbance in Ireland over the payment of tithes to the Church.In 1816 there were the great"bread and blood"riots of April and May. In the summer there was a series of mass meetings demanding parliamentary reform; and in December the Spa Fields riots broke out in Lonodn. A mob armed itself by pillaging a gunsmith's shop and got possession of the central part of the city for a day or two. The next year both the House of Commons and the House of Lords appointed committees to investigate certain dangerous combinations, and these committees brought in alarming reports which held that certain organizations named the Hampden Clubs, in honor of the great orator of medieval times, and certain organizations known as the Spencean Philanthropists were the centers of widespread conspiracy to overthrow the Constitution. It was a frame of mind singularly like that which we witnessed in our own country at the end of the War when every respectable man apparently seemed to fear that every wage earner was in the pay of the Bolshevists.

Owing to this alarmed state of the public mind, Parliament was very readily induced to suspend the Habeas Corpus Act and to authorize vigorous repressive measures on the part of the government. And then it presently appeared - as has been the case so often in similar situations - that the government had been employing spies to discover dangerous organizations and that these spies, possibly in some cases with the collaboration of the government officials themselves, had been trying to magnify their own importance by getting up conspiracies which they might later expose. It is the story that we all know turning up in England a hundred years ago with every feature of aggravation.

In 1818 the improvement of trade caused a diminution in the popular agitation. But, nevertheless, there was a great strike of the spinners and weavers which had to be suppressed by calling out troops. And when the general election came around at the end of that year because Parliament had sat out its term, it was found that the public dissatisfaction was visited upon the ministry so far as the very unequal scheme of parliamentary representation allowed. The government lost some thirty votes, but it still had a sufficient working majority to carry on. Next year, when trade became worse again, the great Peterloo massacre occurred. That was a meeting in St. Peter's Fields, Manchester, where some tens of thousands of people gathered together to hear a speech by Orator Hunt, one of the most popular of the violent working-class agitators of the day. The meeting was presently charged by some ill-trained yeoman recruits and turned into a panic in which eleven of the spectators were killed and between four and five hundred wounded. It was one of the most tragic episodes of the time.*

And in the attempt to make matters perfectly safe, the government decided upon a policy of more rigorous repression. It put through Parliament what were known as the "Six Acts," laws which took away the rights to freedom of moving about the country without permits, which forbade public meetings to be held without express authorization of the authorities, which tried to stop the circulation of cheap newspapers, which forbade people to keep arms (and that in a country where everybody liked to hunt was regarded as a particularly serious deprivation), which forbade bands of people who were not members of the regular military organization to organize maneuvers, put a stop to all the training corps which were so popular. That was, by the reformers of the time, regarded as the crowning peaks of tyranny.

And yet, when in the next year another general election was made necessary by the death of old King George III who had long been mad but who now finally died and was succeeded by his son George IV, the reformers found they could make scarcely any gains at the polls. It was not that the populace was in the least bit contented with the administration, but as the reformers held, it was that the parliamentary machinery of the country, the scheme of suffrage, was so violently unfair that even the most unpopular of governments could return a majority of the House.

*Vide A. Prentice, Historical Sketches of Manchester, 1815, p. 167.

From the outside point of view even the prospect of getting a reform in English institutions seemed pretty nearly hopeless. But that was an outside view. And needless to say, the Philosophical Radicals, living in London, counting among their members some people who were in the midst of political life of the day, and counting among their friends more influential people who were in the midst of things, the Philosophical Radicals knew that the situation was by no means so hopeless as it seemed. The reason it was not so hopeless was that a split was rapidly developing inside the ranks of the Tories themselves.

To the outside it looked as if the Tory policy was guided by Lord Liverpool, by the Chancellor, Lord Eldon, and Lord Castlereagh, the great diplomat who had had a hand in the settlements at the end of the war and who was a firm supporter, in general, of the policies of the Tories, at least so far as the public knew, and of the Duke of Wellington who seemed to have, to his contemporaries, at this time as despotic a temper in politics as he had exhibited in his military life. But opposed to these men, who to the public made up the real representatives of the Tory party, there was a younger set of men who were becoming increasingly dissatisfied with the Castlereagh-Eldon-Wellington policy and men who wanted to revert to that form of Toryism which William Pitt had exhibited in his earlier years before he had been frightened by the French terror. Of these men, George Canning was by all odds the most prominent, but he also had able allies inside the party, particularly in William Huskisson, a London merchant who was very much interested in tariff reform, and the younger Sir Robert Peel, and in two or three other people whose names are less famous.

Now the Philosophical Radicals, as I say, were quite aware of this situation and they took advantage of it. They adopted a policy of "boring from within" as Bentham, I believe phrased it, - the policy of permeating the people in power with their ideas. And they were extraordinarily convenient allies for a man like Huskisson, or Canning, or Sir Robert Peel, because they would do all the hard work which was necessary in getting up the legislative program. They would think out the logical theory to support the propositions; they would gather together the materials which could be used effectively in speeches. If inquiries of any kind were to be made, they would carry them on and not ask for any credit; and, above all, if anybody discovered that they were collaborating with some eminent statesman, the statesman could disown them without any qualms of conscience. The Philosophical Radicals were so eager to get their ideas adopted, they were willing that they should be used in order to achieve their great aims, and, I dare say, they thought the reward would come in the days when Parliament would really be reformed and the most of the people would be able to vote in their own interest. If that was their opinion it turned out to be a mistake.

But they found it was perfectly feasible to work inside this seemingly hopeless Tory group to push what they wanted in an increasing number of details. The program of reform was presently aided in a most illogical fashion by the great royal scandal of 1820. The man who had come to the throne as George IV had long been a notorious character. He had been a bad son; he had been a bad father; he had been a wastrel whose debts Parliament had been compelled to pay several times. His official list of mistresses was finally run up to eighteen and was said to be incomplete at that number. He had been married rather early to a lady for whom he had entertained no great affection and who entertained no great affection for him; and by mutual consent his wife had for years been living on the Continent. But when her husband became king, Queen Caroline returned to England, and she wanted her name inserted in the prayer-book along with that of the king. The king was unwilling to concede any such privilege; and instead, with his ministry, indicted Queen Caroline before the House of Lords for adultery, his own record in this regard apparently making no difference. That led to a most scandalous trial before the House of Lords; - and one in which Queen Caroline was defended by two eminent Whig lawyers: Brougham and Denman, who were apparently more interested in benefiting their party than in simply helping their client; and they used the opportunity most skilfully to discredit all the characters who were concerned in the scandal and to discredit the ministers who had let themselves be used as the king's tools in this affair. The evidence that was presented before the House of Lords - and because it was presented before the House of Lords became privileged matter that any newspaper in the country might publish - was of the most unpleasant character; and it was disseminated through the length and breadth of the land. Everybody read it. It was by all odds the outstanding trial of the generation. It did a great deal to convince the common people that kings and queens were, after all, subject to the grossest of human infirmities. The Queen became, just because she was persecuted, more or less of a popular idol, and the ministry came in for a great deal of the infamy that was endured by the king himself. Those who watched events at the time seemed to believe that this emotional factor of the situation counted rather heavily in diminishing the prestige of the reactionary Tory party; and probably had a great deal to do with the change which presently came over Tory policy; for not long after, in February, 1822, Lord Castlereagh committed suicide.

Castlereagh had been the parliamentary mainstay of the conservative group inside the Tory party. Now it became necessary to find some member of the party who had not incurred odium with the public, to take his place and carry on in the House of Commons. And the only man who was available to do the job was George Canning. And George Canning, you see, was the leader of the modern reformist type of Tory, a man who wanted to go back to William Pitt's tradition of the early days. Canning grasped the strategic strength of his position and he refused to take the lead in the House of Commons and help the Tory ministry out of the predicament into which they seemed to be drifting unless he was given what he called "Castlereagh's full inheritance." He insisted on being installed in the Foreign Office and given great weight in the councils of the party.

The result was that from 1822 to 1827 the ministry which had been dominated by the reactionary powers of Eldon and Castlereagh and Wellington was dominated by the still conservative but, after all, by no means reactionary, in many ways definitely liberal, ideas of George Canning. And under this regime of Canning's ministry the Philosophical Radicals cooperated with Canning and his parliamentary chiefs and began to get some of their ideas enacted into law.

Thus Huskisson became chief of the Board of Trade, and he promptly began the great task of tariff reform. He passed through Parliament a long series of bills in which, broadly speaking, there was effected a genuine reduction of tariff duties. It is impossible to summarize the great number of measures of that sort in any brief statement, but it is perhaps safe to say that, broadly speaking, he reduced the general level of duties on imported goods from something like 40 to 180% ad valorum to ranges of 10 to 35%. Robinson, a Canningite, became Chancellor of the Exchequer, and under the prodding of the Philosophical Radical Joseph Hume, he began to reduce the number of sinecures and effect all sorts of economies in public expenses. Sir Robert Peel became Home Secretary, and he stopped the policy of persecuting free speech and free press. He made the reform of the criminal law which had been pressed, first by Romilly and then by Macintosh. He made that a government policy when Mackintosh died.

Beside that, the ministry as a whole repealed the Anti-Combination Act of 1800 the measure which I spoke of as effecting a sort of union between the agricultural and manufacturing interests against the working classes. That repeal was the greatest single feat of Francis Place's political manipulation. He was a man who had been born a workingman and had gradually risen to a position of affluence. He was most eager to see the laws prohibiting workingmen from forming unions to promote their own interests abolished,not at all because he thought they could accomplish anything;on the contrary he was sure they were not worth while, but he thought it was unjust that workingmen should be prohibited from forming such combinations if they so desired. And by a series of most shrewd maneuvers he got a committee appointed to consider the Anti-Comdination Acts, arranged the evidence which was to be given,got a report written and a bill drawn up,and got it actually passed through Parliament. Many members said in the next session that they did not know what the law contained. Anyway,the law was repealed.And when the next year employers,by the activity of men in forming unions,discovered that the Acts had been repealed and insisted that they be restored, it was Place, supported again by the rather liberal sentiments which dominated the Tory party at that time, who succeeded in getting the bill which was intended to make unions illegal changed in form so that it really gave them a thoroughly sound position at law.

Also this Tory ministry passed Hobhouse's ten and a half hours bill for children, a measure which was intended to prevent the worst excesses in the abuse of child workers.

Now this whole line of policy had two very important effects. On the one hand, it established a sort of truce between Parliament and the people. The government became far less unpopular than it had been in the years before Canning had come more or less into control of Tory policy. Doubtless that improvement in conditions was due very largely to the fact that from about 1822 to 1825 the country was enjoying a period of prosperity. There was far less unemployment,far less suffering all over the country,and that contributed,with this willingness of the government to move in the direction which the reform groups were advocating and gradually rendering popular, to allay the distrust which the populace felt for their scheme of government in very large measure.

But if the Canningite policy brought peace between the public and the government,it brought to the Tories,as a party not peace but a sword. It became the source of an increasingly acrid series of dissensions; so that Canning began to find that his measures were supported in large part by his party opponents and opposed in large part by his nominal party supporters.

In this complicated situation of affairs a new general election had to be held in 1826 because the seven year term of Parliament was expiring. In that election the leading issues were the corn law and the Catholic emancipation,that is, the plan for removing the disability upon Catholics from holding public office.

Now these issues, both of them, cut across party lines. In large part the supporters of the revision of the corn laws and of emancipating the Catholics came from the liberals and the radicals,and in large part the opponents of these measures came from the government in power. The upshot of the election was that the Tories held their majority, neither increasing or diminishing it very much, and matters promised to go on much as they had until in February, 1827 the old Prime Minister, Lord Liverpool, suffered a stroke of apoplexy. Now that made it necessary that the king should choose a new Prime Minister. Of course, he had to be a Tory since the Tories held a majority in Parliament; and among the Tories he had the choice of three possible men: there was Canning, there was Sir Robert Peel, and there was the Duke of Wellington.

The position was a very hard one, but the king finally settled on Canning; and then the quarrels inside the Tory ranks became open. As soon as Canning had been appointed, within forty-eight hours, seven of the twelve ministers in the Cabinet resigned so that the Tory party was split. Those who disapproved of the liberal policy that Canning had been able to carry out, even inside the Liverpool ministry, and felt pretty certain he would go still further in the liberal direction, withdrew. In order to fill his ranks, Canning appealed to the Whigs and asked a number of their leading men to join him. Some of them held out; some of them went with him; so that he built up a new administration that was mixed in political character - Whigs and Tories collaborating together.

What the ministry might have accomplished is quite uncertain; but unfortunately in August of the same year, 1827, Canning, worn out by the labors of office died. And the man who succeeded him, Robinson, the Chancellor of the Exchequer, who had been supporting his policies, and who had now been made Lord Goderich, proved to have not at all the qualities necessary to meet so difficult a political situation, and he finally resigned his position before Parliament met again. He was the only Prime Minister in the whole of English history who resigned without ever meeting a Parliament.

Canning being dead and his particular section of the Tories without an effective leader, the king sent for Wellington. When Wellington came in, the Whigs who had joined Canning promptly resigned, and presently the Canningite Tories also left. So that the country within a very short period of time changed over from a Tory government which promised to have an even more liberal character than Canning had attempted to give it under Liverpool's leadership to a government which promised to have as repressive and illiberal a policy as in the old days when Castlereagh and Eldon and Wellington had been the powers inside the Liverpool ministry. I will have to continue the story from that point at the next meeting.

XXXII

THE PASSAGE OF THE GREAT REFORM BILL OF 1832

On Tuesday I brought the story of how the great social reforms of the first third of the nineteenth century in England were accomplished down to the death of Canning, who, as I said, as the leader of a relatively liberal element in the Tory party had managed to pass through a considerable number of measures such as the social scientists of the day approved.

Now when he died and when his succesor failed to get the cabinet together, the king sent for the Duke of Wellington who was the chief of what was supposed commonly to be the more reactionary element among the Tory party. And when Wellington became Prime Minister, all the Whigs who had joined the Canning cabinet resigned, and then presently Huskisson and the other Canningite Tories retired, so that the ministry was now composed exclusively of people believed to be loyal followers of the "iron duke."

But it turned out that the "iron duke's" ministry itself, illiberal as it was supposed to be in social attitude, was forced, presumably against the inclination of its members, to carry on a considerable part of the program which Canning had installed. Thus, under the leadership of the Duke of Wellington, the Tories had recently thrown out a bill of Huskisson's (you remember he was one of Canning's lieutenants) for reducing the import duties of corn. But the duke's own ministry presently put in and carried through a corn law which provided duties on a sliding scale, duties not quite as low as Huskisson approved, but nevertheless duties which did reduce the sums which imported corn had to pay.

Then they passed an act repealing the old Corporation and Test Acts. These were measures which had been made law in the time of King Charles II and which placed certain disabilities upon dissenters in England. They were among the laws which the Philosophical Radicals were particularly eager to see repealed. They had ceased to be of any considerable moment because dissenters had been in the habit at times of accepting public office though they could not conscientiously sign oaths which involved adherence to the state church. They did so, however, because it had become the prevailing practice year after year to pass an indemnity act in Parliament specifically providing that people who held posts without subscribing to the legal tests should not suffer. So the Acts constituted in practice mainly a standing insult to all dissenters,and when the duke agreed that they should be abolished,in response to widespread public demand, he was taking a step which pleased presumably the majority of the people better than it pleased himself,and which very distinctly displeased a considerable part of his own party.

Then the ministry had to face the question of specie payments. There had been enacted in 1821, if I remember rightly, a bill which provided that the country should at a certain date return to the gold standard.That was a measure that was heartily opposed by a large proportion of the landowning classes on the ground that it would tend to reduce prices and that would make it difficult for their tenants to pay rents. Among the squirearchy there was a very strong opposition to any measure which they thought would render the task of paying rents more difficult. Nevertheless, this part of the program which the Philosophical Radicals supported went through in Wellington's ministry.

Then fourth and more disturbing, Wellington's ministry emancipated the Catholics. And that was a particularly dramatic episode. Among the people whom Wellington included in his cabinet was a Fitzgerald. The Fitzgeralds in those days were among the greatest landed proprietors in Ireland. Since a Fitzgerald was included in the ministry, he had to appeal to his constituency to return him. That was one of the standing British practices. And when Fitzgerald went up for reelection, it was supposed to be a foregone conclusion that his constituents would return him. But by that time Daniel O'Connell, the Irish patriot, had perfected an organization,largely through Catholic priests, and they brought to the polls squadrons of voters,very often led by their priests in full canonical dress, and quite swamped the Fitzgerald vote. Well, it appeared to the duke and to Sir Robert Peel, who was his chief reliance in the cabinet, that they were going to have a civil war in Ireland on their hands if the demand for removing the political disabilities of the Catholics was not met;and so,quite contrary to the general feeling in the party, the duke concluded that the wise measure was to accept that repeal and the measure was put through with a high hand.

Now these reforming acts carried by the Tories under one of their most conservative leaders had a very serious political consequence. It split the Tory party into three groups; on the one hand there were the regulars following the ministry, and in Parliament at least that constituted the bulk of the party; there were also Canningites who were the left wing of the party; and there were the "high" Tories, as they were called, who constituted the right wing. The "high" Tories were so incensed by these reform measures, most of all by the Catholic emancipation, that when Peel came up for reelection in Oxford, (he held the University seat, having been a notably successful scholar and personally very popular there), he was beaten in his own constituency, and had to go back to the pocket borough of Tamworth, and carry forward the measure against this crushing affront.

The ministry's difficulties with its own party were presently aggravated by a recurrence of serious social disorder, a difficulty which Canning managed to allay partly by the popularity of his policy, and partly by the sheer good fortune that his continuancy in power coincided with the relatively good times from 1822 to 1825. In 1825 there had been a bad smash, a great panic in London. The year 1826 was a year of depression. There was a revival of trade in 1827; and the first year of the Wellington ministry, 1828, was a good year. But in 1829 there came a series of relapses - widespread labor unrest and particularly bad harvests - so that there was much more suffering among the agricultural laborers. And all the agitators of the country took advantage of the situation to fan the flames of discontent to a higher heat.

In Birmingham, Thomas Attwood, an irredeemable paper money advocate, formed a political union with the object of getting parliamentary reform, because Attwood thought that a body of sensible men would go in for his patent currency scheme which would straighten out all the ills of the country. He was a banker, a man of large means, but he seems to have been hypnotized by his currency plan and wanted to reform Parliament mainly in order to get an irredeemable currency established according to his specifications; and into his political union he drew a large part of the vigorous manufacturing and business elements.

Outside the metropolis, William Cobbett, the great penny journalist of the time, started out on a series of rides through the various parts of rural England preaching parliamentary reform everywhere he went. He preached parliamentary reform in the interest primarily of the agricultural laborer.

And in London the Rotundardists, the great band of artisan agitators, who believed in giving labor the full value it produced, were carrying on a series of meetings of excited men demanding reforms of a more and more revolutionary sort.

While all this was happening in the manufacturing districts in the west and the north and in London, what they called in those days the "rural war" broke out in the southern counties, those parts least advanced industrially where the plight of the agricultural laborers was probably the saddest. Down in that part of the country that had usually been leading a peaceful, somnolent life, there was a great deal of rick burning and many acts of personal violence were perpetrated.

And just at this time while the ministry was at outs with the "high" Tories and had not made peace with the Canningites, and while agitations were going on from so many sides in such vigorous fashion, King George IV died and a new general election had to be held. The new king was William IV, the brother of the deceased king, and a person who, having personal popularity was at least not so violently unpopular as George IV had deservedly been. In the election, party lines were drawn again. The Whigs were very much helped by a stroke of good luck. The summer of 1830 was a time of unrest on the Continent. It was the time when the Belgians expelled the Dutch and set up an independent government. And what counted still more in the favor of the Whigs, it was the year of the three days of July in Paris, the days of that sudden and bloodless revolution which overturned the Bourbons whom the Holy Alliance had put back on the French throne, and brought in King Louis Phillipe. Both of these revolutions, the one in Belgium and the other in France, were revolutions which seemed to have been engineered primarily by the middle classes. They were highly respectable revolutions; they were accompanied by very little violence, by very little looting; and the parties they established in power were parties that were composed or at least led by people of property and some distinction. It was, in short, a series of European episodes of very considerable interest to Englishmen, in which the Duke of Wellington's Continental friends, the Holy Alliance, were beaten, discredited, and in which people of the rather mildly reformist type of the Whig party succeeded.

That spectacle of a peaceful, law-abiding revolution on the Continent is said greatly to have heartened the Whigs and to have counted very heavily in their favor at the polls because it made Englishmen think that there might be some rather thoroughgoing reforms in England of a sort quite different in character from the French Revolution that had been accompanied by the Terror. However that may be, the outcome at the polls was a series of great gains by the Whigs and by some radicals. The Whig and radical parties together were computed to have gained at least fifty seats, and it was uncertain when the new Parliament met how the balance of power would lie; whether Wellington would still have a working majority, or whether the Whigs would come into the government. The question was soon settled. In his remarks upon the speech from the throne, which is the first important feature of the meeting of any new Parliament, Lord Grey took up the issue which all the radicals of the time talked about, the fundamental one, the issue of parliamentary reform.

Now Grey in his youth had espoused that cause, but by this time, his youth was a far distant event. He had first gone into Parliament when he was very young, in the days when Charles James Fox was still a great power, in the days when William Pitt's ministry was in its earlier years. And he had ranged himself presumably without very mature consideration but in accordance with the sound Whig tradition of his time, on the side of the parliamentary reformers, and had become indeed the chief Whig spokesman for that particular reform, one which they always pushed very vigorously when the Tories were in power, and a reform they might have been less anxious about carrying out had they themselves enjoyed control of Parliament, just as Pitt in his earlier days had been a parliamentary reformist and had given his support to the measure even in the earlier days of his ministry.

For a long while Lord Grey had seemed, at least to the Philosophical Radicals, to be temporizing on the subject of reform; in fact, many of them had come to believe that he really had no heart for any thoroughgoing measure of a democratic sort. The low water mark of his enthusiasm for that particular measure was reached in 1810 when in one of his speeches in the House of Lords he had said:

> I doubt much whether there exist a very general disposition in favor of reform. Whenever this great question shall be taken up by the people of this country seriously and effectively there will then be a fair prospect of accomplishing it, but until the country shall have expressed its opinion on the subject the example of the other nations of Europe shall deter us from any precipitate attempt to hurry a measure upon which the best interests of the nation so doing depends.

It may well be that the agitation of the summer of 1830 and the preceding summer of 1829 had convinved Lord Grey that the nation was "seriously and effectively" taking up the subject of reform. In any case in his remarks on the speech from the throne, he said that the "dangers of the day can be avoided only by securing the affections of our fellow subjects, by reducing their grievances and - My Lords, I will pronounce the words - by reforming Parliament.*

* Smart, Economic Annals, vol. II, p. 565.

That was, of course, a challenge to the ministry and the Duke of Wellington at once made a rejoinder which drew the issue between the Whigs and Tories in the most vigorous fashion. He replied:

> I am fully convinced that the country possesses, at the present moment a legislature which answers all the good purposes of legislation, and this to a greater degree than any legislature ever has answered in any country whatever. I will go further, and say that the legislature and the system of representation possess the full and entire confidence of the country, deservedly possess that confidence, and the discussions in the legislature have a very great influence over the opinions of the country. I will go still further, and say that if at the present moment I had imposed upon me the duty of forming a legislature for any country, and particularly for a country like this, in possession of great property of various descriptions, I do not mean to assert that I would form such a legislature as we possess now - for the nature of man was incapable of reaching it at once - but my great endeavour would be to form some description of legislature which would produce the same results.*

It was, of course, an endorsement of the British Constitution in as strong language as the "iron duke" could use when he was speaking on his feet.

And that meant, as I said, that the outstanding issue of the day between the parties which seemed to be more or less equal in parliamentary votes was to be the issue which the Philosophical Radicals and all the other groups deemed to be the fundamentally important one. Presently the duke's ministry was divided on an issue of comparatively minor importance, and the king had no alternative but to send for Lord Grey and ask him to form a new government. Grey at once invited the leading men among the Canningite Tories to join him, which they did, and thereby increased the power of the Whig party rather materially, giving them what seemed to be, for most purposes, a tolerable working majority. At once Lord Grey appointed a committee to draft the reform bill, - a committee which included his son-in-law Lambton(Lord Durham), Lord John Russell, Sir James Graham, and Lord Duncannon. This measure was submitted to the king before it was put in Parliament and approved by William IV, although he thought it not democratic enough. The king took the ground that the rather narrow democratic reform which Earl Grey proposed was a measure which would give the English people such a measure of reform as would allay the very threatening discontent, but would at the same time keep the mass of the wage-earning population out of the suffrage, would keep the right to vote in the hands of people of some substance.

The bill was introduced into Parliament on the first of March by Lord John Russell. It proposed to abolish altogether some 62 rotten boroughs, boroughs having less than 2,000 population, and to take away one member from some 47 other boroughs which had less than 4,000 people. That would give the ministry 2 times 62 or 124 plus 47 seats, a total of 171 seats, which they proposed to distribute among the large industrial centers of the north that were now altogether unrepresented in Parliament, among certain counties which had been growing rapidly in population, and to the City of London, the representation of which was quite inadequate on a population basis.

---

* Molesworth, W.N., The History of the Reform Bill of 1832, pp. 59-60.

It was proposed also that the complicated medieval schemes of having different bases for the exercise of suffrage in different constituencies should be abolished, and that for it should be substituted a strictly uniform qualification for voting in all the counties, and a second strictly uniform scheme of suffrage for all the boroughs. The scheme involved certain property qualifications. In the boroughs the vote was given to all ten pound householders, that is to say, to all people who held houses of which the rental value was ten pounds per annum. They did not have to own them; if they leased houses at ten pounds per annum they obtained the rights of suffrage. And in the counties all landowners who had estates of ten pounds per annum or more were allowed to vote, and also all people who rented property for which they paid fifty pounds per annum or more.

Now that measure, if it was accepted, would prevent the great mass of the British wage earners from voting. They could not afford to rent ten pound houses in the city or fifty pound farms in the country. It was a measure which would, however, enfranchise a very large part of the middle classes, the lower middle classes. It was a proposal which delighted the Philosophical Radicals and a large part of the agitators for reform outside the working classes proper. For the Philosophical Radicals in their scheme for parliamentary reforms had always stood primarily for the working classes. On the basis of their theories that was largely consistent. Of course, from their point of view, the suffrage ought to be exercised by everyone who was capable of making a sensible association among ideas, - everybody who had a sufficient education and intellectual capacity to entertain a just idea of how to get pleasure and avoid pain. And they believed moreover, quite honestly that this middle class which could not only express intelligent notions concerning their own interests, but would also really represent the best interests of the working classes, - perhaps not on all occasions taking the line the working classes would take for themselves, but taking the line that was good for the working classes. And they felt thoroughly satisfied with the proposal, at least for the time being.

The whole measure was indeed regarded as far more radical in tone than could have been expected from a ministry of large landowners such as Lord Grey had gotten together. One of his boasts, by the way, was that his ministry had a larger average acreage than any that England had ever possessed before.

The Tories, on the other hand, were as much alarmed as the reformers were pleased by the bill. On its first reading they greeted it with jeers, thinking that a measure so radical in character stood very little chance of being enacted. If the bill should be enacted, however, it meant, they believed at the time, a death-blow to the Tory party, for it would break the hold that they held upon a large proportion of parliamentary seats.

One of Canning's political secretaries, Croker, a man who is most famous for having written that very savage review of Keat's first book of poems that is sometimes said to have been a cause of Keat's untimely death, had drawn up for him a schedule of the seats controlled by Tories and Whigs in 1827. According to his computation, there were 203 House of Commons seats in the hands of the Tories, and there were 73 Whig seats. Now this scheme of parliamentary elections would abolish all the rotten boroughs; it would deprive the Whigs of their 73 seats but it would also deprive the Tories of their 203; and it would make it necessary for the Tories hereafter if they wished to control Parliament - at least they believed so - for the time being to adopt a policy that pleased the people instead of a policy that was wise in their own eyes. So the Tories decided to fight the measure tooth and nail.

On the 22d of March the bill passed its second reading by a majority of only one; and then it went into committee, and presently on the 19th of April the government was beaten in one vote by a majority of 8. At once the king who was supporting the ministry prorogued Parliament and called for a new election. That election was held in May, 1831 and resulted in a great popular demonstration in favor of the Whigs. They gained none of the boroughs that they proposed to disfranchise save, of course, the boroughs that were controlled by Whigs, and save for four seats which the Whigs purchased from a traitorous Tory who was in sad need of funds. But they carried all the boroughs where there was a semblance of popular choice; and they got 76 out of 82. So they came back to Parliament with a majority in favor of the bill of 136. That showed that public opinion was unmistakably behind the measure. But this very fact caused a new difficulty to the ministry; that was that the king became alarmed. He began to question whether he was right in saying that this was an aristocratic measure, - whether it was not too popular for a sovereign who ruled by the grace of God to support. For the time being, however, Grey kept him in line, though the task became increasingly difficult as the months went on.

Of course, the new Parliament had to have a new bill submitted to it. The process of passing the measure had to start all over again. The new bill was very much like the first. It passed its second reading on the 6th of July; this went into committee, and the Tories proceeded in their tactics. Through interminable sessions during a very hot summer they fought every clause of the bill with all the vigor that they could command, and by so doing they greatly increased the exasperated state of public opinion. But the Whig majority kept a sufficient number of voters on hand right through the hot summer to make sure no accident should happen in committee.

On the 22d of September the House passed the bill and then it was taken up to the House of Lords. When it got into the House of Lords, it had to run a very dangerous conflict. The whole bunch of bishops without exception opposed the measure, and opposed it with vigor. And so did, of course, pretty much the whole company of Tory peers. Now we think of the House of Lords as being representatives of ancient families, but if one follows the history of the British peerage he will realize that at any time the great majority of the peers are a recent creation. The Tories had been in power at that time for something like a generation, and within that generation they had created, mainly for services to the Tory party, a larger number of peers than was represented by the survivors of the old Whig families. So that the great majority of the late peers joined the bishops in opposition to the bill. And the result was that the bill was allowed to pass its first reading, but thrown out on the 8th of October by a majority of 41.

Then the populace at large took a hand in the proceedings by resorting to their favorite method of expressing their feelings. The Duke of Wellington's windows were broken. Nottingham Castle was burned. A number of Tory peers were stoned in their carriages, and a considerable proportion of the bishops feared to go home from London to their sees. And there was a particularly serious series of riots and incendiary fires in Bristol where it had happened the leader of the parliamentary obstruction to the bill in the House of Commons was going to fulfil certain judicial duties which he had to perform. Also a great impetus was given to the formation of political unions on Attwood's Birmingham model, and to the formation of working class unions to agitate for a reform of Parliament.

Under these circumstances with the nation behind him, Lord Grey decided that the proper thing to do was to start the process over once more, hoping that the outburst of popular anger which had greeted the Lords' action would deter them from being so foolish again. So a third bill was brought into Parliament on the 12th of December 1831, again carried through a committee against the most inveterate obstruction tactics on the part of the Tories.

And while this was happening in the House, the outside agitation was kept going in the most vigorous fashion. The "rural war" in the southern counties broke out again. Attwood and Francis Place, the practical politicians among the Philosophical Radicals, were methodically organizing trained bands, practicing military maneuvers, and preparing to coerce the Lords should that be necessary. Just how much actual influence this prospect of civil war had upon the ultimate fate of the measure is difficult to see. Of course in Parliament these disorders were never mentioned as a reason why the bill should be passed, though they were frequently adduced as a reason why the bill should be thrown out. Lord Grey was continually criticized by the Tories for his failure to maintain order. They charged the responsibility for all the difficulties and indignities which they suffered as a party or as individuals against the inefficiency of the government.

And also if you read the letters of the statesmen of the time you find that they make but casual references to the probability of very serious outbreak of violence in case the Lords remained obdurate. But every now and then one gets a hint that though people were very careful about what they said or wrote on the subject, the spectre of mob violence was a factor of very great importance in influencing the decisions that people came to.

The third bill got through the House of Commons on the 23d of March 1832 and John Russell at the head of the Committee again carried it up to the Lords. That was on the 26th of March. It was in the Lords that the final struggle had to come. There were enough waverers – people who, though they expressed great dislike for the measure, held that it was their duty as public men not to stand in the way of a mistake which the nation as a whole was intent on committing. There were enough waverers to give the ministry a majority of nine on the second reading. But when the bill went into committee in the Lords, there was presently an adverse vote cast, and when that happened Lord Grey at once resigned.

The next day the king appealed to Wellington and asked him whether he could form a ministry and bring in a Tory bill of reform, one which would be acceptable to the country on one side and to the members of his party on the other side. Wellington went to Sir Robert Peel who was by all odds the most powerful Tory member of the House of Commons and asked for his support. Peel had been among those who opposed the bill, though not among the most violent. The choice which was put up to him was one of great difficulty, all the more because he had suffered so much from a change of front. He had only a few years earlier become responsible for the bill for emancipating the Catholics after he stood for years as one of the opponents of that measure. And he came to the conclusion that it would be his political death-knell if he once more changed front on a measure of such great importance and helped to pass a reform measure when for the past two years he had been fighting such a step in the Commons.

Well, when Peel refused to serve, Wellington realized it to be quite impossible for him to carry the measure through without Peel's help. And so he told the king that he could not form a ministry. That left nothing for the king to do except invite the Whig cabinet to accept power again. And, of course, this position put the strong cards in Grey's hands. He told the king he had become by this time very much afraid of the bill because of all the agitation in its favor. He said to the king that it would be impossible for him to accept the responsibility of His Majesty's government unless His Majesty would guarantee to create sufficient new peers to pass the bill over the majority in the House of Lords. That was a measure that the king was exceedingly reluctant to take, and there was a week of hesitation when the various quasi-military organizations that had been formed in the provinces made public preparations for marching on London, and during which Francis Place organized a run on the Bank of England by posting up all over the city posters saying "go for gold," and in which Attwood and his political unions though composed of relatively respectable members of the population took an exceedingly violent tone. Apparently the king came to the conclusion that the only way out of a situation which was becoming almost intolerable to him was the way that Lord Grey insisted upon. And so finally he gave Lord Grey his pledge to create the peers and instructed his private secretary to make that fact known in the House of Lords. The result was that a sufficient number of Tory peers absented themselves when the bill came up for final vote. It passed, and agitation died away as suddenly as it had sprung up.

It was in this way that perhaps the most momentous of all the British reforms of the nineteenth century came about. The reform accomplished in this fashion was in the eyes of the Philosophical Radicals, of course, just the first but by all odds the most important of the measures that should be taken to give the country the sort of political, social and economic organization which their new social sciences called for. For, as they saw things, it was going to make Parliament responsive to the public opinion of the class in whose shrewdness and intelligence they themselves reposed confidence. It meant that the great mass of middle class Englishmen, that class that James Mill liked to refer to as the "virtuous" class, would be able to determine who should be the majority of the law-makers; so that on Bentham's analysis of human nature, it should be a simple, more or less mechanical, matter for the people themselves to determine through their representatives what the laws should be.

So as the Philosophical Radicals saw things, the Reform Bill opened the door to a most gorgeous prospect. It was true that their part in passing the Reform Bill had been an inconspicuous one, that the measure had been carried through by a party which paid no attention to them and, by the way, whose historians have paid no attention to them. But from their point of view as soon as the new measure was in effect, these large landowning aristocratic Whig politicians who had been forced against their will to adopt a measure of genuine democratic significance, these people would not be the sort of folk whom the middle classes would choose as their representatives, but people whom they would choose would understand their interests, as the Philosophical Radicals did. So there was a prospect that the Philosophical Radicals might well become at least the intellectual leaders of a new party which would now have the means of giving the country everything that Bentham had desired. The chief grief to the little group of Philosophical Radicals was that their great leader, Jeremy Bentham, had died, well on in the eighties, just a few months before the Reform Bill was passed.

XXXIII

SIMILARITIES AND CONTRASTS BETWEEN THE PROCESSES OF
SOCIAL REFORM AND REFORM IN METHODS OF PRODUCTION IN ENGLAND.

We spent our last few meetings in discussing the processes by which great social and economic reforms were accomplished in the first third of the nineteenth century in England. Today I want to call your attention to the most instructive

similarities and the equally instructive contrasts between the processes by which
social reform and reform in methods of production were going on in England at
this time. It is one of the common reflections upon the course of history in the
last one hundred or two hundred years that we have made far more progress in the
material arts of life than we have in the arts of living together; that we have
achieved far more in bettering our ways of producing material things than we have
in bettering the social relations which constitute such an important element in
the lives of all of us, which are basic even in this strictly economic matter of
producing and distributing serviceable commodities.

That is a remark that I think is probably justified, but I should like to
go further and, as I say, discuss some of the differences between problems of
improving the social organization and the problems of improving the methods of
producing wealth. These two great processes in England were running apace at much
the same time. The series of great inventions which ushered in the Industrial
Revolution got started just a little before the great developments of the social
sciences in England got under way. It is interesting to remember, as showing how
closely parallel the two processes were, that while Adam Smith was teaching in
Glasgow College and developing the lectures which presently became The Wealth of
Nations, James Watt was a scientific instrument maker in Glasgow College and was
beginning that series of experiments which resulted in his making improvements
upon Newcomen's engine which gave us a steam engine that was really effective
motor power.

And after the time of Adam Smith we have the work of such inventors as
Cartwright who developed the first half-effective power loom; and Arkwright one
of the great inventors of textile machinery and one of the great business organizers of the early factory system; and Stevenson of railroad fame. A whole long
list of mechanical geniuses were working at the same time that Malthus and Benthem and Ricardo and the other Philosophical Radicals were trying to think out
social problems on a new basis. The processes of invention in the social field
and processes of invention in the mechanical field were going on side by side.

Now I think one of the chief reasons why the social inventors seem to us
in retrospect to have accomplished rather less than did the mechanical inventors
is that the social inventors were at a disadvantage as far as trying out their
schemes is concerned. The mechanical inventor has the great advantage of being
able to experiment at will. If he gets what he thinks is a brilliant idea for
improving upon some mechanical device, he can try that out in practice. And he
usually finds, of course, that the happy idea, after all, does not work very
well. And then he can make a series of further experiments and adjustments and
refinings gradually working the crudities out of his machine. Or if he is the
first person who has hit upon the broad problems he is trying to solve but his
labors have not produced a machine which will work, the history of invention has
shown time after time that it will be taken up by somebody else who will have
another inspiration. The great mechanical inventions were not the work of single
individuals. It was a process of accumulation, of betterment accompanied all
the time by practical trials and tests, - practical trials which enabled the
mechanical improvers to build up, and the result of actual experience to devise
methods safer and better than the ways of doing work which they superseded.

In contrast, the people who were inventors in the social field had no such
opportunity to try out their ideas on a small scale. You will observe that not
merely The Wealth of Nations but also Bentham's treatises, Ricardo's Principles
of Economics, and all the classics of English social sciences in the early part
of the century were written on a speculative basis. They represented some

very intelligent and able man's reflections upon how things went at the time, and for the Philosophical Radicals represented also, in very many cases, their ideas how human relations ought to be organized so as to work in a more satisfactory fashion. But Adam Smith could not make any test of his plans for free trade and find out in practice whether the regulations which he believed would enhance the wealth of nations actually did so. Jeremy Bentham could not put into practice although he tried hard to do so, his Panoptican scheme for reforming criminals. Ricardo was not in a position to test out his patent scheme for paying off the war debt by a levy on wealth. Malthus was not in a position to prove by experiment that a change in the poor laws would greatly check the increase of population and redound in the long run to the greater comfort of the working classes. Those men could think out improvements in very much the same way an inventor can get an idea and elaborate it on paper, - draw a lot of blue prints, perhaps, - but the inventor, after he has drawn his designs, can construct a machine and set it to work.

Now all that these men who were working in the social sciences could do was to draw up their designs. They could do a little more than that: they could draw up their designs in the light of similar designs that had been drawn up by their predecessors. The idea is that we get in Ricardo reflections added to those of people like Adam Smith and Malthus and other contemporaries. Of course, not all his ideas are of this nature; there are ideas which Ricardo believed in as a result of his own reflections. But though one social scientist could reflect upon the ideas of his predecessors, and perhaps make improvements, he was not in a position to try them out in practice. There is one of the most serious difficulties in the way of making serviceable social sciences, as contrasted with the ways which can be adopted by men who are interested in reforming the arts of production.

The social scientists labored under a second great disadvantage as compared with the mechanical improvers, and that was that after they had their schemes perfected according to their own test, they had no such simple and easy ways of getting them adopted in practice. When one of the great inventors had succeeded in producing a machine which was really a more efficient producer than the methods which it was intended to displace, in order to get it actually adopted in practice the only thing he needed was capital. And in those days the amount of capital he needed was rather small. Well, of course, the inventors were themselves mainly poor men, and that meant as a rule, before they could get their machines adopted they had to interest someone and induce him to put up the modest sum required for trying the thing out on a commercial scale.

Well, the inventors could do that. That is not a very serious obstacle; and when the machine was tried out on a commercial scale and actually proved that it could turn out more goods and more cheaply than could be done by earlier methods, then the people who had started the innovation of using the new devices could put the most effective kind of pressure on others producing the same kind of goods to take up the new methods in their turn. For, of course, in manufacturing at least, a man who began to spin by using the better machinery which the successive inventions of Cartwright and Arkwright provided could turn out yarn at a price which the people who were still insisting on using old methods could not compete with. That is, in securing the practical application of the device, once it has been sufficiently tested on a commercial scale, the people who were using it could practically coerce laggards in production to adopt their plan; and the people who did not have the adaptability to adopt the new methods were simply put out of business. And it was only a short while before the country was changing its methods of producing its entire supply of yarn.

And the same is true in the history of many of the mechanical industries.

It was true of weaving as well as of spinning. And it became rapidly true of the arts applied to the making of iron and steel, and also of the arts of transportation so far as covering long distances was concerned. Stage-coachers and wagoners could not compete with railroads any more than hand-weavers could compete with the power loom. And the people who were using these new devices, simply by trying to exploit them on a commercial scale, forced the rapid adoption of the improved methods upon the community as a whole.

In agriculture, of course, that was not possible, because people who found improved methods of, let us say, raising mutton sheep could not on the farms under their control, come anywhere near supplying all the mutton that England required. People who invented and first adopted improved methods of crop rotation that gave them larger crops of wheat could not force the rapid adoption of those improvements by all English farmers, because they could not raise more than a small fraction of England's wheat; so that the arts of production in agriculture were not changed nearly as quickly as the arts were changed in most manufacturing processes and in transportation.

But when you pass from agriculture to the social sciences you find that you are making another big step away from a situation which allows the people who are employing the new methods to force a rapid and general adoption to a situation in which the people who are sponsors of the new methods have to adopt other slower and less effective methods. Consider the case of a social scientist who has some new method, which he regards as a great reform, that he wants to see adopted. In some cases, the reforms which the Philosophical Radicals were advocating could be adopted by small groups of people, very much as a new invention, a spinning device could be taken up by a single manufacturing concern. That would be true, for instance, of their schemes for improving schools. You could actually, if you had a brilliant new idea for educating the youth, interest some people who had money enough to start a school and get them to try out your ideas. Well, that is one of the ideas that the Philosophical Radicals had. But when you had done that much, of course, even if your method of teaching children was demonstrably more successful from your viewpoint than the methods of other schools, you had no way of forcing its adoption, although you had demonstrated its superiority to your satisfaction. The results, although perhaps satisfactory to you, might not suit other people. And even if they did, in your school you could train comparatively only a few people; and you could get other schools to adopt your ideas only by a slow process of persuasion; there are no methods of coercion you could employ. You can use only methods even slower than those with which you can push for better methods of agricultural production.

There were comparatively few of the reforms of which the social scientists of that age sought to bring about which could be tried out as new educational schemes might be tried out in schools. Most of the reforms they advocated required the consent of government. Now that did not in all cases mean that before they could get these reforms adopted they had to persuade any large proportion of the members of Parliament of the superiority of what they wanted. They might in a good many cases, and did get new measures adopted by government through the agency of just a few rather eminent people. A good example is afforded by the series of reforms in the criminal law which got pretty well under way even before Bentham's day. Those reforms were taken up first in the House of Commons by Sir Samuel Romilly, one of Bentham's rather independent disciples, following in this one of his schemes most intelligently; and when Sir Samuel Romilly died by his own hand another disciple, Sir James Mackintosh, took up the struggle for reforming the barbarous criminal code of England; and when Sir James Mackintosh died, Sir Robert Peel, though a Tory, took over the task and brought to it the great advantage of his prominence in the party which at that time held control of Parliament. By the time Sir Robert Peel took over the measure, the members of the House of Commons had been largely educated by the long-continued and, for the time being, seemingly vain efforts of Rommily and Mackintosh; and Peel got through a series of measures with comparatively little difficulty. But it was done primarily, so far as one can see, through the continued activity of just a few people and the majority of the members of Parliament apparently knew very little about the matter and paid comparatively little attention to it. When they voted they probably voted largely on the basis of a rather unintelligent acquiescence in what seemed to be simply a common-sense measure.

Another example of a reform that could be worked through the legislature without the need of very close attention from a large number of people is the repeal of the Anti-Combination Acts, those laws passed in 1799 and 1800 which nominally prohibited the formation of organizations among either employees or employers for affecting wages and conditions of working, - laws which stood in the way, of course, of the formation of trade unions. Indeed, through the extremely clever manipulation of Francis Place, Joseph Hume, and a very few colleagues in the House of Commons, they were able to get the Anti-Combination Acts repealed in 1824, and were able to keep the repealing act from being repealed the next year when there was more outcry about it.

And still another measure of the sort is the early Factory Act, the attempt tp prevent the worst abuses of the early factory system which fell so heavily upon children, and pauper children at that. The early factory acts were sponsored by the elder Sir Robert Peel and were passed through a Parliament which understood very little about the matter. Later on, when the attempt was made not simply to protect children but to expand the protection of factory acts to all factory employees, the question became one of far more general interest, was fought with far greater fierceness, and could be carried only when a far larger number of the members of Parliament had been educated, really enlightened, concerning the needs of legislation. But for the time being that went through with even greater ease than the repeal of the Anti-combination Acts or the reform of the criminal law.

On the other hand, when the change that one of the social inventors wanted to make in social arrangements was a change that touched a great number of people, when it was a matter of rather serious importance both in the eyes of the reformers and in the eyes of the people affected, then the reformers could do but a comparatively modest part of the work. Of course, one of their standing demands was for the abolition of all religious disabilities; they wanted to see the Church of England disestablished; and their logical case for the repeal of all sorts of religious disabilities and discriminations was worked out with the same degree of system and attention to logical details, and worked out on the basis of the same conceptions regarding the fundamental characteristics of human nature as were their economic theories. But no set of logical arguments was going to persuade a set of English squires on the seats of Parliament that it was a wise measure to abolish the Catholic disabilities. The weapons of logic there would do part of the work perhaps, they could convert a man here and there, but what brought about Catholic emancipation from the hands of the very reluctant Tory ministry was the pressure applied by Daniel O'Connell, that is, a great popular agitation in which a man who had very few, if any, of the qualities of a social scientist, but who had an abundant supply of the qualities characteristic of a great agitator, in which a man who was primarily a genius at political organization supplied the driving force behind the demand for which the Philosophical Radicals had helped to furnish the reasons.

Or again, take the Great Reform Bill, a matter which they thought was most

important. It meant the providing of that machinery by which all the other reforms in their program could and presumably would be brought about. For long
years the Philosophical Radicals labored to make out a logical case for what they
regarded as the universal scheme of suffrage. They were content, of course, to
confine the suffrage to men and even content with a property qualification; but
they had, as they seemed to think, good logical reasons for treating these limitations as essential. James Mill's arguments in favor of parliamentary reform
on the Utilitarian basis are perhaps even a more elaborate, finer bit of logical
reasoning on the basis of the principles of human nature as laid down by Jeremy
Bentham than anything to be found in James Mill's very beautiful treatise on
political economy. If you want to see about the finest example of Utilitarian
reasoning in the social sciences, you had better read his articles on Government
which he wrote for the Encyclopaedia Britannica. But beautifully as that case
was worked out, strongly as it was argued on the basis of Utilitarian principles,
it was not, of course, popular. To get parliamentary reform a pressure of a
different sort was applied. It was not until the changing economic conditions
of the time which gave the middle classes, who were rapidly increasing in wealth
and intelligence and ambition, an overwhelming desire to get an effective voice
in the public councils, and it was not until a large part of the working classes
themselves had come to think that this was their cause and worth fighting for,
it was not until there was a very highly aroused state of public feeling on the
subject, that a Whig ministry was ready to take up the cause and carry the fight
through to a successful issue.

And so too with reference to that great reform which we usually connect
most closely with the work of the economists, the Philosophical Radicals: free
trade. The Philosophical Radicals were able, by providing arguments and detailed cases to help on the series of minor reforms that Huskisson put through,
just as Adam Smith's argument had much to do with getting that earlier series of
reforms of the tariff adopted. But when it came to the great central issues of
tariff reform in England at that time, the abolition of the import duties of corn,
the economists, the Philosophical Radicals, at large found themselves making
scarcely any headway, even after they had got parliamentary reform. But they continued to agitate the measure. One of John Stuart Mill's great friends brought
up a measure for repealing the corn laws every session in Parliament, but these
rather tiresome economists and Utilitarians could not put any driving power behind their demands. It was only when two great political organizers and agitators,
Cobden and Bright, together with a variety of likeminded allies took up the matter
and began to argue it on all sorts of grounds aside from economic expediency that
the demand for free trade became formidable. And after a series of the most skilfully conducted campaigns in which there was far more evidence of feeling, far
more talk about justice than about expediency, they finally succeeded in forcing
a Tory ministry to accept the measure that they desired.

Now all this means, I take it, not that the social scientists did not play
a very important, indeed a crucially important, role in bringing about the alterations in social life, but it means that in trying to bring about the alterations
they had to work against obstacles, with some of which they were quite unable to
deal by themselves, even with the aid of a small group of allies. When it came
to their more fundamental and more far-reaching changes, they found that the
methods which were native to them were not very effective in producing human
action. They relied upon argument, and on the basis of Bentham's psychology that
ought to have been a sufficient reason why people should act as they pointed
out. For if men are really controlled simply by the desire to get pleasure and
avoid pain, and if their opinions of how to get pleasure and avoid pain are determined by associations among ideas, and if you as a scientist who thought much
upon the matter can work out a series of correct associations between the ideas

of pleasure and certain means to get them, and set forth this chain of reasoning in a clear fashion, then if you have any opinion at all about human intelligence you ought to expect as did the Philosophical Radicals, that a very large proportion of mankind anyway would see the point, would realize that it was to their advantage to adopt the measures which the Philosophical Radicals advocated. And just as soon as they really saw it was to their advantage, they would act. They could not do otherwise if they were controlled, as the Philosophical Radicals thought, by a desire to get pleasure and to avoid pain unless, of course, they tried to meet your arguments and tried to show you were wrong. The Philosophical Radicals were quite ready to meet any arguments brought against them on their own grounds.

Well, of course, the real trouble with their technical position was that their ideas of human nature were curiously schematic and unreal. Men did not prove to be in practice nearly as good reasoning machines as Bentham and his colleagues believed them to be. The human behavior that they were trying to change was not nearly so much the result of calculation as they had supposed, and it was primarily for that reason that the presentation of the series of very clever calculations about how the population at large could increase its pleasures produced such comparatively slight results. And so the Philosophical Radicals had what must have been to them the rather mortifying experience of finding that a great many of the reforms very much at their heart were actually taken up and put over by methods of which they most heartily disapproved. They might be glad to see Daniel O'Connell bring about Catholic emancipation, but they could not approve the methods by which he got people to vote against the Tory candidates. They could hardly approve of the methods which were presently adopted in favor of free trade by Cobden and Bright. They did not understand human nature in such terms, and it was very largely their faulty social psychology that prevented them from being still more effective social reformers than they proved to be in fact. And yet, as we have seen, the greater part of their program was carried out. In fact, all the main points of their program became part of the law of England within two or three generations, saving only the disestablishment of the Church of England, one of the causes which they had much at heart but which has made no headway up to this time.

If the Philosophical Radicals were so much at sea in their opinions of human nature, and if they were so illogical in basing their whole method of reform upon these mistaken notions of human nature, how did it happen that in such large measure their scheme of reforms went through then at the hands of other people? Well, quite obviously, the answer is that the reforms which they were advocating on the basis of their opinions of man's nature were almost all of them reforms in which large parts of the people could believe, and were found ultimately to believe on quite other grounds. That is to say, what they were doing was to work out a series of rather artificial rationalizations of reasons why the aspirations of increasing numbers of increasingly powerful classes should be granted. That is what they did. Just as Adam Smith's scheme of _laissez faire_ as presented in _The Wealth of Nations_ is the rationalization of a practice of personal initiative which had become a mass phenomenon in England by his time; Jeremy Bentham's elaborate proofs of the desirability of mitigating the criminal law, his demonstrations of the illogicality of imposing religious disabilities upon any class of believers, James Mill's beautiful logic showing that the suffrage should be extended, all these things were very pretty rationalizations of reasons why people who had humane instincts ought to reform the criminal laws, why people who believed in something like common treatment of all peaceful citizens before the law should remove religious disabilities, and why people who were coming to have considerable intelligence and considerable practical power and a great stake in the policies of the country, should be allowed to vote.

Well, while working out these rationalizations, the social scientists contributed a good deal to the process of change. They made the people who wanted
the changes more eager, more confident. They presented arguments which the opponents of the changes found it rather difficult to meet. Almost all discussions
of this kind in any human assembly are likely to be treated at some stage on a
logical basis, and the people who won't meet you on a logical ground are at a
disadvantage. And by doing this they helped very materially to put through some
of the most far-reaching and important changes of English social organization
which the time saw.

It is very interesting to observe, however, that at least with reference
to those social struggles which most impressed men, the role played by the
Philosophical Radicals and their allies was never prominent in the public eye,
and is very commonly overlooked in our histories. Take that great movement for
the emancipation of the slaves, a movement that started with Clarkson's and
Wilberforce's attacks on the slave trade, and shortly after Parliament had been
reformed resulted in the abolition of slavery, the freeing of the slaves in the
English sugar islands at an expense of something like twenty million pounds to
the Island of Great Britain. That was one of the measures for which the Philosophical Radicals labored, but the story of emancipation is a story that centers
about the names of Clarkson and Wilberforce, and Jeremy Bentham usually hardly
comes in at all.

In Catholic emancipation the whole tale centered at the time and still
centers in our history around the half comic, half heroic figure of Daniel
O'Connell and the story of parliamentary reform, when told by the old Whig
historians, is solely a story of the wise statesmanship of Lord Grey and his Whig
colleagues. I was very much interested only two or three years ago, when it came
out, to read Trevelyan's biography of Lord Grey of the Reform Bill. Trevelyan
is one who belongs to the old Whig tradition but who presumably is far enough
away from the exciting events of 1832, (the book was published in 1920) to look
at the matter as an impartial student. There is, however, no mention of Jeremy
Bentham or the Philosophical Radicals in the whole volume. It is all still a
story of the immediate political activities and maneuvers which eventuated in
that great change. And when it comes down to the history of the great triumph
of free trade in 1846, the credit goes mainly to Cobden and Bright and perhaps
their colleague William J. Fox. The economists who were working for it may be
given a little credit, particularly Adam Smith who had lived long enough before
not to be at all a dangerous rival for popular favor. These people who think
out the reforms and rationalize them are seldom the people who are able to carry
them through and seldom the people who are remembered afterwards as having been
among the effective agents.

I said a few minutes ago that perhaps one of the chief reasons, at least,
why the Philosophical Radicals were not very effective agents in carrying out
those reforms which required mass movements was because of their curiously mistaken notions about man's rationality. There is, of course, another reason. You
do not expect a mechanical inventor in the majority of cases to make a very good
business executive; or if you do, your view is quite distinctly at variance with
that of the business world. It is not often that the two talents of mechanical
inventiveness and capacity for managing practical affairs on a business basis ever
unite in the same person. It does happen, but it does happen rather rarely. So
you scarcely expect to find the ability to think abstractly and clearly about
social problems and the capacity to organize action for any purpose united in the
same person. The social inventor is as little likely to have that peculiar set
of arts which make one an effective leader of men's movements as he is to have
united in his person, let us say, capacity for abstract speculation and great abil-

ity as a musical virtuoso. There were hardly any members of this group, barring perhaps Francis Place, who were successful in organizing movements, and there you have to admit that Francis Place was more successful as a political manipulator than as a social scientist.

I think these reflections are worthy of your attention, not simply as bearing upon the process by which certain great changes took place a hundred years ago in another country, but also as bearing upon the role that thinking about social problems may play in the future. Presumably social scientists who are working on the basis of conceptions of human nature less artificial than those entertained by the Philosophical Radicals may have a rather better chance of being serviceable, not merely drawing designs for improving social relations but also putting them into effect. And yet, after all, we probably ought, as people who are interested in the social sciences, not adopt any very optimistic notions concerning the immediate and practical effects of our thinking upon human conduct. To do the thinking and to get human conduct changed are two quite distinct tasks, and the people who do the one are not likely in very many cases to be the people who have the capacity to do the other.

XXXIV

POLITICS, SOCIAL REFORM, AND POLITICAL ECONOMY IN THE PERIOD FROM 1832 TO 1848

I brought the story of the social history of classical political economy down to the time when the Great Reform Bill was adopted. Now I want to sketch very briefly the developments of that body of thought from this period forward until the publication of John Stuart Mill's great Principles of Political Economy, and the last few meetings of this semester will be devoted to John Stuart Mill.

The Philosophical Radicals quite naturally built very high hopes upon the Great Reform Bill. They expected that the middle class would have genuine power; and it was, of course, in the middle class that they felt confidence, - that intelligent, that "virtuous rank" as John Stuart Mill called it, - the class from which most of the Philosophical Radicals themselves came, for which they spoke, - the class that was made up of the capitalist employers about whom Ricardo wrote, the people whose profits were most favorable to general prosperity. They supposed that with the new power granted this class in politics it would promptly adopt the painstaking political methods of Francis Place and Joseph Hume; that they would adopt the philosophy of Bentham and James Mill; and that they would use their power to carry through Parliament the series of reforms which had been advocated by Adam Smith, Malthus, Ricardo, and Bentham, - reforms touching upon the economic, political, educational, and religious policy.

But these expectations were not fulfilled. So far as Parliamentary history went, it proved that Bentham and his disciples were wrong and that King William IV and Lord Grey were right. The Great Reform Bill was as aristocratical measure. It is true that that bill enfranchised the middle classes down to a fairly low level. It is true that the Reform Bill broke the strangle hold of the Tories upon the bulk of the seats in general elections. But, after all, the property qualification which had been imposed upon the right of exercising the suffrage in the Reform Bill was high enough to keep out practically all the artisans and agricultural laborers and to leave a somewhat limited mass of voters with whom in practice the gentry continued to have the preponderating influence. They were

able to carry most of the county seats and also those of the small boroughs, so
that the landed interest while shorn of its exclusive control of Parliament -
practically exclusive control - still retained a dominating power, and did so
until at least after the passage of the great Free Trade Bill of 1846, and in
large measure until the passage of John Bright's further suffrage reform of 1867,
a reform which finally admitted a very large proportion of the working classes
to the suffrage.

The Philosophical Radicals during all this period managed to get a few of
their own men into Parliament, for example, George Grote, a particularly faithful disciple of Bentham and James Mill, the great London banker, the man whom
we know as the historian of Greece, who sat term after term. Joseph Hume held a
seat in Parliament and increased somewhat in influence. Then there were lesser
men like Charles Buller; George Villiers, the Earl of Clarendon; and John Arthur
Roebuck. But these Philosophical Radicals never seemed to exercise any great influence upon parliamentary politics. They were rather dry men. They continued to
try to push the measures that they had at heart, primarily by the arts of logical persuasion. They had none of the driving influence of a great emotional appeal
behind them; and the measures which the Philosophical Radicals worked for that
did succeed in getting through Parliament were passed through the instrumentality
of men who were not themselves members of the Philosophical Radical group. The
great instance of that is the chief economic reform of the time: the repeal of
the corn laws in 1846. The active efficient agents in getting that repeal through
were men who did not really belong to the Philosophical Radicals; they were Cobden and Bright, one a great business man with an extraordinary talent for organization and the other a man of most exceptional oratorical powers, a person who
was primarily of the emotional type.

On the whole, politics continued to run after the Reform Bill had passed
much as it had before; that is, the administration alternated between the Whigs
and the Tories who were gradually converting themselves during this period into
parties which we now know as the Conservatives and the Liberals. Lord Grey's
ministry came back into power after the enactment of the Reform Bill with grand
eclat, with an overwhelming majority; and people prophesied that the Whigs would
hold the administration for a long time, as the Tories had before the Reform Bill
had come up. But Lord Brey was old and weary, and he retired presently to his
agreeable country life in the north, leaving Lord Melbourne to succeed him. Lord
Melbourne was a most amiable and accomplished gentleman who is best known for the
impression that he later made upon the young Queen Victoria. He was not, however,
a man of any considerable powers of leadership, and presently he had a dispute
with King William which arose out of the fact that he proposed certain changes
in the collection of the revenue of the Irish Church(The Irish Church, of course,
means the Episcopal Church in Ireland), changes in the use of these revenues
which the king said he could not consent to because they ran counter to certain
clauses in his coronational. So the king called upon Sir Robert Peel to form a
Tory ministry in 1834, - one of the most remarkable examples of English modera-
tion in the whole extraordinary history of that country. The Tory party had been
thrown out of power in 1830. The Whigs had succeeded in passing a revolutionary
reform measure against their bitter opposition, and still only four years after
they had gone out of power, two years after the Great Reform Bill passed, the
Tories came back.

Their hold upon power at this time, however, was very brief. They had the
support of the king, but Peel could not command a majority in Parliament, and so
after less than a year Peel retired and Melbourne came back into power and remained Prime Minister until 1841. During that period the Whig ministry while

controlling Parliament grew continually weaker, and finally in 1841 Peel came in again to begin that great ministry in the course of which the Bank of England was reorganized, the free trade measure passed, and the corn laws repealed.

During this period between 1834 and 1848, when John Stuart Mill's Principles of Political Economy was published, a considerable proportion of the reforms which the economists, the Philosophical Radicals at large had been advocating were put upon the statute books. The first of the great reforms was the bill for emancipating the slaves in the British colonies. That was passed in 1833. Under the terms of this bill the British Government provided twenty million pounds, a very considerable sum for the day, by which the slaves were bought from their owners and bought under terms which provided for their gradual training and complete emancipation.

Also in that same year the first effective Factory Act was passed, an act restricting the hours of work according to certain age limits, the younger employees not being given full freedom to work as long as they liked, the theory being that even from the laissez faire point of view until a person is mature he is not a good judge of his own interests, and it is therefore logical and desirable to control his choice of this important matter of how long he shall work, and presumably how much he shall be allowed to earn, according to governmental decisions.

Also in this year, the first year after the passage of the Reform Bill, the government began the policy of making grants in aid of schools which were intended to educate the children of the poor. Of course, England had long had a very considerable supply of very excellent schools to which the sons of well-to-do people could go, the famous old "public" schools as they were called. In our country they would be called private schools. The central government had theretofore made no provision for the education of the children of the masses; and in this year they made a start, but a very modest one. The government made grants in aid of education to localities amounting to twenty thousand pounds. A few years later that sum was raised to thirty thousand pounds per annum. It meant that the government was backing this one of the great aims of the Philosophical Radicals.

Then in 1834 the poor law amending act was passed. This is one of the famous statutes of the century, a statute which was drawn on Malthusian lines and was intended to substitute for control over the poor by the parishes a considerable measure of centralized direction under a board which was appointed by the royal government.

In the next year another statute, perhaps a law less famous but hardly less important was enacted: a Municipal Reform Act. The local governments, the governments of the municipalities in England at that time were of the most diverse character, resting upon legal instruments some of which were several centuries old, some of which were comparatively modern but presented no general scheme. This was one of the measures which all advocates of rational, systematic government had believed necessary. The government undertook the work and planned a general statute which while not including London and some of the small boroughs was intended to standardize in their broader and more important features the government of most British cities.

In 1836 another act was passed prohibiting the non-residence of the clergy and the holding of pluralities. That was intended to reform certain abuses which had grown up in the Established Church. At that time it was very common that a man would be appointed to a "living" and get the revenue, but would not live in his parish,that he would see that the necessary minimum of clerical duties were administered by some person whom he employed and to whom he paid a pittance of the amount which the "living" itself brought in. Also in those days a good many people held two, three, or four, sometimes a considerable number of different "livings" in the Church. They were the "pluralists." In this way clergymen who had influential friends were sometimes able to acquire for themselves decidedly handsome incomes. Non-residence was by this statute prohibited, and it was also provided that in future no member of the clergy should hold more than one position at a time which required the administration of the usual religious duties.

The next year the Penny Postage Act was passed, the first law, I believe, adopted anywhere in the world which provided what now seems to us such a matter of course: the payment of postage on letters by stamps, and provided also that the stamp for the ordinary letter should cost but one British penny. It is rather interesting to observe that that measure was carried against the ministry by an agitator, Rowland Hill, who devoted many years to work in this particular cause.

In 1842 Peel, who had now become Prime Minister, began a series of tariff reforms. He also reestablished the income tax. And through his non-interference enabled Lord Ashley to put through the bill prohibiting the work of women in mines, thus correcting one of the grievous industrial abuses of the time. Anyone who wants to read some of the most horrible stories that can be collected anywhere regarding the abuses of laborers in the earlier days of the Industrial Revolution can look up the celebrated report which was made to Parliament on the work of women and children in mines, abuses so grievous that when they were once published the bill was passed with very little difficulty.

In 1844 a royal commission was appointed on health in the towns, the commission that started the very important series of practical reforms in municipal sanitation. In that commission one of Bentham's private secretaries, Edwin Chadwick, took a leading hand.

In this year also the Bank of England was reorganized on lines suggested by Ricardo's posthumous pamphlet A Plan for the Establishment of a National Bank, the chief feature of the reorganization being that the department of issue was separated completely from the department of lending and deposit so that the institution became practically two institutions.

Also in this year another Factory Act was passed regulating the hours of women's work. You see, the preceding measure of which I spoke, the one passed in 1833, had limited only the hours of young children. Now the same logic which was used to justify interference with their freedom of action was passed on to another class beginning to be regarded as mentally incompetent, namely the women workers.

In 1846 came the repeal of the corn laws; and finally in 1847 the Ten Hours Bill, a bill which regulated the work of all factories practically to ten hours. It did not nominally include the male workers of full age, but by providing a rigid scheme for preventing factories that employed men, women, and children from working more than ten hours, it practically gave the male operatives themselves the ten hour limit, for in such factories, of course, males could not continue to work after the women and children had left.

Now you see that is a considerable batch of reform, and it is all a series of changes in the direction the Philosophical Radicals wanted, but changes made not through their own intermediacy but through the Whig or the Tory parties.And it is difficult to say which of these two parties had the larger share in carrying out the general program that Bentham and his disciples had laid down.

Class struggles in this period took on quite a different aspect from that they had worn somewhat earlier. Of course, during the French Revolution the line that was drawn was primarily a line between the propertied classes and those who had little property. The capitalist employers on the one side and the agricultural landed interests on the other side were aligned with each other and standing in firm opposition to any popular agitation. We saw how the rise of the corn law question just at the end of the wars in 1814-1815 had broken this alliance between the two great groups of the capitalist class and had lined up the manufacturing interests who wanted cheap food, which they thought would mean low wages, against the landed interests which wanted a high price for their produce.

Now in the struggles which took place during the years after the Great Reform Bill had been passed, conditions kept getting mixed. The chief aim of the capitalist at this time was to secure free trade because he believed that England's prosperity must depend very largely upon her foreign commerce. The capitalists had accepted the doctrine of the economists that a country cannot export on a grand scale unless it is also ready to import freely; and on that ground they were willing to see the protective tariff, which had already been considerably lowered through the reforms of William Huskisson, further reduced at the hands of Sir Robert Peel. But of all the restrictions upon import which they wanted to see removed, the one that they cared most about by far was the duties upon corn. When they were thinking about duties on manufacturing articles, there were two minds about it; the people in the trades protected were usually opposed but most people in the other trades favored reduction of duties. When it came to a reduction of duties of agricultural products they were at one, and they made up the bulk of the party that formed behind Cobden and Bright, the Anti-Corn Law League, that in 1846 secured the abolition of that great stronghold of agricultural protection.

The landlords, on the other hand, subjected to this capitalist attack, responded by viewing with grave disapprobation pretty much all the abuses that were characteristic of the capitalist system. The series of measures for protecting women and child workers, particularly the great bills shortening the hours of labor, the bill prohibiting the employment of women and children in mines, the bills providing for the safeguarding of dangerous machinery, ans so on, were largely carried through Parliament against the opposition by the employing classes by the support of the agricultural interests. So that Parliament to an outside observer presented a disturbing spectacle. Debates alternated between agricultural abuses in which Philippic speeches were delivered by the manufacturing class, and debates upon manufacturing abuse in which the charges were brought by agricultural interests. And, broadly speaking, the welfare of the wage-earning population was promoted about equally by the manufacturers and by the agriculturalists; but all the benefits which the manufacturing population got came from the landed interests, and pretty much all the benefits the agricultural laborers got came from the manufacturing interests.

The working classes themselves were becoming far more keenly alive to their own interest, beginning to believe that their chance of getting adequate recognition in the country's government must depend less on what benevolent gentry or benevolent employers would do for them that what they might do for themselves. They would take an eager advantage of the abolition of the Anti-Combination Acts to form trade unions. They experimented very widely but soon found that trade unions as a more or less emergency organization to be employed to get a great advance of wages were worse than useless. They had led to strikes that were almost invariably lost, and then they would turn for a while to some grand schemes for social reorganization which were headed mainly by Robert Owen

the great Utopian socialist, and found that his cooperative scheme did not work
very well. And then thinking that, after all, what they needed was primarily
a new constitution for the country at large, one that would give them control of
the government, they went in for a decade for Chartism, a great political movement in its immediate aspects, but a movement that interested them primarily
because of the economic measures that they thought they would succeed in passing
if they had the Charter, the most important of which were universal manhood
suffrage, secret ballot, and annual Parliaments. With universal manhood suffrage
they thought they could outvote all other classes. With the secret ballot they
could all dare to vote as they liked. With annual Parliaments they would be able
to retire any person who did not suit the most of the voters. But the great
Chartist movement, despite the extraordinary enthusiasm which it aroused for a
while, was not successful; and so the working classes toward the end of the period which I have in mind now, that is, the later 40's, were settling down to a
rather constructive policy. They would build up that series of suitable trade
unions pursuing a rather conservative policy that for several decades, in fact
till after the end of the century, seems to have formed the backbone of the English labor movement.

During this time political economy in one sense came into its own in a
very much more striking and effective fashion than at any earlier period. The
successes of the economists in getting public recognition were found in various
places. A number of professorships, for instance, were established in different
schools. Of course, economics had been taught in England for a long while. You
remember that when Adam Smith went to Glasgow as a college student he heard
lectures on economic subjects given by Francis Hutcheson. And later in life he,
although he was not a professor of economics but of logic and moral philosophy,
lectured on that subject. And after he had retired, Dugald Stewart followed him.
So too, Malthus had been made a professor of economics and history in 1807 down
in the East India Company's college at Haileybury. But the regular chairs of
economics in which a person was employed to teach this subject alone came considerably later.

The earliest chair to be established was that at Oxford in 1825. It was
founded by Henry Drummond, a rather eccentric banker who was somewhat equally
interested in economics and a curious brand of theology. He provided a fund
which enabled Oxford to have a series of professors of economics. Though a modest
one, the fund was supposed to keep a man working only for a short term each year.

Three years later, in 1828, George Pryme, who had been lecturing on political economy at Cambridge rather informally, succeeded in getting a chair established there, a chair which he occupied for a very long while, the chair which
was later well known through being held by Henry Fawcett and Alfred Marshall.
The Oxford chair was long held by Professor Edgeworth. In 1832 Dublin established
a chair, and presently thereafter the University College in Edinburgh and Queen's
College, Ireland, followed suit.

It cannot be said that political economy profited greatly by these professorships except that held by Marshall and except for Senior's rather brief
term of office at Oxford. The chairs called simply for a few lectures. Most of
the statutes provided that the professor should publish at least one lecture
each year. That accounts for the peculiar character of a number of the classical
writings that you will find on our book-shelves. Senior, who held the Oxford
chair, has a number of little books, Three Lectures on Money, Three Lectures on
Wages, etc. Those were published simply to meet the formal requirements of the
professorship which he held,

The chairs were, as a rule, taken by ambitious young men who for some reason could not get a regular university fellowship. They provided a supplementary source of income while studying law or casting about to secure a seat in Parliament. They did not lead to professional studies in economics perhaps in any case.

More important than these teaching professorships was the employment of the economists by the government. It became more and more the practice when a question that involved important economic issues was before the country to call in one or more of the recognized experts in the science and get his views about administrative procedure or about the drawing of new statutes. Thus Senior was consulted about the new poor law, William Jones had a considerable hand in the efforts that were made to reform the matter of tithes to the Church, or rather to clergymen. William Jacobs was sent to the Continent to study the condition of agriculture. And McCulloch in due season, for good and sufficient services rendered to the Whig party, was given a post in the Stationery Office where he was in more or less regular contact with at least the prominent officials of succeeding administrations.

There was also a pretty definite effort made not only by people regarded as scientifically interested in the subject, but also by people who believed in popularizing the subject. The Society for the Diffusion of Useful Knowledge issued a great many small text-books and lectures, and devoted a considerable part of its attention to this particular science. Text-books were written not only for use in the schools but also for the use of governesses. Of course, the large proportion of the children of the better class families were brought up by a governess until they were of age to go to school or until ready to enter society. Among the amusing products of the books of the time, you find little treatises of one or two hundred pages in which some amiable lady who stands for the governess carries on a series of enlightening talks on political economy with some small girl.

And then came Harriet Martineau, that extraordinary woman who hit on the happy device of teaching economics under the form of fiction. I do not know if any of you had the pleasure of reading her tales; but she published a long series of them, each story pointing out some economic moral showing into what sad difficulties people get if they disregarded economics. Those tales had extraordinary success. It was said that ten thousand copies were sold each year; they were among the best sellers of their day.

At the same time economics was winning a measure of popular authority which it had never enjoyed before. The economists were inclined to speak in an authoritative tone and they were likely to be listened to. They talked about economic laws in much the same tone in which their contemporaries interested in physics and chemistry talked about natural laws. The implication that there are laws of economics which are immutable, which cannot be broken no matter how powerful the governmental agency is behind such vain attempt, was one that seemed to have been accepted far more readily by many of the politicians and many of the business people of the time than it was accepted even by the economists themselves and some of them went pretty far in that particular direction.

Of course, the prestige of political economy was greatly enhanced by the gradual adoption of one after another of the measures which the economists had been advocating. Most of all its prestige was enhanced by the repeal of the corn laws in 1846 and by the great national prosperity which followed for a couple of decades after that change had been made. Nowadays we are inclined to question whether this extraordinary prosperity in the 50's and 60's and early 70's was due as much to free trade as advocates of that measure at the time were inclined to think, but those people quite naturally got the benefit of the doubt just as nowadays the political administration in the United States which happens to come up for reelection at a time when the country is prosperous is likely to claim and is likely by perhaps the majority of the people to be credited for the good times which the country is having. It seemed that political economy had made good. It might be dry, hard-headed doctrine, but it was true that if the country would only follow the dictates of the economists then it would stand a better chance of being really prosperous, of being made up of people who were as happy as it was possible for men to be in a world where, after all, the food was limited.

Now a very large measure, probably the largest measure, of the popular support accorded the economists in this period was due to the fact that the measures which they advocated recommended themselves to the class that was coming to exercise increasing power, that is, the class of the capitalist employers. Anybody who reads nowadays the classics cannot help but feel that the writers were far more keenly alive to the viewpoint of the employing class than they were to the viewpoint of the mass of the workers. One cannot help feeling that these men, however honest they tried to be with themselves, however benevolent their dispositions may have been as individuals, were still people who continually believed that the way to make the country prosperous was to increase profits, which Ricardo said so definitely and the classical economists agreed with him as a whole. It did not take a great deal of persuasion to turn that supposedly scientific analysis of the relation between different classes in society into a very plain defense of pretty much all the measures that the employing class desired to see enacted because they thought these measures were really beneficial to the country as a whole, and to turn it into a refutation of the various doctrines that were being advocated by the wage-earning classes. For example, we had occasion to see how strongly not only Bentham but also Ricardo insisted upon the security of property as necessary to economic prosperity, Ricardo arguing explicitly that if people were not going to be secure in the fruits of their industry they would not work, they would not save, and so the country would not have capital and that would mean that they would not have employment. So the security of property is a measure of interest most of all to the wage earners who are at times misled into denying it.

Also classical political economy, particularly the doctrine associated with the name of Malthus, was very convenient, very comforting, because it proved that the working-men were responsible for their own poverty and distress. That general view that the only way in which wages could be raised to a satisfactory level was by practicing wise continence about marriage and begetting children was a doctrine which anyone could use to relieve his conscience from feeling any responsibility for the distress he might see about him. It meant that the remedy for working-class distress was in the hands of the working class themselves, and that remedy in their hands was not at all to attack property and try to get better wages through stikes but was simply to be prudent about marriage.

And then when it came to the efforts of the working classes to get higher wages by forming unions and attempting to use their combined power to extort better terms from employers, political economy provided convenient proof that such action was bound to be futile. This proof was supplied by the celebrated doctrine of the wages fund, a doctrine which you do not find explicitly set forth in Ricardo but which was developed by some of his successors and then turned to practical use against trade unions, the theory being that the general level of wages in a country was determined by the ratio between capital and population, or more correctly, was determined by the ratio between the amount of capital which is destined to the payment of wages, that is, the wages fund, and the number of wage earners. That being true, trade unions could at most divert an unfair part of the wages fund to the benefit of members of the trade in which the unions belonged. But if members of that particular trade got more than their fair share of wages, they got it not at the expense of the employers but at the expense of other employees. The trade union could not do anything to increase the amount of the wages fund, - at least so it was argued.

The theory of laissez faire could also be used to rationalize opposition to factory acts. And in general the tenor of that rather capitalistically supported doctrine was of a sort which made it very welcome not only to the minds but also the feelings of the capitalist employing class, and that was the class at the time, as I say, gaining rapidly in power; it was the one class which was most interested in economics because it affected their emotional and practical needs so well. It was quite natural that the science itself should be held in very high esteem at least in this quarter.

It is interesting to note that despite these extraordinary successes of political economy, and the fact that the science was getting so much recognition on various sides, scientific progress was very slow. But that is the theme which leads up to the discussion of John Stuart Mill.

XXXV

FURTHER REMARKS ON THE PERIOD PRECEDING JOHN
STUART MILL ; HIS EARLY LIFE

At the preceding meeting I was discussing the general state of economics in the period following the passing of the Great Reform Bill, which is also the early part of the period during which occurred the great outburst of activity which culminated in John Stuart Mill's Principles of Political Economy. I pointed out that during this period a certain considerable number of the causes for which the Philosophical Radicals, including the economists, had been working were accomplished; that it was a period when political economy was gaining social recognition on an unprecedented scale. That it was being accepted as an authoritative social science, particularly by the class in the community who were most interested in the development of the social sciences.

I have now to add rather briefly that it was a period when the science as a science made scarcely any advance. It was a period of external recognition, but of scientific sterility, - a very familiar remark, but one which is nevertheless true. If you take the publications on economics in the generation that followed upon the publication of Ricardo's Principles, you will indeed find inceptions of most of the fruitful ideas which at a later period were developed in economics. But the fruitful ideas which were published at this time came almost altogether from unorthodox sources. They were little regarded, and they remained for the most part latent suggestions, - suggestions which have been observed only in these later years when economists have become very much interested in the history of their subject and have been delving round in forgotten pamphlets and articles and neglected books to see how far back some of the ideas which, let us say, within the last fifty years or so have been made much of in economics can be traced. For example, Malthus's book on political economy which was published in 1820 and then again in 1836 represents a far more realistic type of treatment than did Ricardo's. From the present point of view it seems in many ways a much more modern book, much clearer in many ways, but it was not accepted by its generation as possessing anything like the scientific value of Ricardo's treatise. Mal-

thus's whole temperamental attitude of attempting so far as possible to build
up economic theory on the basis of personal observation supplemented by such
statistics as were available, that whole attitude was generally deemed to be a
mistaken one that would lead to no satisfactory results.

Richard Jones, who was one of Malthus's colleagues at Haileybury College,
a Church of England minister, began applying what we may call the comparative
historical method to the study of economic problems. He set out to study the
institutions bearing upon the distribution of wealth. He never got further in
the execution of this plan than to publish one not very large book* dealing with
one share in distribution, namely rent. But in that book his way of working was
very different from the Ricardian classical way at large. He traveled rather
extensively upon the continent of Europe and read still more extensively and thus
discovered that the principles which regulate the payment for the use of land
which is cultivated by a person not its owner are in very many quarters of the
world, in fact for most of the world, altogether different in character from those
in the orthodox Ricardian theory of rent. Thus he pointed out that the metayer
rents which were so common on the Continent, rents which consisted in a share of
the produce, were fixed by custom, the proportion varying in different parts of
Europe from say perhaps one-third in some places to more than one-half in other
places. He dealt with rents that prevailed at that time under the curious medieval
survivals in Russian villages, with the cottier rents in Ireland, and with the
rents that were paid by the oppressed cultivators in India, finally coming to the
conclusion that farm rents of the Ricardian type were to be found in very few
places of the world outside of England and a part of the Netherlands, eliminating
on the basis of comparative studies a problem which he had seen in a far wider
light than that of Ricardo. Ricardo, without saying anything about the subject,
set out to discuss the distribution of wealth supposedly in extenso, but really
confining his whole analysis to the way in which shares of distribution are divided up among the classes under a very definite and at that time by no means
widely dispersed set of economic institutions.** But this book of Jones' attracted
comparatively little attention. Englishmen were not interested in finding out how
payments of the various shares of distribution were effected in other countries.

Then too, there was a very vigorous development of what for want of a more
precise name we have to call socialistic theory, perhaps most notable at the hands
of William Thompson who was a very curious person, an Irishman who had been one
of Jeremy Bentham's secretaries and who accepted Bentham's Utilitarian doctrines
and used his analysis to prove that the whole product of labor which included the
whole value of what is produced in industry should go to the workingmen as wages,
a view that was more clearly worked out presently by Hodgskin, a man who had been
in the British navy and then had traveled extensively on foot through Germany,
became acquainted with James Mill, and turned his very considerable powers of
logical analysis against the doctrines which James Mill and McCulloch in particular were excogitating.

As I shall have occasion to remark in a moment, James Mill and McCulloch
altered the Ricardian doctrine of value by dropping completely out of sight Ricardo's occasional wavering references to a second factor in cost, the factor that
Marshall calls "waiting." They set up a labor cost theory of value by holding

---

* Essay on the Distribution of Wealth, London, 1831.

**For a full discussion of various criticisms of the Ricardian theory see Diehl,
Ricardo's Volkswirtschaft und Besteurung; Leipzig, 1905; vol.II,pp.199 ff.

that the capital cost can itself be reduced without residual into the labor cost of making capital. Well, Hodgskin taking up this view held that in the last resort the value of everything is determined on Ricardian lines, but the value of freely reproducible goods is determined by cost in the long run. And then accepting James Mill's and McCulloch's emendation of that rule, proceeded to argue technically and in very elaborate fashion as William Thompson had done, that all value should go to the laborer.

So too, there were metaphysical inquiries into economic theory started at this time by William Whewell, a man who is best known from his History of the Inductive Sciences; a book to which John Stuart Mill owed a great deal. And these studies of Whewell in metaphysical terms were presently developed with vastly greater ability by Auguste Comte in France. Utility analysis, that is, the development of the fundamental conception of marginal utility and the beginnings of its application to the explanation of value is found fairly well developed in the writings of Mountifort Longfield and by William Forster Lloyd; Longfield being an Irish lawyer who held one of the professorships in economics in Trinity College, Dublin, and Lloyd holding an Oxford professorship.*

So too, what has more recently been called the "social value" type of economic theory was rather definitely exploited by John Rae, a Scotchman who traveled somewhat extensively in Canada and who had an excellent opportunity to see the economic processes of a highly developed country in clear light by virtue of the contrast between the economic life lived in England and the economic life which he saw among the natives in America, the Indians.

But all these suggestions, though nowadays they seem to us in many cases highly significant, for the time being bore little fruit. The writers like Jones, Whewell, Longfield, Lloyd, William Thompson, and Hodgskin, even Malthus in so far as he advocated any economic theory different from Ricardo, - all these writers were generally regarded as being on useless trails that would lead nowhere. The central line of economic theory was carried on rather by James Mill, John Ramsay McCulloch, Nassau Senior, and a small group of less important people who with them enjoyed the title of being orthodox representatives.

Now it cannot be said that these orthodox writers really made any very important contribution to the body of economic analysis as it stood at the time of Ricardo's death. As I just had occasion to remark incidentally, James Mill and John Ramsay McCulloch took at least one rather significant backward step. It was presumably in his desire to make the science of economics more elegant that James Mill followed by McCulloch tried to show that the cost of capital can be resolved into labor cost, and it is therefore possible to explain the cost of all reproducible goods in the long run in terms of a single factor.

From that point of view Nassau Senior stood in a very much better position, for while Ricardo had in his first chapter on value in several passages intimated, as we know, that you cannot make allowance for the time that is required to produce certain articles in considering their total cost, he had not been clear or emphatic on the point, but Senior was. He set up a doctrine of value involving two elements of cost; the cost of labor on the one hand, and the cost of abstinance on the other hand. It was Senior's type of value theory that was followed in the later writings. But that, while an important correction of James Mill and McCulloch,

*On Longfield see Cannon, History of Theories of Production and Distribution, and Seligman, Some Neglected British Economists. On Lloyd see Professor T.S. Adams' article on "Index Numbers" in the Journal of Political Economy, Dec. 1901, p. 19.

was after all not a very important advance upon Ricardo, for it was only bringing
out clearly and forcibly a part of the analysis which was definitely present in
Ricardo's chapter, though present in a form in which it was quite easy for readers
to overlook, quite possible for professed disciples like James Mill and McCulloch
to explain away.

During the greater part, pretty much the whole period between the death of
Ricardo and the appearance of John Stuart Mill's great treatise, economics was
standing very high in the esteem of the people who counted, and as a social science
it was being more and more looked to as a safe and authoritative guide of public
policy. One after another of its policies was adopted in large part as the basis
for the country's policy; it was getting taught in the universities and was spread
so far as possible among classes that did not go to the universities through the
training of young children and through popular lectures.

But economics was at the same time making little progress. The reasons why
it made comparatively little progress in this time are, of course, matters that
we can only speculate about. I am inclined to think there were two particularly
important reasons; but if anyone doubts it I am not in a position to prove that
these are the most important. One reason, I think, was that as economists came
into the position of having to defend their theories in public discussions on a
formal basis they adopted an unfortunate line of defense against their critics.
Economics was, when taken in a strictly logical fashion, a set of hypothetical discussions built up on certain assumptions. When anybody challenged the correctness
of an economist's conclusions he might say "yes I admit the facts that you cite
are not consistent with the theory, but you must recall that this theory is a hypothetical construction; it rests upon certain assumptions. From those assumptions
it is deduced by a consistent body of reasoning, and therefore the theory is true.
That the facts do not correspond with it means simply that the conditions which prevail in actual life are not conditions closely corresponding to the hypothetical
assumptions on the basis of which the economists have reasoned."

Now that is a perfectly logical position and it is a position that economists
to this day continually find themselves taking. It is a position with which no
one can quarrel from the logical viewpoint. But people who feel perfectly satisfied with their science when it has to be defended by taking this sort of stand
are missing a most valuable spur to progress. That is, the economists who felt that
a theory which led to conclusions not applicable to the important facts of the
social situation were people who were contenting themselves with a theory which
did not seem of much use in explaining experience. And in this way they were really
going back on the example of their great masters Adam Smith, Malthus, and Ricardo.
It is perfectly true that the reasoning of Adam Smith, Malthus, and Ricardo was
from the logical point of view built up on the basis of certain assumptions which
might or might not correspond with conditions that prevail in the world at large;
but most certainly Adam Smith, and Malthus, and Ricardo had very little use for a
theory which did not help one to explain experience. Their view was that in their
reasoning they should use assumptions which at least corresponded substantially to
the important features of actual life in order that their conclusions might really
be a valued guide to discussions of public policy. They certainly would not have
been content with a theory, however perfectly logical, that did not help people
to decide what was the wise thing for the country to do with reference to, let us
say, duties upon foreign goods, or the treatment of labor unions, or the treatment
of the poor, or monetary problems. Their theory might have been hypothetical, but
the hypotheses on the basis of which they argued were socially significant in the
sense that they answered, broadly speaking, the social conditions. And their
followers continued to follow the letter of their law even when the letter of their
law ran counter to general observation; and the type of economic theory they wanted

was at the same time doing violence to the real example that masters had set.

. So this art of self-defense which the economists used was one of the reasons, I think, why people did not vigorously push forward, after the fashion of Ricardo's generation and try to deal successfully with the problems which were coming to the fore in that generation as their predecessors had done with earlier problems.

The second even more important possible reason for the scientific sterility of economics in this period is, I think, the intensely practical use to which the doctrines were being put in very many quarters. You see, economic theory had in the hands of Adam Smith, Malthus, and Ricardo been regarded as the safest guide to public policy. In this later generation, people were inclined, - perhaps less the economists than their practical disciples, - to hold up the great text-books of economic theory as a sort of Bible, to deduce from them the kind of conclusions which were agreeable to the disciples and to hold that a science which led to such splendid conclusions was something that ought not be tampered with, - particularly the people who wanted to use economics in order to break down the corn laws, people who wanted to use it in order to justify the new poor law, people who wanted to use it in order to show that trade unions at the very best were of no use to the working-man, for in the majority of cases they might allow one set of working people to exploit other sets of working people unjustly; people who wanted to use the theories of political economy in these intensely practical ways found that it was very much better for propagandist purposes to ascribe to the teachings of political economy a character of immutability, of laws, to hold that the most important of these laws had already been discovered, to regard the whole subject not as a developing science, but as a set of established doctrines.

People who treat economics in that way, of course, render themselves perhaps stronger as practical propagandists, but certainly much weaker as theoretical inquirers. No science is likely to prosper unless it is being subjected to ever new criticisms, unless the people who cultivate it are not only willing but eager to find all the conditions which inhere in the science as it has been passed on to them, people who are regarding the work even of their greatest predecessors with unrelenting skeptical criticism. Well, that sort of eager criticism was notably absent among the majority of people who were interested in economics during this generation. And it is, I think, notable that the way in which people used to defend economic doctrines that seemed to be at variance with fact was, I am inclined to believe, the chief reason for the fact that so little was accomplished toward coordinating the work which Adam Smith, and Malthus, and Ricardo had started, that is, between 1817 and 1848, the latter year being the one when John Stuart Mill's Principles was published. That is the last of the great classical treatises; and what remains of our time will be devoted to a discussion of its general character-istics.

First, however, as in dealing with Mill's predecessors, I want to give you a general idea at least of the forces which formed Mill as a social scientist. He came from the very heart of the Benthamite group. He was born in 1806 in London, just before his father became acquainted with Jeremy Bentham, and he grew up, in his earlier years, on Bentham's own premises. For a time James Mill lived in a small house belonging to Bentham near the latter's London mansion; and during these years James Mill was not only intellectually the ablest of Bentham's disciples but also the man in closest touch with him.

Now James Mill was not only a very vigorous Benthamite, but he was also a Scotchman who had been trained for the Church and who retained all through his life that fundamental, that primary interest, in ethical problems which is so character-istic of the Scotch, and that intense belief that a person can accomplish anything

which he tries hard enough to do,which is also characteristic of the Scotch. He
set himself as a father to make his eldest son the best kind of man that could be
turned out. Well, of course, one of the notions which James Mill shared with
Jeremy Bentham was that a person's mind is made up of associations among ideas,
and it ought, therefore, be possible for you, if you controlled the making of a
mind, to make just as good a machine as you yourself are capable of. James Mill
took his duty toward his eldest son very seriously, taught him himself, and in all
this teaching proceeded with the greatest system to turn out a person who would
have admitted into his head only elements that would be useful as forming conclusions among properly associated ideas. He started the child to learn Greek when he
was three, and when he was seven or eight he had already gone through Zenophon and
Herodotus, a part of Lucian; and was then set in due season to learning Latin. And
when he had gotten on to a certain point his father decided it was time for mathematics, and he was turned into that field. Finally, in his early teens his father
thought that he now had the tools of learning at his command and could have his
attention directed to the most important matters of human concern, namely, philosophy and the social sciences. Philosophy with James Mill meant primarily the study
of how the mind is made up by associations among the ideas; and the social sciences
for him meant that variegated batch of disciplines which Jeremy Bentham was excogitating and which his several disciples were elaborating.

Probably nobody about whom we have intimate knowledge has ever had a more
rigorous intellectual training than John Stuart Mill had. From his father's point
of view, his extraordinarily rapid progress was simply an exemplification of the
merits of the Benthamite scheme of education. Most modern commentators think it
also reflects considerable credit on the native powers of the boy's mind. Few
people, I suppose, would be willing to admit that the average boy picked up at ran-
dom and brought up under James Mill's method could have accomplished anything like
what this bright youngster did. He had done far more intellectual work by the time
he was fifteen or sixteen than the great majority of Englishmen of his generation
accomplished by the time they were twenty-five. He had a long start toward an
intellectual life by the time that the ordinary youngster is, let us say, ready to
enter high school.

This formal education at his father's hands was fairly completed by the time
he was fifteen, and he was set to work then upon the first of his large undertakings. That was the editing of one of Bentham's most important works on evidence.An
enormous heap of manuscripts on this highly technical subject was turned over to
the lad. It was his duty to go through the mass, to arrange it in order, to discard
the less desirable portions when there were two or three different discussions of
the same subject, to provide such connective tissue which would combine the several
parts into a work. He spent upwards of four years on this task and turned out a
really wonderful piece of editing. Those of you who are at all interested in Bentham's works might like to look over this large treatise on evidence. In comparing
it with the treatises put together by other disciples, you will be inclined to
agree that even in his later teens John Stuart Mill was showing constructive powers
of a far higher order than the rest of Bentham's helpers, with the possible exception of his own father.

He had begun to come into contact with a considerable number of young people.
When he did so, he learned for the first time how unusual he was . One of his
father's principles had been not to allow him to discover that he was accomplishing
more than the ordinary boy, not to let him believe that he was in any way a remarkable person. From James Mill's point of view,the theory would be too that this was
a boy who had a remarkable father;one who was able and willing to give him a most
extraordinary education. When he started out for himself, he found his associates
quite naturally among people who were from seven to ten years older than himself,

able youngsters down from the universities come to London to make their way; and these people seem to have accepted him very promptly as one of themselves, which means that out of his strict training he got not only a facile control and command over the ordinary tools of thought and some acquaintance with modern philosophy, but had also come to a point where he commanded these materials so that he was able to talk in an interesting way about them in a fashion that commanded the respect of men who had gone through the usual university training.

And with these young people John Stuart Mill presently went through another course of mutual education, supplementing his training from his father's hands with the training that the other men had gotten from their schools, a sort of training not very different from that which a good many of you I suppose are getting from each other in your study groups. And just as you often feel that you derive really a great deal more intellectual benefit from discussing these intellectual problems systematically among yourselves than you do from listening to university lectures or even participating in discussion courses, so John Stuart Mill found that by joining the groups that took up for serious and systematic discussion problems that were interesting to them, he widened the range of his knowledge and greatly improved his powers of analysis.

I want to refer to a little passage in which he speaks of this matter in his Autobiography, I hope that as many of you who have not read John Stuart Mill's Autobiography will take this occasion to become acquainted with that wonderful book. It really gives you, I think, perhaps the best opportunity to see the development of a mind that is interested in intellectual problems which is afforded by any volume that has ever been published. Mill had a rare candor about his own intellectual difficulties, as much candor as a person of his generation could well be expected to have when speaking about personal matters. What makes the Autobiography so exceptionally interesting, so exceptionally worthy of studying to us is that here was a man whose life was so much wrapped up in intellectual pursuits, a man whose energy went far less than is the case with the overwhelming majority into merely social or emotional channels, a man whose intellectual pursuits were his passion. It gives you a certain sense of forces in the intellectual life itself that you hardly can get elsewhere. That part of his story Mill tells very fully and clearly in his later years when this book was written.* In this particular passage he is speaking**about these youngsters with whom he discussed matters of interest:Charles Austin, son of John Austin who wrote the great Benthamite textbook on jurisprudence and who in his day was even more brilliant than Macaulay as a talker;William Thompson,that secretary of Jeremy Bentham's who wrote a great book on the Distribution of Wealth, giving a socialistic twist to the Utilitarian doctrines; he saw a little of McCulloch, though he was an older man and one to whom they did not take; Charles Villiers, afterwards Earl of Clarendon, and one of the greatest of the English diplomats of the century;also his brothers Hyde and Charles;and Romilly,afterwards Lord Romilly; Thomas Macaulay; Samuel Wilberforce, afterwards Bishop of Oxford, to whom Huxley made the celebrated retort about preferring to be descended from a race of animals rather than from human beings who were willing to distort the truth; Edward and Henry Lytton-Bulwer; Fonblanque, the journalist; and others

* The original manuscript from which the 1873 edition was printed is now in the library of Columbia University. It was published by the Columbia University Press in 1924.

**C.U. Press ed., p. 88.

All these people, representing widely divergent viewpoints, spent regularly a certain number of hours devoted to debating almost always questions of a fundamentally social nature, so that Mill got from those talks an acquaintance with views altogether different from those which had been implanted in him by his father, and he also learned how to marshal his arguments against skeptics, learned how difficult it was to convince people who did not set out with his presumptions, and learned the very important arts of how to put his argumentation in the most effective fashion.

XXXVI

THE LIFE OF JOHN STUART MILL

At our meeting on Tuesday I described John Stuart Mill's early education at the hands of his father, and that somewhat more miscellaneous education that he got for himself in conversation with a brilliant group of men not many years older, organized in small discussion groups. When he was seventeen years of age his father, who as the author of the History of British India, had received an appointment in the India Office and had become a power there, secured him a clerkship. For pretty much of his life that office gave him his livelihood, his chief business occupation. He was promoted gradually from post to post until in 1856 when the old East India Company was taken over by the British Government he was retired upon a pension. Toward the end of his days in the India Office he was receiving a salary of £2,000 per annum. This meant that all his life long he was, so far as money matters are concerned, in a secure position. He was, of course, deprived of the prospect of ever accumulating a fortune, but on the other hand he had an income of a fairly adequate amount, and he had also security of tenure with the prospect of a pension when he reached the retiring age.

He himself regarded that position as one peculiarly favorable to the conduct of intellectual work, holding that the kind of duties which he had to perform at the India Office were themselves of a nature which worked in very nicely with the scientific occupations to which his leisure hours were devoted. He seems to have had sufficient physical and mental energy to carry his full share of the load at the Office and on the side to do much more intellectual labor than most men accomplish even when they have far less exacting duties. In particular, he thought that the practical duties performed at the India Office taught him a great deal about the ways of getting ideas into people's heads. Whenever he had some policy which he wanted to promote, he found it necessary to convince his colleagues of the wisdom of his measure. He learned how to put his ideas into such shape that they would readily be admitted into other minds. He learned to make the kind of compromises which are most inevitably necessary when some large action is being carried on by a group.

In outward ways his life was singularly uneventful. The only important things which happened to him, aside from this appointment at the India Office, was his retirement at a relatively early age, and then after his retirement serving a term in the House of Commons, of which later. He lived, I suppose, about as exciting an intellectual life as was possible for an Englishman at his time. That life started, as we saw on Tuesday, with a most extraordinary schooling, first in the classics, and then in a set of elaborately worked out philosophical and social doctrines.

When he was about twenty years of age, he passed through a period of mental crisis which his biographers are inclined to think must have had a physiological basis, perhaps to have resulted from his very strenuous labors as editor of Jeremy Bentham's book on evidence combined with his work at the office and activity as a member of several discussion groups. But in his own eyes it was a crisis of a strictly mental sort. Let me read you a passage or two from the <u>Autobiography</u>. I will read you first what he himself has to say about the attitude of the Philosophical Radicals toward feeling as a factor in life and in human behavior.

> ...my father's teachings tended to the undervaluing of feeling. It was not that he was himself cold-hearted or insensible; I believe it was rather from the contrary quality; he thought that feeling could take care of itself;that there was sure to be enough of it if actions were properly cared about. Offended by the frequency with which, in ethical and philosophical controversy, feeling is made the ultimate reason and justification of conduct, instead of being itself called on for a justification, in practice, actions, the effect of which on human happiness is mischievous, are defended as being required by feeling, and the character of a person of feeling obtains a credit for desert, which he thought only due to actions, he had a real impatience of attributing praise to feeling, or of any but the most sparing reference to it, either in the estimation of persons or in the discussion of things. In addition to the influence which this characteristic in him had on me and others, we found all the opinions to which we attached most importance, con stantly attacked on the ground of feeling. Utility was denounced as cold calculation; political economy as hard-hearted; anti-population doctrines as repulsive to the natural feelings of mankind. We retorted by the word "sentimentality,"which, along with "declamation" and "vague generalities," served us as common terms of opprobrium. Although we were generally in the right, as against those who were opposed to us, the effect was that the cultivation of feeling (except the feelings of public and private duty), was not in much esteem among us, and had very little place in the thoughts of most of us, myself in particular. What we principally thought of, was to alter people's opinions; to make them believe according to evidence and know what was their real interest, which when they once knew, they would, we thought, by the instrument of opinion, enforce a regard to it upon one another. While fully recognizing the superior excellence of unselfish benevolence and love of justice, we did not expect the regeneration of mankind from any direct action on those sentiments, but from the effect of educated intellect, enlightening the selfish feelings.*

Now that was a position which he had imbibed as a pupil immediately of his father, and at one remove a pupil of Jeremy Bentham; and it was this attitude which became intolerable to him during his period of mental crisis.

> From the winter of 1821, when I first read Bentham, and especially from the commencement of the Westminster Review, I had what might truly be called an object in life; to be a reformer of the world.My conception of my own happiness was entirely identified with this object.The personal sympathies I wished for were those of fellow labourers in this enterprise. I endeavoured to pick up as many flowers as I could by the way;but as a serious and permanent personal satisfaction to rest upon, my whole reliance was placed on this; and I was accustomed to felicitate myself on the certainty of a happy life which I enjoyed, through placing my happiness in something durable and distant,in which some progress might be always making, while it could never be exhausted by complete attainment. This did very well for several years, during which the general improvement going on in the world and the idea of myself as engaged with others in struggling to promote it,seemed enough to fill up an interesting and animated existence.But the time came when I awakened from this as from

---

*Autobiography; C.U. Press ed. pp. 77-78. All references to the Autobiography will be given to the C.U. Press ed.

a dream. It was in the autumn of 1826. I was in a dull state of nerves, such as everybody is occasionally liable to; unsusceptible to enjoyment of pleasurable excitement; one of those moods when what is pleasure at other times, becomes insipid or indifferent; the state, I should think, in which converts to Methodism usually are, when smitten by their first "conviction of sin." In this frame of mind it occurred to me to put the question directly to myself: "Suppose that all your objects in life were realized; that all the changes in institutions and opinions which you are looking forward to, could be completely effected at this very instant, would this be a great joy and and happiness to you?" And an irrepressible self-consciousness distinctly answered, "No!" At this my heart sank within me: the whole foundation on which my life was constructed fell down. All my happiness was to have been found in the continual pursuit of this end. The end had ceased to charm, and how could there ever again be any interest in the means? I seemed to have nothing left to live for.*

From this period of depression which seems to have weighed most heavily upon him for some months, he was gradually roused, - roused by a change in his outlook on life and particularly by a new valuation of the factor of feeling.

In the first place, they led me to adopt a theory of life, very unlike that on which I had before acted, and having much in common with what at that time I certainly had never heard of, the anti-self-consciousness theory of Carlyle. I never, indeed, wavered in the conviction that happiness is the test of all rules of conduct, and the end of life. But I now thought that this end was only to be attained by not making it the direct end. Those only are happy (I thought) who have their minds fixed on some object other than their own happiness; on the happiness of others, on the improvement of mankind, even on some art or pursuit, followed not as a means, but as itself an ideal end. Aiming thus at something else, they find happiness by the way. The enjoyments of life (such was now my theory) are sufficient to make it a pleasant thing, when they are taken en passant, without being made a principal object. Once make them so, and they are immediately felt to be insufficient. They will not bear a scrutinizing examination. Ask yourself whether you are happy, and cease to be so. The only chance is to treat, not happiness but some end external to it, as the purpose of life. Let your self-consciousness, your scrutiny, your self-interrogation, exhaust themselves on that; and if otherwise fortunately circumstanced you will inhale happiness with the air you breathe, without dwelling on it or thinking about it, without either forestalling it in imagination, or putting it to flight by fatal questioning. This theory now became the basis of my philosophy of life.**

Now you see here is a Benthamite convincing himself that after all although the greatest happiness is the proper rule of conduct, still in the conduct of one's own life one is almost certain to fail if he aims at happiness directly. He may get happiness by fixing his regard upon some object external to it and then living a full and vigorous life in that basis.

The other important change which my opinions at this time underwent, was that I, for the first time, gave its proper place, among the prime necessities of human well-being, the internal culture of the individual. I ceased to attach almost exclusive importance to the ordering of outward circumstances, and the training of the human being for speculation and for action.

* Ibid., pp. 93-94.

**Ibid., pp. 99-100.

I had now learnt by experience that the passive susceptibilities needed to be cultivated as well as the active capacities, and required to be nourished and enriched as well as guided. I did not, for an instant, lose sight of, or undervalue, that part of the truth which I had seen before; I never turned recreant to intellectual culture, or ceased to consider the power and practice of analysis as an essential condition both of individual and of social improvement. But I thought that it had consequences which required to be corrected, by joining other kinds of cultivation with it. The maintenance of a due balance among the faculties, now seemed to me of primary importance. The cultivation of the feelings became one of the cardinal points in my ethical and philosophical creed.*

That is, he also reacted very strongly against that particular element in Benthamism which was perhaps most pronounced in his father; disregard of feeling as a factor in behavior. He goes on to explain in a most interesting way what extraordinary help he got at this time from reading Wordsworth's poems:

What made Wordsworth's poems a medicine for my state of mind, was that they expressed, not mere outward beauty, but states of feeling, and of thought coloured by the very culture of the feelings, which I was in quest of. In them I seemed to draw from a source of inward joy, of sympathetic and imaginative pleasure, which could be shared in by all human beings; which had no connection with struggle or imperfection, but would be made richer by every improvement in the physical or social condition of mankind. From them I seemed to learn what would be the perennial sources of happiness, when all the greater evils of life shall have been removed. And I felt myself at once better and happier as I came under their influence. There have certainly been, even in our own age, greater poets than Wordsworth; but poetry of deeper and loftier feeling could not have done for me at that time what his did. I needed to be made to feel that there was real, permanent happiness in tranquil contemplation. Wordsworth taught me this, not only without turning away from, but with a greatly increased interest in the common feelings and common destiny of human beings. And the delight which these poems gave me, proved that with culture of this sort, there was nothing to dread from the most confirmed habit of analysis. At the conclusion of the poems came the famous Ode, falsely called Platonic, "Intimations of Immortality;" in which, along with more than his usual sweetness of melody and rhythm, and along with the two passages of grand imagery but bad philosophy so often quoted, I found that he too had had similar experience to mine; that he also had felt that the first freshness of youthful enjoyment of life was not lasting; but that he had sought for compensation, and found it, in the way in which he was now teaching me to find it. The result was that I gradually, but completely, emerged from my habitual depression, and was never again subject to it.**

The immediate result of this curious but very intense mental experience was that the lad began to cultivate a new set of contacts. Among the several discussion groups to which he belonged were a number of people who looked up to Samuel Taylor Coleridge, the poet, as their intellectual and spiritual leader. He had seemed from most points of view to represent the very antithesis of the philosophy of life from Bentham. But now Mill began to find that in some of Coleridge's younger disciples he had points of similarity which he had hitherto not suspected. Like him, they were interested in the feelings. They were sensitive to a whole range of human experiences which were notably absent in the rather bare Benthamite viewpoint. They got Mill into the habit of reading Goethe and other German authors. They brought

* Ibid., pp.100-101.
**Ibid., pp.104-105.

him presently into contact with Carlyle; and between these two men, so different
in their antecedents, their general philosophy of life, there sprang up a very
close feeling. For a considerable time they thought themselves indeed very largely
at one on most fundamental issues, though as time went on Carlyle worked more and
more into the position of worshipping the hero, defending autocracy; and particularly when he was believed to have come out as the champion of slavery Mill's
moral sense revolted.

Now this change in Mill's attitude toward life had very important reactions
upon his intellectual preoccupations. He was one of those people who take the line
of thought as the real thing which should concern a human being. These changes in
his valuation of feeling meant that he could not simply alter his ordinary day to
day occupations but had to go back and reconsider his philosophy. In particular
this led him into a series of reflections which for the time being centered upon
his father's theory of government. In an article which James Mill had published in
the Encyclopaedia Britannica on government, you can find perhaps one of the most
extraordinary examples of Benthamite reasoning in social science to be picked up
in the whole range of the Philosophical Radical literature. There James Mill had
drawn up what seemed to be a set of governmental institutions as necessary conclusions from certain broad principles that he laid down as characteristic of human
nature, the whole argument being conducted very much on the plan of a demonstration
in Euclidean geometry. Several years after this article had appeared, Macaulay (he
was not yet a Lord) had attacked it most savagely in the Edinburgh Review. In his
attack Macaulay had taken the ground that, after all, government cannot be made
the subject of a science; the only way in which we can satisfactorily think about
these great practical problems is in an empirical way; the proper leader for us to
follow in this field is not Jeremy Bentham but Edmund Burke; it is quite possible
to learn a great deal concerning government by reflecting upon experiences in the
past, the kind of experiences which are treasured up in history, but there is no
opening there for a science.

John Stuart Mill, of course, was very deeply concerned in this controversy
between Macaulay and his father. He says:

I was not at all satisfied with the mode in which my father met the criticism
of Macaulay. He did not, as I thought he ought to have done, justify himself
by saying,"I was not writing a scientific treatise on politics, I was writing
an argument for parliamentary reform." He treated Macaulay's argument as simply
irrational; an attack upon the reasoning faculty; an example of the saying of
Hobbes, that when reason is against a man, a man will be against reason. This
made me think that there was really something more fundamentally erroneous in
my father's conception of philosophical method, as applicable to politics, than
I had hitherto supposed there was. But I did not at first see clearly what the
error might be. At last it flashed upon me all at once in the course of other
studies.*

These other studies which brought him illumination concerning his father's methods
in treating the problems of government were a set of logical studies on which he
had embarked as one of the results of his membership in discussion groups. In thinking about the problems of how we really arrive at our conclusions in the social
sciences,he thought that it can be most helped by considering the processes of
reaching scientific conclusions which were practiced with success in more highly
developed branches of learning.And for his purposes the one that seemed to him most
instructive to study for the time being was the theory of the composition of forces.

*Ibid., p.111.

On examining, accordingly, what the mind does when it applies the principle of the Composition of Forces, I found that it performs a simple act of addition. It adds the separate effect of the one force to the separate effect of the other, and puts down the sum of these separate effects as the joint effect. But is this a legitimate process? In dynamics, and in all the mathematical branches of physics, it is; but in some other cases, as in chemistry, it is not; and I then recollected that something not unlike this was pointed out as one of the distinctions between chemical and mechanical phenomena, in the introduction to that favourite of my boyhood, Thomson's System of Chemistry. This distinction at once made my mind clear as to what was perplexing me in respect to the philosophy of politics. I now say, that a science is either deductive or experimental, according as, in the province it deals with, the effects of causes when conjoined, are or are not the sums of the effects which the same produce when separate

Now you are probably expecting Mill to go on to the conclusion that the problems presented by human society are like those of chemistry. When you have two forces combining with each other, the net effect is not always to be ascertained by adding the two forces together, the procedure which works so well with the composition of forces as a physical problem, but has to be ascertained as in so many chemical cases when you put two substances together and it can be determined only by experiment what sort of thing they make. At least in Mill's day chemistry was in that state; it was only by experiment that you could really tell what two substances mixed together would produce. But you find Mill taking the opposite ground; that in the social sciences the proper procedure is that which is followed in dealing with the composition of forces. You must proceed by adding together the factors in order to find out what the end vector will be, and you must not proceed on the experimental basis. He says:

> It followed that politics must be a deductive science. It thus appeared, that both Macaulay and my father were wrong; the one in assimilating the method of philosophizing in politics to the purely experimental method in chemistry; while the other, though right in adopting a deductive method, had made a wrong selection of one, having taken as the type of deduction, not the appropriate process, that of the deductive branches of natural philosophy, but the inappropriate one of pure geometry, which, not being a science of causation at all, does not require or admit of any summing-up of effects. A foundation was thus laid in my thoughts for the principal chapters of what I afterwards published on the Logic of the Moral Sciences; and my new position in respect to my old political creed, now became perfectly definite.**

Well, now you see this means that the boy who had been so strictly brought up by his father had come not only to doubt the philosophy of life which included an undervaluation of feeling, but also had come to have very definite doctrinal objections to the methods which his father was applying in the social sciences. And that made him another set of problems; not that he fell back into a state of melancholy such as had marked his great moral crisis, but that now the father to whom he was so enormously attached seemed to him to be proceeding, at least in certain respects, along a mistaken path. And the question came what he should do about it. He was a highly conscientious person, and yet, as he says, his father was not a person with whom one could readily differ.

> My father's tone of thought and feeling, I now felt myself at a great distance from: greater, indeed, that a full and calm explanation and reconsideration on both sides, might have shown to exist in reality. But my father was not

___
* Ibid., pp. 112-113.
**Ibid., p. 113.

one with whom calm and full explanations on fundamental points of doctrine could be expected, at least with one whom he might consider as, in some sort, a deserter from his standard.*

And so he really felt more or less bottled up inside himself. He was not free to follow out, as under other circumstances he might have been, these new ideas which were stirring within him. And probably in order to relieve these mental strains, he turned his thoughts for the time being to certain technical questions of an economic order. It was in this period that he wrote the Essays on Some Unsettled Questions of Political Economy, though after he had written them he did not get them published for a while. In fact, it was only some considerable number of years later, after his System of Logic had made a great reputation, that he succeeded in finding someone to bring out that small but highly technical economic treatise. And he also began writing quietly on logical problems proper; but his logical problems soon brought him to an impasse, particularly on the problem of induction. He says he had come to the end of his tether and could make nothing satisfactory of induction at this time because he did not have an adequate survey at hand of the inductive processes as practiced in the natural sciences; and it was not until Whewell's History of the Inductive Sciences appeared that he was able to satisfy himself on that side.

Meanwhile his father died. That event occurred in 1836 when John Stuart Mill was thirty years old. This gave him at least freedom to express his dissent from the strict Benthamite doctrine. He took fairly early opportunity to explain very clearly what doubts he had come to entertain, his position being publicly presented in two articles, one of them on Bentham, and the other on Coleridge, which were published in the London and Westminster Review in 1838 and 1840. (The London and Westminster Review being the successor of the old Westminster Review which had been the particular organ of the Benthamites.) You will see how his attitude toward Bentham changed from the following brief extract from the essay on the first of these men:

It (Bentham's philosophy) can teach the means of organizing and regulating the merely business part of the social arrangements. ...He committed the mistake of supposing that the business part of human affairs was the whole of them; all at least that the legislator and the moralist had to do with.

...A philosophy of laws and institutions, not founded on a philosophy of national character is an absurdity. But what could Bentham's opinion be worth on national character? How could he, whose mind contained so few and so poor types of individual character, rise to that higher generalization?**

It is not unnatural that after Mill had published an article of reflections of that sort that the stricter Benthamites among his father's and his own friends began to feel that he was straying away from the fold. And meanwhile the young man had become very much dissatisfied with the conduct of the Philosophical Radicals as a party. There

had taken place the election of the first Reformed Parliament, which included several of the most notable of my Radical friends and acquaintances - Grote, Roebuck, Buller, Sir William Molesworth, John and Edward Romilly, and several more; besides Warburton Strutt, and others, who were in parliament already.

* Ibid., p. 126
**Dissertations and Discussions; London, 1875, vol. I, p. 366

Those who thought themselves, and were called by their friends the philosophic
radicals, had now, it seemed, a fair opportunity, in a more advantageous position than they had ever before occupied, for showing what was in them; and I,
as well as my father, founded great hopes on them. These hopes were destined
to be disappointed. The men were honest, and faithful to their opinions, as
far as votes were concerned; often in spite of much discouragement. When
measures were proposed, flagrantly at variance with their principles, such
as the Irish Coercion Bill, or the Canada coercion in 1837, they came forward manfully, and braved any amount of hostility and prejudice rather than
desert the right. But on the whole they did very little to promote any opinions; they had little enterprise, little activity: they left the lead of
the radical portion of the House to the old hands, to Hume and O'Connell.
A partial exception must be made in favour of one or two of the younger men;
and in the case of Roebuck, it is his title to permanent remembrance, that
in the very first year during which he sat in Parliament, he originated (or
re-originated after the unsuccessful attempt of Mr. Brougham) the parliamentary movement for National Education; and that he was the first to commence,
and for years carried on almost alone, the contest for the self-government
of the Colonies. Nothing, on the whole equal to these two things, was done
by any other individual, even of those from whom most was expected. And now,
on a calm retrospect, I can perceive that the men were less in fault than we
supposed, and that we had expected too much from them. They were in un-
favourable circumstances. Their lot was cast in the ten years of inevitable
reaction, when, the Reform excitement being over, and the few legislative
improvements which the public really called for having been rapidly effected,
power gravitated back in its natural direction, to those who were for keeping
things as they were; when the public mind desired rest, and was less disposed than at any other period since the peace, to let itself be moved by
attempts to work up the reform feeling into fresh activity in favour of new
things. It would have required a great political leader, which no one is to
be blamed for not being, to have effected really great things by parliamentary
discussion when the nation was in this mood.*

Now that disappointment over the activity of the Philosophical Radicals as a
party about 1840 had further important consequences in his life. In his early years
he had been a very eager propagandist, and his interest in propaganda had not been
changed by his mental crisis. But now he found that the particular group with
whom he still had a great deal of sympathy was disintegrating. They had accomplished
hardly anything and he saw very little chance that he himself or he and association
with any other group then in existence could accomplish practical results of any
large value. The consequence was that he withdrew himself after 1840 both from interest in politics and from writing any political reviews, and even from ordinary
society; and devoted himself more to philosophical speculation of one sort and
another. He was indeed inclined to justify this policy of his on high grounds:

Being now released from any active concern in temporary politics, and
from any literary occupation involving personal communication with contributors
and others, I was enabled to indulge the inclination, natural to thinking
persons when the age of boyish vanity is once past, for limiting my own society
to a very few persons. General society, as now carried on in England, is so insipid an affair, even to the persons who make it what it is, that it is kept up
for any reason rather than the pleasure it affords. All serious discussion on
matters on which opinions differ, being considered ill-bred, and the national
deficiency in liveliness and sociability having prevented the cultivation of the
art of talking agreeably on trifles, in which the French of the last century so

*Autobiography, p. 136-137.

much excelled, the sole attraction of what is called society to those who
are not at the top of the tree, is the hope of being aided to climb a little
higher in it; while to those who are already at the top, it is chiefly a com-
pliance with custom, and with the supposed requirements of their station..
...A person of high intellect should never go into unintellectual society unless he can enter it as an apostle; yet he is the only person with high objects who can safely enter it at all. Persons even of intellectual aspirations had much better, if they can, make their habitual associates of at least
their equals, and, as far as possible, their superiors, in knowledge, intellect,
and elevation of sentiment. Moreover, if the character is formed, and the mind
made up, on the few cardinal points of human opinion, agreement of conviction and
feeling on these, has been felt in all times to be an essential requisite of
anything worthy the name of friendship, in a really earnest mind.*

And Mill's mind was eminently an earnest one.

So from about 1840 the man led to an increasing degree a life of retirement
and gave himself much less to periodical writing of one sort and another and much
more to the production of the large seriously-considered treatised which became such
factors in the further development of thought in England. Of these the first was
his System of Logic, a book which had its origin in his early experiences as a
member of discussion groups. It had long been a matter of serious concern with him,
largely because of his doubts about the methodological procedure of his father and
the other Benthamites, and which had finally become possible to complete when Whewell's History of the Inductive Sciences had given Mill the opportunity to review
the recent advances in physics and chemistry particularly, and so had made far
clearer to him the subject of induction which had formerly been his stumbling block.
Doubtless many of you are acquainted with this book, a work of substantially the same
size as the Political Economy, a work on which Mill spent far more time, and a work
which I suppose has an importance in the development of modern thought greater than
that of his economic treatise. It is a systematic discussion of logical procedures.
But it is interesting to observe that when Mill toward the end of his life was writing his Autobiography he underestimated the importance of this treatise. He thought
of its real importance not in terms that have to do with logical procedure as such
but have to do with the general welfare of mankind.

I have never indulged the illusion that the book had made any considerable
impression on philosophical opinion.

That was a modest estimation. It had; - perhaps not at the time Mill was writing,
but certainly had before the century was over produced a considerable impression on
philosophical opinion.

The German, or a priori view of human knowledge, and of the knowing faculties,
is likely for some time longer (though it may be hoped in a diminishing degree)
to predominate among those who occupy themselves with such inquiries, both here
and on the Continent. But the "System of Logic" supplies what was much wanted,
a text-book of the opposite doctrine - that which derives all knowledge from
experience, and all moral and intellectual qualities principally from the direction given to the associations.**

That means, of course, associations among ideas. As I have said, Mill attached much importance to this doctrine that all knowledge is derived from experience
instead of being knowledge a priori. Now why did he think it important that all
moral and intellectual qualities are derived from the direction given to the associa-

* Ibid., pp. 159-160.
**Ibid., p. 157.

The notion that truths external to the mind may be known by intuition or consciousness, independently of observation and experience, is, I am persuaded,
in these times, the great intellectual support of false doctrines and bad
institutions.*

And here you see the Benthamite coming strongly to the fore: that philosophical
doctrine that we get knowledge intuitively is the great support of false doctrines
and bad institutions. He continues:

By the aid of this theory, every inveterate belief and every intense feeling,
of which the origin is not remembered, is enabled to dispense with the obligation of justifying itself by reason, and is erected into its own all-
sufficient voucher and justification. There never was such an instrument
devised for consecrating all deep-seated prejudices.**

You see Mill with his doctrine that all our knowledge comes ultimately from
experience does put one philosophically into a position to challenge every belief
that people assert, no matter how great it claims to be, and to try its wholesomeness
for society; whereas people who hold a priori theories of human nature can always
escape a challenge of that sort. It was the social consequences of the philosophical theory which he was challenging in his Logic; and that was, I think, the real
service which that book rendered.

The effect of the publication of the Logic in 1834 was to give Mill immediately a place of prominence among the philosophers of his country and his generation.
The book had extraordinary popularity for one dealing with such a subject. It
passed through eight editions between the date of publication and Mill's death in
1873, a period of thirty years. And a minor, but for us interesting, result was
that the great popular success of the Logic commercially enabled Mill to get a
publisher for his old set of Essays on the Unsettled Problems of Political Economy,
and also encouraged him to set about writing a treatise on economic theory at large.

Now quite clearly he could not have been thinking very actively about
economic problems during the years which had elapsed between writing these essays
(they were written in his twenties) and the date when he published them. He just
pulled the manuscript out of his desk, made ordinary changes, and sent them off to
the printer. Also when he set about writing his Political Economy he planned to do
the whole job and did it far more quickly that he had done his Logic. He began
writing his Political Economy in 1845 and eighteen months later the two volumes
were ready for the printer, despite the fact that he had been doing his office work
and had spent most of his leisure time for six months writing a series of newspaper
articles on Irish land tenure. It was a book written, you see, at a very high rate
of speed, a book that could be written at a very high rate of speed only because John
Stuart Mill his life long had been thinking more or less about these problems and
also because to him political economy was a pretty wellfinished product. It did not
present any very great problems of an intellectual sort that had to be solved; no
difficulties turned up in writing his Political Economy such as turned up while he
was engaged in writing his Logic; it was a matter of arranging an ordered exposition
of principles which had been found out by his predecessors.

Books of that sort you do not expect to be a real contribution, but Jogn Stuart

* Ibid., p. 158.
**Ibid., p. 158

Mill's <u>Political Economy</u> is certainly an exception. While it was written in this very rapid fashion; while it did not represent an effort to solve any very significant new problems; while it was primarily an exposition of views which others had developed, it still did put the whole subject of political economy in quite a new light. It became the authoritative final formulation of the classical doctrines on the one hand and the starting point of a whole series of new endeavors to work out the economic science in the years that followed.

The two books, the <u>Logic</u> and the <u>Political Economy</u> together, gave John Stuart Mill a position in English life and thought such as no economist had enjoyed before him and such as no economist has enjoyed since his day in any country. On the one hand, he was revered as a great philosopher, a philosopher particularly adapted to the severest branch of philosophy, logic; and on the other hand, he was looked upon as the greatest expert in technical economic theory. And also because of the spirit which infuses both these books he was looked upon as a great spiritual leader, a man who stood for all that was best and finest in the moral aspirations of these who pinned their faith on the use of human intelligence as a means of bettering the doubtful lot of mankind.

XXXVII

JOHN STUART MILL'S PRINCIPLES OF POLITICAL ECONOMY

I want to occupy our last meeting of the Winter Session by pointing out certain broad characteristics of Mill's <u>Political Economy</u>. That book is notable for its double message, a double message which is indicated by the title which Mill chose. He called his book <u>Principles of Political Economy with Some of Their Applications to Social Philosophy</u>. That means that he has on the one hand a systematic presentation of economic principles, more complete and systematic that you find in Ricardo; and then on the other hand a discussion of many social problems in the light of economic theory. As you look through the book you have no difficulty in separating out these two parts, the pure economic theory on the one side and the applications of economic principles, the social philosophy, on the other side.

It is also notable that Mill himself thought that the second part of his book, at least the part he put second in his sub-title, was of the greater importance. He wrote to his German translator, Professor Carl D. Heinrich Rau, of Heidelberg, in 1852, that is, four years after the book appeared in England:

> I confess that I regard the purely abstract investigations of political economy (beyond those elementary ones which are necessary for the correction of mischievous prejudices), as of very minor importance compared with the great practical questions which the progress of democracy and the spread of Socialist opinions are pressing on, and for which both governing and the governed classes are very far from being in a fit state of preparation.*

The thing that seemed to him particularly important was not simply to expound a system to economic principles but to show the bearing of these principles upon the questions which were already of importance and which he thought were presently going to become of a still more pressing character. And in this he was true to the Utilitarian tradition.

Political economy was to him primarily one of the great agencies for guiding public policy and for thus contributing to human welfare. And these contributions

* <u>Letters</u>, vol. I, p. 170.

were what justified a thinker in spending considerable time in excogitating principles with the greatest possible accuracy. He had less interest, presumably, in the purely theoretical part of his work because he seems to have felt that economics perhaps had already attained a highly satisfactory form. Certainly the major part of his economic principles are borrowed by John Stuart Mill from his great predecessors, from Ricardo most of all, from whom he got his ideas about the theory of value, theories of wages, profits, and rent, the theory of money, theory of international trade, and theories of the long time tendencies of rent, wages, and profits, as well as his theories on the questions of taxation.

With this central core of Ricardian doctrines he incorporated with masterly expository skill the Malthusian theory of population, together with a variety of the most important points of doctrine derived from Adam Smith, from his father, from J. B. Say, from Nassau Senior, from De Quincey, who had written a most charming essay upon value, from John Rae, that interesting and original economist who had lived for a considerable time in the wilds of Canada, from Richard Jones who, as I mentioned incidentally the other day, was trying to use the comparative historical method of attacking economic problems, from Colonel Torrens, and from John Ramsay McCulloch. It is interesting, by the way, to notice that when he quotes McCulloch it is usually with the purpose of showing he was wrong, McCulloch in his mind representing the worst form of the old political economy.

With this general framework of economic theory we may feel sure that Mill was pretty well satisfied, because of the speed with which his book was written. As I said last Thursday, this whole book which in the first edition ran to one thousand crown octavo pages was composed within about eighteen months, and that despite the fact that during this brief period Mill devoted some six months mainly to writing an elaborate series of newspaper articles upon land tenure in Ireland. More than that, we find Mill expressing explicitly his satisfaction concerning what since Ricardo's time we have been in the habit of regarding as the central problem of economic theory, namely, the theory of value. He ventured the remark which has in recent years been so often quoted that it is familiar to you:

Happily, there is nothing in the laws of value which remains for the present or any future writer to clear up.....*

Apparently to him that central theory at least was in final form.

And so far as the other economic doctrines of the book are concerned, he did not make any very important additions to them, made no pretense of doing so. He accomplished a very considerable service in bringing these various doctrines all into a beautifully articulated discussion, in expounding them with a higher degree of literary and artistic skill than any of his predecessors. But they were, after all, - barring minor improvements here and there which he had found necessary - discoveries of other people. And yet, Mill did feel very clearly that his book represented a considerable change in the position of political economy as compared with these predecessors. He speaks, for instance, toward the end of his Political Economy a bit contemptuously of what he calls "political economists of the old school" and seems to be setting himself off as representing something new. And so in his Autobiography somewhat later he speaks of the "common run" of political economists, again as if that was a category to which he did not belong. And to his friend W.T. Thornton he wrote in 1867, some thirteen years after his book had been published, about a forthcoming treatise of Thornton's:

* Principles, Bk. III, sec. 1; Ashley ed. p. 436.

To mention only one thing, the book will
be very serviceable in carrying on what
may be called the emancipation of political economy - its liberation from the
kind of doctrines of the old school (now
taken up by well-to-do people)which treat
what they call commercial laws, demand
and supply for instance, as if they were
laws of inanimate matter, not amenable
to the will of the human beings from whose
feelings, interests, and principles of action
they proceed. This is one of the queer
mental confusions which will be wondered
at by-and-by, and you are helping very much
in the good work of clearing it up.*

You see he was very unfavorably affected by that process of vulgarization
through which political economy had gone in the generation immediately after
Ricardo, a vulgarization which adapted it to all sorts of partisan use, which
made political economy in the hands of the well-to-do people a rationalization of
their view about the proper treatment of the poor, of their views about the in-
effectiveness and worse of trade unions, their views about the undesirability of a
protective tariff, - a process that had made political economy, which professed to
be a science, practically a weapon adapted to the use of class warfare.

Indeed, for political economy of that sort John Stuart Mill had no use. And
while he took his economic principles with no very large changes from his predecessors, he felt that his book certainly had a tone, a meaning of a new sort.
What was it,in his eyes, that distinguished his book from political economy of the
old school? What set him off from the"common run" of political economists? What
feature of his purpose was it that contributed to the emancipation of political
economy, this liberation from the kind of "doctrines of the old school now taken
up by well-to-do people?" It was the distinction to which he attributed fundamental importance between the character of the laws of production and the character of the laws of distribution. I want to read you a few sentences in which
he sets forth his conception of this fundamental difference.

*Letters, vol. II, p. 90.

> The laws and conditions of the Production of Wealth
> partake of the character of physical truths. There
> is nothing optional or arbitrary in them. Whatever
> mankind produce, must be produced in the modes, and
> under the conditions, imposed by the constitution
> of external structure............
>
> It is not so with the Distribution of
> Wealth. That is a matter of human institution solely.
> The things once there, mankind, individually or
> collectively, can do with them as they like. They can
> place them at the disposal of whomsoever they please,
> and on whatever terms. Further, in the social state,
> in every state except total solitude, any disposal
> whatever of them can only take place by the consent of
> society, or rather of those who dispose of its active
> force. Even what a person has produced by his indi-
> vidual toil, unaided by any one, he cannot keep, unless
> by the permission of society. Not only can society
> take it from him, but individuals could and would take
> it from him, if society only remained passive; if it
> did not either interfere en masse, or employ and pay
> people for the purpose of preventing him from being
> disturbed in the possession. The distribution of
> wealth, therefore, depends on the laws and customs of
> society. The rules by which it is determined are
> what the opinions and feelings of the ruling portion of
> the community make them, and are very different in
> different ages and countries; and might be still more
> different, if mankind so chose.*

Mill felt that it was this distinction between the physical character and
therefore the changeless form of the laws of production, and the social character
and therefore the possibility of change in the laws of distribution that gave his
book that "general tone by which it is distinguished from all previous expositions
of political economy." This phrase I am quoting from his Autobiography.** And
he is very much interested in tracing the origin of this grand ideal in his own
mind. He tells us in his Autobiography that it was "partially learnt....from the
thoughts awakened in me by the speculations of St. Simonians" *** that group of
speculative French socialists with whom Mill was for a long time in sympathetic
contact until at last they developed a religion in which he could not share. He
goes on to say "but it was made a living principle pervading and animating the
book by my wife's promptings." *** And if you care to dig out the passage you
will find that among numerous extraordinary intellectual benefits which in Mill's
eyes she had conferred upon him this was perhaps the most important.

---

* Principles, Bk. II, Ch. I: Ashley ed. p. 199-200
** p. 174.
***p. 175.

HOW MILL SAW THE FUTURE: CONTRASTED WITH MALTHUS AND RICARDO

Why is that distinction so important? It seems perhaps after all a matter of a rather trivial sort. It was important because it allowed a man to cherish a prospect of indefinite increase in human felicity; it elevated economics from the position of a dismal science to the position of a science which promised an illimitable gradual development in the lot of mankind. You recall the very drab view of the future taken by Malthus, and the view scarcely less drab taken by Ricardo, who when he looked forward, thought that he saw the progressive state in which men lived in his time gradually running down into what he called the "stationary" state, a state in which profits would be reduced to a minimum, in which laborers would find it very difficult to maintain even their then existing low standard of living, and in which the greater part of the proceeds of production would be going to the recipients of tithes and taxes, a body of people who made no substantial contribution to human welfare. And that was a prospect which Ricardo thought inevitable as a matter of fact the best that could happen to mankind, because it was inevitable if the existing institutions of property were to be maintained. And he also thought that any attack upon the security of property would make things immediately far worse for the bulk of mankind inasmuch as if property were not secure there would be no motive for the accumulation of capital; and if there were no capital in abundance there would not be the wherewithal to pay wages and cultivate land.

All that seemed a source of inevitable deductions from the principles of human nature and the physical characteristics of the environment in which men lived. That is one of the views in which Mill was inexorably drilled by his father in his youth. Now from the St. Simonians and his wife he got this different perspective of mankind's lot. It is true he continued to think that the laws which regulate production cannot be altered; it is always going to remain true, for instance, that production will be limited by capital. In that he was a good Ricardian. It is always going to remain true that successive applications of labor and capital to a given piece of land will yield diminishing returns after a certain period. It was also true, apparently, - though this is a point that he did not argue out - that we cannot expect any improvements in the arts of transportation and manufacturing to offset the great importance of the law of diminishing returns. And therefore it looks as if the amount of wealth per capita which society can produce in the future is not likely to increase as fast as numbers may multiply.

But after all, granting the truth of these fundamental propositions concerning production, Mill saw a ray of hope in the changes which can be made in the distribution of products. Those laws of distribution have nothing inevitable about them like the laws of production; they are matters of human institution. And as men grow wiser they can adapt the institutions regulating the production of wealth so as to achieve a much higher degree of equality in distribution, so as to give a

---

* p. 174.

**p. 175.

much more effective stimulus to the development of the right kind of social equalities, the right kind of social beings. And while this meant that strictly as an economist he was allowed to entertain not such gorgeous views of the possibility of rapid improvement in human kind as Robert Owen had entertained, or such views as William Godwin had expounded shortly after the outbreak of the French Revolution to the scandal of Malthus, but a tempered view of a possibility of a slow but steady and gradual evolution of human intelligence and its application to economic institutions which would elevate our race from a position in which the great majority of it lived lives of uncertainty and deprivation to a position in which all the worthy members of it might have a secure, rich, and varied life.

And the means of achieving that advance in which Mill believed were presumably the means upon which the Philosophical Radicals as a whole had always laid chief stress. Now Mill continued to the end to hold the same fundamental conceptions of human nature which Jeremy Bentham and his father had propounded; that is, he believed that our knowledge is derived from experience. You remember that on Thursday I read you a passage in which he said that the whole purpose of the Logic was to give a text-book of the view that our minds are formed by experience instead of being stereotyped by a set of a priori notions which according to German metaphysics was the case. Well, now as a person who believed that minds are formed by experience and the process of forming minds is that of establishing associations among ideas, Mill not only hoped but expected that we would gradually become far more intelligent creatures than we ever had been in the past; that we would apply this intelligence - we would come to the point where we would do so - and would be able to apply this intelligence not only to the regulation of our problems as individual beings but to the regulation of our social institutions. For one thing, - and this was, of course, to him of great importance - he believed that the slow growth of intelligence would gradually enable men to master the promptings of their sexual passions. Passion to him meant something bad; it meant an unreflecting line of attack, a way of acting that did not count the consequences; it was not calculated. To be certain of producing good results, therefore, the first duty of man is to think what lines of action are productive of pleasure and what are productive of harm. Well, if people become calculating to the extent that they are able to repress the promptings of sexual passion in considerable measure, then the increase in human numbers perhaps will be diminished. That is, we need not envisage the future as did Malthus and Ricardo as holding no possibility of increasing the standard of living for the majority of mankind.

Mill believed heartily with Malthus and Ricardo in their hypothetical proposition that if men did continue to take advantage of any increase in their material condition in order to marry somewhat earlier and have larger families then wages could not rise and the benefits of improvements in the arts would all be swallowed up by the adverse action of the law of diminishing returns in agriculture; that any gains we made in our ability to transport and manufacture goods would no more than compensate for the loss in our efforts to get food for greater numbers out of the same extent of soil. But Mill said: well, that is all right as a hypothetical proposition; there is no reason to believe that men are always going to continue to be as stupid as they are at present. On the contrary, the chances are that they will become enlightened concerning their own interest. Their rate of propagation will diminish. And as their rate of propagation diminishes it will not be necessary to wring increases of the food supply from a soil which yields diminishing returns; but you can keep perhaps a standard of population in existence with a given amount of food, and all the improvements that you make in the arts of transportation, exchange, and fabrication can be used to give people a larger real income. And more than that, as people get wiser they will learn ways of distributing this larger real income among their members which are less unfair and which give a larger proportion of the total population the opportunity of having a satisfactory life.

And he went on in some of his wonderful later chapters on the future of the laboring classes to point out what changes in the institutions regulating distribution he thought were likely to prove most beneficial. The changes on which he pinned his hope were developments from a plan of producers' cooperation. He deemed it not ridiculous to dream that bodies of workingmen would come to the point where they could carry on, in a way more satisfactory than employing capitalists, a large part of the world's work; that by taking over, at a fair valuation, business enterprises first organized perhaps upon a strictly capitalistic basis, they would themselves come as wage earners to supplement their wages with the shares of income that now go to lenders and the active business organizers. And more than that, when they became themselves the recipients of profits as well as the recipients of interest and of wages, they would have an enhanced incentive to productivity. As a matter of fact, this enhanced incentive to productivity made Mill believe that the cooperative workshop might in a not distant future come to be an increasingly important form of organization, for groups of cooperating laborers with their greater incentive to efficiency would succeed in producing at a lower cost than capitalistically organized industries, and on the theory of competition the odds would be that rather rapidly a large proportion of the capitalistically managed enterprises would pass into the hands of cooperating workingmen. So that in a quiet, peaceful fashion, without any violent expropriation of the owners of the world's present business enterprises, society might transform itself into an organization where all had an interes much more definite than the wage system gives us, where all producers had an interest in efficiency, where everybody realized that he was producing for himself at the same time he was producing for his customers. And that state of society would be an infinitely better one, not only than the future state of society which was pictured in the somewhat dismal view of Ricardo and Malthus, but also a vastly better state than that in which society stood in Mill's own day.

So you see this rather technical distinction between the laws of production as unchanging in character and the laws of distribution as subject to man's own determination really made an enormous difference, as Mill saw things, in the kind of conclusions concerning the future of the race which one draws from the study of economics. It changed, as I have already said, the dismal science into a science that entertained most cheerful hopes for the future of mankind. It is no wonder that Mill regarded this distinction as by far the most important of his contributions to economics, or rather of the contributions which his wife and in less measure the St. Simonians had made through their influence upon his thinking.

One other matter perhaps deserves some mention in this course, although it is by no means so interesting: Mill introduced a distinction between statics and dynamics, a distinction which can be traced in earlier writers but which had not been by any of them so clearly and explicitly avowed. In the realm of statics he professed himself to include his discussion of production, distribution, and exchange. His discussion of dynamics included his treatment of the influence of the progress of society on production and distribution.* This distinction Mill presumably got in the first place from Comte, but he gave it a somewhat different twist. From his viewpoint, social statics is the theory of the relations existing between the different parts of the social organization at a given time, and social dynamics is the theory of society considered in the state of progressive movement. That is the language he uses in the Logic. A little more specifically one finds that in the Political Economy Mill considers under the head of dynamics the effect of an increase of population, an increase of capital, and of improvement in the arts upon society, without supposing any change in economic institutions other than that which can come about gradually through the enlightenment of our understandings. Still that change which can come about gradually through the enlightenment of our understanding, particularly the diminished rate of increase of population and the elaborate plan of organizing business enterprises with its resulting changes in the distribution of

* See Principles, Bk. IV, CH.I; Ashley ed. p. 695.

wealth can, given time enough to run, effect a revolution as he sees it, of the greatest moment in human affairs.

In later writings this distinction between statics and dynamics gets developed on a grand scale. The time comes when you will find people saying that the portion of economics which can be regarded as really scientific, as worked out with a considerable measure of certainty, is the part which deals with static problems; and that the portion of economics which we have for the most part to speculate about is that more difficult portion in which people advance from the supposition of an unchanging state to consider the effects of alternatives resulting from such factors as Mill had in mind: increases of capital, population, improvements in the arts, and perhaps other more sudden changes in human arrangements.

The distinction, as Mill makes it, really is giving names of a definite sort to two different classes of problems which had been comprised within the scope of English political economy very definitely at least since the days of Ricardo; for you remember that Ricardo set up two different sets of laws about distribution: one set of laws stating what determines wages, rents, and profits, as matters constant, and a second set concerning the long run tendencies of wages, rent, and profits. What Mill did was to say the first set of laws is a discussion of static problems, the second set of laws is a discussion of dynamic problems.

I may also perhaps comment upon Mill's general conception of what economics is, though this again is a matter of secondary interest; the subject matter of political economy, said Mill, is wealth. That is, in his formal definition he talks about economics as if it were an analysis of the various things which constitute the material means for satisfying our wants; and then he proceeds to show that this is not what he is talking about at all. Economics is not, on his showing, a discussion of wealth, but a discussion of what people do to get wealth, how people conduct themselves in exchanging it, what are their institutions for distributing wealth, how these institutions may change in the future. That is, he sets out by stating that he is discussing wealth and then goes on, in fact, to discuss human behavior with reference to wealth. Economics in Mill, despite his definition, is really a discussion of certain phases of human behavior, a discussion of human behavior with reference to producing, exchanging, valuing, and distributing wealth.

In this way too the book has a modern character. When one reads the volume as a whole, when one notes with what charm it is written, how attractive it makes the possibility of human development, one need not be surprised that it very rapidly eclipsed in popular favor all the preceding treatises in England. It came very soon to be, not merely in England but also in the United States and in the countries of Europe into whose languages it was rapidly translated, not only the most popular but also scientifically the most valued book, summing up and restating in a modern perspective all the chief results of the school of thought it represented. And on the other hand it became the point of departure from which most of the effective workers upon economic theory in the generation or two that followed took their start. It was not, as a matter of fact, until perhaps two generations after the book had been published that its hold upon the scientific and the popular public came to be challenged. It had, in other words, as long a period of primacy among books on political economy as The Wealth of Nations and a longer period than Ricardo's Principles.

XXXVIII

SOME SHORTCOMINGS OF THE CLASSICAL ECONOMISTS

Inasmuch as John Stuart Mill's Principles of Political Economy was the most important systematic, authoritative exposition of classical political economy, it is well worth while to inquire somewhat carefully into the general character of the science which the great English masters had built up, beginning with the epoch-making work of Adam Smith and going on through the discoveries of Malthus, Ricardo, and their followers, to the final masterly summary of their work by the younger Mill.

Let us begin with the subject matter of classical political economy. Mill tells us on his first page that the subject of political economy is wealth, and then he tells us immediately that it is not. This explanation of the statement that political economy deals with wealth says that what he is really concerned with is one aspect of human behavior:

> Writers on Political Economy profess to teach, or to investigate, the nature of Wealth, and the laws of its production and distribution: including, directly or remotely, the operation of all the causes by which the condition of mankind, or of any society of human beings, in respect to this universal object of human desire, is made prosperous or the reverse.*

Well, of course, what it really deals with is the production of wealth, its distribution among different members of society, its exchange, the effect of an increase of wealth upon production and distribution, and the influence of government upon these processes. To say that the science deals with wealth is elliptical to a degree. The classical masters, in due succession, misdefined their own subject. That is a rather obvious and perhaps not very important observation. But I think that they would have seen their problems more clearly had they been in the habit of observing that what they were really doing was trying to give a scientific account of one basically important phase of the behavior of men in society.

The second observation I want to make concerns the organization of Mill's treatise. I had something to say about the very curious order in which the analysis written by Adam Smith in The Wealth of Nations developed. Then I pointed out the very considerable disorder that characterizes the miscellaneous arrangement of the chapters in Ricardo's Political Economy . Mill in one sense is far more systematic, far more orderly in his arrangement than either Smith or Ricardo. The order which he follows is that suggested by Say, worked out somewhat further by his own father, and then developed in detail by himself. And it is an order that is open to most of the objections which lie against Ricardo's far less systematic development. He begins with Production and then goes on in Book II to Distribution; and he disposes of both of these topics before he goes on in Book III, which is entitled Exchange, to a discussion of the problem of value. The result of that order is that Mill cannot systematize his analysis in that convenient and highly integrated form which has been characteristic of more recent treatises, namely, making the problem of value the center of discussion. If you do not take up the problem of value until after you have treated both production and distribution, then you are prevented from showing the interrelations which really exist between the propositions concerning the value of commodities and the propositions that you want to lay down concerning the value of the services in production which are themselves the instruments through which the distribution of wealth is effected. If you begin with the analysis of the conditions which determine the value of commodities or the prices that are paid for them and work out as Mill does, when he gets around to that topic, the scheme of analysis that turns on supply and demand, then you can apply this central feature of economic doctrines to the particular problems which are offered by the theory of distribution,

* Ashley, ed. p. 1.

namely, the problem how the value or the price of labor is determined, how the value of the uses of capital is determined, and finally how the value of whatever it is that the business organizer contributes to the economic process is determined. Well, Mill had no more insight into these close logical relations between the theory of value and the theory of distribution than was vouchsafed to Ricardo. And the consequence is that we find his book highly systematic though it be, from one viewpoint far less closely organized in its fundamental logic than are the books that have been written since, - Marshall above all others, who hit upon a better mode of treatment.

Next, I want to call your attention to the topic that I call the four levels of analysis. I spent some time in pointing out that in dealing with economic problems Ricardo sometimes carried on his discussion in terms of money, thinking of business men as aiming at money profits, wage earners aiming at money wages, capitalists as getting money interest, landlords receiving money rents, - treating the processes in a rather realistic fashion as if the human beings whose behavior is analyzed by economists were really thinking and acting much like the human beings that we can observe in the market places of the world. But at times Ricardo found it desirable to give what he conceived to be a lower and more fundamental level of analysis: real wages to him were the sums of money that men get for a day's or a week's work in the form of commodities that could be bought with their money wages. And so too, with the income of any class. People are not interested in money as money itself to them, from this point of view, is little more than a means for getting the goods which they really desire, and these goods are the commodities and services which they require. Even that point of view is not getting down to the bottom of the problem because just as you can say what people want money for is commodities and what people want commodities and services for is to satisfy their needs, to gratify their wants, you can also say it is not until you penetrate to this most fundamental level of analysis, if your psychology runs on the lines Ricardo accepted, it is not until you penetrate to this level of analysis that you are talking about the real forces which control economic behavior.

Mill's practice is very much like Ricardo's. He talks about economic activity sometimes as if it were an effort to get money, sometimes as if it were an effort to get commodities, and occasionally in a rather casual manner he penetrates to the level of real forces. For example, in talking about the law of the increase of capital he says:

> The lowest rate of profit which can permanently exist, is that which
> is barely adequate, at the given place and time, to afford an equivalent for
> the abstinence, risk, and exertion implied in the employment of capital.*

That is, by implication, people won't undergo abstaining from personal consumption which is required for capital, capital is not going to be saved, unless they are paid for it. They won't assume risks of loss unless they expect adequate compensation. They won't undergo the exertion which is involved in the business use of capital without remuneration. Here are the ultimate forces, and these ultimate forces are quite obviously on the level of feeling; in Bentham's terminology they are the pains of abstinence, the pains of assuming risk, the pains of exertion. But for the most part Mill is content to carry his analysis on rather in terms of commodities or of money. And much interested as he was in psychology, thoroughly grounded in the psychological notions not only of Bentham but also of his father, and although considerable is the attention he gave to certain types of psychological problems in the last Book of his treatise on logic, he did not seem to think it necessary or expedient in his treatise on political economy to attempt all the time to carry on his discussion in terms of real forces. He does not even give us any systematic analysis

---

* Ashley ed., p. 407.

of the relation of these real forces to the commodities or the money about which he talks most of the time. Had he attempted an analysis of that sort, it is quite possible that he might have been the first to develop the utilitarian analysis which had already been worked out in principle by one or two of these very little known predecessors, predecessors of whom Mill however knew nothing or of the consequences of whose ideas he had no adequate ground. He left it to others to work out the implications for economics of the ideas of human nature which he had been brought up in and which he helped somewhat to develop.

The most interesting thing, however, about the level of analysis in Mill's <u>Political Economy</u> is his forthright statement concerning the insignificance of money as a factor in economic behavior. He tells us in the seventh chapter of his book on Exchange where he begins the formal treatment of money, - he tells us

> There cannot, in short, be intrinsically a more insignificant thing, in the economy of society, than money; except in the character of a contrivance for sparing time and labour. It is a machine for doing quickly and commodiously, what would be done, though less quickly and commodiously, without it; and like many other kinds of machinery, it only exerts a distinct and independent influence of its own when it gets out of order.*

Well, now this notion which Mill held and which has a definite relationship to similar notions that Adam Smith sets forth in <u>The Wealth of Nations</u> covers from sight a variety of problems, some of which are only coming at the present time to be adequately appreciated as problems with which an economist ought to be dealing. One of the characteristic features of Mr. John Maynard Keynes's recent work, for instance, is his much belated discovery of the fact that economic activities are in modern commercial nations for the most part carried on as parts of an attempt to make money profits. I say one of the most characteristic features of Mr. Keynes's recent work is that discovery and it stands out in bold contrast to the Marshallian tradition in which Mr. Keynes has grown up, and stands in bold contrast to the work which has been done by the majority of Mr. Keynes's contemporaries at Cambridge today. And yet when you stop to think of it you will realize that it is not only when a monetary system gets out of order that it exerts a distinct and independent influence of its own. It exerts such a distinct and independent influence whenever the general business system gets out of order. The fact has long been recognized, for instance, that almost all business undertakings are carried on upon a bookkeeping basis, in the anticipation of realizing a sum of money from sales greater than the cost, and that these business enterprises commonly involve borrowing from others in the anticipation of repayment. It is obvious enough that this whole complicated way in which we organize most of our activities exposes business to very grave difficulties whenever for any reason there is a credit strain, whenever there is common difficulty about repaying the loans that have been obtained by business men at any time when these loans fall due. Now difficulties of that sort occur, usually at the climax of every succeeding period of cyclical prosperity which the commercial nations have undergone. During a period of great business activity loans expand rapidly, they ordinarily expand so rapidly as to lead to some diminution in the ability of the banks to meet further demands upon them. If, then, when the credit resources of the country are already strained somewhat there is for any reason an alarm created regarding the ability of people to repay their loans, you find there will begin to develop at a rapid rate throughout the commercial system a process of liquidation, that is, a demand that people repay the money that is owed by them. This liquidation may give rise to failures; if so, it enhances the crisis, and the upshot may be a commercial panic.

---

* <u>Ibid</u>., p. 488.

I have cited this as much the simplest and most obvious way in which without there being anything wrong with the monetary system as such, the fact that we organize our common traffic in goods on the basis of trying to make money does exercise a most indubitable influence upon our economic behavior. And if one wants to take a somewhat larger veiw of the problems which concern economists, then it is very simple to see that the pecuniary organization of society, the use of money, has had an enormously potent influence upon the fortunes of mankind. The breakdown of the old feudalistic organization of society before the rising commercial interests of men was due directly to an increase in the use of money. People began to revamp their old economic relationships based largely on payment in services or in kind into payments in money. The possession of money began to be a matter of first class significance to military powers. The old order of thinking which characterized men and their aims in life altered as they went more and more into a state of human relationships which were based upon money payments. The rise of capitalism as the successor of feudalism was associated in the most intimate fashion with the growing use of money. And needless to say this reorganization of society has had not only a very powerful influence upon the kind of activities that people engage in but also had a most powerful influence upon the amount of wealth that can be produced from capital and the way in which that wealth is distributed. Now problems of that sort you see were hidden from Mill by this curious superficial notion that money is intrinsically an insignificant thing, except in the character of a contrivance for sparing time, that it is something which merely enables people to do things quickly and commodiously.

Indeed, if you take a long historical perspective it would be hard to make a statement which is more demonstrably false than that people who made very little use of money did, less quickly and commodiously, what people are enabled to do when they have developed full-fledged pecuniary institutions. Indeed, I think it possible to go a good deal further than this and to hold that the use of money has been a most potent influence in shaping the development of culture at large and economic activities as an inherent part of culture. Also I think it is perfectly clear that the use of money has come to exercise a very great disciplinary influence over our thoughts in all sorts of direct and all sorts of subtle and indirect ways. The use of money affects our habits of thought. The very calculating frame of mind which is one of the essential characteristics of the psychology that Bentham developed and which John Stuart Mill accepted is, I think, in very large measure a quality that men have learned in the use of money. Certainly our most elaborate calculations of an economic sort are those we carry on in connection with our business Accountancy has become in these latter days an extremely refined art; some of its practicioners would say a science. It represents on the whole a high elaboration of the type of calculations which Jeremy Bentham so naively supposed to be carried on by all of us in conducting the simplest affairs of life. Had Bentham lived in a society of savages where money was in very little use, it would never have occurred to him as plausible to think of men as calculating machines, to suppose that they were addicted to the practice of dividing up their pleasures into units of intensit; and multiplying these units by numbers. Still less would it have occurred to him to discount pleasures and pains because of their futurity or because of their uncertainty. These are elaborate intellectual habits which the race acquired primarily because in taking on that money-making habit of activity they had perforce developed a bookkeeping technique. And, when that habit is thoroughly developed in a population, a person whose ideas about human nature have a strong individualist cast, as had Jeremy Bentham's, finds it plausible to suppose that we carry back into our subtle half - conscious thinking as individuals of our pleasures and pains, these habits which have become so firmly established, so firmly recognized in our business dealings. So you have in this dictum of Mill's a statement that is characteristic of the classical school at large, of thinking, in which he was brought up, and the statement of a view which covers from sight a host of problems of very profound

concern to anyone who wants to understand the character of human nature as it is
accepted in economic behavior or wants to understand anything at all of the process
by which we have been enabled to go so far as we have toward the organization of a
highly efficient and elaborate scheme for mutual service to one another in the satisfaction of our wants.

I want to speak about Mill's conception about the place of competition in
economics. His chief dictum on this point is that which occurs near the beginning
of the Fourth Chapter of his Second Book "Of Competition and Custom". His chief
dictum is that

> only through the principle of competition has political economy an pretension
> to the character of a science.*

That would rule out from the science of economics the discussion of the distribution
of wealth, let us say, or the production of wealth under non-competitive conditions.
It would mean that in so far as distribution is controlled by tradition or custom
in any of its forms there is no scientific basis for explaining why the existing
arrangements are as they are. If you want an explanation of customary traditional
arrangements you can perhaps get at least a quasi-answer to your problems by means
of historical research; you can trace the growth of certain customs. And Mill
points out that you can explain the consequences to which these customs give rise,
but you cannot analyze the customary situation and give an explanation of it
scientifically in the same fashion as you can give an explanation of a competitive
situation. And not only that, but it would seem, if you take Mill here literally,
that the economist is not in a position to deal with the problem of monopoly. In
fact, if you go over his discussions of the theory of value you will find that in
fact his remarks upon monopoly are of an exceedingly vague and from the modern
viewpoint unsatisfactory character. He says:

> There are but few commodities which are naturally and necessarily limited
> in supply. But any commodity whatever may be artificially so. Any commodity may
> be the subject of a monopoly: like tea, in this country, up to 1834: tobacco in
> France, opium in British India, at present.**

and so on. So he raises the question too, what it is that determines monopoly
prices and what he has to tell us about that is that we must not think that monopoly
prices are altogether arbitrary, depending upon the will of the monopolist.

> This is in one sense true, but forms no exception, nevertheless, to the de-
> pendence of the value on supply and demand. The monopolist can fix the value
> as high as he pleases, short of what the consumer either could not or would
> not pay; but he can only do so by limiting the supply. ....Monopoly value, there-
> fore,   does not depend on any particular principle but is a mere variety
> of the ordinary case of demand and supply.***

Now that is the gist of Mill's theory of monopoly prices. And you see from
the modern viewpoint how slender and inadequate it is. The reason why Mill probably did not think it necessary to go further into the problem of monopoly prices
is, as you will realise, that it was a nest of problems rather than a single one,
that it contained cases not only of complete monopoly on the part of the seller but
also complete monopoly on the part of the buyers with competition on the part of the
sellers and then a whole variety of cases in which competition and monopoly are mixe

---

* _Ibid._, p. 242.
** _Ibid._, p. 448.
***_Ibid._, p. 449.

together in various degrees, - a reason why he did not explore that subject; and
so his conviction that that subject was not of first class importance. From his
point of view the class of cases that was equally practical and theoretical was that
of commodities which admit of indefinite multiplication; and these commodities he
seems to have assumed without much of an inquiry are produced and are bought under
conditions of competition. Exactly what competition implies or involves, Mill did
not stop to show. He seems to have taken it for granted that our off-hand rough
and ready notion of a competitive situation is quite adequate for purposes of an
economic inquiry. And if he had stopped to think about this point also he doubtless
would have discovered, what later writers have, how exceedingly difficult it is to
define in any satisfactory fashion the essential conditions of competition. And
possibly if he had come further afield he would have seen a good many cases in which,
after all, goods in his own time and country were being bought and sold under conditions which were affected in more or less considerable measure by monopolistic control, cases in which certainly the competition going on did not answer his conception. He, of course, could not be expected to have any vision of the way in which
the rule of competition in business would in the decades to come establish limits
to competition. He could not be expected to see that the drastic effect of sharp
competition in limiting profits would lead to a great effort on the part of business
men themselves to escape from the trammels of competition to build up a situation
in which the business enterprises could exercise a protective control over prices,
a practice which of course has gone far enough in these modern days to make it impossible for anyone who is dealing with problems of value and price at large to
assume that the great mass of commodities are bought and sold under strictly competitive conditions, a process which has gone so far that it makes us feel nowadays that
if economics is to give us valuable light upon the practices which prevail in the
modern world it must have at least as careful an analysis of prices under impure
competition as it has of prices under pure competition. And there are those nowadays
who go so far as to say that in fact there are no cases of really pure competition,
that the problem of prices from start to finish is a problem which presents mixed
combinations of monopolistic elements on the one side and competitive elements on
the other side. That is another of the great problems of the future which escaped
the attention of the classical political economists, even at the hands of their last
and greatest systematic expositor.

Finally, I want to say something about the problem of method. Just as one
might have expected that Mill's interest in psychology might have led him to dealing
at much greater length than he did with the real forces that are supposed to control
economic behavior, so one might have expected that his highly developed interests
in logic would have led him to dress his treatise on political economy with a disquisition upon method or would have led him at least to set forth from time to time
rather definitely the character of the proofs that he was giving, - let him call
his readers' attention to the logical properties that he was employing. I suppose
if you had put this proposition to Mill himself he might have answered "It is precisely because I have dealt with these problems of method at such length elsewhere
that I did not feel myself called upon to treat them in my political economy. If
you want to learn my views about the methods that are best employed in developing
the social sciences in general, and political economy in particular, if you want to
know the kind of methods which I myself employ, then by all means read the last book
of my System of Logic." Or, if that is an undertaking that overtaxes your time,
possibly your ability, at least he might have said "I recommend that you read my
essay 'On the Definition of Political Economy;and on the Method of Investigation
Proper to It' in the little volume on Essays on Some Unsettled Questions of Political
Economy." The fact is that, whether or not Mill would have taken this ground, this
was his practice. If we want to know what methods he recommends for political economy we have to turn from the treatise on that subject either to his volume of Essays
or to his System of Logic. And if we want to find out what methods he actually em-

ploys in building up the theorems of the <u>Political Economy</u> itself, we have to do the thinking, we have to stop and ask ourselves "Well, what is the proof of this proposition? Suppose we take a critical attitude, how can we establish the validity of Mill's statements or propositions, how can we show that Mill's statements are wrong? When we meet again I want to spend a little time in examining very briefly Mill's formal ideas about what method ought to be as he set them forth in his methodologica <u>Essay</u>.

XXXIX

JOHN STUART MILL'S METHOD OF ANALYSIS

As I said, I want to close the first half-year by discussing the methods of demonstration which are employed by Mill in the <u>Political Economy</u>, a book that can be properly regarded, I think, as the final flower of classical political economy in its earlier form. As I remarked at the end of the last hour, Mill does not give a formal discussion of the methods of economics in his treatise on political economy If asked why not, his answer would probably have been that he treated that subject at considerable length, first in an essay "On the Definition of Political Economy; and On the Method of Investigation Proper to It" which he published in a magazine in 1836 and which he republished in his little volume of <u>Essays on Some Unsettled Questions of Political Economy</u> four years before the <u>Political Economy</u> came out; and because he dealt with the subject at still greater length in his <u>System of Logic</u> published five years before the <u>Political Economy</u>. So if we want to know what his formal views on the problem of method were, we must turn to this essay and to the <u>System of Logic</u>.

I want to begin by calling your attention to the chief point argued in his essay published in 1836 "On the Definition of Political Economy; and On the Method of Investigation Proper to It;" and the one which he finally accepts runs as follows.

The science which traces the laws of such of the phenomena of society as arise from the combined operations of mankind for the production of wealth, in so far as those phenomena are not modified by the pursuit of any other object.*

Now there are several features of that definition which call for remark. In the first place, it is a science which deals with laws. Mill takes it for granted that there are generalizations in this particular field that can be established. He uses "laws" in that sense, - "The science which traces the laws of such of the phenomena of society.." Now observe this makes economics a social science; it deals with the "phenomena of society as arise from the combined operations of mankind..."; it is not concerned with the actions of isolated individuals; emphasis, you see, upon social character of the activities "for the production of wealth.." It is evident that though Mill came directly out of the Benthamic school, he does not undertake to treat economics as a science which deals with utility or with pleasure and pains. It is "the combined operations of mankind for the production of wealth"; and, as we shall see in other passages, wealth is conceived as desirable commodities. Finally it is "the science which traces the laws of such of the phenomena of society as arise from the combined operations of mankind for the production of wealth, in so far as those phenomena are not modified by the pursuit of any other object." That is to say, it is a science which discusses operations which are guided by just one motive according to this definition, and that motive is a desire for wealth.

This definition Mill points out necessarily makes ploitical economy an abstract

---

*Essays on Some Unsettled Questions of Political Economy, 2d. ed., 1874, p. 140.

science because it abstracts all motives of human behavior except one. It does not undertake to discuss the actual conduct of mankind, only to discuss that conduct in so far as it is concerned with the production of wealth and has no other motive. There is, of course, an heroic abstraction. And also this definition makes the a priori method, the one of reasoning on the basis of assumptions, the inevitable method to choose because you are not dealing with the actual situation in which mankind behave. You are supposing them to be other than they are: to be acting from a single motive. And all you can learn about their operations has to be learned by reasoning on the basis of this assumption. Mill makes that a little clearer in comments which follow. Political economy, he says

> reasons, and, as we contend, must necessarily reason, from assumptions, not from facts. It is built upon hypotheses......

of which the chief is this hypothesis that the sole motive animating the behavior of man is the desire for wealth.

> ...Political Economy presuppose(s) an arbitrary definition of man,

and here the homo oeconomicus appears –

> as a being who invariably does that by which he may obtain the greatest amount of necessaries, conveniences, and luxuries,......

You see, wealth here becomes commodities which you can classify as "necessaries, conveniences, and luxuries"

> with the smallest quantity of labour

and here you find him admitting the introduction of another factor among his psychological premises –

> with the smallest quantity of labour and physical self-denial with which they can be obtained in the existing state of knowledge. It is true that this definition of man is not formally prefixed to any work on Political Economy, as the definition of a line is prefixed to Euclid's Elements; and in proportion as by being so prefixed it would be less in danger of being forgotten, we may see ground for regret that this is not done.*

and yet when Mill came to write his own treatise on political economy he did not follow the lines suggested here. That is, he did not prefix his arbitrary definition of a man to his treatise.

> The conclusions of Political Economy, consequently, like those of geometry, are only true, as the common phrase is, in the abstract; ...
>   This ought not to be denied by the political economist. If he deny it, then, and only then, he places himself in the wrong. .....

The economists have

> to do only with those parts of human conduct which have pecuniary advantage for their direct and principal object;.....
>   But we go farther than to affirm that the method a priori is a legitimate mode of philosophical investigation in the moral sciences; we contend that it is the only mode. We affirm that the method a posteriori, or that of specific ex-

*Ibid., p. 144.

-256-

perience, is altogether inefficacious in those sciences, as a means of arriving
at any considerable body of valuable truth; though it admits of being usefully
applied in aid of the method a priori, and even forms an indispensable supplement
to it. *

That is to say after you have established your conclusions by reasoning on
the basis of your artificial definition of a man you can oftentimes to very great advantage verify your results by observing in how far they concur with actual experience. That is a point on which we shall presently find him more specific in the
System of Logic. The real reason why it is not feasible to argue a posteriori in
economics by observation is that this is one of the sciences in which we cannot experiment. That is, we cannot arrange conditions for the specific purpose of getting
the clear-cut observations which are needed in scientific work. Could we experiment,
then economics might be built up as chemistry is supposed by Mill to be built up,
a posteriori, by trying out combinations under controlled conditions, observing what
differences in result arise from the differences in combinations. But inasmuch as
economics deals with social phenomena and these social phenomena cannot be arranged
according to his desire by any investigator inasmuch as no one simply by virtue of
being a political economist has any right to interfer with the lives of other people,
experiment is not feasible. And so the economist has to fall back upon general
reasoning based upon arbitrary definitions. His result must accordingly always be
an hypothetical result. They do not profess to give an account of actual human behavior.

That is the ground that Mill takes in an essay written when he was a young man,
And when he came as a result of his long and strenuous labors upon the System of
Logic to treat the subject in his concluding Book VI "On the Logic of the Moral
Sciences," he takes substantially the same ground. It is worth while, however, to see
how he chooses his ground in this latter place, partly because stated in somewhat
different form it will make the position adopted in the essay more clear. This
Book "On the Logic of the Moral Sciences" begins by saying that the backward state
of the moral sciences - and moral sciences is a term which in Mill's time meant substantially the same thing that the term social sciences does now, with the possible
exception that moral would have included ethics and we do not think of ethics as one
of the social sciences - the backward state of the moral sciences can only be remedie
by applying to them the method of the physical sciences, duly extended and genaralize
The fundamental science in this group is psychology. It is on the basis laid by
psychology that sociology at large, economics and all the other moral sciences in
particular, necessarily rest. And psychology does lay down certain general laws.
Mill gives us examples; for example, the law that every mental impression has its
ideal. And then again at greater length he expounds the laws of associations among
ideas. Association among ideas depends upon the similarity of different ideas and
their contiguity, that is, the relation between the occurrence of two different ideas
When those ideas occur contiguously with one another they are consequently associated
in the mind. When they do not occur contiguously the association is much less likely
to be established. And these associations, based on similarities and contiguity
are reinforced by frequency of occurrence, and by intensity of the impression which
the idea makes on the person to whom it occurs.

You will observe from this that when Mill thought of psychology he thought as
people of his time commonly did of little beyond that part of psychology which is
supposed to deal with the intellectual content of the mind. Sensations come in, but
come in as making up ideas. He gives comparatively little of habit except in so far
as habit is of very great importance in establishing certain associations in our mind
that is, frequency of a sensation or frequency of association between two ideas which
you can regard as more or less an habitual association if you like, strengthens the
bond between ideas.

* Ibid., pp. 144-146.

Now this psychology then is the fundamental moral science. And then second there is a science which Mill talks about a good deal in his Logic and which he there claims has not been developed but might be developed by a constant thinker who set himself to the job: the science of what he calls ethology - not ethnology, but ethology. This is the science which has to deal with the laws of the formation of character. One of Mill's deeplying convictions about mankind was that the character of people found in different countries and even to a considerable extent the character of people who lived at considerably separated periods in the same country, is considerably different. And he thought that it should be feasible to investigate the conditions of greatest significance in forming the character of men, investigate these conditions in a fashion which would go far at least toward explaining differences of character. If you did that, then you might account for the fact, for instance, that the British public of his day had a certain character in economic transactions which he thought quite appreciably different from the character exhibited by the French, or Germans, or other continentals. He seems to have had a desire of building up the science of ethology himself. If so, he did not succeed. When you read the System of Logic in which he kept passages relating to ethology through to the seventh edition, the last one published in his lifetime, you get the impressic that the desire to develop this particular science was one of Mill's leading ambitions. If you turn to the Autobiography in which he gives such an interesting story of his intellectual life, you find scarcely any reference to the subject. Just what it was that stood in his way we do not learn. Anyway that proved to be an abortive scheme.

The fundamental moral science then is psychology. On that there should be erected a science of ethology; and finally comes the science of sociology. Ethology is the science of the formation of individual character; sociology is the science of man in society. Now he says there are three or four different methods of developing the science of sociology which have been recommended or adopted. And he proceeds, as proper to a person discussing questions of logic, to analyze the merits and the shortcomings of these several methods. The first is what he calls the chemical or experimental method. That is not feasible fundamentally because in dealing with social phenomena experiment is ruled out. The second is what he calls the geometrical or abstract method, a method that is applied with the most brilliant success in Euclidian geometry. The trouble with that method in sociology, he says, is that it dealswith but one factor at a time, whereas one of the most notable features of sociological phenomena is that they are indissolubly interrelated. You cannot really account for social phenomena on the basis of following through one factor at a time. You must deal with a conjunction of factors; and if you do that then the geometrical method is inapplicable.

So he decides on what he calls the physical or concrete deductive method as the one which is proper to employ in sociology at large and in special sociological sciences like political economy. That method is justifiable, he thinks, because in social phenomena while you have to deal with a good many different forces you find that these forces can be handled in the same fashion in which different forces are handled in physics in problems that relate to the composition of forces. That is, different social forces stand in the relation such that you can add them together or you can subtract them from the others. They do not enter into strange new combinations with one another such as appear oftentimes when you put two chemical elements together; they may make something the nature of which you could not anticipate in the least from what you know about the two separate elements. But in society that is not true. The ultimate factors in society are individuals. And there is no alteration in the character of the individual which you have to take account of because of the fact that individuals live together in society. I want to read you a passage in which he makes this what now seems to us a remarkable statement:

The laws of the phenomena of society are, and can be, nothing but the laws of the actions and passions of human beings united together in the social state. Men, however, in a state of society are still men; their actions and passions are obedient to the laws of individual human nature. Men are not, when brought together, converted into another kind of substance, with different properties; as hydrogen and oxygen are different from water, or as hydrogen, oxygen, carbon, and azote, are different from nerves, muscles, and tendons. Human beings in society have no properties but those which are derived from, and may be resolved into, the laws of the nature of individual man. In social phenomena the Composition of Causes is the universal law.*

Well, now, or course, Mill does not mean here that a man who grows up in society is going to be the same sort of character as the man who grows up, let us say, in a very small savage group. He does not mean that the man who grows up in London is going to turn out to be the same kind of individual as would grow up in one of the isolated islands off the coast of Scotland. What he means simply is, given individuals with the character that has been formed in them according to the laws of the non-existent science of ethology, the fact that they live together in a society does not produce any other changes in their individual characters which the sociologist need take into account.

In later times, we have speculations that look to a very different sort of result. For instance, I dare say not a few of you are familiar with the theory of crowds which has been developed by Le Bon, the French psychologist, a man who undertook to argue in a plausible and effective fashion that after all the behavior of men in a mob is very different from the behavior of which the individual members of that mob could conceivably perform as separate individuals. Cases of that sort however, had not come to the attention of people in Mill's time: and with a strong individualistic tradition behind him, Mill felt, without going into the question at any time further than here, that he was safe in saying that human beings in society have no properties which are different from their nature as individual men.

That being the case, Mill thought it safe to argue that if you have different forces brought to bear upon individuals you can investigate these forces one at a time and then add their effects together and in this way gradually build up an account of social behavior. And the way to do that, since you could not experiment, was to reason on the basis of the effect which known forces brought to bear on individuals will give rise to. You take the individual desire for children, for instance, as one of your premises and you can argue out at least certain important phases of human conduct that will result from that. Or you take the desire for wealth as another one of the forces which men in society are subject to, and you can argue out the result to which that desire must necessarily lead. And this means, as he said in his essay, that your method of investigation in sociology at large must be deductive. Your fundamental premises are those laws of human nature which psychology gives you. In the last resort they are the laws of associations among ideas. And then you really ought to have the aid of the science of ethology with its laws about the formation of character. And on the basis of the ruling principle provided by the fundamental moral sciences you should be able to take one incentive to action after another to deduce the kind of behavior which each one of these distinguishing incentives would give rise to.

This means then that in building up sociology it is not only desirable, it is necessary that you should recognize restrictive sociological sciences, of which political economy is the one best developed, and the one to which he gives most attention And when he comes to discussing the peculiar problem of method that this science presents us he says that it must be based on restricted psychological premises.

---

* A System of Logic; 8th ed., p. 608.

Political Economy...concerns itself only with such of the phenomena
of the social state as take place in consequence of the pursuit of wealth. It
makes entire abstraction of every other human passion or motive; except those

and here you see he is developing the idea a little more clearly

except those which may be regarded as perpetually antagonizing principles to the
desire of wealth, namely, aversion to labor, and desire of the present enjoyment
of costly indulgences.*

That is, a man is supposed to be ruled by the desire for wealth and two opposing
forces: his aversion to labor, and second his preference for present enjoyment.
Then he goes on:

The political economist inquires, what are the actions which would be produced
by this desire, if within the departments in question it were unimpeded by any
other. In this way a nearer approximation is obtained than would otherwise be
practicable to the real order of human affairs in those departments. This
approximation has then to be corrected by making proper allowance for the effects
of any impulses of a different description, which can be shown to interfere with
the result in any particular case. Only in a few of the most striking cases
(such as the important one of the principle of population) are these corrections
interpolated into the expositions of political economy itself; the strictness of
purely scientific arrangement being thereby somewhat departed from, for the sake
of practical utility.**

That is, he starts out with his standardized definition of man subject to the
desire for wealth opposed by aversion to labor and preference for present enjoyment,
and reasons on that basis; but he corrects his conclusions drawn from these general
premises when he is dealing with certain phenomena, notably those of wages, by
bringing in another psychological factor, the principle of population, that is,
the preference particularly characteristic of the wage earning classes for marriage
and a family over an increase in the standard of living. That is a clear case of
another factor triumphing in a measure over the desire for wealth.

Mill tells us that while sociology at large and economics in particular must
reason this way they must observe that their calculations apply only to those states
of society in which actual conditions conform more or less to their assumptions.

In political economy, for instance, empirical laws of human nature are tacitly
assumed by English thinkers, which are calculated only for Great Britain and the
United States. Among other things, an intensity of competition is constantly
supposed, which, as a general mercantile fact, exists in no country in the world
except those two.***

That is, political economy, though an abstract science, as a valid piece of reasoning is applicable in a serious sense only to countries where competition is intense; and Mill thinks that really limits it to two: Great Britain and the United
States. He goes on:

An English political economist, like his countrymen in general, has seldom learned
that it is possible that men, in conducting the business of selling their goods

* Ibid., p. 624.
** Ibid., p. 625.
***Ibid., p. 627.

over a counter, should care more about their cases or their vanity than about their pecuniary gain.*

And then he remarks that an Englishman's frame of mind is not at all representative of tradesmen on the continent.

Finally, he points out that an indispensable part of the physical method is verification; an

indispensable element in all deductive sciences, Verification by Specific Experience - comparison between the conclusions of reasoning and the results of observation.**

How are you going to get to verify the deductions of sociology and of political economy? Well, he points out that we have certain general methods of observing, among others the statistical method which enables us in some cases to establish empirical generalizations which we could establish on no other basis. For example, he says that he has before him a newspaper in which one of the official assignees in bankruptcy, after reviewing the bankruptcies which occurred in Great Britain in recent years and inquiring into their causes, draws a conclusion that the number of failures caused by misconduct greatly preponderate over those arising from all other causes together. Mill says:

Nothing but specific experience could have given sufficient ground for a conclusion of this purport. To collect, therefore, such empirical laws (which are never more than approximate generalizations) from direct observation, is an important part of the process of sociological inquiry.***

And he tells us further that in a good many cases the way we can find out the causes at work is to observe the effects produced and then argue back from the effects to the kind of causes that must have been at work. But the extent to which we can, as a matter of fact, use specific experiences, even in this process of verification, is limited by the great variety of conditions under which given causes operate. Mill illustrates by proposing a problem of how you can verify the economist's reasoning concerning the results produced by protective tariffs through an appeal to specific experience. Take, he says, the Corn Laws, those laws which imposed duties upon the importation of grain into Great Britain. The fact is that these Corn Laws were operating in Great Britain at the same time that a great many other factors were at work. And you cannot by any method of analyzing the results of observation disentangle the effects due to the Corn Laws themselves from the effects that may have been introduced by, say, production of articles under competition, or production by the monopolistic countries, or introduced by changes in the level of prices. All these different factors are interacting at the same time; and simply by studying the results you cannot tell what the effect of the Corn Laws was. The only way to apply that test, he says, would be to have a large number of different nations which under varied conditions had imposed corn laws and then study the results in detail and you might be able to argue, if you had cases enough, that there were certain common elements among the phenomena in all these cases which could be attributed to the corn laws. But we cannot get that number of cases and consequently we can seldom make much use of that type of direct verification.

On the other hand, he thinks that an indirect verification which is of scarcely less value is always practicable.

* Ibid., p. 627.
** Ibid., p. 628.
***Ibid., p. 628

The conclusion drawn as to the individual case can only be directly verified
in that case; but it is verified indirectly, by the verification of other
conclusions drawn in other individual cases from the same laws.*

That is to say, if you are interested in the result of protection you would not
really be limited in your inquiries to the effects produced by putting import duties
on grains. You could take account of the different facts which you might deduce
would result from putting duties upon a variety of other articles. That is, you
would not get a direct verification of your argument about the effect of the Corn
Laws, but by taking analogous problems you would be able to establish results indirectly. If you could demonstrate that your conclusions regarding other things
were borne out in some measure by different facts, that tends strongly to support
the validity of the reasoning you had adopted with reference to the Corn Laws.

The method that Mill recommends for use by political economists, then is
the method that rests fundamentally on psychological premises. And he thinks that
it is necessary to split up a human being, so far as his motives are concerned,
into small parts; to take some over-masteringly important motives that dominate
various branches of human activity and on the basis of these abstractions, which
are necessary to simplify your problem, argue out what kind of behavior will result.
And then after you have carried through your argumentation to certain conclusions
you should do the best that conditions make possible to verify your results by
seeing what way these results that you have reasoned out are or are not in accord
with facts which are open to observation.

* * * * *